Connecting Networks v6
Companion Guide

Cisco Networking Academy

Cisco Press

800 East 96th Street

Indianapolis, Indiana 46240 USA

Connecting Networks v6 Companion Guide

Cisco Networking Academy

Copyright © 2018 Cisco Systems, Inc.

Published by:
Cisco Press
800 East 96th Street
Indianapolis, IN 46240 USA

Printed in the United States of America

1   17

Library of Congress Control Number: 2017950140

ISBN-13: 978-1-58713-432-6

ISBN-10: 1-58713-432-2

Warning and Disclaimer

This book is designed to provide information about the Cisco Networking Academy Connecting Networks course. Every effort has been made to make this book as complete and as accurate as possible, but no warranty or fitness is implied.

The information is provided on an "as is" basis. The authors, Cisco Press, and Cisco Systems, Inc. shall have neither liability nor responsibility to any person or entity with respect to any loss or damages arising from the information contained in this book or from the use of the discs or programs that may accompany it.

The opinions expressed in this book belong to the author and are not necessarily those of Cisco Systems, Inc.

This book is part of the Cisco Networking Academy® series from Cisco Press. The products in this series support and complement the Cisco Networking Academy curriculum. If you are using this book outside the Networking Academy, then you are not preparing with a Cisco trained and authorized Networking Academy provider.

For more information on the Cisco Networking Academy or to locate a Networking Academy, Please visit www.netacad.com

Editor-in-Chief
Mark Taub

Alliances Manager, Cisco Press
Ron Fligge

Product Line Manager
Brett Bartow

Executive Editor
Mary Beth Ray

Managing Editor
Sandra Schroeder

Development Editor
Christopher Cleveland

Senior Project Editor
Tonya Simpson

Copy Editor
Chuck Hutchinson

Technical Editor
Rick McDonald

Editorial Assistant
Vanessa Evans

Cover Designer
Chuti Prasertsith

Composition
codeMantra

Indexer
Lisa Stumpf

Proofreader
H S Rupa

Trademark Acknowledgments

All terms mentioned in this book that are known to be trademarks or service marks have been appropriately capitalized. Cisco Press or Cisco Systems, Inc., cannot attest to the accuracy of this information. Use of a term in this book should not be regarded as affecting the validity of any trademark or service mark.

Special Sales

For information about buying this title in bulk quantities, or for special sales opportunities (which may include electronic versions; custom cover designs; and content particular to your business, training goals, marketing focus, or branding interests), please contact our corporate sales department at corpsales@pearsoned.com or (800) 382-3419.

For government sales inquiries, please contact governmentsales@pearsoned.com.

For questions about sales outside the U.S., please contact intlcs@pearson.com.

Feedback Information

At Cisco Press, our goal is to create in-depth technical books of the highest quality and value. Each book is crafted with care and precision, undergoing rigorous development that involves the unique expertise of members from the professional technical community.

Readers' feedback is a natural continuation of this process. If you have any comments regarding how we could improve the quality of this book, or otherwise alter it to better suit your needs, you can contact us through email at feedback@ciscopress.com. Please make sure to include the book title and ISBN in your message.

We greatly appreciate your assistance.

CISCO

Americas Headquarters	Asia Pacific Headquarters	Europe Headquarters
Cisco Systems, Inc.	Cisco Systems (USA) Pte. Ltd.	Cisco Systems International BV Amsterdam,
San Jose, CA	Singapore	The Netherlands

Cisco has more than 200 offices worldwide. Addresses, phone numbers, and fax numbers are listed on the Cisco Website at **www.cisco.com/go/offices.**

Cisco and the Cisco logo are trademarks or registered trademarks of Cisco and/or its affiliates in the U.S. and other countries. To view a list of Cisco trademarks, go to this URL: www.cisco.com/go/trademarks. Third party trademarks mentioned are the property of their respective owners. The use of the word partner does not imply a partnership relationship between Cisco and any other company. (1110R)

About the Contributing Authors

Bob Vachon is a professor at Cambrian College in Sudbury, Ontario, Canada, where he teaches networking infrastructure courses. He has worked and taught in the computer networking and information technology field since 1984. Since 2002, he has collaborated on various CCNA, CCNA Security, CCNP, Cybersecurity, and IoT projects for the Cisco Networking Academy as team lead, lead author, and subject matter expert. He enjoys playing guitar and being outdoors.

Allan Johnson entered the academic world in 1999 after 10 years as a business owner/operator to dedicate his efforts to his passion for teaching. He holds both an MBA and an MEd in training and development. He taught CCNA courses at the high school level for seven years and has taught both CCNA and CCNP courses at Del Mar College in Corpus Christi, Texas. In 2003, Allan began to commit much of his time and energy to the CCNA Instructional Support Team providing services to Networking Academy instructors worldwide and creating training materials. He now works full time for Cisco Networking Academy as Curriculum Lead.

Contents at a Glance

Contents

Reader Services

Register your copy at www.ciscopress.com/title/9781587134326 for convenient access to downloads, updates, and corrections as they become available. To start the registration process, go to www.ciscopress.com/register and log in or create an account*. Enter the product ISBN 9781587134326 and click Submit. When the process is complete, you will find any available bonus content under Registered Products.

*Be sure to check the box that you would like to hear from us to receive exclusive discounts on future editions of this product.

Icons Used in This Book

Router

Wireless Router

PIX Firewall

WLAN Controller

Workgroup Switch

Route/Switch Processor with and without Si

Modem

Access Point

Cisco ASA 5500

Cisco CallManager

NAT

Cisco 5500 Family

File/Application Server

Hub

Key

PC

Laptop

IP Phone

Phone

Headquarters

Branch Office

Home Office

Network Cloud

Line: Ethernet

Wireless Connectivity

Command Syntax Conventions

The conventions used to present command syntax in this book are the same conventions used in the IOS Command Reference. The Command Reference describes these conventions as follows:

- **Boldface** indicates commands and keywords that are entered literally as shown. In actual configuration examples and output (not general command syntax), boldface indicates commands that are manually input by the user (such as a **show** command).

- *Italic* indicates arguments for which you supply actual values.

- Vertical bars (|) separate alternative, mutually exclusive elements.

- Square brackets ([ ]) indicate an optional element.

- Braces ({ }) indicate a required choice.

- Braces within brackets ([{ }]) indicate a required choice within an optional element.

Introduction

Connecting Networks v6 Companion Guide is the official supplemental textbook for the Cisco Network Academy CCNA Connecting Networks course. Cisco Networking Academy is a comprehensive program that delivers information technology skills to students around the world. The curriculum emphasizes real-world practical application, while providing opportunities for you to gain the skills and hands-on experience needed to design, install, operate, and maintain networks in small- to medium-sized businesses, as well as enterprise and service provider environments.

This textbook provides a ready reference to explain the same networking concepts, technologies, protocols, and devices as the online curriculum. This book emphasizes key topics, terms, and activities and provides some alternate explanations and examples as compared with the course. You can use the online curriculum as directed by your instructor and then use this Companion Guide's study tools to help solidify your understanding of all the topics.

Who Should Read This Book

The book, as well as the course, is designed as an introduction to data network technology for those pursuing careers as network professionals as well as those who need only an introduction to network technology for professional growth. Topics are presented concisely, starting with the most fundamental concepts and progressing to a comprehensive understanding of network communication. The content of this text provides the foundation for additional Cisco Networking Academy courses, and preparation for the CCNA Routing and Switching certification.

Book Features

The educational features of this book focus on supporting topic coverage, readability, and practice of the course material to facilitate your full understanding of the course material.

Topic Coverage

The following features give you a thorough overview of the topics covered in each chapter so that you can make constructive use of your study time:

- **Objectives:** Listed at the beginning of each chapter, the objectives reference the core concepts covered in the chapter. The objectives match the objectives stated in the corresponding chapters of the online curriculum; however, the question format in the Companion Guide encourages you to think about finding the answers as you read the chapter.

- **Notes:** These are short sidebars that point out interesting facts, timesaving methods, and important safety issues.

- **Chapter summaries:** At the end of each chapter is a summary of the chapter's key concepts. It provides a synopsis of the chapter and serves as a study aid.

- **Practice:** At the end of chapter, there is a full list of all the labs, class activities, and Packet Tracer activities to refer back to for study time.

Readability

The following features have been updated to assist your understanding of the networking vocabulary:

- **Key terms:** Each chapter begins with a list of key terms, along with a page-number reference from inside the chapter. The terms are listed in the order in which they are explained in the chapter. This handy reference allows you to find a term, flip to the page where the term appears, and see the term used in context. The Glossary defines all the key terms.

- **Glossary:** This book contains an all-new Glossary with 347 terms.

Practice

Practice makes perfect. This new Companion Guide offers you ample opportunities to put what you learn into practice. You will find the following features valuable and effective in reinforcing the instruction that you receive:

- **Check Your Understanding questions and answer key:** Updated review questions are presented at the end of each chapter as a self-assessment tool. These questions match the style of questions that you see in the online course. Appendix A, "Answers to the 'Check Your Understanding' Questions," provides an answer key to all the questions and includes an explanation of each answer.

- **Labs and activities:** Throughout each chapter, you will be directed back to the online course to take advantage of the activities created to reinforce concepts. In addition, at the end of each chapter, a practice section collects a list of all the labs and activities to provide practice with the topics introduced in this chapter. The labs, class activities, and Packet Tracer instructions are available in the companion *Connecting Networks v6 Labs & Study Guide* (ISBN 9781587134296). The Packet Tracer PKA files are found in the online course.

- **Page references to online course:** After headings, you will see, for example, (1.1.2.3). This number refers to the page number in the online course so that you can easily jump to that spot online to view a video, practice an activity, perform a lab, or review a topic.

Lab Study Guide

The supplementary book *Connecting Networks v6 Labs & Study Guide*, by Allan Johnson (ISBN 9781587134296), includes a Study Guide section and a Lab section for each chapter. The Study Guide section offers exercises that help you learn the concepts, configurations, and troubleshooting skills crucial to your success as a CCNA exam candidate. Some chapters include unique Packet Tracer activities available for download from the book's companion website. The Labs and Activities section contains all the labs, class activities, and Packet Tracer instructions from the course.

About Packet Tracer Software and Activities

Interspersed throughout the chapters, you'll find many activities to work with the Cisco Packet Tracer tool. Packet Tracer allows you to create networks, visualize how packets flow in the network, and use basic testing tools to determine whether the network would work. When you see this icon, you can use Packet Tracer with the listed file to perform a task suggested in this book. The activity files are available in the course. Packet Tracer software is available only through the Cisco Networking Academy website. Ask your instructor for access to Packet Tracer.

How This Book Is Organized

This book corresponds closely to the Cisco Academy Introduction to Networking course and is divided into eight chapters, one appendix, and a glossary of key terms:

- **Chapter 1, "WAN Concepts":** This chapter discusses basic WAN operations and services including private and public WAN technologies. It also discusses how to select the appropriate WAN protocol and service for a specific network requirement.

- **Chapter 2, "Point-to-Point Connections":** This chapter examines point-to-point serial communications using the PPP and HDLC protocols. It describes the features and benefits of PPP over HDLC and examines the PPP-layered architecture and the functions of LCP and NCP. PPP configuration and PPP authentication commands are also covered.

- **Chapter 3, "Branch Connections":** This chapter discusses how users and enterprises connect to the Internet using cable, DSL, and wireless broadband solutions. It explains how ISPs use PPPoE to provide the authentication, accounting, and link management features to their customers. It introduces how VPNs are implemented to address Internet security concerns and how GRE is used to create a virtual point-to-point connection between two remote points. Finally, the chapter discusses BGP as the routing protocol used between service providers and how to implement BGP on a single-homed network.

- **Chapter 4, "Access Control Lists":** This chapter describes how to use ACLs to filter traffic. Configuration, verification, and troubleshooting of standard and extended IPv4 ACLs are covered. Securing remote access with an ACL is also discussed.

- **Chapter 5, "Network Security and Monitoring":** This chapter discusses common Layer 2 network attacks and how they can be mitigated. Network monitoring is discussed next using SNMP. Finally, SPAN is discussed to provide network traffic mirroring to packet analyzers or IPS devices.

- **Chapter 6, "Quality of Service":** This chapter discusses QoS tools used to guarantee that certain traffic types are prioritized over traffic that is not as time-sensitive. Specifically, the chapter describes network transmission quality, traffic characteristics, queueing algorithms, QoS models, and QoS implementation techniques.

- **Chapter 7, "Network Evolution":** This chapter discusses how network must evolve to support new technology such as the IoT using innovative new technology including cloud computing, virtualization, and SDN.

- **Chapter 8, "Network Troubleshooting":** This chapter discusses how network documentation is used to troubleshoot network issues. It describes the general troubleshooting problems using a systematic layered approach to troubleshooting.

- **Appendix A, "Answers to the 'Check Your Understanding' Questions":** This appendix lists the answers to the "Check Your Understanding" review questions that are included at the end of each chapter.

- **Glossary:** The glossary provides you with definitions for all the key terms identified in each chapter.

CHAPTER 1

WAN Concepts

Objectives

Upon completion of this chapter, you will be able to answer the following questions:

- What is the purpose of a WAN?
- How do WANs operate?
- What WAN services are available?
- What are the differences between private WAN technologies?

- What are the differences between public WAN technologies?
- What is the appropriate WAN protocol and service for a specific network requirement?

Key Terms

This chapter uses the following key terms. You can find the definitions in the Glossary.

Introduction (1.0)

Businesses must connect LANs to provide communications between them, even when these LANs are far apart. Wide-area networks (WANs) are used to connect remote LANs. A WAN may cover a city, country, or global region. A WAN is owned by a service provider, and a business pays a fee to use the provider's WAN network services.

Different technologies are used for WANs than for LANs. This chapter introduces WAN standards, technologies, and purposes. It covers selecting the appropriate WAN technologies, services, and devices to meet the changing business requirements of an evolving enterprise.

Class Activity 1.0.1.2: Branching Out

Your medium-sized company is opening a new branch office to serve a wider, client-based network. This branch will focus on regular, day-to-day network operations but will also provide TelePresence, web conferencing, IP telephony, video on demand, and wireless services.

Although you know that an ISP can provide WAN routers and switches to accommodate the branch office connectivity for the network, you prefer to use your own customer premises equipment (CPE). To ensure interoperability, Cisco devices have been used in all other branch-office WANs.

As the branch-office network administrator, you are responsible for researching possible network devices for purchase and use over the WAN.

WAN Technologies Overview (1.1)

In this section, you learn about WAN access technologies available to small- to medium-sized business networks.

Purpose of WANs (1.1.1)

In this topic, you learn the purpose of the WAN.

Why a WAN? (1.1.1.1)

A WAN operates beyond the geographic scope of a LAN. As shown Figure 1-1, WANs are used to interconnect the enterprise LAN to remote LANs in branch sites and telecommuter sites.

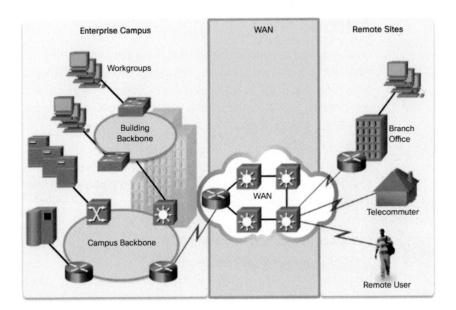

Figure 1-1   WANs Interconnect Users and LANs

A WAN is owned by a *service provider*. A user must pay a fee to use the provider's network services to connect remote sites. WAN service providers include carriers, such as a telephone network, cable company, or satellite service. Service providers provide links to interconnect remote sites for the purpose of transporting data, voice, and video.

In contrast, LANs are typically owned by an organization. They are used to connect local computers, peripherals, and other devices within a single building or other small geographic area.

Are WANs Necessary? (1.1.1.2)

Without WANs, LANs would be a series of isolated networks. LANs provide both speed and cost-efficiency for transmitting data over relatively small geographic areas. However, as organizations expand, businesses require communication among geographically separated sites. The following are some examples:

- Regional or branch offices of an organization need to be able to communicate and share data with the central site.

- Organizations need to share information with other customer organizations. For example, software manufacturers routinely communicate product and promotional information to distributors that sell their products to end users.

- Employees who travel on company business frequently need to access information that resides on their corporate networks.

Home computer users also need to send and receive data across increasingly larger distances. Here are some examples:

- Consumers now commonly communicate over the Internet with banks, stores, and a variety of providers of goods and services.
- Students do research for classes by accessing library indexes and publications located in other parts of their country and in other parts of the world.

It is not feasible to connect computers across a country, or around the world, with physical cables. Therefore, different technologies have evolved to support this communication requirement. Increasingly, the Internet is being used as an inexpensive alternative to enterprise WANs. New technologies are available to businesses to provide security and privacy for their Internet communications and transactions. WANs used by themselves, or in concert with the Internet, allow organizations and individuals to meet their wide-area communication needs.

WAN Topologies (1.1.1.3)

Interconnecting multiple sites across WANs can involve a variety of service provider technologies and WAN topologies. Common WAN topologies are

- *Point-to-point topology*
- *Hub-and-spoke topology*
- *Full mesh topology*
- *Dual-homed topology*

Point-to-Point

A point-to-point topology, as shown in Figure 1-2, employs a point-to-point circuit between two endpoints. Typically involving dedicated *leased-line* connections like a *T1* or an *E1* line, a point-to-point connection provides a Layer 2 transport service through the service provider network. Packets sent from one site are delivered to the other site and vice versa. A point-to-point connection is transparent to the customer network, as if there was a direct physical link between two endpoints.

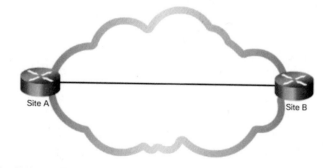

Figure 1-2 Point-to-Point Topology

Hub-and-Spoke

If a private network connection between multiple sites is required, a point-to-point topology with multiple point-to-point circuits is one option. Each point-to-point circuit requires its own dedicated hardware interface that will require multiple routers with multiple WAN interface cards. This interface can be expensive. A less expensive option is a point-to-multipoint topology, also known as a hub-and-spoke topology.

With a hub-and-spoke topology, all spoke circuits can share a single interface to the *hub*. For example, spoke sites can be interconnected through the hub site using virtual circuits and routed subinterfaces at the hub. A hub-and-spoke topology is also an example of a single-homed topology. Figure 1-3 displays a sample hub-and-spoke topology consisting of four routers with one router as a hub connected to the other three spoke routers across a WAN cloud.

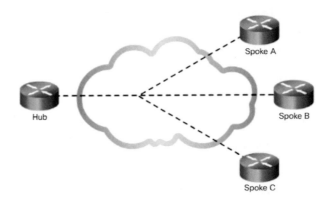

Figure 1-3   Hub-and-Spoke Topology

Full Mesh

One of the disadvantages of hub-and-spoke topologies is that all communication has to go through the hub. With a full mesh topology using virtual circuits, any site can communicate directly with any other site. The disadvantage here is the large number of virtual circuits that need to be configured and maintained. Figure 1-4 displays a sample full mesh topology consisting of four routers connected to each other across a WAN cloud.

Dual-homed Topology

A dual-homed topology provides redundancy. As shown in Figure 1-5, the spoke routers are dual-homed and redundantly attached to two hub routers across a WAN cloud. The disadvantage to dual-homed topologies is that they are more expensive to implement than a *single-homed topology*. The reason is that they require additional networking hardware, like additional routers and switches. Dual-homed topologies are also more difficult to implement because they require additional, and more complex, configurations. However, the advantage of dual-homed topologies is that they offer enhanced network redundancy, load balancing, distributed computing or processing, and the ability to implement backup service provider connections.

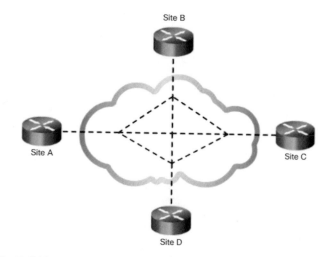

Figure 1-4   Full Mesh Topology

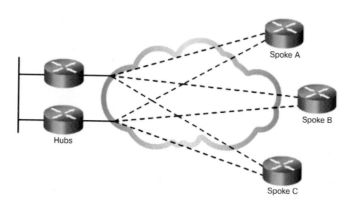

Figure 1-5   Dual-Homed Topology

Evolving Networks (1.1.1.4)

Every business is unique, so how an organization grows depends on many factors. These factors include the types of products or services the business sells, the management philosophy of the owners, and the economic climate of the country in which the business operates.

In slow economic times, many businesses focus on increasing their profitability by improving the efficiency of their existing operations, increasing employee productivity, and lowering operating costs. Establishing and managing networks can represent significant installation and operating expenses. To justify such a large expense, companies expect their networks to perform optimally and to be able to deliver an ever-increasing array of services and applications to support productivity and profitability.

The example used in this chapter and shown in Figure 1-6 is of a fictitious company called SPAN Engineering. This topic will illustrate how SPAN's network requirements change as the company grows from a small, local business into a global enterprise.

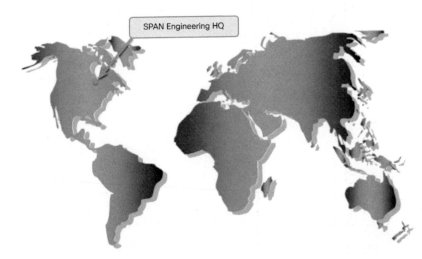

SPAN Engineering HQ

Figure 1-6   SPAN Engineering

Small Office (1.1.1.5)

SPAN Engineering, an environmental consulting firm, has developed a special process for converting household waste into electricity and is developing a small pilot project for a municipal government in its local area. The company, which has been in business for four years, is a small office consisting of 15 employees: six engineers, four computer-aided drawing (CAD) designers, a receptionist, two senior partners, and two office assistants.

SPAN Engineering's management is working to win full-scale contracts after the pilot project successfully demonstrates the feasibility of the company's process. Until then, the company must manage its costs carefully.

As shown in Figure 1-7, SPAN Engineering uses a single LAN to share information between computers and to share peripherals, such as a printer, a large-scale plotter (to print engineering drawings), and fax equipment.

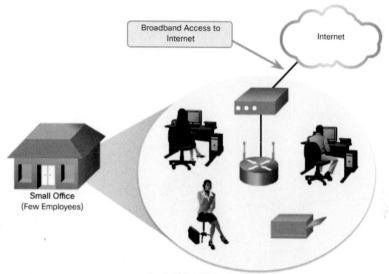

Small single LAN for sharing peripherals and Internet access

Figure 1-7   Connecting a Small Office

The company has recently upgraded its LAN to provide inexpensive *voice over IP (VoIP)* service to save on the costs of separate phone lines for employees.

Internet connectivity is provided using a common *broadband service* called *digital subscriber line (DSL)*, which is supplied by the local telephone service provider. Because SPAN has so few employees, bandwidth is not a significant problem.

The company cannot afford in-house IT support staff, so it uses support services purchased from the DSL provider. The company also uses a hosting service rather than purchasing and operating its own FTP and email servers.

Campus Network (1.1.1.6)

Five years later, SPAN Engineering has grown rapidly. The company was contracted to design and implement a full-size waste conversion facility soon after the successful implementation of its first pilot plant. Since then, SPAN has won other projects in neighboring municipalities and in other parts of the country.

To handle the additional workload, the business has hired more staff and leased more office space. It is now a small- to medium-sized business with several hundred employees. Many projects are being developed at the same time, and each requires a project manager and support staff. The company has organized itself into functional departments, with each department having its own organizational team. To meet its growing needs, the company has moved into several floors of a larger office building.

As the business has expanded, the network has also grown. Instead of a single small LAN, the network now consists of several subnetworks, each devoted to a different department. For example, all the engineering staff is on one LAN, while the marketing staff is on another LAN. These multiple LANs are joined to create a company-wide network, or campus, which spans several floors of the building.

Figure 1-8 shows an example of SPAN's campus network.

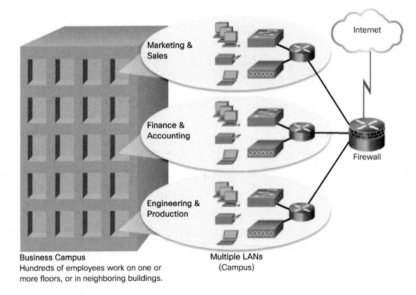

Figure 1-8   Connecting a Campus Network

The business now has in-house IT staff to support and maintain the network. The network includes dedicated servers for email, data transfer, and file storage, and web-based productivity tools and applications. In addition, a company intranet provides in-house documents and information to employees. An extranet provides project information to designated customers.

Branch Networks (1.1.1.7)

Another six years later, SPAN Engineering has been so successful with its patented process that demand for its services has skyrocketed. New projects are underway in multiple cities. To manage those projects, the company has opened small branch offices closer to the project sites.

This situation presents new challenges to the IT team. To manage the delivery of information and services throughout the company, SPAN Engineering now has a data center, which houses the various databases and servers of the company. To ensure that all parts of the business are able to access the same services and applications regardless of where the offices are located, the company must now implement a WAN.

For its branch offices that are in nearby cities, the company decides to use private *dedicated lines* through a local service provider, as shown in Figure 1-9. However, for those offices that are located in other countries, the Internet is an attractive WAN connection option. Although connecting offices through the Internet is economical, this approach introduces security and privacy issues that the IT team must address.

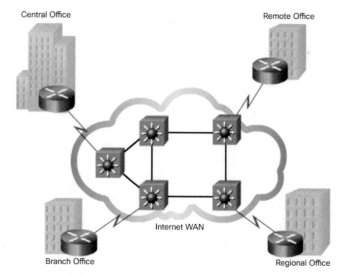

Figure 1-9   Connecting Branch Networks

Distributed Network (1.1.1.8)

SPAN Engineering has now been in business for 20 years and has grown to thousands of employees distributed in offices worldwide, as shown in Figure 1-10.

The cost of the *enterprise network* and its related services is a significant expense. The company is looking to provide its employees with the best network services at the lowest cost. Optimized network services would allow each employee to work at a high rate of efficiency.

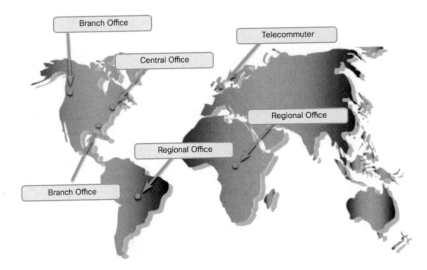

Figure 1-10 SPAN Engineering

To increase profitability, SPAN Engineering must reduce its operating expenses. It has relocated some of its office facilities to less expensive areas. The company is also encouraging *teleworking* and virtual teams. Web-based applications, including web conferencing, e-learning, and online collaboration tools, are being used to increase productivity and reduce costs. Site-to-site and remote-access *virtual private networks (VPNs)* enable the company to use the Internet to connect easily and securely with employees and facilities around the world. To meet these requirements, the network must provide the necessary converged services and secure Internet WAN connectivity to remote offices and individuals, as shown in Figure 1-11.

As seen in this example, network requirements of a company can change dramatically as the company grows over time. Distributing employees saves costs in many ways, but it puts increased demands on the network.

A network not only must meet the day-to-day operational needs of the business but also must be able to adapt and grow as the company changes. Network designers and administrators meet these challenges by carefully choosing network technologies, protocols, and service providers. They must also optimize their networks by using many of the network design techniques and architectures described in this course.

Interactive Graphic

Activity 1.1.1.9: Identify WAN Topologies

Refer to the online course to complete this activity.

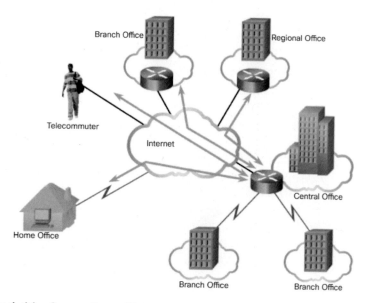

Figure 1-11   Connecting a Global Enterprise Network

WAN Operations (1.1.2)

In this topic, you learn how WANs operate.

WANs in the OSI Model (1.1.2.1)

WAN operations focus primarily on the physical layer (OSI Layer 1) and the data link layer (OSI Layer 2), as illustrated in Figure 1-12. WAN access standards typically describe both physical layer delivery methods and data link layer requirements. The data link layer requirements include physical addressing, flow control, and encapsulation.

WAN access standards are defined and managed by a number of recognized authorities:

- *Telecommunications Industry Association (TIA)*
- *Electronic Industries Alliance (EIA)*
- *International Organization for Standardization (ISO)*
- *Institute of Electrical and Electronics Engineers (IEEE)*

Layer 1 protocols describe how to provide electrical, mechanical, operational, and functional connections to the services of a communications service provider.

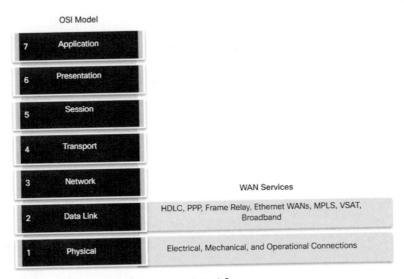

OSI Model

		WAN Services
7	Application	
6	Presentation	
5	Session	
4	Transport	
3	Network	
2	Data Link	HDLC, PPP, Frame Relay, Ethernet WANs, MPLS, VSAT, Broadband
1	Physical	Electrical, Mechanical, and Operational Connections

Figure 1-12   WANs Operate in Layers 1 and 2

Layer 2 protocols define how data is encapsulated for transmission toward a remote location and the mechanisms for transferring the resulting frames. A variety of different technologies are used, such as the *Point-to-Point Protocol (PPP)*, *Frame Relay*, and *Asynchronous Transfer Mode (ATM)*. Some of these protocols use the same basic framing or a subset of the *High-Level Data Link Control (HDLC)* mechanism.

Most WAN links are point-to-point. For this reason, the address field in the Layer 2 frame is usually not used.

Common WAN Terminology (1.1.2.2)

One primary difference between a WAN and a LAN is that a company or organization must subscribe to an outside WAN service provider to use WAN carrier network services. A WAN uses data links provided by carrier services to access the Internet and connect different locations of an organization to each other. These data links also connect to locations of other organizations, to external services, and to remote users.

The physical layer of a WAN describes the physical connections between the company network and the service provider network. Figure 1-13 illustrates the terminology commonly used to describe WAN connections:

■ *Customer premises equipment (CPE)*: The CPE consists of the devices and inside wiring located on the enterprise edge connecting to a carrier link. The subscriber (that is, customer) either owns the CPE or leases the CPE from the service provider. A subscriber, in this context, is a company that arranges for WAN services from a service provider.

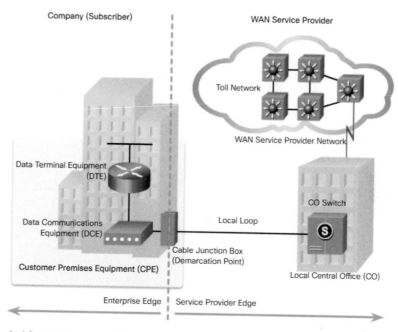

Figure 1-13 WAN Terminology

- *Data communications equipment (DCE)*: This is an EIA term. Also called data circuit-terminating equipment by the ITU. The DCE consists of devices that put data on the local loop. The DCE primarily provides an interface to connect subscribers to a communication link on the WAN cloud.

- *Data terminal equipment (DTE)*: These customer devices pass the data from a customer network or host computer for transmission over the WAN. The DTE connects to the local loop through the DCE.

- *Demarcation point*: This point is established in a building or complex to separate customer equipment from service provider equipment. Physically, the demarcation point is the cabling junction box, located on the customer premises, that connects the CPE wiring to the local loop. It is usually placed so that a technician can access it easily. The demarcation point is the place where the responsibility for the connection changes from the user to the service provider. When problems arise, it is necessary to determine whether the user or the service provider is responsible for troubleshooting or repair.

- *Local loop*: This loop is the actual copper or fiber cable that connects the CPE to the CO of the service provider. The local loop is also sometimes called the *last-mile*.

- *Central office (CO)*: The CO is the local service provider facility or building that connects the CPE to the provider network.

■ *Toll network*: This network consists of the long-haul, all-digital, fiber-optic communications lines, switches, routers, and other equipment inside the WAN provider network.

WAN Devices (1.1.2.3)

Many types of devices are specific to WAN environments, as shown in Figure 1-14, and are described in the list that follows.

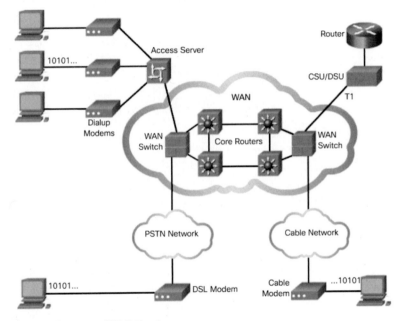

Figure 1-14   Common WAN Devices

■ *Dialup modem*: Voiceband modems are considered to be a legacy WAN technology. A voiceband modem *modulates* (that is, converts) the digital signals produced by a computer into voice frequencies. These frequencies are then transmitted over the analog lines of the public telephone network. On the other side of the connection, another modem *demodulates* the sounds back into a digital signal for input to a computer or network connection.

■ *Access server*: This server controls and coordinates dialup modem, dial-in, and dial-out user communications. Considered to be a legacy technology, an access server may have a mixture of analog and digital interfaces and support hundreds of simultaneous users.

■ *Broadband modem*: This type of digital modem is used with high-speed DSL or cable Internet service. Both operate in a similar manner to the voiceband modem but use higher broadband frequencies to achieve higher transmission speeds.

- *Channel service unit/data service unit (CSU/DSU)*: Digital leased lines require a CSU and a DSU. A CSU/DSU can be a separate device like a modem, or it can be an interface on a router. The CSU provides termination for the digital signal and ensures connection integrity through error correction and line monitoring. The DSU converts the line frames into frames that the LAN can interpret and vice versa.

- *WAN switch*: This multiport internetworking device is used in service provider networks. These devices typically switch traffic, such as Frame Relay or ATM, and operate at Layer 2.

- **Router:** This device provides internetworking and WAN access interface ports that are used to connect to the service provider network. These interfaces may be serial connections, Ethernet, or other WAN interfaces. With some types of WAN interfaces, an external device, such as a DSU/CSU or modem (analog, cable, or DSL), is required to connect the router to the local service provider.

- **Core router/Multilayer switch:** This router or multilayer switch resides within the middle or backbone of the WAN, rather than at its periphery. To fulfill this role, a router or multilayer switch must be able to support multiple telecommunications interfaces of the highest speed used in the WAN core. It must also be able to forward IP packets at full speed on all of those interfaces. The router or multilayer switch must also support the routing protocols being used in the core.

Note

The preceding list is not exhaustive, and other devices may be required, depending on the WAN access technology chosen.

WAN technologies are either circuit-switched or packet-switched. The type of device used depends on the WAN technology implemented.

Circuit Switching (1.1.2.4)

A *circuit-switched network* is one that establishes a dedicated circuit (or channel) between nodes and terminals before the users may communicate. Specifically, circuit switching dynamically establishes a dedicated virtual connection for voice or data between a sender and a receiver. Before communication can start, it is necessary to establish the connection through the network of the service provider, as shown in Figure 1-15.

As an example, when a subscriber makes a telephone call, the dialed number is used to set switches in the exchanges along the route of the call so that there is a continuous circuit from the caller to the called party. Because of the switching operation used to establish the circuit, the telephone system is called a circuit-switched network. If the telephones are replaced with modems, the switched circuit is able to carry computer data.

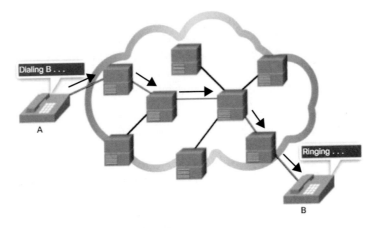

Figure 1-15   Circuit-Switched Network

If the circuit carries computer data, the usage of this fixed capacity may not be efficient. For example, if the circuit is used to access the Internet, a burst of activity occurs on the circuit while a web page is transferred. This burst could be followed by no activity while the user reads the page and then another burst of activity while the next page is transferred. This variation in usage between none and maximum is typical of computer network traffic. Because the subscriber has sole use of the fixed capacity allocation, switched circuits are generally an inefficient way of moving data.

The two most common types of circuit-switched WAN technologies are the *public switched telephone network (PSTN)* and the *Integrated Services Digital Network (ISDN).*

Packet Switching (1.1.2.5)

In contrast to circuit switching, a *packet-switched network (PSN)* splits traffic data into packets that are routed over a shared network. Packet-switching networks do not require a circuit to be established, and they allow many pairs of nodes to communicate over the same channel.

The switches in a PSN determine the links that packets must be sent over based on the addressing information in each packet. The following are two approaches to this link determination:

- **Connectionless systems:** Full addressing information must be carried in each packet. Each switch must evaluate the address to determine where to send the packet. An example of a connectionless system is the Internet.

- **Connection-oriented systems:** The network predetermines the route for a packet, and each packet only has to carry an identifier. The switch determines the onward route by looking up the identifier in tables held in memory. The set of entries in the tables identifies a particular route or circuit through the system. When the circuit is established temporarily while a packet is traveling through it and then breaks down again, it is called a *virtual circuit (VC)*. An example of a connection-oriented system is Frame Relay. In the case of Frame Relay, the identifiers used are called *data-link connection identifiers (DLCIs)*.

Note

Frame Relay systems are commonly being replaced by Ethernet WANs.

Because the internal links between the switches are shared between many users, the cost of packet switching is lower than that of circuit switching. However, *latency* (delays) and *jitter* (variability of delay) are greater in packet-switched networks than in circuit-switched networks. The reason is that the links are shared, and packets must be entirely received at one switch before moving to the next. Despite the latency and jitter inherent in shared networks, modern technology allows satisfactory transport of voice and video communications on these networks.

In Figure 1-16, SRV1 is sending data to SRV2. As packets traverse the provider network, they arrive at the first provider switch. Packets are added to the queue and forwarded after other packets in the queue have been forwarded. Eventually, the packets reach SRV2.

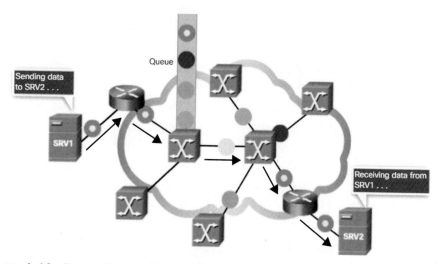

Figure 1-16   Packet-Switched Network

Activity 1.1.2.6: Identify WAN Terminology

Refer to the online course to complete this activity.

Selecting a WAN Technology (1.2)

In this section, you learn how to select WAN access technologies to satisfy business requirements.

WAN Services (1.2.1)

In this topic, you learn about different WAN services available.

WAN Link Connection Options (1.2.1.1)

ISPs can use are several WAN access connection options to connect the local loop to the enterprise edge. These WAN access options differ in technology, speed, and cost. Each has distinct advantages and disadvantages. Familiarity with these technologies is an important part of network design.

As shown in Figure 1-17 and described in the list that follows, an enterprise can get WAN access in two ways.

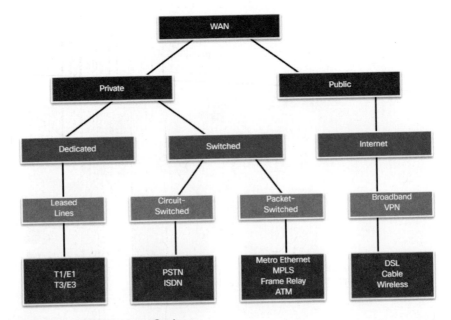

Figure 1-17   WAN Access Options

- *Private WAN infrastructure*: Service providers may offer dedicated point-to-point leased lines, circuit-switched links, such as PSTN or ISDN, and packet-switched links, such as Ethernet WAN, ATM, or Frame Relay.

- *Public WAN infrastructure*: Service providers provide Internet access using broadband services such as DSL, cable, and satellite access. *Broadband connections* are typically used to connect small offices and telecommuting employees to a corporate site over the Internet. Data traveling between corporate sites over the public WAN infrastructure should be protected using VPNs.

Note

Frame Relay systems are commonly being replaced by Ethernet WANs.

The topology in Figure 1-18 illustrates some of these WAN access technologies.

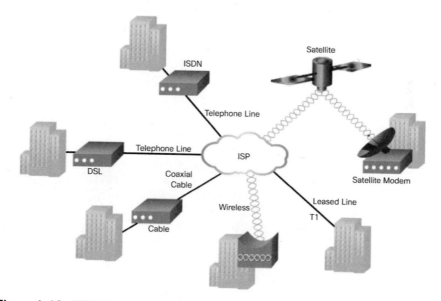

Figure 1-18   WAN Access Technologies

Service Provider Network Infrastructure (1.2.1.2)

When a WAN service provider receives data from a client at a site, it must forward the data to the remote site for final delivery to the recipient. In some cases, the remote site may be connected to the same service provider as the originating site. In other cases, the remote site may be connected to a different ISP, and the originating ISP must pass the data to the connecting ISP.

Long-range communications are usually those connections between ISPs, or between branch offices in very large companies.

Service provider networks are complex. They consist mostly of high-bandwidth fiber-optic media, using either the *Synchronous Optical Networking (SONET)* or *Synchronous Digital Hierarchy (SDH)* standard. These standards define how to transfer multiple data, voice, and video traffic over optical fiber using lasers or *light-emitting diodes (LEDs)* over great distances.

Note

SONET is an American-based ANSI standard, while SDH is a European-based ETSI and ITU standard. Both are essentially the same and, therefore, often listed as SONET/SDH.

A newer fiber-optic media development for long-range communications is called *dense wavelength division multiplexing (DWDM)*. DWDM multiplies the amount of bandwidth that a single strand of fiber can support, as illustrated in Figure 1-19.

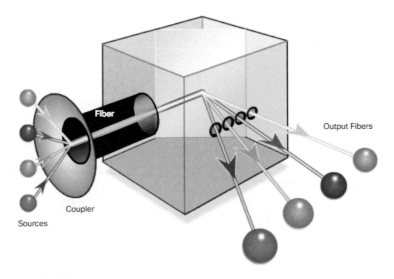

Figure 1-19   DWDM

DWDM enables long-range communication in several ways:

- DWDM enables bidirectional (for example, two-way) communications over one strand of fiber.

- It can *multiplex* more than 80 different channels of data (that is, wavelengths) onto a single fiber.

- Each channel is capable of carrying a 10 Gb/s multiplexed signal.

- It assigns incoming optical signals to specific wavelengths of light (that is, frequencies).

- It can amplify these wavelengths to boost the signal strength.

- It supports SONET and SDH standards.

DWDM circuits are used in all modern submarine communications cable systems and other long-haul circuits, as illustrated in Figure 1-20.

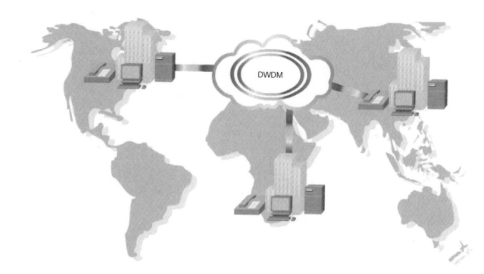

Figure 1-20   Service Provider Networks Use DWDM

Activity 1.2.1.3: Classify WAN Access Options

Refer to the online course to complete this activity.

Private WAN Infrastructures (1.2.2)

In this topic, you compare private WAN technologies.

Leased Lines (1.2.2.1)

When permanent dedicated connections are required, a point-to-point link is used to provide a pre-established WAN communications path from the customer premises to the provider network. Point-to-point lines are usually leased from a service provider and are called leased lines.

Leased lines have existed since the early 1950s; for this reason, they are referred to by different names such as leased circuits, serial link, serial line, point-to-point link, and T1/E1 or T3/*E3* lines.

The term *leased line* refers to the fact that the organization pays a monthly lease fee to a service provider to use the line. Leased lines are available in different capacities and are generally priced based on the bandwidth required and the distance between the two connected points.

In North America, service providers use the T-carrier system to define the digital transmission capability of a serial copper media link, while Europe uses the E-carrier system, as shown in Figure 1-21. For instance, a T1 link supports 1.544 Mb/s, an E1 supports 2.048 Mb/s, a T3 supports 43.7 Mb/s, and an E3 connection supports 34.368 Mb/s. *Optical carrier (OC)* transmission rates are used to define the digital transmitting capacity of a fiber-optic network.

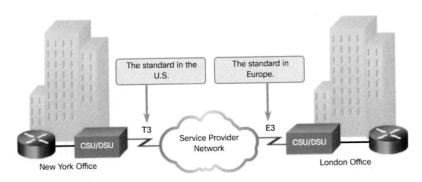

Figure 1-21   Sample Leased-Line Topology

Table 1-1 describes the advantages and disadvantages of using leased lines.

Table 1-1   Advantages/Disadvantages of Leased Lines

Advantages	Disadvantages
Simplicity: Point-to-point communication links require minimal expertise to install and maintain.	**Cost:** Point-to-point links are generally the most expensive type of WAN access. The cost of leased-line solutions can become significant when they are used to connect many sites over increasing distances. In addition, each endpoint requires an interface on the router, which increases equipment costs.

Advantages	Disadvantages
Quality: Point-to-point communication links usually offer high service quality, if they have adequate bandwidth. The dedicated capacity removes latency or jitter between the endpoints.	**Limited flexibility:** WAN traffic is often variable, and leased lines have a fixed capacity, so the bandwidth of the line seldom matches the need exactly. Any change to the leased line generally requires a site visit by ISP personnel to adjust capacity.
Availability: Constant availability is essential for some applications, such as e-commerce. Point-to-point communication links provide permanent, dedicated capacity, which is required for VoIP or Video over IP.	

The Layer 2 protocol is usually HDLC or PPP.

Dialup (1.2.2.2)

Dialup WAN access may be required when no other WAN technology is available. For example, a remote location could use modems and analog dialed telephone lines to provide low capacity and dedicated switched connections, as shown in Figure 1-22. Dialup access is suitable when intermittent, low-volume data transfers are needed.

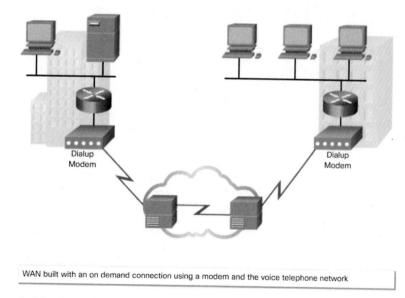

WAN built with an on demand connection using a modem and the voice telephone network

Figure 1-22   Sample Dialup Topology

Traditional telephony uses a copper cable, called the local loop, to connect the telephone handset in the subscriber premises to the CO. The signal on the local loop during a call is a continuously varying electronic signal that is a translation of the subscriber voice into an analog signal.

Traditional local loops can transport binary computer data through the voice telephone network using a dialup modem. The modem modulates the binary data into an analog signal at the source and demodulates the analog signal to binary data at the destination. The physical characteristics of the local loop and its connection to the PSTN limit the rate of the signal to less than 56 kb/s.

For small businesses, these relatively low-speed dialup connections are adequate for the exchange of sales figures, prices, routine reports, and email. Using automatic dialup at night or on weekends for large file transfers and data backup can take advantage of lower off-peak rates. These rates, often referred to as tariffs or toll charges, are based on the distance between the endpoints, time of day, and the duration of the call.

The advantages of modem and analog lines are simplicity, availability, and low implementation cost. The disadvantages are the low data rates and a relatively long connection time. The dedicated circuit has little delay or jitter for point-to-point traffic, but voice or video traffic does not operate adequately at these low bit rates.

Note

Although very few enterprises support dialup access, it is still a viable solution for remote areas with limited WAN access options.

ISDN (1.2.2.3)

Integrated Services Digital Network (ISDN) is a circuit-switching technology that enables the local loop of a PSTN to carry digital signals, resulting in higher capacity switched connections.

ISDN changes the internal connections of the PSTN from carrying analog signals to *time-division multiplexed (TDM)* digital signals. TDM allows two or more signals, or bit streams, to be transferred as subchannels in one communication channel. The signals appear to transfer simultaneously; but physically, the signals are taking turns on the channel.

Figure 1-23 displays a sample ISDN topology. The ISDN connection may require a terminal adapter (TA), which is a device used to connect ISDN *Basic Rate Interface (BRI)* connections to a router.

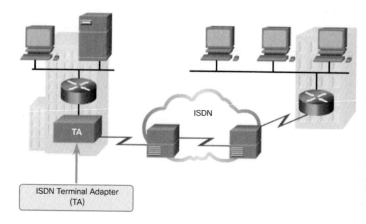

Figure 1-23   Sample ISDN Topology

The two types of ISDN interfaces are as follows:

■ **Basic Rate Interface (BRI):** ISDN BRI is intended for the home and small enterprise and provides two 64 kb/s bearer channels (B) for carrying voice and data and a 16 kb/s delta channel (D) for signaling, call setup, and other purposes. The BRI D channel is often underused because it has only two B channels to control (see Figure 1-24).

Figure 1-24   ISDN BRI

■ *Primary Rate Interface (PRI):* ISDN is also available for larger installations. In North America, PRI delivers 23 B channels with 64 kb/s and one D channel with 64 kb/s for a total bit rate of up to 1.544 Mb/s. This includes some additional overhead for synchronization. In Europe, Australia, and other parts of the world, ISDN PRI provides 30 B channels and one D channel, for a total bit rate of up to 2.048 Mb/s, including synchronization overhead (see Figure 1-25).

Figure 1-25   ISDN PRI

BRI has a call setup time that is less than a second, and the 64 kb/s B channel provides greater capacity than an analog modem link. In comparison, the call setup time of a dialup modem is approximately 30 or more seconds with a theoretical maximum of 56 kb/s. With ISDN, if greater capacity is required, a second B channel can be activated to provide a total of 128 kb/s. This permits several simultaneous voice conversations, a voice conversation and data transfer, or a video conference using one channel for voice and the other for video.

Another common application of ISDN is to provide additional capacity as needed on a leased-line connection. The leased line is sized to carry average traffic loads while ISDN is added during peak demand periods. ISDN is also used as a backup if the leased line fails. ISDN tariffs are based on a per-B channel basis and are similar to those of analog voice connections.

With PRI ISDN, multiple B channels can be connected between two endpoints. This allows for videoconferencing and high-bandwidth data connections with no latency or jitter. However, multiple connections can be very expensive over long distances.

Note

Although ISDN is still an important technology for telephone service provider networks, it has declined in popularity as an Internet connection option with the introduction of high-speed DSL and other broadband services.

Frame Relay (1.2.2.4)

Frame Relay is a simple Layer 2 *nonbroadcast multi-access (NBMA)* WAN technology used to interconnect enterprise LANs. A single router interface can be used to connect to multiple sites using *permanent virtual circuits (PVCs)*. PVCs are used to carry both voice and data traffic between a source and destination, and support data rates up to 4 Mb/s, with some providers offering even higher rates.

An edge router requires only a single interface, even when multiple VCs are used. The leased line to the Frame Relay network edge allows cost-effective connections between widely scattered LANs.

Frame Relay creates PVCs, which are uniquely identified by a data-link connection identifier (DLCI). The PVCs and DLCIs ensure bidirectional communication from one DTE device to another.

For instance, in Figure 1-26, R1 will use DLCI 102 to reach R2 while R2 will use DLCI 201 to reach R1.

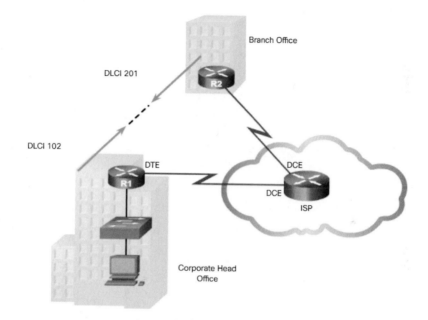

Figure 1-26   Sample Frame Relay Topology

ATM (1.2.2.5)

Asynchronous Transfer Mode (ATM) technology is capable of transferring voice, video, and data through private and public networks. It is built on a cell-based architecture rather than on a frame-based architecture. ATM cells are always a fixed length of 53 bytes. The ATM cell contains a 5-byte ATM header followed by 48 bytes of ATM payload. Small, fixed-length cells are well suited for carrying voice and video traffic because this traffic is intolerant of delay. Video and voice traffic do not have to wait for larger data packets to be transmitted, as shown in Figure 1-27.

The 53-byte ATM cell is less efficient than the bigger frames and packets of Frame Relay. Furthermore, the ATM cell has at least 5 bytes of overhead for each 48-byte payload. When the cell is carrying segmented network layer packets, the overhead is higher because the ATM switch must be able to reassemble the packets at the

destination. A typical ATM line needs almost 20 percent greater bandwidth than
Frame Relay to carry the same volume of network layer data.

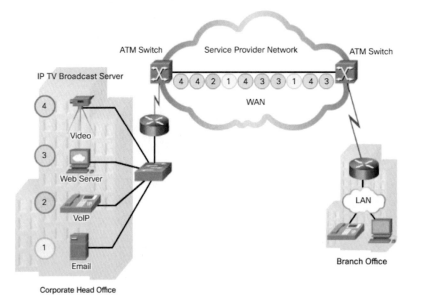

Figure 1-27   Sample ATM Topology

ATM was designed to be extremely scalable and to support link speeds of T1/E1 to
OC-12 (622 Mb/s) and faster.

As with other shared technologies, ATM allows multiple VCs on a single leased-line
connection to the network edge.

Note

ATM networks are now considered to be a a legacy technology.

Ethernet WAN (1.2.2.6)

Ethernet was originally developed to be a LAN access technology. Originally, Ethernet was not suitable as a WAN access technology because at that time, the maximum
cable length was one kilometer. However, newer Ethernet standards using fiber-optic
cables have made Ethernet a reasonable WAN access option. For instance, the IEEE
1000BASE-LX standard supports fiber-optic cable lengths of 5 km, while the IEEE
1000BASE-ZX standard supports cable lengths up to 70 km.

Service providers now offer Ethernet WAN service using fiber-optic cabling. The
Ethernet WAN service can go by many names, including *Metropolitan Ethernet*

(MetroE), *Ethernet over MPLS (EoMPLS)*, and *Virtual Private LAN Service (VPLS)*. A sample Ethernet WAN topology is shown in Figure 1-28.

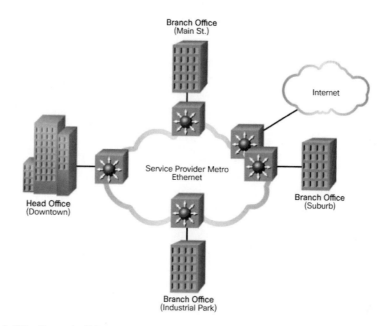

Figure 1-28   Sample Ethernet WAN Topology

An Ethernet WAN offers several benefits:

■ **Reduced expenses and administration:** Ethernet WAN provides a switched, high-bandwidth Layer 2 network capable of managing data, voice, and video all on the same infrastructure. This characteristic increases bandwidth and eliminates expensive conversions to other WAN technologies. The technology enables businesses to inexpensively connect numerous sites in a metropolitan area, to each other, and to the Internet.

■ **Easy integration with existing networks:** Ethernet WAN connects easily to existing Ethernet LANs, reducing installation costs and time.

■ **Enhanced business productivity:** Ethernet WAN enables businesses to take advantage of productivity-enhancing IP applications that are difficult to implement on TDM or Frame Relay networks, such as hosted IP communications, VoIP, and streaming and broadcast video.

Note

Ethernet WANs have gained in popularity and are now commonly being used to replace the traditional Frame Relay and ATM WAN links.

MPLS (1.2.2.7)

Multiprotocol Label Switching (MPLS) is a multiprotocol high-performance WAN technology that directs data from one router to the next. MPLS is based on short path labels rather than IP network addresses.

MPLS has several defining characteristics. It is multiprotocol, meaning it has the ability to carry any payload including IPv4, IPv6, Ethernet, ATM, DSL, and Frame Relay traffic. It uses labels that tell a router what to do with a packet. The labels identify paths between distant routers rather than endpoints, and while MPLS actually routes IPv4 and IPv6 packets, everything else is switched.

MPLS is a service provider technology. Leased lines deliver bits between sites, and Frame Relay and Ethernet WAN deliver frames between sites. However, MPLS can deliver any type of packet between sites. MPLS can encapsulate packets of various network protocols. It supports a wide range of WAN technologies including T-carrier/E-carrier links, Carrier Ethernet, ATM, Frame Relay, and DSL.

The sample topology in Figure 1-29 illustrates how MPLS is used. Notice that the different sites can connect to the MPLS cloud using different access technologies.

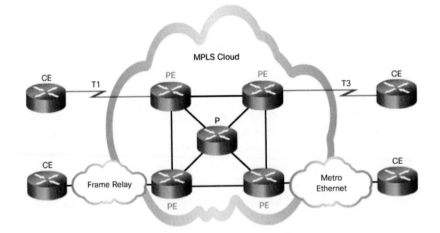

Figure 1-29   Sample MPLS Topology

In the Figure 1-29, CE refers to the customer edge; PE is the provider edge router, which adds and removes labels; and P is an internal provider router, which switches MPLS labeled packets.

VSAT (1.2.2.8)

All private WAN technologies discussed so far used either copper or fiber-optic media. What if an organization needed connectivity in a remote location where no service providers offer WAN service?

Very small aperture terminal (VSAT) is a solution that creates a private WAN using satellite communications. A VSAT is a small satellite dish similar to those used for home Internet and TV. VSATs create a private WAN while providing connectivity to remote locations.

Specifically, a router connects to a satellite dish that is pointed to a service provider's satellite. This satellite is in geosynchronous orbit in space. The signals must travel approximately 35,786 kilometers (22,236 miles) to the satellite and back.

The example in Figure 1-30 displays a VSAT dish on the roofs of the buildings communicating with a satellite thousands of kilometers away in space.

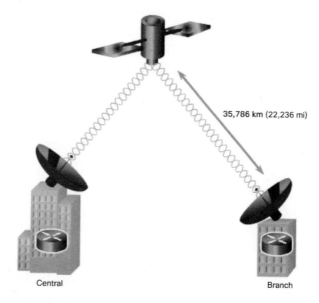

Figure 1-30   Sample VSAT Topology

Interactive
Graphic

Activity 1.2.2.9: Identify Private WAN Infrastructure Terminology

Refer to the online course to complete this activity.

Public WAN Infrastructure (1.2.3)

In this topic, you compare public WAN technologies.

DSL (1.2.3.1)

DSL technology is an always-on connection technology that uses existing twisted-pair telephone lines to transport high-bandwidth data, and provides IP services to subscribers. A *DSL modem* converts an Ethernet signal from the user device to a DSL signal, which is transmitted to the central office.

Multiple DSL subscriber lines are multiplexed into a single, high-capacity link using a *DSL access multiplexer (DSLAM)* at the provider location referred to as the *point of presence (POP)*. DSLAMs incorporate TDM technology to aggregate many subscriber lines into a single medium, generally a T3 connection. Current DSL technologies use sophisticated coding and modulation techniques to achieve fast data rates.

There is a wide variety of DSL types, standards, and emerging standards. DSL is now a popular choice for enterprise IT departments to support home workers. Generally, a subscriber cannot choose to connect to an enterprise network directly but must first connect to an ISP, and then an IP connection is made through the Internet to the enterprise. Security risks are incurred in this process but can be mediated with security measures.

The topology in Figure 1-31 displays a sample DSL WAN connection.

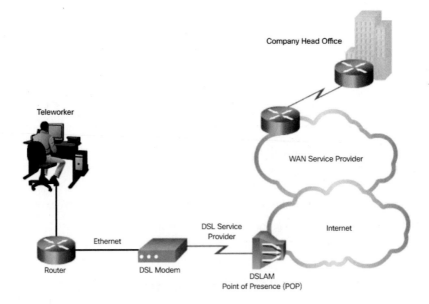

Figure 1-31   Sample DSL Topology

Cable (1.2.3.2)

Coaxial cable is widely used in urban areas to distribute television signals. Network access is available from many cable television providers. This access allows for greater bandwidth than the conventional telephone local loop.

Cable modems (CMs) provide an always-on connection and a simple installation. A subscriber connects a computer or LAN router to the cable modem, which translates the digital signals into the broadband frequencies used for transmitting on a cable television network. The local cable TV office, which is called the cable *headend*, contains the computer system and databases needed to provide Internet access. The most important component located at the headend is the *cable modem termination system (CMTS)*, which sends and receives digital cable modem signals on a cable network and is necessary for providing Internet services to cable subscribers.

Cable modem subscribers must use the ISP associated with the service provider. All the local subscribers share the same cable bandwidth. As more users join the service, available bandwidth may drop below the expected rate.

The topology in Figure 1-32 displays a sample cable WAN connection.

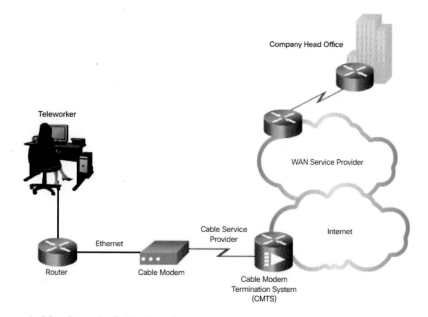

Figure 1-32   Sample Cable Topology

Wireless (1.2.3.3)

Wireless technology uses the unlicensed radio spectrum to send and receive data. The unlicensed spectrum is accessible to anyone who has a wireless router and wireless technology in the device he or she is using.

Until recently, one limitation of wireless access has been the need to be within the local transmission range (typically less than 100 feet) of a wireless router or a wireless modem that has a wired connection to the Internet. The following new developments in broadband wireless technology are changing this situation:

- *Municipal Wi-Fi*: Many cities have begun setting up municipal wireless networks. Some of these networks provide high-speed Internet access for free or for substantially less than the price of other broadband services. Others are for city use only, allowing police and fire departments and other city employees to do certain aspects of their jobs remotely. To connect to a municipal Wi-Fi, a subscriber typically needs a wireless modem, which provides a stronger radio and directional antenna than conventional wireless adapters. Most service providers provide the necessary equipment for free or for a fee, much like they do with DSL or cable modems.

- *WiMAX*: Worldwide Interoperability for Microwave Access (WiMAX) is a new technology that is just beginning to come into use. It is described in the IEEE standard 802.16. WiMAX provides high-speed broadband service with wireless access and provides broad coverage like a cell phone network rather than through small Wi-Fi hotspots. WiMAX operates in a similar way to Wi-Fi, but at higher speeds, over greater distances, and for a greater number of users. It uses a network of WiMAX towers that are similar to cell phone towers. To access a WiMAX network, subscribers must subscribe to an ISP with a WiMAX tower within 30 miles of their location. They also need some type of WiMAX receiver and a special encryption code to get access to the base station.

- *Satellite Internet*: Typically, rural users use this type of technology where cable and DSL are not available. A VSAT provides two-way (upload and download) data communications. The upload speed is about one-tenth of the 500 kb/s download speed. Cable and DSL have higher download speeds, but satellite systems are about 10 times faster than an analog modem. To access satellite Internet services, subscribers need a satellite dish, two modems (uplink and downlink), and coaxial cables between the dish and the modem.

Figure 1-33 displays an example of a WiMAX network.

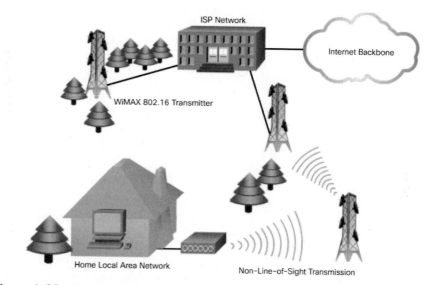

Figure 1-33   Sample Wireless Topology

3G/4G Cellular (1.2.3.4)

Increasingly, cellular service is another wireless WAN technology being used to connect users and remote locations where no other WAN access technology is available, as shown in Figure 1-34. Many users with smartphones and tablets can use cellular data to email, surf the web, download apps, and watch videos.

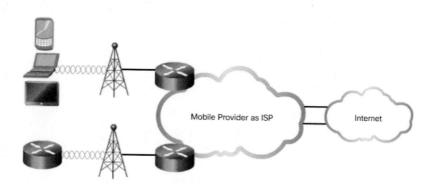

Figure 1-34   Sample Cellular Topology

Phones, tablet computers, laptops, and even some routers can communicate through to the Internet using cellular technology. These devices use radio waves to communicate through a nearby mobile phone tower. The device has a small radio antenna, and the provider has a much larger antenna sitting at the top of a tower somewhere within miles of the phone.

These are two common cellular industry terms:

- *3G/4G Wireless*: Abbreviation for third-generation and fourth-generation cellular access. These technologies support wireless Internet access.

- *Long-Term Evolution (LTE)*: Refers to a newer and faster technology and is considered to be part of fourth-generation (4G) technology.

VPN Technology (1.2.3.5)

Security risks are incurred when a *teleworker* or a remote office worker uses a broadband service to access the corporate WAN over the Internet. To address security concerns, broadband services provide capabilities for using VPN connections to a network device that accepts VPN connections, which are typically located at the corporate site.

A VPN is an encrypted connection between private networks over a public network, such as the Internet. Instead of using a dedicated Layer 2 connection, such as a leased line, a VPN uses virtual connections called VPN tunnels, which are routed through the Internet from the private network of the company to the remote site or employee host.

Using VPN offers several benefits:

- **Cost savings:** VPNs enable organizations to use the global Internet to connect remote offices, and to connect remote users to the main corporate site. This eliminates expensive, dedicated WAN links and modem banks.

- **Security:** VPNs provide the highest level of security by using advanced encryption and authentication protocols that protect data from unauthorized access.

- **Scalability:** Because VPNs use the Internet infrastructure within ISPs and devices, it is easy to add new users. Corporations are able to add large amounts of capacity without adding significant infrastructure.

- **Compatibility with broadband technology:** VPN technology is supported by broadband service providers such as DSL and cable. VPNs allow mobile workers and telecommuters to take advantage of their home high-speed Internet service to access their corporate networks. Business-grade, high-speed broadband connections can also provide a cost-effective solution for connecting remote offices.

There are two types of VPN access:

- *Site-to-site VPNs*: Site-to-site VPNs connect entire networks to each other; for example, they can connect a branch office network to a company headquarters network, as shown in Figure 1-35. Each site is equipped with a VPN gateway, such as a router, firewall, VPN concentrator, or security appliance. In the Figure 1-35, a remote branch office uses a site-to-site-VPN to connect with the corporate head office.

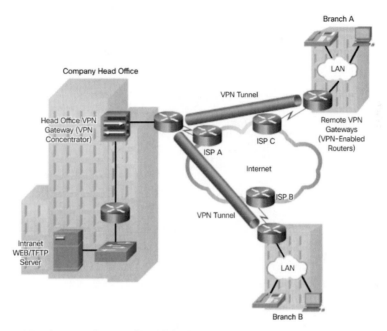

Figure 1-35   Sample Site-to-Site VPN Topology

- *Remote-access VPNs*: Remote-access VPNs enable individual hosts, such as telecommuters, mobile users, and extranet consumers, to access a company network securely over the Internet. Each host (Teleworker 1 and Teleworker 2) typically has VPN client software loaded or uses a web-based client, as shown in Figure 1-36.

Interactive Graphic

Activity 1.2.3.6: Identify Public WAN Infrastructure Terminology

Refer to the online course to complete this activity.

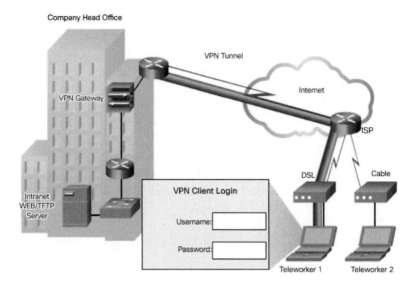

Figure 1-36   Sample Remote-Access VPN Topology

Selecting WAN Services (1.2.4)

In this topic, you learn how to select the appropriate WAN protocol and service for a specific network requirement.

Choosing a WAN Link Connection (1.2.4.1)

There are many important factors to consider when choosing an appropriate WAN connection. For a network administrator to decide which WAN technology best meets the requirements of a specific business, he or she must answer the following questions:

What is the purpose of the WAN?

There are a few issues to consider:

- Will the enterprise connect local branches in the same city area, connect remote branches, or connect to a single branch?

- Will the WAN be used to connect internal employees, or external business partners and customers, or all three?

- Will the enterprise connect to customers, connect to business partners, connect to employees, or some combination of these?

- Will the WAN provide authorized users limited or full access to the company intranet?

What is the geographic scope?

There are a few issues to consider:

- Is the WAN local, regional, or global?
- Is the WAN one-to-one (single branch), one-to-many branches, or many-to-many (distributed)?

What are the traffic requirements?

There are a few issues to consider:

- What type of traffic must be supported (data only, VoIP, video, large files, streaming files)? This determines the quality and performance requirements.
- What volume of traffic type (voice, video, or data) must be supported for each destination? This determines the bandwidth capacity required for the WAN connection to the ISP.
- What Quality of Service is required? This may limit the choices. If the traffic is highly sensitive to latency and jitter, eliminate any WAN connection options that cannot provide the required quality.
- What are the security requirements (data integrity, confidentiality, and security)? These are important factors if the traffic is of a highly confidential nature, or if it provides essential services, such as emergency response.

Choosing a WAN Link Connection (Cont.) (1.2.4.2)

In addition to gathering information about the scope of the WAN, the administrator must also determine the following:

- **Should the WAN use a private or public infrastructure?** A private infrastructure offers the best security and confidentiality, whereas the public Internet infrastructure offers the most flexibility and lowest ongoing expense. The choice depends on the purpose of the WAN, the types of traffic it carries, and available operating budget. For example, if the purpose is to provide a nearby branch with high-speed secure services, a private dedicated or switched connection may be best. If the purpose is to connect many remote offices, a public WAN using the Internet may be the best choice. For distributed operations, a combination of options may be the solution.

- **For a private WAN, should it be dedicated or switched?** Real-time, high-volume transactions have special requirements that could favor a dedicated line, such as traffic flowing between the data center and the corporate head office. If the enterprise is connecting to a local single branch, a dedicated leased line could be used. However, that option would become very expensive for a WAN connecting multiple offices. In that case, a switched connection might be better.

- **For a public WAN, what type of VPN access is required?** If the purpose of the WAN is to connect a remote office, a site-to-site VPN may be the best choice. To connect teleworkers or customers, remote-access VPNs are a better option. If the WAN is serving a mixture of remote offices, teleworkers, and authorized customers, such as a global company with distributed operations, a combination of VPN options may be required.

- **Which connection options are available locally?** In some areas, not all WAN connection options are available. In this case, the selection process is simplified, although the resulting WAN may provide less than optimal performance. For example, in a rural or remote area, the only option may be VSAT or cellular access.

- **What is the cost of the available connection options?** Depending on the option chosen, the WAN can be a significant ongoing expense. The cost of a particular option must be weighed against how well it meets the other requirements. For example, a dedicated leased line is the most expensive option, but the expense may be justified if it is critical to ensure secure transmission of high volumes of real-time data. For less demanding applications, a less expensive switched or Internet connection option may be more suitable.

Using the preceding guidelines, as well as those described by the Cisco Enterprise Architecture, a network administrator should be able to choose an appropriate WAN connection to meet the requirements of different business scenarios.

Lab 1.2.4.3: Researching WAN Technologies

In this lab, you will complete the following objectives:

Part 1: Investigate Dedicated WAN Technologies and Providers

Part 2: Investigate a Dedicated Leased-Line Service Provider in Your Area

Summary (1.3)

Class Activity 1.3.1.1: WAN Device Modules

Your medium-sized company is upgrading its network. To make the most of the equipment currently in use, you decide to purchase WAN modules instead of new equipment.

All branch offices use either Cisco 1900 or 2911 series ISRs. You will be updating these routers in several locations. Each branch has its own ISP requirements to consider.

To update the devices, focus on the following WAN module access types:

- Ethernet
- Broadband
- T1/E1 and ISDN PRI
- BRI
- Serial
- T1 and E1 Trunk Voice and WAN
- Wireless LANs and WANs

A business can use private lines or the public network infrastructure for WAN connections. A public infrastructure connection can be a cost-effective alternative to a private connection between LANs, as long as security is also planned.

WAN access standards operate at Layers 1 and 2 of the OSI model, and are defined and managed by the TIA/EIA, ISO, and IEEE. A WAN may be circuit-switched or packet-switched.

There is common terminology used to identify the physical components of WAN connections and who, the service provider or the customer, is responsible for which components.

Service provider networks are complex, and the service provider's backbone networks consist primarily of high-bandwidth fiber-optic media. The device used for interconnection to a customer is specific to the WAN technology that is implemented.

Permanent, dedicated point-to-point connections are provided by using leased lines. Dialup access, although slow, is still viable for remote areas with limited WAN options. Other private connection options include ISDN, Frame Relay, ATM, Ethernet WAN, MPLS, and VSAT.

Public infrastructure connections include DSL, cable, wireless, and 3G/4G cellular. Security over public infrastructure connections can be provided by using remote-access or site-to-site VPNs.

Practice

The following activities provide practice with the topics introduced in this chapter. The Labs and Class Activities are available in the companion *Connecting Networks Labs & Study Guide* (ISBN 9781587134296). The Packet Tracer Activities PKA files are found in the online course.

 Class Activities

Class Activity 1.0.1.2: Branching Out

Class Activity 1.3.1.1: WAN Device Modules

 Labs

Lab 1.2.4.3: Researching WAN Technologies

Check Your Understanding Questions

Complete all the review questions listed here to test your understanding of the topics and concepts in this chapter. The appendix "Answers to the 'Check Your Understanding' Questions" lists the answers.

1. A small company with 10 employees uses a single LAN to share information between computers. Which type of connection to the Internet would be appropriate for this company?

   A. A broadband service, such as DSL, through the company's local service provider

   B. A dialup connection that is supplied by the local telephone service provider

   C. Private dedicated lines through the local service provider

   D. A VSAT connection to a service provider

2. Which network scenario will require the use of a WAN?

   A. Employee workstations need to obtain dynamically assigned IP addresses.

   B. Employees in the branch office need to share files with the headquarters office that is located in a separate building on the same campus network.

   C. Employees need to access web pages that are hosted on the corporate web servers in the DMZ within their building.

   D. Employees need to connect to the corporate email server through a VPN while traveling.

3. Which statement describes a characteristic of a WAN?

   A. A WAN operates within the same geographic scope of a LAN but has serial links.

   B. A WAN provides end-user network connectivity to the campus backbone.

   C. All serial links are considered WAN connections.

   D. WAN networks are owned by service providers.

4. Which two devices are needed when a digital leased line is used to provide a connection between the customer and the service provider? (Choose two.)

   A. Access server

   B. CSU

   C. Dialup modem

   D. DSU

   E. Layer 2 switch

5. What is a requirement of a connectionless packet-switched network?

   A. A virtual circuit is created for the duration of the packet delivery.

   B. Each packet has to carry only an identifier.

   C. Full addressing information must be carried in each data packet.

   D. The network predetermines the route for a packet.

6. What is an advantage of packet-switched technology over circuit-switched technology?

   A. Packet-switched networks are less susceptible to jitter than circuit-switched networks are.

   B. Packet-switched networks can efficiently use multiple routes inside a service provider network.

C. Packet-switched networks do not require an expensive permanent connection to each endpoint.

D. Packet-switched networks usually experience lower latency than circuit-switched networks experience.

7. What is a long-distance fiber-optic media technology that supports both SONET and SDH, and assigns incoming optical signals to specific wavelengths of light?

A. ATM

B. DWDM

C. ISDN

D. MPLS

8. What is the recommended technology to use over a public WAN infrastructure when a branch office is connected to the corporate site?

A. ATM

B. ISDN

C. Municipal Wi-Fi

D. VPN

9. What are two common high-bandwidth fiber-optic media standards? (Choose two.)

A. ANSI

B. ATM

C. ITU

D. SDH

E. SONET

10. Which WAN technology establishes a dedicated constant point-to-point connection between two sites?

A. ATM

B. Frame Relay

C. ISDN

D. Leased lines

11. A hospital is looking for a solution to connect multiple, newly established remote branch medical offices. Which consideration is important when selecting a private WAN connection rather than a public WAN connection?

    A. Data security and confidentiality during transmission

    B. Higher data transmission rate

    C. Lower cost

    D. Website and file exchange service support

12. A new corporation needs a data network that must meet certain requirements. The network must provide a low-cost connection to salespeople dispersed over a large geographical area. Which two types of WAN infrastructure would meet the requirements? (Choose two.)

    A. Dedicated

    B. Internet

    C. Private infrastructure

    D. Public infrastructure

    E. Satellite

13. Which wireless technology provides Internet access through cellular networks?

    A. LTE

    B. Municipal Wi-Fi

    C. Satellite

    D. WiMAX

14. Which equipment is needed for an ISP to provide Internet connections through cable service?

    A. Access server

    B. CMTS

    C. CSU/DSU

    D. DSLAM

15. A customer needs a WAN virtual connection that provides high-speed, dedicated bandwidth between two sites. Which type of WAN connection would best fulfill this need?

    A. Circuit-switched network

    B. Ethernet WAN

    C. MPLS

    D. Packet-switched network

CHAPTER 2

Point-to-Point Connections

Objectives

Upon completion of this chapter, you will be able to answer the following questions:

- What are the fundamentals of point-to-point serial communication across a WAN?

- How do you configure HDLC encapsulation on a point-to-point serial link?

- What are differences between PPP and HDLC?

- What is the PPP-layered architecture?

- What are the functions of LCP and NCP?

- How does PPP establish a session?

- How do you configure PPP encapsulation on a point-to-point serial link?

- How do you configure PPP authentication?

- How do you troubleshoot PPP using **show** and **debug** commands?

Key Terms

This chapter uses the following key terms. You can find the definitions in the Glossary.

Introduction (2.0)

One of the most common types of WAN connections, especially in long-distance communications, is a point-to-point connection, also called a serial or leased-line connection. Because these connections are typically provided by a carrier, such as a telephone company, boundaries between what is managed by the carrier and what is managed by the customer must be clearly established.

This chapter covers the terms, technology, and protocols used in serial connections. The *High-Level Data Link Control (HDLC)* and *Point-to-Point Protocol (PPP)* are introduced. HDLC is the default protocol on a Cisco router serial interface. PPP is a protocol that is able to handle authentication, compression, and error detection; monitor link quality; and logically bundle multiple serial connections together to share the load.

Class Activity 2.0.1.2: PPP Persuasion

Your network engineering supervisor recently attended a networking conference where Layer 2 protocols were discussed. He knows that you have Cisco equipment on the premises, but he would also like to offer security and advanced TCP/IP options and controls on that same equipment by using the Point-to-Point Protocol (PPP).

After researching the PPP protocol, you find it offers some advantages over the HDLC protocol, currently used on your network.

Create a matrix listing the advantages and disadvantages of using the HDLC versus PPP protocols. When comparing the two protocols, include

- Ease of configuration

- Adaptability to nonproprietary network equipment

- Security options

- Bandwidth usage and compression

- Bandwidth consolidation

Share your chart with another student or class. Justify whether or not you would suggest sharing the matrix with the network engineering supervisor to justify a change being made from HDLC to PPP for Layer 2 network connectivity.

Serial Point-to-Point Overview (2.1)

In this section, you learn how to configure HDLC encapsulation.

Serial Communications (2.1.1)

In this topic, you learn the fundamentals of point-to-point serial communication across a WAN.

Serial and Parallel Ports (2.1.1.1)

A common type of WAN connection is the point-to-point connection. As shown in Figure 2-1, point-to-point connections are used to connect LANs to service provider WANs and to connect LAN segments within an enterprise network.

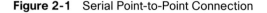

Figure 2-1   Serial Point-to-Point Connection

A LAN-to-WAN point-to-point connection is also referred to as a *serial connection* or *leased-line connection*. The reason is that the lines are leased from a carrier (usually a telephone company) and are dedicated for use by the company leasing the lines. Companies pay for a continuous connection between two remote sites, and the line is continuously active and available. Leased lines are a frequently used type of WAN access, and they are generally priced based on the bandwidth required and the distance between the two connected points.

Understanding how point-to-point serial communication across a leased line works is important to an overall understanding of how WANs function.

Communication across a serial connection is a method of data transmission in which the bits are transmitted sequentially over a single channel. Imagine the task of moving balls from one bin to another via a pipe only wide enough to fit one ball at a time. Multiple balls can go into the pipe, but only one at a time, and they have only one exit point, the other end of the pipe. A serial port is bidirectional and often referred to as a bidirectional port or a communications port.

This serial communication is in contrast to parallel communications in which bits can be transmitted simultaneously over multiple wires. Figure 2-2 illustrates the difference between serial and parallel connections.

A parallel connection theoretically transfers data eight times faster than a *serial connection*. Based on this theory, a *parallel connection* sends a byte (eight bits) in the time that a serial connection sends a single bit. However, parallel communications do have issues with crosstalk across wires, especially as the wire length increases.

Clock skew is also an issue with parallel communications. Clock skew occurs when data across the various wires does not arrive at the same time, creating synchronization issues. Finally, many parallel communications support only one-direction, outbound-only communication, but some support half-duplex communication (two-way communication, but only one way at a time).

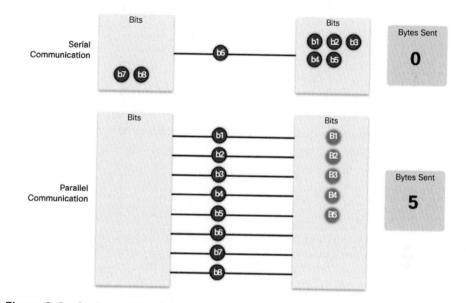

Figure 2-2   Serial and Parallel Communication

At one time, most PCs included both serial and parallel ports. Parallel ports were used to connect printers, computers, and other devices that required relatively high bandwidth. Parallel ports were also used between internal components. For external communications, a serial bus was primarily used to connect to phone lines and devices that could potentially be a further distance than a parallel transfer would allow. Because serial communications are less complex and require simpler circuitry, serial communications are considerably less expensive to implement. Serial communications use fewer wires, cheaper cables, and fewer connector pins.

On most PCs, *parallel ports* and *RS-232 serial ports* have been replaced by the higher speed serial *universal serial bus (USB) interfaces*. For long-distance communication, many WANs also use serial transmission.

Point-to-Point Communication Links (2.1.1.2)

When permanent dedicated connections are required, a point-to-point link is used to provide a single, pre-established WAN communications path. This path goes from the customer premises, through the provider network, to a remote destination, as shown in Figure 2-3.

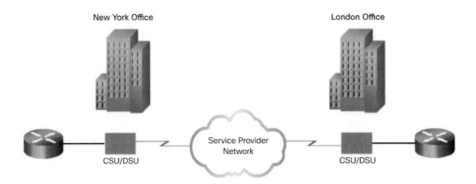

Figure 2-3 Point-to-Point Communication Links

A point-to-point link can connect two geographically distant sites, such as a corporate office in New York and a regional office in London. For a point-to-point line, the carrier dedicates specific resources for a line that is leased by the customer (leased line).

Note

Point-to-point connections are not limited to connections that cross land. Hundreds of thousands of miles of undersea fiber-optic cables connect countries and continents worldwide. An Internet search of "undersea Internet cable map" produces several cable maps of these undersea connections.

Point-to-point links are usually more expensive than shared services. The cost of leased-line solutions can become significant when used to connect many sites over increasing distances; however, sometimes the benefits outweigh the cost of the leased line. The dedicated capacity removes latency or jitter between the endpoints. Constant availability is essential for some applications such as voice or video over IP.

Serial Bandwidth (2.1.1.3)

Bandwidth refers to the rate at which data is transferred over the communication link. The underlying carrier technology will dictate how much bandwidth is available. There is a difference in bandwidth points between the North American (T-carrier) specification and the European (E-carrier) system. Optical networks also use a different bandwidth hierarchy, which again differs between North America and Europe. In the United States, optical carrier (OC) defines the bandwidth points.

In North America, the bandwidth is usually expressed as a *digital signal level (DS)* number (DS0, DS1, and so on), which refers to the rate and format of the signal. The most fundamental line speed is 64 kb/s, or DS0, which is the bandwidth required for an uncompressed, digitized phone call. Serial connection bandwidths can be incrementally increased to accommodate the need for faster transmission. For example, 24

DS0s can be bundled to get a DS1 line (also called a T1 line) with a speed of 1.544 Mb/s. Also, 28 DS1s can be bundled to get a DS3 line (also called a T3 line) with a speed of 44.736 Mb/s. Leased lines are available in different capacities and are generally priced based on the bandwidth required and the distance between the two connected points.

OC transmission rates are a set of standardized specifications for the transmission of digital signals carried on SONET fiber-optic networks. The designation uses OC, followed by an integer value representing the base transmission rate of 51.84 Mb/s. For example, OC-1 has a transmission capacity of 51.84 Mb/s, whereas an OC-3 transmission medium would be three times 51.84 Mb/s or 155.52 Mb/s.

Table 2-1 lists the most common line types and the associated bit rate capacity of each.

Table 2-1   Serial Line Bandwidth Capacities

Line Type	Bit Rate Capacity
56	56 kb/s
64	64 kb/s
T1	1.544 Mb/s
E1	2.048 Mb/s
J1	2.048 Mb/s
E3	34.064 Mb/s
T3	44.736 Mb/s
OC-1	51.84 Mb/s
OC-3	155.54 Mb/s
OC-9	466.56 Mb/s
OC-12	622.08 Mb/s
OC-18	933.12 Mb/s
OC-24	1.244 Gb/s
OC-36	1.866 Gb/s
OC-48	2.488 Gb/s
OC-96	4.976 Gb/s
OC-192	9.954 Gb/s
OC-768	39.813 Gb/s

Note

E1 (2.048 Mb/s) and E3 (34.368 Mb/s) are European standards like T1 and T3, but with different bandwidths and frame structures.

HDLC Encapsulation (2.1.2)

In this topic, you configure HDLC encapsulation on a point-to-point serial link.

WAN Encapsulation Protocols (2.1.2.1)

On each WAN connection, data is encapsulated into frames before crossing the WAN link. To ensure that the correct protocol is used, you must configure the appropriate Layer 2 encapsulation type. The choice of protocol depends on the WAN technology and the communicating equipment. Figure 2-4 displays the more common WAN protocols and where they are used.

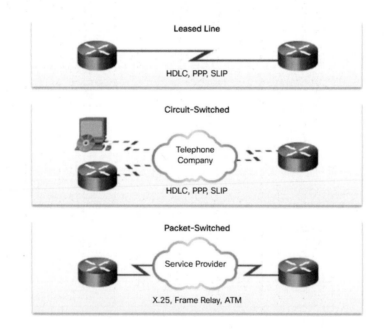

Figure 2-4   WAN Encapsulation Protocols

The following are short descriptions of each type of WAN protocol:

■ **HDLC:** This protocol is the default encapsulation type on point-to-point connections, dedicated links, and circuit-switched connections when the link uses two Cisco devices. HDLC is now the basis for synchronous PPP used by many servers to connect to a WAN, most commonly the Internet.

- **PPP:** This protocol provides router-to-router and host-to-network connections over *synchronous circuits* and *asynchronous circuits*. PPP works with several network layer protocols, such as IPv4 and IPv6. PPP is based on the HDLC encapsulation protocol but also has built-in security mechanisms such as *Password Authentication Protocol (PAP)* and *Challenge Handshake Authentication Protocol (CHAP)*.

- *Serial Line Internet Protocol (SLIP)*: This standard protocol for point-to-point serial connections uses TCP/IP. SLIP has been largely displaced by PPP.

- *X.25*: This ITU-T standard defines how connections between a DTE and DCE are maintained for remote terminal access and computer communications in public data networks. X.25 specifies *Link Access Procedure, Balanced (LAPB)*, a data link layer protocol. X.25 is a predecessor to Frame Relay.

- **Frame Relay:** This industry standard, switched, data link layer protocol handles multiple virtual circuits. Frame Relay is a next-generation protocol after X.25. Frame Relay eliminates some of the time-consuming processes (such as error correction and flow control) employed in X.25.

- **ATM:** This is the international standard for cell relay in which devices send multiple service types, such as voice, video, or data, in fixed-length (53-byte) cells. Fixed-length cells allow processing to occur in hardware, thereby reducing transit delays. ATM takes advantage of high-speed transmission media such as E3, SONET, and T3.

HDLC and PPP are the focus of this course. The other WAN protocols listed are considered either legacy technologies or beyond the scope of this course.

HDLC Encapsulation (2.1.2.2)

HDLC is a *bit-oriented* synchronous data link layer protocol developed by the International Organization for Standardization (ISO). The current standard for HDLC is ISO 13239. HDLC was developed from the *Synchronous Data Link Control (SDLC)* standard proposed in the 1970s. HDLC provides both connection-oriented and connectionless service.

HDLC uses synchronous serial transmission to provide error-free communication between two points. HDLC defines a Layer 2 framing structure that allows for flow control and error control through the use of acknowledgments. Each frame has the same format, whether it is a data frame or a control frame.

When frames are transmitted over synchronous or asynchronous links, those links have no mechanism to mark the beginning or end of frames. For this reason, HDLC uses a frame delimiter, or flag, to mark the beginning and the end of each frame.

Cisco has developed an extension to the HLDC protocol to solve the inability to provide multiprotocol support. Although Cisco HLDC (also referred to as cHDLC) is proprietary, Cisco has allowed many other network equipment vendors to implement it. Cisco HDLC frames contain a field for identifying the network protocol being encapsulated. Figure 2-5 compares standard HLDC to Cisco HLDC.

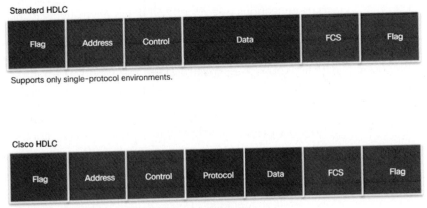

Figure 2-5   Standard and Cisco HDLC Frame Format

Configuring HDLC Encapsulation (2.1.2.3)

Cisco HDLC is the default encapsulation method that Cisco devices use on synchronous serial lines.

Use Cisco HDLC as a Point-to-Point Protocol on leased lines between two Cisco devices. If connecting non-Cisco devices, use synchronous PPP.

If the default encapsulation method has been changed, use the **encapsulation hdlc** interface configuration mode command to re-enable HDLC.

Example 2-1 displays how to re-enable HDLC on a serial interface.

Example 2-1 Configuring HDLC Encapsulation

```
Router(config)# interface s0/0/0
Router(config-if)# encapsulation hdlc
```

Troubleshooting a Serial Interface (2.1.2.4)

The output of the **show interfaces serial** command displays information specific to serial interfaces. Add the specific interface number you want to investigate, such as **show interface serial 0/0/0**.

When HDLC is configured, "encapsulation HDLC" should be reflected in the output, as highlighted in Example 2-2.

Example 2-2 Verifying a Serial Interface

```
R1# show interface serial 0/0/0
Serial0/0/0 is up, line protocol is up
  Hardware is GT96K Serial
  Internet address is 172.16.0.1/30
  MTU 1500 bytes, BW 1544 Kbit/sec, DLY 20000 usec,
     reliability 255/255, txload 1/255, rxload 1/255
  Encapsulation HDLC, loopback not set
  Keepalive set (10 sec)
  CRC checking enabled
  Last input 00:00:05, output 00:00:04, output hang never
  Last clearing of "show interface" counters never
  Input queue: 0/75/0/0 (size/max/drops/flushes); Total output drops: 0
  Queueing strategy: weighted fair
  Output queue: 0/1000/64/0 (size/max total/threshold/drops)
     Conversations  0/1/256 (active/max active/max total)
     Reserved Conversations 0/0 (allocated/max allocated)
     Available Bandwidth 1158 kilobits/sec
  5 minute input rate 0 bits/sec, 0 packets/sec
  5 minute output rate 0 bits/sec, 0 packets/sec
     5 packets input, 1017 bytes, 0 no buffer
     Received 5 broadcasts (0 IP multicasts)
     0 runts, 0 giants, 0 throttles
     0 input errors, 0 CRC, 0 frame, 0 overrun, 0 ignored, 0 abort
     4 packets output, 395 bytes, 0 underruns
     0 output errors, 0 collisions, 4 interface resets
     0 unknown protocol drops
     0 output buffer failures, 0 output buffers swapped out
     2 carrier transitions
     DCD=up  DSR=up  DTR=up  RTS=up  CTS=up
```

The highlighted section, "Serial 0/0/0 is up, line protocol is up," indicates that the line is up and functioning while the "encapsulation HDLC" highlighted section indicates that the default serial encapsulation (HDLC) is enabled.

The **show interfaces serial** command returns one of six possible states:

- Serial x is up, line protocol is up
- Serial x is down, line protocol is down (DTE mode)
- Serial x is up, line protocol is down (DTE mode)
- Serial x is up, line protocol is down (DCE mode)
- Serial x is up, line protocol is up (looped)
- Serial x is up, line protocol is down (disabled)
- Serial x is administratively down, line protocol is down

Of the seven possible states, six are problem states. Table 2-2 lists the six possible problem states, the issues associated with the problem states, and how to troubleshoot a problem state.

Table 2-2 Troubleshooting a Serial Interface

Line State	Possible Condition(s)	Problem/Solution
Serial x is up, line protocol is up	This is the proper status line condition.	No action is required.
Serial x is down, line protocol is down (DTE mode)	■ The router is not sensing a *Carrier Detect (CD) signal*. ■ A WAN service provider problem has occurred, which means the line is down or is not connected to CSU/DSU. ■ Cabling is faulty or incorrect. ■ Hardware failure has occurred (CSU/DSU).	1. Check the LEDs on the CSU/DSU to see whether the CD is active. 2. Verify that the proper cable and interface are being used. 3. Contact the service provider to see whether a problem has occurred. 4. Swap faulty parts. 5. Use another serial line to see if the connection comes up, indicating the previously connected interface has a problem.
Serial x is up, line protocol is down (DTE mode)	■ A local or remote router is misconfigured. ■ *Keepalives* are not being sent by the remote router. ■ A leased-line or other carrier service problem has occurred, which means a noisy line or misconfigured or failed switch.	1. Many DCE devices (e.g., modems and CSU/DSUs) have a local loopback self-check mechanism to verify the connection between the DCE and DTE (e.g., router). Enable this mechanism and use the **show interfaces serial** command on the router. If the line protocol comes up between the DCE and DTE, the problem is most likely a WAN service provider problem. 2. If the problem appears to be on the remote end, repeat Step 1 on the remote DCE.

Line State	Possible Condition(s)	Problem/Solution
	■ A timing problem has occurred on the cable. ■ A local or remote CSU/DSU has failed. ■ Router hardware, which could be either local or remote, has failed.	3. Verify that the correct cabling has been used and that the DTE is correctly connected to the DCE and that the DCE is correctly connected to the service provider network-termination point. Use the **show controllers** EXEC command to determine which cable is attached to which interface. 4. Enable the **debug serial interface** EXEC command. 5. If the line protocol comes up and the keepalive counter increments, the problem is not in the local router. 6. If the line protocol does not come up in local loopback mode, and the **debug serial interface** command output does not indicate incrementing keepalives, a router hardware problem is likely. Swap the router interface hardware. 7. If faulty router hardware is suspected, change the serial line to an unused port. If the connection comes up, the previously connected interface has a problem.
Serial x is up, line protocol is down (DCE mode)	■ The **clockrate** interface configuration command is missing. ■ The DTE device does not support the DCE timing. ■ The remote CSU or DSU has failed.	1. Add the **clockrate** *bps* interface configuration command on the serial interface. Use the question mark (?) to verify valid *bps* values. 2. If the problem appears to be on the remote end, repeat Step 1 on the remote DCE. 3. Verify that the correct cable is being used. 4. If the line protocol is still down, there is a possible hardware failure or cabling problem. 5. Replace faulty parts as necessary.
Serial x is up, line protocol is up (looped)	■ A loop exists in the circuit. The sequence number in the keepalive packet changes to a random number when a loop is initially detected. If the same random number is returned over the link, a loop exists.	1. Use the **show running-config** privileged EXEC command to look for any loopback interface configuration command entries. 2. If there is a loopback interface configuration command entry, use the **no loopback interface** global configuration command to remove the loopback.

Line State	Possible Condition(s)	Problem/Solution
		3. If there is no loopback interface configuration command, examine the CSU/DSU to determine whether they are configured in manual loopback mode. If they are, disable manual loopback.
		4. After disabling loopback mode on the CSU/DSU, reset the CSU/DSU and inspect the line status. If the line protocol comes up, no other action is needed.
		5. If, upon inspection, the CSU or DSU cannot be manually set, contact the leased-line or other carrier service for line troubleshooting assistance.
Serial x is up, line protocol is down (disabled)	■ A high error rate has occurred due to a WAN service provider problem. ■ A CSU or DSU hardware problem has occurred. ■ Router hardware (interface) is bad.	1. Troubleshoot the line with a serial analyzer and breakout box. Look for toggling CTS and DSR signals. 2. Loop CSU/DSU (DTE loop). If the problem continues, it is likely that there is a hardware problem. If the problem does not continue, it is likely that there is a WAN service provider problem. 3. Swap out bad hardware as required (CSU, DSU, switch, local or remote router).
Serial x is administratively down, line protocol is down	■ The router configuration includes the **shutdown** interface configuration command. ■ A duplicate IP address exists.	1. Check the router configuration for the **shutdown** command. 2. Use the **no shutdown** interface configuration command to remove the **shutdown** command. 3. Verify that there are no identical IP addresses using the **show running-config** privileged EXEC command or the **show interfaces** EXEC command. 4. If there are duplicate addresses, resolve the conflict by changing one of the IP addresses.

The **show controllers** command is another important diagnostic tool when troubleshooting serial lines, as shown in Example 2-3.

Example 2-3 Verifying the Controller Settings

```
R1# show controllers serial 0/0/0
Interface Serial0/0/0
Hardware is GT96K
DCE V.35, clock rate 64000
idb at 0x66855120, driver data structure at 0x6685C93C
<output omitted>
```

The output indicates the state of the interface channels and whether a cable is attached to the interface. In the example, interface serial 0/0/0 has a V.35 DCE cable attached. The command syntax varies, depending on the platform.

Note

Cisco 7000 series routers use a cBus controller card for connecting serial links. With these routers, use the **show controllers cbus** command.

If the electrical interface output displays as "UNKNOWN" instead of "V.35," "EIA/TIA-449," or some other electrical interface type, the likely problem is an improperly connected cable. A problem with the internal wiring of the card is also possible. If the electrical interface is unknown, the corresponding display for the **show interfaces serial** command shows that the interface and line protocol are down.

Packet Tracer
☐ **Activity**

Packet Tracer 2.1.2.5: Troubleshooting Serial Interfaces

Background/Scenario

You have been asked to troubleshoot WAN connections for a local telephone company (telco). The telco router is supposed to communicate with four remote sites, but none of them are working. Use your knowledge of the OSI model and a few general rules to identify and repair the errors in the network.

PPP Operation (2.2)

In this section, you learn how PPP operates across a point-to-point serial link.

Benefits of PPP (2.2.1)

In this topic, you learn how to compare PPP with HDLC.

Introducing PPP (2.2.1.1)

HDLC is the default serial encapsulation method when connecting two Cisco routers. With an added protocol type field, the Cisco version of HDLC is proprietary. Therefore, Cisco HDLC can work only with other Cisco devices. However, as shown in Figure 2-6, use PPP encapsulation when you need to connect to a non-Cisco router.

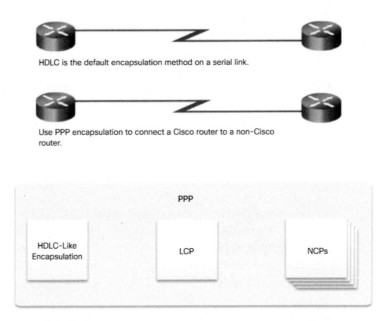

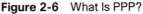

Figure 2-6   What Is PPP?

PPP is commonly used as a data link layer protocol for connection over synchronous and asynchronous circuits. PPP encapsulation has been carefully designed to retain compatibility with most commonly used supporting hardware. PPP encapsulates data frames for transmission over Layer 2 physical links. It establishes a direct connection using serial cables, phone lines, *trunk lines*, cellular telephones, specialized radio links, or fiber-optic links.

PPP contains three main components:

- HDLC-like framing for transporting multiprotocol packets over point-to-point links.

- *Link Control Protocol (LCP)* for establishing, configuring, and testing the data-link connection.

- Family of *Network Control Protocols (NCPs)* for establishing and configuring different network layer protocols. PPP allows the simultaneous use of multiple network layer protocols. The most common NCPs are IPv4 Control Protocol and IPv6 Control Protocol.

Note

Other NCPs include AppleTalk Control Protocol, Novell IPX Control Protocol, Cisco Systems Control Protocol, SNA Control Protocol, and Compression Control Protocol.

Advantages of PPP (2.2.1.2)

PPP originally emerged as an encapsulation protocol for transporting IPv4 traffic over point-to-point links. It provides a standard method for transporting multiprotocol packets over point-to-point links.

There are many advantages to using PPP, including the fact that it is not proprietary. PPP includes many features not available in HDLC:

- The *link quality management (LQM)* feature monitors the quality of the link. LQM can be configured with the interface command **ppp quality** *percentage*. If the error percentage falls below the configured threshold, the link is taken down and packets are rerouted or dropped.

- PPP supports PAP and CHAP authentication. This feature is explained and configured in the next section.

LCP and NCP (2.2.2)

In this topic, you learn about the PPP-layered architecture and the functions of LCP and NCP.

PPP-Layered Architecture (2.2.2.1)

A layered architecture is a logical model, design, or blueprint that aids in communication between interconnecting layers. Figure 2-7 maps the layered architecture of PPP against the Open System Interconnection (OSI) model. PPP and OSI share the same physical layer, but PPP distributes the functions of LCP and NCP differently.

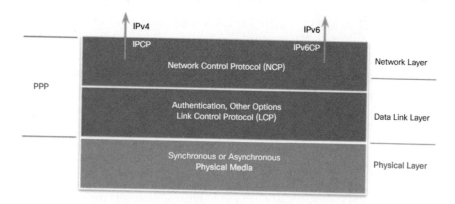

Figure 2-7   PPP-Layered Architecture: Physical Layer

At the physical layer, you can configure PPP on a range of interfaces. The only absolute requirement imposed by PPP is that it can operate using a full-duplex circuit. The physical layer standards are transparent to PPP link layer frames. PPP does not impose any restrictions regarding transmission rate.

Most of the work done by PPP happens at the data link and network layers, by LCP and NCPs.

PPP: Link Control Protocol (LCP) (2.2.2.2)

LCP functions within the data link layer and has a role in establishing, configuring, and testing the data link connection. LCP establishes the point-to-point link. LCP also negotiates and sets up control options on the WAN data link, which are handled by the NCPs, as shown in Figure 2-7.

LCP provides automatic configuration of the interfaces at each end:

- Handling varying limits on packet size

- Detecting common misconfiguration errors

- Terminating the link

- Determining when a link is functioning properly or when it is failing

After the link is established, PPP also uses LCP to agree automatically on encapsulation formats such as authentication, compression, and error detection.

PPP: Network Control Protocol (NCP) (2.2.2.3)

PPP permits multiple network layer protocols to operate on the same communications link. For every network layer protocol used, PPP uses a separate NCP, as shown in Figure 2-7. For example, IPv4 uses *IP Control Protocol (IPCP)* and IPv6 uses *IPv6 Control Protocol (IPv6CP)*.

NCPs include functional fields containing standardized codes to indicate the network layer protocol that PPP encapsulates. Table 2-3 lists the PPP protocol field numbers. Each NCP manages the specific needs required by its respective network layer protocols. The various NCP components encapsulate and negotiate options for multiple network layer protocols.

Table 2-3 Protocol Field Names

Value (in Hex)	Protocol Name
8021	Internet Protocol (IPv4) Control Protocol
8057	Internet Protocol version 6 (IPv6) Control Protocol
8023	OSI Network Layer Control Protocol

Value (in Hex)	Protocol Name
8029	Appletalk Control Protocol
802b	Novell IPX Control Protocol
c021	Link Control Protocol
c023	Password Authentication Protocol
c223	Challenge Handshake Authentication Protocol

PPP Frame Structure (2.2.2.4)

A PPP frame consists of six fields. The following descriptions summarize the PPP frame fields illustrated in Figure 2-8:

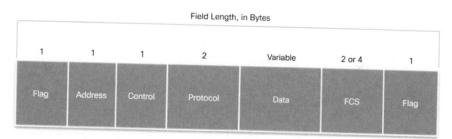

Figure 2-8   PPP Frame Fields

- **Flag:** A single byte that indicates the beginning or end of a frame. The Flag field consists of the binary sequence 01111110.

- **Address:** A single byte that contains the binary sequence 11111111, the standard broadcast address. PPP does not assign individual station addresses.

- **Control:** A single byte that contains the binary sequence 00000011, which calls for transmission of user data in an unsequenced frame.

- **Protocol:** Two bytes that identify the protocol encapsulated in the information field of the frame. The 2-byte Protocol field identifies the protocol of the PPP payload.

- **Data:** Zero or more bytes that contain the datagram for the protocol specified in the protocol field.

- **Frame Check Sequence (FCS):** This is normally 16 bits (2 bytes). If the receiver's calculation of the FCS does not match the FCS in the PPP frame, the PPP frame is silently discarded.

LCPs can negotiate modifications to the standard PPP frame structure. Modified frames, however, are always distinguishable from standard frames.

Interactive
Graphic

Activity 2.2.2.5: Identify PPP Features and Operations

Refer to the online course to complete this activity.

PPP Sessions (2.2.3)

In this topic, you learn how PPP establishes a session.

Establishing a PPP Session (2.2.3.1)

Establishing a PPP session entails three phases, as shown in Figure 2-9 and described in the list that follows.

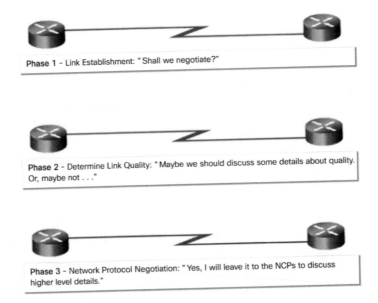

Phase 1 - Link Establishment: "Shall we negotiate?"

Phase 2 - Determine Link Quality: "Maybe we should discuss some details about quality. Or, maybe not . . ."

Phase 3 - Network Protocol Negotiation: "Yes, I will leave it to the NCPs to discuss higher level details."

Figure 2-9   Establishing a PPP Session

- **Phase 1: Link establishment and configuration negotiation:** Before PPP exchanges any network layer datagrams, such as IP, the LCP must first open the connection and negotiate configuration options. This phase is complete when the receiving router sends a configuration-acknowledgment frame back to the router initiating the connection.

- **Phase 2: Link quality determination (optional):** The LCP tests the link to determine whether the link quality is sufficient to bring up network layer protocols.

The LCP can delay transmission of network layer protocol information until this phase is complete.

- **Phase 3: Network layer protocol configuration negotiation:** After the LCP has finished the link quality determination phase, the appropriate NCP can separately configure the network layer protocols, and bring them up and take them down at any time. If the LCP closes the link, it informs the network layer protocols so that they can take appropriate action.

The link remains configured for communications until explicit LCP or NCP frames close the link, or until some external event occurs such as an inactivity timer expiring or an administrator intervening.

The LCP can terminate the link at any time. This is usually done when one of the routers requests termination but can happen because of a physical event, such as the loss of a carrier or the expiration of an idle-period timer.

LCP Operation (2.2.3.2)

LCP operation includes provisions for link establishment, link maintenance, and link termination. LCP operation uses three classes of LCP frames to accomplish the work of each of the LCP phases:

- *Link-establishment frames* establish and configure a link (Configure-Request, Configure-Ack, Configure-Nak, and Configure-Reject).

- *Link-maintenance frames* manage and debug a link (Code-Reject, Protocol-Reject, Echo-Request, Echo-Reply, and Discard-Request).

- *Link-termination frames* terminate a link (Terminate-Request and Terminate-Ack).

Link Establishment

Link establishment is the first phase of LCP operation, as seen in Figure 2-10. This phase must complete successfully before any network layer packets can be exchanged. During link establishment, the LCP opens the connection and negotiates the configuration parameters. The link-establishment process starts with the initiating device sending a Configure-Request frame to the responder. The Configure-Request frame includes a variable number of configuration options needed to set up on the link.

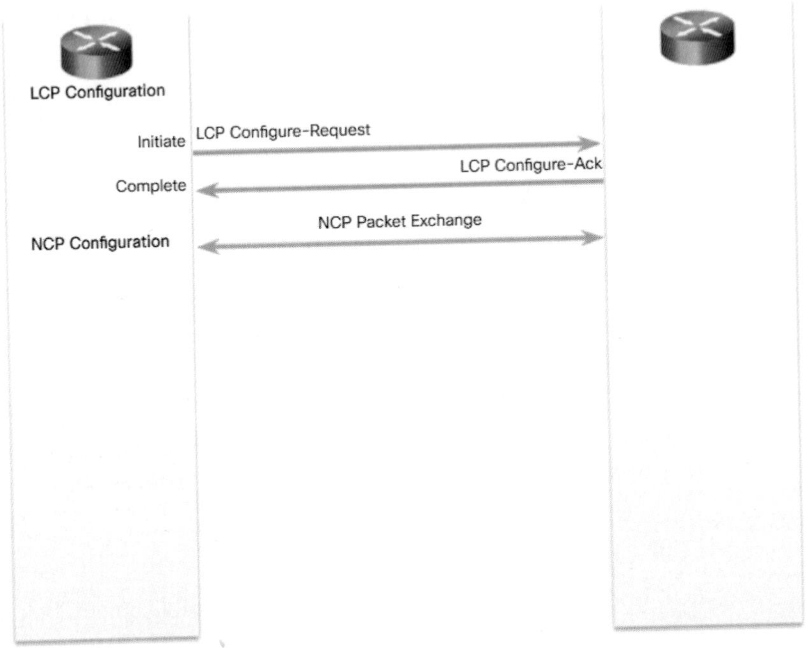

Figure 2-10   PPP Link Establishment

The initiator includes the options for how it wants the link created, including protocol or authentication parameters. The responder processes the request:

- If the options are not acceptable or not recognized, the responder sends a Configure-Nak or Configure-Reject message. If this occurs and the negotiation fails, the initiator must restart the process with new options.

- If the options are acceptable, the responder responds with a Configure-Ack message and the process moves on to the authentication stage. The operation of the link is handed over to the NCP.

When NCP has completed all necessary configurations, including validating authentication if configured, the line is available for data transfer. During the exchange of data, LCP transitions into link maintenance.

Link Maintenance

During link maintenance, LCP can use messages to provide feedback and test the link, as shown in Figure 2-11:

- **Echo-Request, Echo-Reply, and Discard-Request:** These frames can be used for testing the link.

- **Code-Reject and Protocol-Reject:** These frame types provide feedback when one device receives an invalid frame. The sending device will resend the packet.

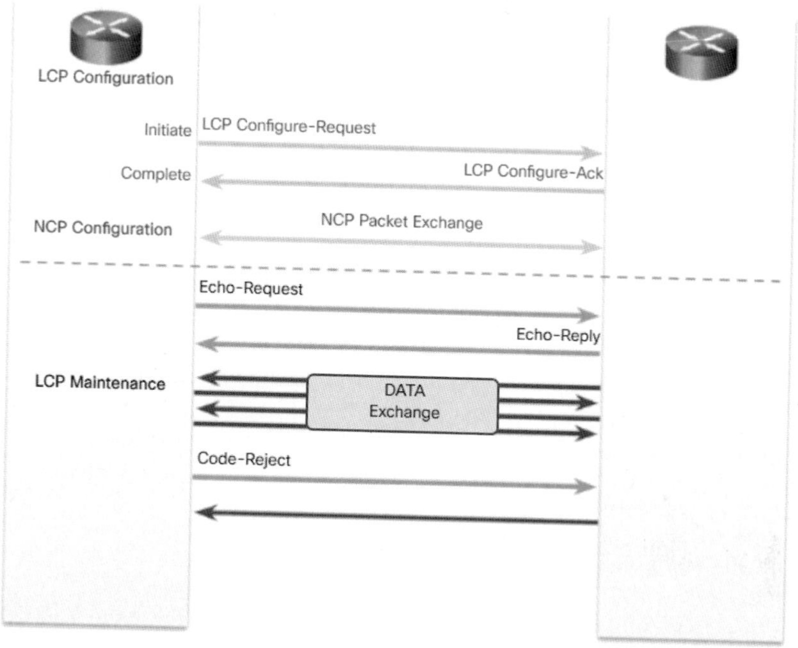

Figure 2-11   PPP Link Maintenance

Link Termination

After the transfer of data at the network layer completes, the LCP terminates the link, as shown in Figure 2-12. NCP terminates only the network layer and NCP link. The link remains open until the LCP terminates it. If the LCP terminates the link before NCP, the NCP session is also terminated.

PPP can terminate the link at any time. This might happen because of the loss of the carrier, authentication failure, link quality failure, the expiration of an idle-period timer, or the administrative closing of the link. The LCP closes the link by exchanging Terminate packets. The device initiating the shutdown sends a Terminate-Request message. The other device replies with a Terminate-Ack. A termination request indicates that the device sending it needs to close the link. When the link is closing, PPP informs the network layer protocols so that they may take appropriate action.

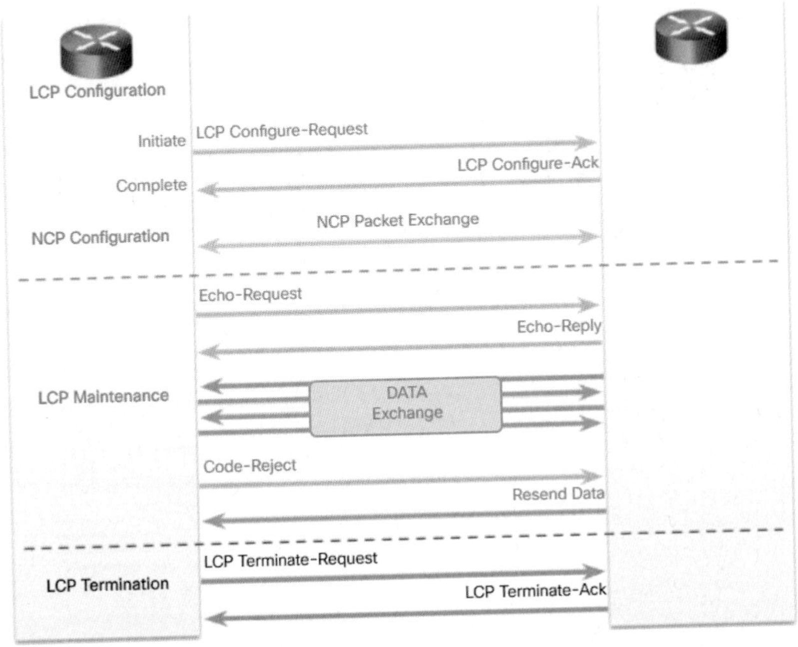

Figure 2-12   PPP Link Termination

PPP Configuration Options (2.2.3.3)

PPP can be configured to support various optional functions. There are three optional functions:

- Authentication using either PAP or CHAP
- Compression using either Stacker or Predictor
- Multilink that combines two or more channels to increase the WAN bandwidth

NCP Explained (2.2.3.4)

After the LCP has configured and authenticated the basic link, the appropriate NCP is invoked to complete the specific configuration of the network layer protocol being used. When the NCP has successfully configured the network layer protocol, the network protocol is in the open state on the established LCP link. At this point, PPP can carry the corresponding network layer protocol packets.

IPCP Example

As an example of how the NCP layer works, Figure 2-13 shows the NCP configuration of IPv4. After LCP has established the link, the routers exchange IPCP messages, negotiating options specific to IPv4. IPCP is responsible for configuring, enabling, and disabling the IPv4 modules on both ends of the link.

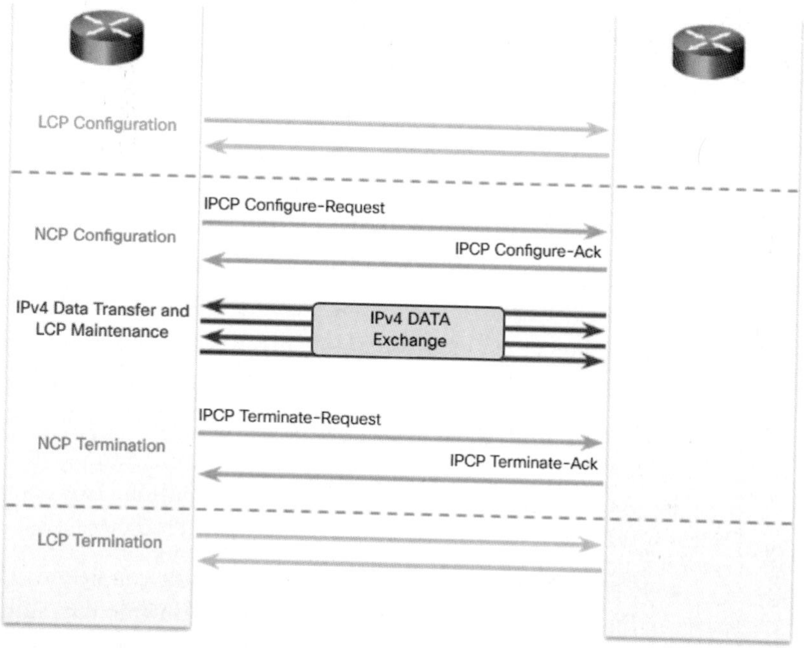

Figure 2-13   PPP NCP Operation

IPCP negotiates two options:

- **Compression:** Allows devices to negotiate an algorithm to compress TCP and IP headers and save bandwidth. The Van Jacobson TCP/IP header compression reduces the size of the TCP/IP headers to as few as 3 bytes. This can be a significant improvement on slow serial lines, particularly for interactive traffic.

- **IPv4-Address:** Allows the initiating device to specify an IPv4 address to use for routing IP over the PPP link, or to request an IPv4 address for the responder. Prior to the advent of broadband technologies such as DSL and cable modem services, dialup network devices commonly used the IPv4 address option.

After the NCP process is complete, the link goes into the open state and LCP takes over again in a link maintenance phase. Link traffic consists of any possible combination of LCP, NCP, and network layer protocol packets. When data transfer is complete, NCP terminates the protocol link and LCP terminates the PPP connection.

Interactive
Graphic

Activity 2.2.3.5: Identify the Steps in the LCP Link Negotiation Process

Refer to the online course to complete this activity.

PPP Implementation (2.3)

In this section, you learn how to configure PPP encapsulation.

Configure PPP (2.3.1)

In this topic, you configure PPP encapsulation on a point-to-point serial link.

PPP Configuration Options (2.3.1.1)

The previous section introduced configurable LCP options to meet specific WAN connection requirements. PPP may include several LCP options:

- **Authentication:** Peer routers exchange authentication messages. Two authentication choices are Password Authentication Protocol (PAP) and Challenge Handshake Authentication Protocol (CHAP).

- **Compression:** This option increases the effective throughput on PPP connections by reducing the number of bits that must travel across the link. The protocol decompresses the frame at its destination. Two compression protocols available in Cisco routers are Stacker and Predictor.

- **Error detection:** This option identifies fault conditions. The Quality and Magic Number options help ensure a reliable, loop-free data link. The Magic Number field helps in detecting links that are in a looped-back condition. Until the Magic-Number Configuration Option has been successfully negotiated, the Magic-Number must be transmitted as zero. Magic numbers are generated randomly at each end of the connection.

- *PPP callback*: PPP callback is used to enhance security. With this LCP option, a Cisco router can act as a callback client or a callback server. The client makes the initial call, requests that the server call it back, and terminates its initial call. The callback router answers the initial call and makes the return call to the client based on its configuration statements.

- *Multilink PPP*: This alternative provides load balancing over the router interfaces that PPP uses. Multilink PPP, also referred to as MP, MPPP, MLP, or Multilink, provides a method for spreading traffic across multiple physical WAN links while providing packet fragmentation and reassembly, proper sequencing, multivendor interoperability, and load balancing on inbound and outbound traffic.

When options are configured, a corresponding field value is inserted into the LCP option field, as shown in Table 2-4.

Table 2-4 PPP Configuration Options

Option Name	Option Type	Option Length	Description
Maximum Receive Unit (MRU)	1	4	MRU is the maximum size of a PPP frame and cannot exceed 65,535. The default is 1500, and if neither peer is changing the default, it is not negotiated.
Asynchronous Control Character Map (ACCM)	2	6	This is a bitmap that enables character escapes for asynchronous links. By default, character escapes are used.
Authentication Protocol	3	5 or 6	This field indicates the authentication protocol, either PAP or CHAP.
Magic Number	5	6	This is a random number chosen to distinguish a peer and detect looped-back lines.
Protocol Compression	7	2	This flag indicates that the PPP protocol ID be compressed to a single octet when the 2-byte protocol ID is in the range 0x00-00 to 0x00-FF.
Address and Control Field Compression	8	2	This flag indicates that the PPP Address field (always set to 0xFF) and the PPP Control field (always set to 0x03) be removed from the PPP header.
Callback	13 or 0x0D	3	This 1-octet indicator determines how callback is to be determined.

PPP Basic Configuration Command (2.3.1.2)

To set PPP as the encapsulation method used by a serial interface, use the **encapsulation ppp** interface configuration command. The command has no arguments. Remember that if PPP is not configured on a Cisco router, the default encapsulation for serial interfaces is HDLC.

Figure 2-14 shows a two-router topology used to demonstrate PPP configuration.

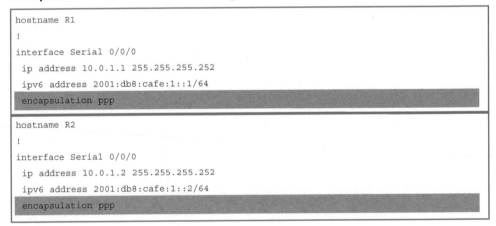

Figure 2-14   PPP Basic Configuration

Example 2-4 shows the configuration for R1 and R2 with both an IPv4 and an IPv6 address on the serial interfaces. PPP is a Layer 2 encapsulation that supports various Layer 3 protocols including IPv4 and IPv6.

Example 2-4 R1 and R2 PPP Basic Configuration

```
hostname R1
!
interface Serial 0/0/0
 ip address 10.0.1.1 255.255.255.252
 ipv6 address 2001:db8:cafe:1::1/64
 encapsulation ppp
hostname R2
!
interface Serial 0/0/0
 ip address 10.0.1.2 255.255.255.252
 ipv6 address 2001:db8:cafe:1::2/64
 encapsulation ppp
```

PPP Compression Commands (2.3.1.3)

Point-to-point software compression on serial interfaces can be configured after PPP encapsulation is enabled. Because this option invokes a software compression process, it can affect system performance. If the traffic already consists of compressed files, such as .zip, .tar, or .mpeg, do not use this option.

Use the **compress [predictor | stac]** interface configuration command to enable PPP compression.

Table 2-5 shows the options for the **compress** command.

Table 2-5   PPP **compress** Command

Keyword	Description
predictor	(Optional) Specifies that a predicator compression algorithm will be used
stac	(Optional) Specifies that a Stacker (LZS) compression algorithm will be used

Example 2-5 shows the configuration for R1 and R2 to use predictor compression.

Example 2-5 R1 and R2 PPP Compression Configuration

```
hostname R1
!
interface Serial 0/0/0
 ip address 10.0.1.1 255.255.255.252
 ipv6 address 2001:db8:cafe:1::1/64
 encapsulation ppp
 compress predictor

hostname R2
!
interface Serial 0/0/0
 ip address 10.0.1.2 255.255.255.252
 ipv6 address 2001:db8:cafe:1::2/64
 encapsulation ppp
 compress predictor
```

PPP Link Quality Monitoring Command (2.3.1.4)

LCP provides an optional link quality determination phase. In this phase, LCP tests the link to determine whether the link quality is sufficient to use Layer 3 protocols.

The **ppp quality** *percentage* interface configuration command ensures that the link meets the quality requirement set; otherwise, the link closes down. The *percentage* value specifies the link quality threshold using a range between 1 and 100.

The percentages are calculated for both incoming and outgoing directions. The outgoing quality is calculated by comparing the total number of packets and bytes sent, to the total number of packets and bytes received by the destination node. The incoming quality is calculated by comparing the total number of packets and bytes received to the total number of packets and bytes sent by the destination node.

If the link quality percentage is not maintained, the link is deemed to be of poor quality and is taken down. LQM implements a time lag so that the link does not bounce up and down.

The configuration **ppp quality 80**, shown in Example 2-6, sets minimum quality to 80 percent.

Example 2-6 R1 and R2 PPP Link Quality Configuration

```
hostname R1
!
interface Serial 0/0/0
 ip address 10.0.1.1 255.255.255.252
 ipv6 address 2001:db8:cafe:1::1/64
 encapsulation ppp
 compress predictor
 ppp quality 80

hostname R2
!
interface Serial 0/0/0
 ip address 10.0.1.2 255.255.255.252
 ipv6 address 2001:db8:cafe:1::2/64
 encapsulation ppp
 compress predictor
 ppp quality 80
```

PPP Multilink Commands (2.3.1.5)

Multilink PPP (also referred to as MP, MPPP, MLP, or Multilink) provides a method for spreading traffic across multiple physical WAN links. Multilink PPP also provides packet fragmentation and reassembly, proper sequencing, multivendor interoperability, and load balancing on inbound and outbound traffic.

MPPP allows packets to be fragmented and sends these fragments simultaneously over multiple point-to-point links to the same remote address. The multiple physical links come up in response to a user-defined load threshold. MPPP can measure the load on just inbound traffic or on just outbound traffic, but not on the combined load of both inbound and outbound traffic.

Figure 2-15 shows a PPP multilink topology.

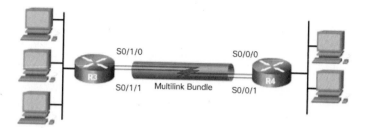

Figure 2-15   PPP Multilink

Configuring MPPP requires two steps:

Step 1.   Create a multilink bundle.

- Use the **interface multilink** *number* global configuration command to create the multilink interface.

- In interface configuration mode, assign an IPv4 and/or IPv6 address to the multilink interface.

- Use the **ppp multilink** interface configuration command to enable multilink PPP.

- Use the **ppp multilink group** *number* interface configuration command to assign the multilink group number.

Step 2.   Assign each physical interface to the multilink bundle.

- Use the **ppp encapsulation** interface configuration command to enable PPP.

- Use the **ppp multilink** interface configuration command to enable multilink PPP.

- Use the **ppp multilink group** *number* interface configuration command to assign the multilink group number.

Example 2-7 shows the configuration for R3 and R4.

Example 2-7 R3 and R4 PPP Multilink Configuration

```
hostname R3
!
interface Multilink 1
 ip address 10.0.1.1 255.255.255.252
 ipv6 address 2001:db8:cafe:1::1/64
 ppp multilink
 ppp multilink group 1
!
interface Serial 0/1/0
 no ip address
 encapsulation ppp
 ppp multilink
 ppp multilink group 1
!
interface Serial 0/1/1
 no ip address
 encapsulation ppp
 ppp multilink
 ppp multilink group 1
```

```
hostname R4
!
interface Multilink 1
 ip address 10.0.1.2 255.255.255.252
 ipv6 address 2001:db8:cafe:1::2/64
 ppp multilink
 ppp multilink group 1
!
interface Serial 0/0/0
 no ip address
 encapsulation ppp
 ppp multilink
 ppp multilink group 1
!
interface Serial 0/0/1
 no ip address
 encapsulation ppp
 ppp multilink
 ppp multilink group 1
```

To disable PPP multilink, use the **no ppp multilink** interface configuration command on each of the bundled interfaces.

Verifying PPP Configuration (2.3.1.6)

Use the **show interfaces serial** command to verify proper configuration of HDLC or PPP encapsulation. The command output in Example 2-8 shows a PPP configuration.

Example 2-8 Verifying the Serial PPP Encapsulation Configuration

```
R2# show interfaces serial 0/0/0
Serial0/0/0 is up, line protocol is up
  Hardware is GT96K Serial
  Internet address is 10.0.1.2/30
  MTU 1500 bytes, BW 1544 Kbit/sec, DLY 20000 usec,
     reliability 255/255, txload 1/255, rxload 1/255
  Encapsulation PPP, LCP Open
  Open: IPCP, IPV6CP, CCP, CDPCP, loopback not set
  Keepalive set (10 sec)
  CRC checking enabled
  Last input 00:00:02, output 00:00:02, output hang never
  Last clearing of "show interface" counters 01:29:06
  Input queue: 0/75/0/0 (size/max/drops/flushes); Total output drops: 0
  Queueing strategy: weighted fair
  Output queue: 0/1000/64/0 (size/max total/threshold/drops)
     Conversations  0/1/256 (active/max active/max total)
     Reserved Conversations 0/0 (allocated/max allocated)
     Available Bandwidth 1158 kilobits/sec
  5 minute input rate 0 bits/sec, 0 packets/sec
  5 minute output rate 0 bits/sec, 0 packets/sec
     1944 packets input, 67803 bytes, 0 no buffer
     Received 0 broadcasts (0 IP multicasts)
     0 runts, 0 giants, 0 throttles
     0 input errors, 0 CRC, 0 frame, 0 overrun, 0 ignored, 0 abort
     1934 packets output, 67718 bytes, 0 underruns
     0 output errors, 0 collisions, 5 interface resets
     1 unknown protocol drops
     0 output buffer failures, 0 output buffers swapped out
     8 carrier transitions
     DCD=up  DSR=up  DTR=up  RTS=up  CTS=up

R2#
```

When you configure HDLC, the output of the **show interfaces serial** command should display "encapsulation HDLC." When PPP is configured, the command also displays the LCP and NCP states. Notice that NCPs IPCP and IPV6CP are open for IPv4 and IPv6 because R1 and R2 were configured with both IPv4 and IPv6 addresses.

Table 2-6 summarizes commands used when verifying PPP.

Table 2-6   PPP Verification Commands

Command	Description
show interfaces	Displays statistics for all interfaces configured on the router
show interfaces serial	Displays information about a serial interface
show ppp multilink	Displays information about a PPP multilink interface

The **show ppp multilink** command verifies that PPP multilink is enabled on R3, as shown in Example 2-9. The output indicates the interface Multilink 1, the hostnames of both the local and remote endpoints, and the serial interfaces assigned to the multilink bundle.

Example 2-9 Verifying PPP Multilink Configuration

```
R3# show ppp multilink
Multilink1
  Bundle name: R4
  Remote Endpoint Discriminator: [1] R4
  Local Endpoint Discriminator: [1] R3
  Bundle up for 00:01:20, total bandwidth 3088, load 1/255
  Receive buffer limit 24000 bytes, frag timeout 1000 ms
    0/0 fragments/bytes in reassembly list
    0 lost fragments, 0 reordered
    0/0 discarded fragments/bytes, 0 lost received
    0x2 received sequence, 0x2 sent sequence
  Member links: 2 active, 0 inactive (max 255, min not set)
    Se0/1/1, since 00:01:20
    Se0/1/0, since 00:01:06
No inactive multilink interfaces
R3#
```

Configure PPP Authentication (2.3.2)

In this topic, you configure PPP authentication.

PPP Authentication Protocols (2.3.2.1)

PPP defines an LCP that allows negotiation of an authentication protocol for authenticating its peer before allowing network layer protocols to transmit over the link. RFC 1334, *PPP Authentication Protocols*, defines two protocols for authentication, PAP and CHAP, as shown in Figure 2-16.

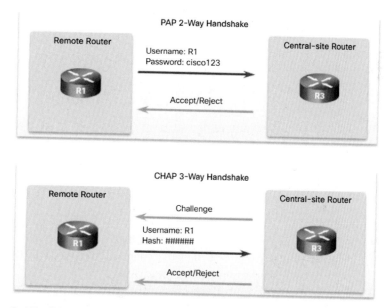

Figure 2-16   PPP Authentication Protocols

PAP is a basic two-way process. There is no encryption. The username and password are sent in plaintext. If it is accepted, the connection is allowed. CHAP is more secure than PAP. It involves a three-way exchange of a shared secret.

The authentication phase of a PPP session is optional. If used, the peer is authenticated after LCP establishes the link and chooses the authentication protocol. Authentication takes place before the network layer protocol configuration phase begins.

The authentication options require that the calling side of the link provide authentication information. This helps ensure that the user has the permission of the network administrator to make the call. Peer routers exchange authentication messages.

Password Authentication Protocol (PAP) (2.3.2.2)

PAP provides a simple method for a remote node to establish its identity using a two-way handshake. PAP is not interactive. When the **ppp authentication pap** interface configuration command is used, the username and password are sent as one LCP data package, as shown in Figure 2-17, rather than one PPP device sending a login prompt and waiting for a response as in some authentication mechanisms.

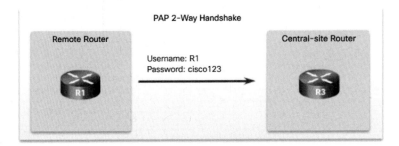

Figure 2-17   Initiating PAP

PAP Process

After PPP completes the link establishment phase, the remote node repeatedly sends a username-password pair across the link until the receiving node acknowledges it or terminates the connection.

At the receiving node, the device running PPP checks the username-password. This device either allows or denies the connection. An accept or reject message is returned to the requester, as shown in Figure 2-18.

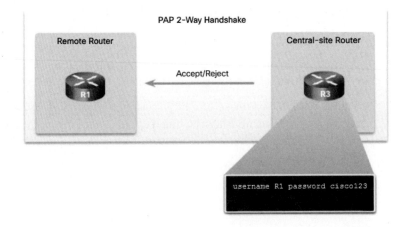

Figure 2-18   Completing PAP

PAP is not a strong authentication protocol. Using PAP, passwords are sent across the link in plaintext, and there is no protection from playback or repeated trial-and-error attacks. The remote node is in control of the frequency and timing of the login attempts.

Nonetheless, using PAP can be justified sometimes. Despite its shortcomings, PAP may be used in the following environments:

- A large installed base of client applications that do not support CHAP
- Incompatibilities between different vendor implementations of CHAP
- Situations in which a plaintext password must be available to simulate a login at the remote host

Challenge Handshake Authentication Protocol (CHAP) (2.3.2.3)

PAP authenticates only once. After authentication is established with PAP, it does not re-authenticate, thus leaving the network vulnerable to attack.

CHAP is more secure as it conducts periodic challenges to make sure that the remote node still has a valid password value. The password value is variable and changes unpredictably while the link exists.

CHAP is configured using the **ppp authentication chap** interface configuration command.

CHAP Process

After the PPP link establishment phase is complete, the local router sends a challenge message to the remote node, as shown in Figure 2-19.

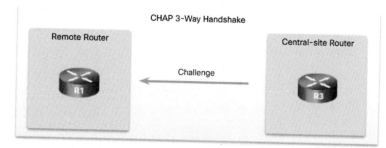

Figure 2-19   Initiating CHAP

The remote node responds with a value that is calculated using a one-way hash function. This is typically *Message Digest 5 (MD5)* based on the password and challenge message, as shown in Figure 2-20.

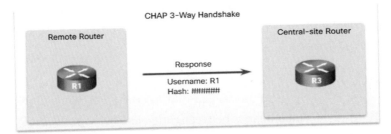

Figure 2-20 Responding CHAP

The local router checks the response against its own calculation of the expected hash value. If the values match, the initiating node acknowledges the authentication, as shown in Figure 2-21. If the values do not match, the initiating node immediately terminates the connection.

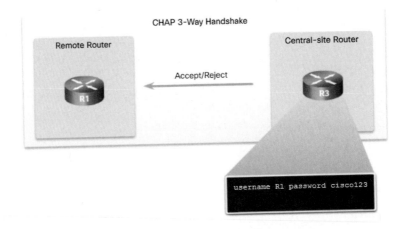

Figure 2-21 Completing CHAP

CHAP provides protection against a playback attack by using a variable challenge value that is unique and unpredictable. Because the challenge is unique and random, the resulting hash value is also unique and random. The use of repeated challenges limits the time of exposure to any single attack. The local router, or a third-party authentication server, is in control of the frequency and timing of the challenges.

PPP Authentication Command (2.3.2.4)

PAP, CHAP, or both can be enabled. If both methods are enabled, the first method specified is requested during link negotiation. If the peer suggests using the second method or simply refuses the first method, the second method should be tried. Some remote devices support CHAP only and some PAP only. The order in which you specify the methods is based on your concerns about the ability of the remote device to correctly negotiate the appropriate method as well as your concern about data line security.

To specify the order in which the CHAP or PAP protocols are requested on the interface, use the **ppp authentication** {**chap** | **chap pap** | **pap chap** | **pap**} interface configuration command.

Table 2-7 shows the description for each keyword in the **ppp authentication** command.

Table 2-7   The **ppp authentication** Command

Keyword	Description
chap	Enables CHAP on a serial interface
pap	Enables PAP on a serial interface
chap pap	Enables both CHAP and PAP, and performs CHAP authentication before PAP
pap chap	Enables both CHAP and PAP, and performs PAP authentication before CHAP

Use the **no** form of the command to disable this authentication.

Configuring PPP with Authentication (2.3.2.5)

Figure 2-22 displays the two-router topology used for demonstrating PPP authentication configurations.

Figure 2-22   PAP and CHAP Configuration Topology

Configuring PAP Authentication

Example 2-10 shows a two-way PAP authentication configuration. Both routers authenticate and are authenticated, so the PAP authentication commands mirror each other. Use the **ppp pap sent-username** *name* **password** *password* interface configuration command to specify the username and password parameters that a router will send. This username and password combination must match those specified with the **username** *name* **password** *password* command of the other receiving router.

Example 2-10 R1 and R2 PAP Configuration

```
hostname R1
username R2 password sameone
!
interface Serial0/0/0
 ip address 10.0.1.1 255.255.255.252
 ipv6 address 2001:DB8:CAFE:1::1/64
 encapsulation ppp
 ppp authentication pap
 ppp pap sent-username R1 password sameone
hostname R2
username R1 password 0 sameone
!
interface Serial 0/0/0
 ip address 10.0.1.2 255.255.255.252
 ipv6 address 2001:db8:cafe:1::2/64
 encapsulation ppp
 ppp authentication pap
 ppp pap sent-username R2 password sameone
```

PAP provides a simple method for a remote node to establish its identity using a two-way handshake. This is done only on initial link establishment. The hostname on one router must match the username the other router has configured for PPP. The passwords must also match.

Configuring CHAP Authentication

Always configure CHAP instead of PAP because CHAP is more secure than PAP. CHAP periodically verifies the identity of the remote node using a three-way handshake. The hostname on one router must match the username the other router has configured. The passwords must also match. This occurs on initial link establishment and can be repeated any time after the link has been established.

Example 2-11 shows a CHAP configuration.

Example 2-11 R1 and R2 CHAP Configuration

```
hostname R1
username R2 password sameone
!
interface Serial0/0/0
 ip address 10.0.1.1 255.255.255.252
 ipv6 address 2001:DB8:CAFE:1::1/64
 encapsulation ppp
 ppp authentication chap
hostname R2
username R1 password 0 sameone
!
interface Serial 0/0/0
 ip address 10.0.1.2 255.255.255.252
 ipv6 address 2001:db8:cafe:1::2/64
 encapsulation ppp
 ppp authentication chap
```

Notice how the CHAP configuration is also simpler than PAP.

Packet Tracer 2.3.2.6: Configuring PAP and CHAP Authentication

Background/Scenario

In this activity, you practice configuring PPP encapsulation on serial links. You also configure PPP PAP authentication and PPP CHAP authentication.

Lab 2.3.2.7: Configuring Basic PPP with Authentication

In this lab, you complete the following objectives:

- Part 1: Configure Basic Device Settings
- Part 2: Configure PPP Encapsulation
- Part 3: Configure PPP CHAP Authentication

Troubleshoot WAN Connectivity (2.4)

In this section, you learn how to troubleshoot PPP.

Troubleshoot PPP (2.4.1)

In this topic, you troubleshoot PPP using **show** and **debug** commands.

Troubleshooting PPP Serial Encapsulation (2.4.1.1)

The privileged EXEC mode **debug** command is very useful for troubleshooting. The command generates real-time output information about various router operations, related traffic generated or received by the router, and any error messages.

However, the **debug** command is a resource-intensive process. It can consume a significant amount of CPU resources as the router is forced to process-switch the packets being debugged. Therefore, the **debug** command is not something we enable to regularly monitor the network. The command is meant to be used for a short period of time when troubleshooting. Therefore, always remember to disable **debug** commands using the **no debug** or **undebug all** privileged EXEC command.

Use the **debug ppp** {packet | negotiation | error | authentication | compression} privileged EXEC mode command to display information about the operation of PPP.

Table 2-8 describes the options for the **debug ppp** command.

Table 2-8   Options for the **debug ppp** Command

Keyword	Description
packet	Displays PPP packets being sent and received.
negotiation	Displays PPP packets transmitted during PPP startup. It is useful to see how PPP options are negotiated.
error	Displays protocol errors and error statistics associated with PPP connection negotiation and operation.
authentication	Displays PAP and CHAP authentication protocol messages.
compression	Displays information specific to the exchange of PPP connections using packet compression.

Use the **no** form of this command to disable debugging output.

Use the **debug ppp** command when trying to search the following:

- NCPs that are supported on either end of a PPP connection
- Any loops that might exist in a PPP internetwork
- Nodes that are (or are not) properly negotiating PPP connections
- Errors that have occurred over the PPP connection
- Causes for CHAP session failures
- Causes for PAP session failures

- Information specific to the exchange of PPP connections using the Callback Control Protocol (CBCP), used by Microsoft clients

- Incorrect packet sequence number information where MPPC compression is enabled

Debugging PPP (2.4.1.2)

A useful command to use when troubleshooting serial interface encapsulation is the **debug ppp packet** privileged EXEC mode command, as shown Example 2-12.

Example 2-12 debug ppp packet Command Output

```
R1# debug ppp packet
PPP packet display debugging is on
R1#
*Apr  1 16:15:17.471: Se0/0/0 LQM: O state Open magic 0x1EFC37C3 len 48
*Apr  1 16:15:17.471: Se0/0/0 LQM:    LastOutLQRs 70 LastOutPackets/Octets 194/9735
*Apr  1 16:15:17.471: Se0/0/0 LQM:    PeerInLQRs 70 PeerInPackets/Discards/Errors/
 Octets 0/0/0/0
*Apr  1 16:15:17.471: Se0/0/0 LQM:    PeerOutLQRs 71 PeerOutPackets/Octets 197/9839
*Apr  1 16:15:17.487: Se0/0/0 PPP: I pkt type 0xC025, datagramsize 52 link[ppp]
*Apr  1 16:15:17.487: Se0/0/0 LQM: I state Open magic 0xFE83D624 len 48
*Apr  1 16:15:17.487: Se0/0/0 LQM:    LastOutLQRs 71 LastOutPackets/Octets 197/9839
*Apr  1 16:15:17.487: Se0/0/0 LQM:    PeerInLQRs 71 PeerInPackets/Discards/Errors/
 Octets 0/0/0/0
*Apr  1 16:15:17.487: Se0/0/0 LQM:    PeerOutLQRs 71 PeerOutPackets/Octets 196/9809
*Apr  1 16:15:17.535: Se0/0/0 LCP: O ECHOREQ [Open] id 36 len 12 magic 0x1EFC37C3
*Apr  1 16:15:17.539: Se0/0/0 LCP-FS: I ECHOREP [Open] id 36 len 12 magic
 0xFE83D624
*Apr  1 16:15:17.539: Se0/0/0 LCP-FS: Received id 36, sent id 36, line up
*Apr  1 16:15:18.191: Se0/0/0 PPP: I pkt type 0xC025, datagramsize 52 link[ppp]
*Apr  1 16:15:18.191: Se0/0/0 LQM: I state Open magic 0xFE83D624 len 48
*Apr  1 16:15:18.191: Se0/0/0 LQM:    LastOutLQRs 71 LastOutPackets/Octets 197/9839
*Apr  1 16:15:18.191: Se0/0/0 LQM:    PeerInLQRs 71 PeerInPackets/Discards/Errors/
 Octets 0/0/0/0
*Apr  1 16:15:18.191: Se0/0/0 LQM:    PeerOutLQRs 72 PeerOutPackets/Octets 198/9883
*Apr  1 16:15:18.191: Se0/0/0 LQM: O state Open magic 0x1EFC37C3 len 48
*Apr  1 16:15:18.191: Se0/0/0 LQM:    LastOutLQRs 72 LastOutPackets/Octets 198/9883
*Apr  1 16:15:18.191: Se0/0/0 LQM:    PeerInLQRs 72 PeerInPackets/Discards/Errors/
 Octets 0/0/0/0
*Apr  1 16:15:18.191: Se0/0/0 LQM:    PeerOutLQRs 72 PeerOutPackets/Octets 199/9913
*Apr  1 16:15:18.219: Se0/0/0 LCP-FS: I ECHOREQ [Open] id 36 len 12 magic
 0xFE83D624
*Apr  1 16:15:18.219: Se0/0/0 LCP-FS: O ECHOREP [Open] id 36 len 12 magic
 0x1EFC37C3
R1# un all
```

The example depicts packet exchanges under normal PPP operation.

The **debug ppp negotiation** privileged EXEC mode command enables the network administrator to view the PPP negotiation transactions, identify the problem or stage when the error occurs, and develop a resolution.

Example 2-13 displays the output of the **debug ppp negotiation** command in a normal negotiation, where both sides agree on NCP parameters.

Example 2-13 Output of **debug ppp negotiation** Command

```
R1# debug ppp negotiation
PPP protocol negotiation debugging is on
R1#
*Apr  1 18:42:29.831: %LINK-3-UPDOWN: Interface Serial0/0/0, changed state to up
*Apr  1 18:42:29.831: Se0/0/0 PPP: Sending cstate UP notification
*Apr  1 18:42:29.831: Se0/0/0 PPP: Processing CstateUp message
*Apr  1 18:42:29.835: PPP: Alloc Context [66A27824]
*Apr  1 18:42:29.835: ppp2 PPP: Phase is ESTABLISHING
*Apr  1 18:42:29.835: Se0/0/0 PPP: Using default call direction
*Apr  1 18:42:29.835: Se0/0/0 PPP: Treating connection as a dedicated line
*Apr  1 18:42:29.835: Se0/0/0 PPP: Session handle[4000002] Session id[2]
*Apr  1 18:42:29.835: Se0/0/0 LCP: Event[OPEN] State[Initial to Starting]
*Apr  1 18:42:29.835: Se0/0/0 LCP: O CONFREQ [Starting] id 1 len 23
*Apr  1 18:42:29.835: Se0/0/0 LCP:    AuthProto CHAP (0x0305C22305)
*Apr  1 18:42:29.835: Se0/0/0 LCP:    QualityType 0xC025 period 1000
  (0x0408C025000003E8)
*Apr  1 18:42:29.835: Se0/0/0 LCP:    MagicNumber 0x1F887DD3 (0x05061F887DD3)
<Output omitted>
*Apr  1 18:42:29.855: Se0/0/0 PPP: Phase is AUTHENTICATING, by both
*Apr  1 18:42:29.855: Se0/0/0 CHAP: O CHALLENGE id 1 len 23 from "R1"
<Output omitted>
*Apr  1 18:42:29.871: Se0/0/0 IPCP: Authorizing CP
*Apr  1 18:42:29.871: Se0/0/0 IPCP: CP stalled on event[Authorize CP]
*Apr  1 18:42:29.871: Se0/0/0 IPCP: CP unstall
<Output omitted>
*Apr  1 18:42:29.875: Se0/0/0 CHAP: O SUCCESS id 1 len 4
*Apr  1 18:42:29.879: Se0/0/0 CHAP: I SUCCESS id 1 len 4
*Apr  1 18:42:29.879: Se0/0/0 PPP: Phase is UP
*Apr  1 18:42:29.879: Se0/0/0 IPCP: Protocol configured, start CP. state[Initial]
*Apr  1 18:42:29.879: Se0/0/0 IPCP: Event[OPEN] State[Initial to Starting]
*Apr  1 18:42:29.879: Se0/0/0 IPCP: O CONFREQ [Starting] id 1 len 10
*Apr  1 18:42:29.879: Se0/0/0 IPCP:    Address 10.0.1.1 (0x03060A000101)
*Apr  1 18:42:29.879: Se0/0/0 IPCP: Event[UP] State[Starting to REQsent]
*Apr  1 18:42:29.879: Se0/0/0 IPV6CP: Protocol configured, start CP. state[Initial]
*Apr  1 18:42:29.883: Se0/0/0 IPV6CP: Event[OPEN] State[Initial to Starting]
```

```
*Apr  1 18:42:29.883: Se0/0/0 IPV6CP: Authorizing CP
*Apr  1 18:42:29.883: Se0/0/0 IPV6CP: CP stalled on event[Authorize CP]
<Output omitted>
*Apr  1 18:42:29.919: Se0/0/0 IPCP: State is Open
*Apr  1 18:42:29.919: Se0/0/0 IPV6CP: State is Open
*Apr  1 18:42:29.919: Se0/0/0 CDPCP: State is Open
*Apr  1 18:42:29.923: Se0/0/0 CCP: State is Open
*Apr  1 18:42:29.927: Se0/0/0 Added to neighbor route AVL tree: topoid 0, address
  10.0.1.2
*Apr  1 18:42:29.927: Se0/0/0 IPCP: Install route to 10.0.1.2
*Apr  1 18:42:39.871: Se0/0/0 LQM: O state Open magic 0x1F887DD3 len 48
*Apr  1 18:42:39.871: Se0/0/0 LQM:    LastOutLQRs 0 LastOutPackets/Octets 0/0
*Apr  1 18:42:39.871: Se0/0/0 LQM:    PeerInLQRs 0 PeerInPackets/Discards/Errors/
  Octets 0/0/0/0
*Apr  1 18:42:39.871: Se0/0/0 LQM:    PeerOutLQRs 1 PeerOutPackets/Octets
  3907/155488
*Apr  1 18:42:39.879: Se0/0/0 LQM: I state Open magic 0xFF101A5B len 48
*Apr  1 18:42:39.879: Se0/0/0 LQM:    LastOutLQRs 0 LastOutPackets/Octets 0/0
*Apr  1 18:42:39.879: Se0/0/0 LQM:    PeerInLQRs 0 PeerInPackets/Discards/Errors/
  Octets 0/0/0/0
*Apr  1 18:42:39.879: Se0/0/0 LQM:    PeerOutLQRs 1 PeerOutPackets/Octets
  3909/155225
<Output omitted>
```

In this case, protocol types IPv4 and IPv6 are proposed and acknowledged. The output includes the LCP negotiation, authentication, and NCP negotiation.

The **debug ppp error** privileged EXEC mode command is used to display protocol errors and error statistics associated with PPP connection negotiation and operation, as shown in Example 2-14.

Example 2-14 Output of **debug ppp error** Command

```
R1# debug ppp error
PPP Serial3(i): rlqr receive failure. successes = 15
PPP: myrcvdiffp = 159 peerxmitdiffp = 41091
PPP: myrcvdiffo = 2183 peerxmitdiffo = 1714439
PPP: threshold = 25
PPP Serial2(i): rlqr transmit failure. successes = 15
PPP: myxmitdiffp = 41091 peerrcvdiffp = 159
PPP: myxmitdiffo = 1714439 peerrcvdiffo = 2183
PPP: l->OutLQRs = 1 LastOutLQRs = 1
PPP: threshold = 25
PPP Serial3(i): lqr_protrej() Stop sending LQRs.
PPP Serial3(i): The link appears to be looped back.
```

Troubleshooting a PPP Configuration with Authentication (2.4.1.3)

Authentication is a feature that needs to be implemented correctly; otherwise, the security of your serial connection may be compromised. Always verify your configuration with the **show interfaces serial** command, in the same way as you did without authentication.

Never assume the authentication configuration works without testing it using the previously covered **show** commands. If you discover issues, debugging enables you to verify the issue is with authentication and correct any deficiencies.

For debugging PPP authentication, use the **debug ppp authentication** privileged EXEC mode command as shown in Example 2-15.

Example 2-15 Troubleshooting PPP Authentication Process

```
R2# debug ppp authentication
Serial0: Unable to authenticate. No name received from peer
Serial0: Unable to validate CHAP response. USERNAME pioneer not found.
Serial0: Unable to validate CHAP response. No password defined for USERNAME pioneer
Serial0: Failed CHAP authentication with remote. Remote message is Unknown name
Serial0: remote passed CHAP authentication.
Serial0: Passed CHAP authentication with remote.
Serial0: CHAP input code = 4 id = 3 len = 48
```

The following is an interpretation of the output:

- Line 1 informs us that the router is unable to authenticate on interface Serial0 because the peer did not send a name.

- Line 2 says the router was unable to validate the CHAP response because the username "pioneer" was not found in the local router database.

- Line 3 says no password was found for "pioneer."

- In the last line, code 4 means that a failure has occurred (other code values include 1 – Challenge, 2 – Response, and 3 – Success). The last line also displays the ID number of the LCP packet (that is, id – 3) and its packet length (that is, len – 48) without the header.

Packet Tracer
☐ Activity

Packet Tracer 2.4.1.4: Troubleshooting PPP with Authentication

Background/ Scenario

The routers at your company were configured by an inexperienced network engineer. Several errors in the configuration have resulted in connectivity issues. Your boss has asked you to troubleshoot and correct the configuration errors and document your work. Using your knowledge of PPP and standard testing methods, find and correct the errors. Make sure that all the serial links use PPP CHAP authentication and that all the networks are reachable. The passwords are "cisco" and "class."

Lab 2.4.1.5: Troubleshooting Basic PPP with Authentication

In this lab, you complete the following objectives:

- Part 1: Build the Network and Load Device Configurations
- Part 2: Troubleshoot the Data Link Layer
- Part 3: Troubleshoot the Network Layer

Summary

Class Activity 2.5.1.1: PPP Validation

Three friends who are enrolled in the Cisco Networking Academy want to check their knowledge of PPP network configuration.

They set up a contest in which each person will be tested on configuring PPP with defined PPP scenario requirements and varying options. Each person devises a different configuration scenario.

The next day they get together and test each other's configuration using their PPP scenario requirements.

Packet Tracer 2.5.1.2: Skills Integration Challenge

Background/Scenario

This activity enables you to practice a variety of skills including configuring VLANs, PPP with CHAP, static and default routing, using IPv4 and IPv6. Due to the sheer number of graded elements, feel free to click Check Results and Assessment Items to see if you correctly entered a graded command. Use the passwords "cisco" and "class" to access EXEC modes of the CLI for routers and switches.

Serial transmissions sequentially send one bit at a time over a single channel. A serial port is bidirectional. Synchronous serial communications require a clocking signal.

Point-to-point links are usually more expensive than shared services; however, the benefits may outweigh the costs. Constant availability is important for some protocols, such as VoIP.

SONET is an optical network standard that uses STDM for efficient use of bandwidth. In the United States, OC transmission rates are standardized specifications for SONET.

The bandwidth hierarchy used by carriers is different in North America (T-carrier) and Europe (E-carrier). In North America, the fundamental line speed is 64 kb/s, or DS0. Multiple DS0s are bundled together to provide higher line speeds.

The demarcation point is the point in the network where the responsibility of the service provider ends and the responsibility of the customer begins. The CPE, usually a router, is the DTE device. The DCE is usually a modem or CSU/DSU.

Cisco HDLC is a bit-oriented synchronous data link layer protocol extension of HDLC; many vendors use it to provide multiprotocol support. This is the default encapsulation method used on Cisco synchronous serial lines.

Synchronous PPP is used to connect to non-Cisco devices, to monitor link quality, provide authentication, or bundle links for shared use. PPP uses HDLC for encapsulating datagrams. LCP is the PPP protocol used to establish, configure, test, and terminate the data link connection. LCP can optionally authenticate a peer using PAP or CHAP. The PPP protocol uses a family of NCPs to simultaneously support multiple network layer protocols. Multilink PPP spreads traffic across bundled links by fragmenting packets and simultaneously sending these fragments over multiple links to same remote address, where they are reassembled.

PPP optionally supports authentication using PAP, CHAP, or both PAP and CHAP protocols. PAP sends authentication data in plaintext. CHAP uses periodic challenge messaging and a one-way hash that helps protect against playback attacks.

Practice

The following activities provide practice with the topics introduced in this chapter. The Labs and Class Activities are available in the companion *Connecting Networks v6 Labs & Study Guide* (ISBN 9781587134296). The Packet Tracer Activity instructions are also in the *Labs & Study Guide*. The PKA files are found in the online course.

Class Activities

Class Activity 2.0.1.2: PPP Persuasion

Class Activity 2.5.1.1: PPP Validation

Labs

Lab 2.3.2.7: Configuring Basic PPP with Authentication

Lab 2.4.1.5: Troubleshooting Basic PPP with Authentication

Packet Tracer
☐ Activity

Packet Tracer Activities

Packet Tracer 2.1.2.5: Troubleshooting Serial Interfaces

Packet Tracer 2.3.2.6: Configuring PAP and CHAP Authentication

Packet Tracer 2.4.1.4: Troubleshooting PPP with Authentication

Packet Tracer 2.5.1.2: Skills Integration Challenge

Check Your Understanding Questions

Complete all the review questions listed here to test your understanding of the topics and concepts in this chapter. The appendix "Answers to the 'Check Your Understanding' Questions" lists the answers.

1. Which command can be used to view the cable type that is attached to a serial interface?

   A. Router(config)# **show interfaces**

   B. Router(config)# **show controllers**

   C. Router(config)# **show ip interface**

   D. Router(config)# **show ip interface brief**

2. Which serial 0/0/0 interface state will be shown if no serial cable is attached to the router, but everything else has been correctly configured and turned on?

   A. Serial 0/0/0 is administratively down, line protocol is down

   B. Serial 0/0/0 is down, line protocol is down

   C. Serial 0/0/0 is up (disabled)

   D. Serial 0/0/0 is up (looped)

   E. Serial 0/0/0 is up, line protocol is down

   F. Serial 0/0/0 is up, line protocol is up

3. Which is an advantage of using PPP on a serial link instead of HDLC?

   A. Fixed-size frames

   B. Higher speed transmission

   C. Option for authentication

   D. Option for session establishment

4. How does PPP interface with different network layer protocols?

    A. By encoding the information field in the PPP frame

    B. By negotiating with the network layer handler

    C. By specifying the protocol during link establishment through LCP

    D. By using separate NCPs

5. Which three are types of LCP frames used with PPP? (Choose three.)

    A. Link-acknowledgment frames

    C. Link-control frames

    D. Link-establishment frames

    E. Link-maintenance frames

    F. Link-negotiation frames

    G. Link-termination frames

6. Which protocol will terminate the PPP link after the exchange of data is complete?

    A. CDPCP

    B. IPCP

    C. IPV6CP

    D. LCP

    E. NCP

7. Which three statements are true about PPP? (Choose three.)

    A. PPP can be used only between two Cisco devices.

    B. PPP can use synchronous and asynchronous circuits.

    C. PPP carries packets from several network layer protocols in LCPs.

    D. PPP is a default encapsulation of serial interfaces on Cisco routers.

    E. PPP uses LCPs to agree on format options such as authentication, compression, and error detection.

    F PPP uses LCPs to establish, configure, and test the data link connection.

8. What PPP information will be displayed if a network engineer issues the **show ppp multilink** command on a Cisco router?

    A. The IP addresses of the link interfaces

    B. The link LCP and NCP status

    C. The queuing type on the link

    D. The serial interfaces participating in the multilink

9. A network engineer is monitoring an essential but poor-quality PPP WAN link that periodically shuts down. An examination of the interface configurations shows that the **ppp quality 90** command has been issued. What action could the engineer take to reduce the frequency with which the link shuts down?

   A. Issue the command **ppp quality 70**.

   B. Issue the command **ppp quality 100**.

   C. Set the DCE interface to a lower clock rate.

   D. Use the **bandwidth** command to increase the bandwidth of the link.

10. In which situation would the use of PAP be preferable to the use of CHAP?

   A. When a network administrator prefers it because of ease of configuration

   B. When multilink PPP is used

   C. When plaintext passwords are needed to simulate login at the remote host

   D. When router resources are limited

CHAPTER 3

Branch Connections

Objectives

Upon completion of this chapter, you will be able to answer the following questions:

- What are the remote-access broadband connection options for small- to medium-sized businesses?

- What is the appropriate broadband connection for a given network requirement?

- What is PPPOE and how does it operate?

- What is the basic configuration for a PPPoE connection on a client router?

- What are the benefits of VPN technology?

- What are the features of site-to-site and remote-access VPNs?

- What is the purpose and what are the benefits of GRE tunnels?

- How do you troubleshoot a site-to-site GRE tunnel?

- What are the basic BGP features?

- What are the basic BGP design considerations?

- How do you configure an eBGP branch connection?

Key Terms

This chapter uses the following key terms. You can find the definitions in the Glossary.

PPP over Ethernet (PPPoE)   Page 103

Internet Protocol Security (IPsec)   Page 103

Border Gateway Protocol (BGP)   Page 103

radio frequency (RF)   Page 104

hybrid fiber-coaxial (HFC)   Page 104

Data over Cable Service Interface Specification (DOCSIS)   Page 104

antenna site   Page 105

transportation network   Page 105

distribution network   Page 105

central office (CO)   Page 105

amplifier   Page 105

subscriber drop   Page 105

node   Page 106

downstream   Page 106

upstream   Page 106

asymmetric DSL (ADSL)   Page 107

symmetric DSL (SDSL)   Page 107

DSL transceiver   Page 108

DSL micro filter   Page 108

Cellular/mobile   Page 109

Introduction (3.0)

Broadband solutions provide teleworkers with high-speed connection options to business locations and to the Internet. Small branch offices can also connect using these same technologies. This chapter covers commonly used broadband solutions, such as cable, DSL, and wireless.

Note

Teleworking is a broad term referring to conducting work by connecting to a workplace from a remote location, with the assistance of telecommunications.

ISPs value the Point-to-Point Protocol (PPP) because of the authentication, accounting, and link management features. Customers appreciate the ease and availability of the Ethernet connection. Ethernet links do not natively support PPP. A solution to this problem was created: *PPP over Ethernet (PPPoE)*. This chapter covers the implementation of PPPoE.

Security is a concern when using the public Internet to conduct business. Virtual private networks (VPNs) are used to improve the security of data across the Internet. A VPN is used to create a private communication channel (also called a tunnel) over a public network. Data can be secured by using encryption in this tunnel through the Internet and by using authentication to protect data from unauthorized access. VPN technology provides security options for data running over these connections. This chapter describes some basic VPN implementations.

Note

VPNs rely on *Internet Protocol Security (IPsec)* to provide security across the Internet. IPsec is beyond the scope of this course.

Generic Routing Encapsulation (GRE) is a tunneling protocol developed by Cisco that can encapsulate a wide variety of protocol packet types inside IP tunnels. GRE creates a virtual point-to-point link to Cisco routers at remote points, over an IP internetwork. The chapter covers the basic GRE implementation.

The *Border Gateway Protocol (BGP)* is routing protocol used between autonomous systems. This chapter concludes with a discussion of BGP routing and an implementation of BGP in a single-homed network.

Class Activity 3.0.1.2: Broadband Varieties

Telework employment opportunities are expanding in your local area every day. You have been offered employment as a teleworker for a major corporation. The new employer requires teleworkers to have access to the Internet to fulfill their job responsibilities.

Research the following broadband Internet connection types that are available in your geographic area:

- DSL

- Cable

- Satellite

Consider the advantages and disadvantages of each broadband variation as you notate your research, which may include cost, speed, security, and ease of implementation or installation.

Remote-Access Connections (3.1)

In this section, you learn how to select broadband remote-access technologies to support business requirements.

Broadband Connections (3.1.1)

In this topic, you compare remote-access broadband connection options for small- to medium-sized businesses.

What Is a Cable System? (3.1.1.1)

Accessing the Internet through a cable network is a popular option that teleworkers use to access their enterprise network. The cable system uses a coaxial cable that carries *radio frequency (RF)* signals across the network. Coaxial cable is the primary medium used to build cable TV systems.

Visit this website to learn more about the history of cable:

https://www.calcable.org/learn/history-of-cable/

Modern cable systems offer customers advanced telecommunications services, including high-speed Internet access, digital cable television, and residential telephone service. Cable operators typically deploy *hybrid fiber-coaxial (HFC)* networks to enable high-speed transmission of data to cable modems located in a small office/home office (SOHO).

The *Data over Cable Service Interface Specification (DOCSIS)* is the international standard for adding high-bandwidth data to an existing cable system.

Figure 3-1 shows an example of a cable system.

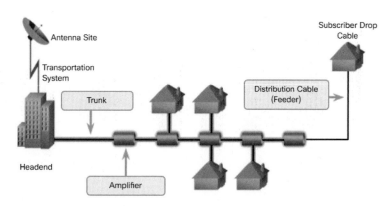

Figure 3-1   Cable System

The following describes the components shown in Figure 3-1:

- *Antenna site*: The location of an antenna site is chosen for optimum reception of over-the-air, satellite, and sometimes point-to-point signals. The main receiving antennas and satellite dishes are located at the antenna site.

- *Transportation network*: A transportation network links a remote antenna site to a headend or a remote headend to the *distribution network*. The transportation network can be microwave, coaxial, or fiber optic.

- **Headend:** This is where signals are first received, processed, formatted, and then distributed downstream to the cable network. The headend facility is usually unmanned, under security fencing, and is similar to a telephone company *central office (CO)*.

- *Amplifier*: This is a device that regenerates an incoming signal to extend further through the network. Cable networks use various types of amplifiers in their transportation and distribution networks.

- *Subscriber drop*: A subscriber drop connects the subscriber to the cable services. The subscriber drop is a connection between the feeder part of a distribution network and the subscriber terminal device (e.g., cable modem). The type of cable commonly used in a subscriber drop consists of radio grade (RG) series 6 (RG6) or series 59 (RG59) coaxial cable.

Cable Components (3.1.1.2)

Figure 3-2 shows an end-to-end cable topology.

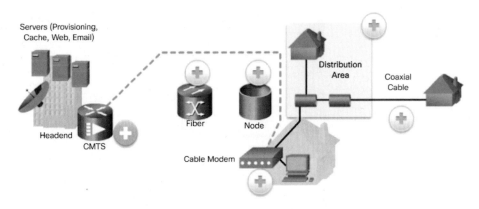

Figure 3-2   End-to-End Data Propagation over Cable

The following describes the components shown in Figure 3-2:

- **Cable modem termination system (CMTS):** A CMTS is a component that exchanges digital signals with cable modem on a cable network. A headend CMTS communicates with CMs that are located in subscriber homes.

- **Fiber:** The trunk portion of the cable network is usually fiber-optic cable.

- *Node*: Nodes convert optical signals to RF signals.

- **Distribution area:** A distribution network segment (feeder segment) is from 500 to as many as 2000 subscribers.

- **Coaxial cable:** Coaxial feeder cables originate from the node and carry RF signals to the subscribers.

- **Cable modem:** A cable modem enables you to receive data at high speeds. Typically, the cable modem attaches to a standard Ethernet card in the computer.

A headend CMTS communicates with CMs located in subscriber homes. The headend is actually a router with databases for providing Internet services to cable subscribers. The architecture is relatively simple, using an HFC network. The HFC network is a mixed optical-coaxial network in which optical fiber replaces the lower bandwidth coaxial cable. The fiber carries the same broadband content for Internet connections, telephone service, and streaming video as the coaxial cable carries.

In a modern HFC network, typically 500 to 2000 active data subscribers are connected to a cable network segment, all sharing the upstream and downstream bandwidth. DOCSIS standards are used to specify how data is exchanged between cable modem and the headend. For instance, the DOCSIS 3.1 standard supports *downstream* bandwidths (that is, from the headend to the subscriber) up to 10 Gb/s and *upstream* bandwidths (that is, from the subscriber to the headend) of 1 Gb/s.

What Is DSL? (3.1.1.3)

A digital subscriber line (DSL) is a means of providing high-speed connections over installed copper wires. DSL is one of the key teleworker solutions available.

Figure 3-3 shows a representation of bandwidth space allocation on a copper wire for *asymmetric DSL (ADSL)*. The area labeled POTS (Plain Old Telephone System) identifies the frequency range used by the voice-grade telephone service. The area labeled ADSL represents the frequency space used by the upstream and downstream DSL signals. The area that encompasses both the POTS area and the ADSL area represents the entire frequency range supported by the copper wire pair.

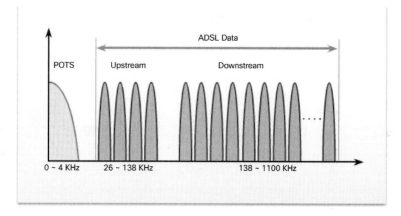

Figure 3-3   Asymmetric DSL in the Electromagnetic Spectrum

Another form of DSL technology is *symmetric DSL (SDSL)*. All forms of DSL service are categorized as ADSL or SDSL, and there are several varieties of each type. ADSL provides higher downstream bandwidth to the user than upload bandwidth. SDSL provides the same capacity in both directions.

The different varieties of DSL provide different bandwidths, some with capabilities exceeding 40 Mb/s. The transfer rates are dependent on the actual length of the local loop, and the type and condition of the cabling. For satisfactory ADSL service, the loop must be less than 3.39 miles (5.46 km).

DSL Connections (3.1.1.4)

Service providers deploy DSL connections in the local loop. The connection is set up between a pair of modems on either end of a copper wire that extends between the customer premises equipment (CPE) and the DSL access multiplexer (DSLAM). A DSLAM is the device located at the CO of the provider; it concentrates connections from multiple DSL subscribers. A DSLAM is often built into an aggregation router.

Figure 3-4 shows the equipment needed to provide a DSL connection to a SOHO.

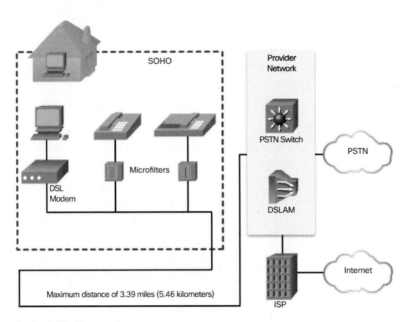

Figure 3-4   DSL Connections

The two important components in this topology are the DSL transceiver and the DSLAM:

- *DSL transceiver:* Connects the computer of the teleworker to the DSL. Usually, the transceiver is a DSL modem connected to the computer using a USB or Ethernet cable. Typically, DSL transceivers are built into small routers with multiple switch ports suitable for home office use.

- **DSLAM:** Located at the CO of the carrier, the DSLAM combines individual DSL connections from users into one high-capacity link to an ISP, and therefore, to the Internet.

A *DSL micro filter* (also known as a DSL filter) is required to connect devices such as phones or fax machines on the DSL network.

Figure 3-5 depicts modern DSL routers and broadband aggregation routers.

The advantage that DSL has over cable technology is that DSL is not a shared medium. Each user has a separate direct connection to the DSLAM. Adding users does not impede performance, unless the DSLAM Internet connection to the ISP, or the Internet, becomes saturated.

Figure 3-5   Example of DSL Routers

Wireless Connection (3.1.1.5)

Developments in broadband wireless technology are increasing wireless availability through three main technologies:

- Municipal Wi-Fi
- *Cellular/mobile*
- Satellite Internet

The sections that follow describe these technologies in more detail.

Municipal Wi-Fi

Many municipal governments, often working with service providers, are deploying wireless networks. Some of these networks provide high-speed Internet access at no cost or for substantially less than the price of other broadband services. Other cities reserve their Wi-Fi networks for official use, providing police, firefighters, and city workers remote access to the Internet and municipal networks.

Most municipal wireless networks use a mesh of interconnected access points, as shown in Figure 3-6. Each access point is in range and can communicate with at least two other access points. The mesh blankets a particular area with radio signals.

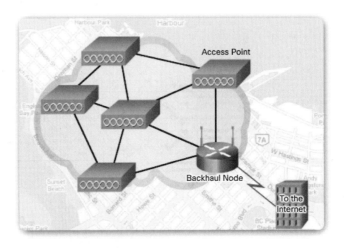

Figure 3-6   Municipal Wireless Network

Cellular/Mobile

Mobile phones use radio waves to communicate through nearby cell towers. The mobile phone has a small radio antenna. The provider has a much larger antenna that sits at the top of a tower, as shown in Figure 3-7.

Figure 3-7   Cellular Tower

Three common terms are used when discussing cellular/mobile networks:

- **Wireless Internet:** A general term for Internet services from a mobile phone or from any device that uses the same technology.

- **2G/3G/4G wireless:** Major changes to the mobile phone companies' wireless networks through the evolution of the second, third, and fourth generations of wireless mobile technologies.

- **Long-Term Evolution (LTE):** A newer and faster technology considered to be part of 4G technology.

Cellular/mobile broadband access consists of various standards such as 4G using LTE. A mobile phone subscription does not necessarily include a mobile broadband subscription. Cellular speeds continue to increase. For example, 4G LTE Category 10 supports up to 450 Mb/s download and 100 Mb/s upload.

Note

Under development is a proposed 5G standard rumored to support higher bandwidth than 4G LTE.

Satellite Internet

Satellite Internet services are used in locations where land-based Internet access is not available or for temporary installations that are mobile. Internet access using satellites is available worldwide, including for providing Internet access to vessels at sea, airplanes in flight, and vehicles moving on land.

Figure 3-8 illustrates a two-way satellite system that provides Internet access to a home subscriber. Upload speeds are about one-tenth of the download speed. Download speeds range from 5 Mb/s to 25 Mb/s.

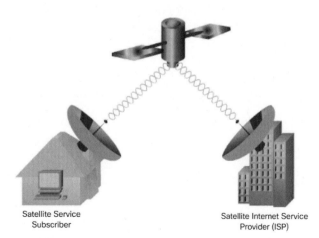

Satellite Service
Subscriber

Satellite Internet Service
Provider (ISP)

Figure 3-8   Two-Way Satellite Implementation

The primary installation requirement is for the antenna to have a clear view toward the equator, where most orbiting satellites are stationed. Trees and heavy rains can affect reception of the signals.

Note

WiMAX (Worldwide Interoperability for Microwave Access) is a wireless technology for both fixed and mobile implementations. WiMAX may still be relevant for some areas of the world. However, in most of the world, WiMAX has largely been replaced by LTE for mobile access and cable or DSL for fixed access.

Interactive Graphic

Activity 3.1.1.6: Identify Broadband Connection Terminology

Refer to the online course to complete this activity.

Select a Broadband Connection (3.1.2)

In this topic, you select an appropriate broadband connection for a given network requirement.

Comparing Broadband Solutions (3.1.2.1)

Each broadband solution has advantages and disadvantages. The ideal is to have a fiber-optic cable directly connected to the SOHO network. Some locations have only one option, such as cable or DSL. Some locations have only broadband wireless options for Internet connectivity.

If multiple broadband solutions are available, a cost-versus-benefit analysis should be performed to determine the best solution.

Some factors to consider in making a decision include

- **Cable:** Bandwidth is shared by many users; upstream data rates are often slow during high-usage hours in areas with oversubscription.

- **DSL:** Limited bandwidth is distance sensitive (in relation to the ISP's central office); the upstream rate is proportionally quite small compared to the downstream rate.

- **Cellular/mobile:** Coverage is often an issue, even within a SOHO where bandwidth is relatively limited.

- **Wi-Fi mesh:** Most municipalities do not have a mesh network deployed; if it is available and the SOHO is in range, it is a viable option.

- **Satellite Internet:** This option is expensive, has limited capacity per subscriber, but often provides access where no other access is possible.

Lab 3.1.2.2: Researching Broadband Internet Access Technologies

In this lab, you complete the following objectives:

- Part 1: Investigate Broadband Distribution
- Part 2: Research Broadband Access Options for Specific Scenarios

PPPoE (3.2)

In this section, you configure a Cisco router with PPPoE.

PPPoE Overview (3.2.1)

In this topic, you learn how PPPoE operates.

PPPoE Motivation (3.2.1.1)

In addition to understanding the various technologies available for broadband Internet access, it is also important to understand the underlying data link layer protocol that the ISP uses to form a connection.

A data link layer protocol commonly used by ISPs is Point-to-Point Protocol (PPP). PPP can be used on all serial links, including those links created with dialup analog and ISDN modems. To this day, the link from a dialup user to an ISP, using analog modems, likely uses PPP.

Figure 3-9 shows a basic representation of that analog dial connection with PPP.

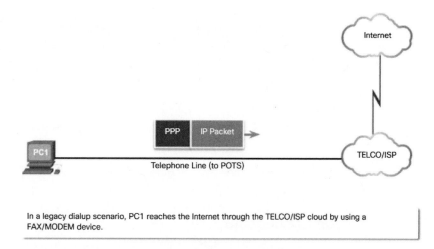

Figure 3-9   PPP Frames over Legacy Dialup Connection

Additionally, ISPs often use PPP as the data link protocol over broadband connections. There are several reasons for this. First, PPP supports the ability to assign IP addresses to remote ends of a PPP link. With PPP enabled, ISPs can use PPP to assign each customer one public IPv4 address. More importantly, PPP supports CHAP authentication. ISPs often want to use CHAP to authenticate customers because during authentication, ISPs can check accounting records to determine whether the customer's bill is paid prior to letting the customer connect to the Internet.

These technologies came to market in the following order, with varying support for PPP:

1. Analog modems for dialup that could use PPP and CHAP

2. ISDN for dialup that could use PPP and CHAP

3. DSL, which did not create a point-to-point link and could not support PPP and CHAP

ISPs value PPP because of the authentication, accounting, and link-management features. Customers appreciate the ease and availability of the Ethernet connection; however, Ethernet links do not natively support PPP. PPP over Ethernet (PPPoE) provides a solution to this problem. As shown in Figure 3-10, PPPoE sends PPP frames encapsulated inside Ethernet frames.

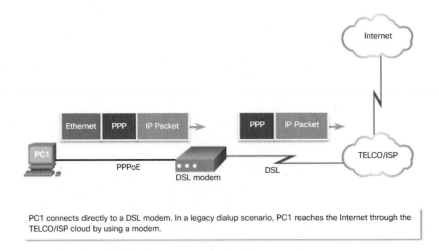

PC1 connects directly to a DSL modem. In a legacy dialup scenario, PC1 reaches the Internet through the TELCO/ISP cloud by using a modem.

Figure 3-10   PPP Frames over an Ethernet Connection (PPPoE)

PPPoE Concepts (3.2.1.2)

As shown in Figure 3-11, the customer's router is usually connected to a DSL modem using an Ethernet cable. PPPoE creates a PPP tunnel over an Ethernet connection.

This allows PPP frames to be sent across the Ethernet cable to the ISP from the customer's router. The modem converts the Ethernet frames to PPP frames by stripping the Ethernet headers. The modem then transmits these PPP frames on the ISP's DSL network.

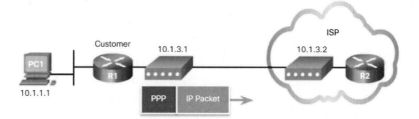

Figure 3-11   Tunneling to Create a PPP Link over Ethernet

Implement PPPoE (3.2.2)

In this topic, you implement a basic PPPoE connection on a client router.

PPPoE Configuration (3.2.2.1)

With the ability to send and receive PPP frames between the routers, the ISP could continue to use the same authentication model as with analog and ISDN. To make it all work, the client and ISP routers need additional configuration, including PPP configuration, as shown in Figure 3-12.

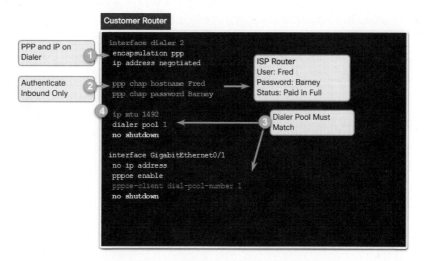

Figure 3-12   Steps for a PPPoE Customer Configuration

To understand the configuration, consider the following:

1. To create a PPP tunnel, the configuration uses a *dialer interface*. A dialer interface is a virtual interface. The PPP configuration is placed on the dialer interface, not the physical interface. The dialer interface is created using the **interface dialer** *number* global configuration command. The client can configure a static IP address but will more likely be automatically assigned a public IP address by the ISP.

2. The PPP CHAP configuration usually defines one-way authentication; therefore, the ISP authenticates the customer. The hostname and password configured on the customer router must match the hostname and password configured on the ISP router. Notice in Figure 3-12 that the CHAP username and password match the settings on the ISP router.

3. The physical Ethernet interface that connects to the DSL modem is then enabled with the **pppoe enable** interface configuration command. This command enables PPPoE and links the physical interface to the dialer interface. The dialer interface is linked to the Ethernet interface with the **dialer pool** *number* and **pppoe-client dial-pool-number** *number* interface configuration commands, using the same *number*. The dialer interface number does not have to match the dialer pool number.

4. The *maximum transmission unit (MTU)* should be lowered to 1492, versus the default of 1500, to accommodate the PPPoE headers.

PPPoE Verification (3.2.2.2)

As shown in Figure 3-13, the customer's router is connected to the ISP router using DSL. Both routers have been configured for PPPoE.

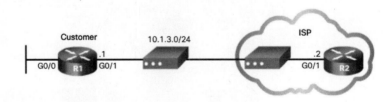

Figure 3-13   Verifying the PPPoE Configuration

In Example 3-1, the **show ip interface brief** command is issued on R1 to verify the IPv4 address automatically assigned to the dialer interface by the ISP router.

Example 3-1 Verifying the Dialer Interface Is Up

```
R1# show ip interface brief
Interface                    IP-Address   OK?  Method  Status                   Protocol
Embedded-Service-Engine0/0   unassigned   YES  unset   administratively down    down
GigabitEthernet0/0           unassigned   YES  unset   administratively down    down
GigabitEthernet0/1           unassigned   YES  unset   up                       up
Serial0/0/0                  unassigned   YES  unset   administratively down    down
Serial0/0/1                  unassigned   YES  unset   administratively down    down
Dialer2                      10.1.3.1     YES  IPCP    up                       up
Virtual-Access1              unassigned   YES  unset   up                       up
Virtual-Access2              unassigned   YES  unset   up                       up
R1#
```

As shown in Example 3-2, the **show interface dialer** command on R1 verifies the MTU and PPP encapsulation configured on the dialer interface.

Example 3-2 Verifying the MTU Size and Encapsulation

```
R1# show interface dialer 2
Dialer2 is up, line protocol is up (spoofing)
  Hardware is Unknown
  Internet address is 10.1.3.1/32
  MTU 1492 bytes, BW 56 Kbit/sec, DLY 20000 usec,
      reliability 255/255, txload 1/255, rxload 1/255
  Encapsulation PPP, LCP Closed, loopback not set
  Keepalive set (10 sec)
  DTR is pulsed for 1 seconds on reset
<output omitted>
```

Example 3-3 displays the routing table on R1.

Example 3-3 Verifying the R1 Routing Table

```
R1# show ip route | begin Gateway

Gateway of last resort is 0.0.0.0 to network 0.0.0.0

S*     0.0.0.0/0 is directly connected, Dialer2
       10.0.0.0/32 is subnetted, 2 subnets
C         10.1.3.1 is directly connected, Dialer2
C         10.1.3.2 is directly connected, Dialer2
R1#
```

Notice that two /32 host routes for 10.0.0.0 have been installed in R1's routing table. The first host route is for the address assigned to the dialer interface. The second host route is the IPv4 address of the ISP. The installation of these two host routes is the default behavior for PPPoE.

As shown in Example 3-4, the **show pppoe session** command enables you to display information about currently active PPPoE sessions.

Example 3-4 Viewing the Current PPPoE Sessions

```
R1# show pppoe session
     1 client session

Uniq ID   PPPoE   RemMAC          Port        VT    VA       State
          SID     LocMAC                            VA-st    Type
     N/A    1     30f7.0da3.1641  Gi0/1       Di2   Vi2      UP
                  30f7.0da3.0da1                    UP
R1#
```

The output displays the local and remote Ethernet MAC addresses of both routers. The Ethernet MAC addresses can be verified by using the **show interfaces** command on each router.

PPPoE Troubleshooting (3.2.2.3)

After you ensure that the client router and DSL modem are connected with the proper cables, the cause of a PPPoE connection not functioning properly is usually one or more of the following reasons:

- Failure in the PPP negotiation process

- Failure in the PPP authentication process

- Failure to adjust the TCP *maximum segment size (MSS)*

PPPoE Negotiation (3.2.2.4)

Verify PPP negotiation using the **debug ppp negotiation** command. Example 3-5 displays part of the debug output after R1's G0/1 interface has been enabled.

Example 3-5 Examining the PPP Negotiation Process

```
R1# debug ppp negotiation
*Sep 20 19:05:05.239: Vi2 PPP: Phase is AUTHENTICATING, by the peer
*Sep 20 19:05:05.239: Vi2 LCP: State is Open
<output omitted>
*Sep 20 19:05:05.247: Vi2 CHAP: Using hostname from interface CHAP
*Sep 20 19:05:05.247: Vi2 CHAP: Using password from interface CHAP
```

```
*Sep 20 19:05:05.247: Vi2 CHAP: O RESPONSE id 1 len 26 from "Fred"
*Sep 20 19:05:05.255: Vi2 CHAP: I SUCCESS id 1 len 4
<output omitted>
*Sep 20 19:05:05.259: Vi2 IPCP:    Address 10.1.3.2 (0x03060A010302)
*Sep 20 19:05:05.259: Vi2 IPCP: Event[Receive ConfAck] State[ACKsent to Open]
*Sep 20 19:05:05.271: Vi2 IPCP: State is Open
*Sep 20 19:05:05.271: Di2 IPCP: Install negotiated IP interface address 10.1.3.2
*Sep 20 19:05:05.271: Di2 Added to neighbor route AVL tree: topoid 0, address
  10.1.3.2
*Sep 20 19:05:05.271: Di2 IPCP: Install route to 10.1.3.2
R1# undebug all
```

The output is an example of what should be generated when PPP is correctly configured.

The four main points of failure in a PPP negotiation are as follows:

- No response from the remote device (the ISP)

- Link Control Protocol (LCP) not open

- Authentication failure

- IP Control Protocol (IPCP) failure

PPPoE Authentication (3.2.2.5)

After confirming with the ISP that it uses CHAP, verify that the CHAP username and password are correct. Example 3-6 shows the CHAP configuration on the dialer2 interface.

Example 3-6 Verify the CHAP Configuration

```
R1# show running-config | section interface Dialer2
interface Dialer2
 mtu 1492
 ip address negotiated
 encapsulation ppp
 dialer pool 1
 ppp authentication chap callin
 ppp chap hostname Fred
 ppp chap password 0 Barney
R1#
```

Re-examining the output of the **debug ppp negotiation** command in Example 3-7 verifies that the CHAP username is correct.

Example 3-7 Verify the CHAP Username

```
R1# debug ppp negotiation
*Sep 20 19:05:05.239: Vi2 PPP: Phase is AUTHENTICATING, by the peer
*Sep 20 19:05:05.239: Vi2 LCP: State is Open
<output omitted>
*Sep 20 19:05:05.247: Vi2 CHAP: Using hostname from interface CHAP
*Sep 20 19:05:05.247: Vi2 CHAP: Using password from interface CHAP
*Sep 20 19:05:05.247: Vi2 CHAP: O RESPONSE id 1 len 26 from "Fred"
*Sep 20 19:05:05.255: Vi2 CHAP: I SUCCESS id 1 len 4
<output omitted>
*Sep 20 19:05:05.259: Vi2 IPCP:    Address 10.1.3.2 (0x03060A010302)
*Sep 20 19:05:05.259: Vi2 IPCP: Event[Receive ConfAck] State[ACKsent to Open]
*Sep 20 19:05:05.271: Vi2 IPCP: State is Open
*Sep 20 19:05:05.271: Di2 IPCP: Install negotiated IP interface address 10.1.3.2
*Sep 20 19:05:05.271: Di2 Added to neighbor route AVL tree: topoid 0, address
   10.1.3.2
*Sep 20 19:05:05.271: Di2 IPCP: Install route to 10.1.3.2
R1# undebug all
```

If the CHAP username or password were incorrect, the output from the **debug ppp negotiation** command would show an authentication failure message such as shown in Example 3-8.

Example 3-8 Authentication Failure Message

```
R1#
*Sep 20 19:05:05.247: Vi2 CHAP: I FAILURE id 1 Len 26 MSG is "Authentication
   failure"
R1#
```

PPPoE MTU Size (3.2.2.6)

Accessing some web pages might be a problem with PPPoE. When the client requests a web page, a TCP three-way handshake occurs between the client and the web server. During the negotiation, the client specifies the value of its TCP maximum segment size (MSS). The TCP MSS is the maximum size of the data portion in the TCP segment.

A host determines the value of its MSS field by subtracting the IP and TCP headers from the Ethernet maximum transmission unit (MTU). On an Ethernet interface, the default MTU is 1500 bytes. Subtracting the IPv4 header of 20 bytes and the TCP header of 20 bytes, the default MSS size will be 1460 bytes, as shown in Figure 3-14.

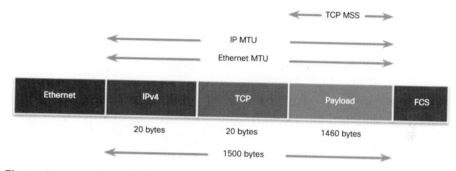

Figure 3-14   MTU and MSS

The default MSS size is 1460 bytes, when the default MTU is 1500 bytes; however, PPPoE supports an MTU of only 1492 bytes to accommodate the additional 8-byte PPPoE header, as shown in Figure 3-15.

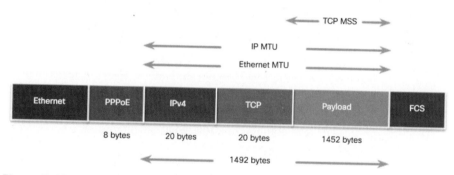

Figure 3-15   Adjusted MSS with PPPoE Header

You can verify the PPPoE MTU size in running configuration, as shown in Example 3-9. This disparity between the host and PPPoE MTU size can cause the router to drop 1500-byte packets and terminate TCP sessions over the PPPoE network.

Example 3-9 Verifying the MTU Size on the Dialer Interface

```
R1# show running-config | section interface Dialer2
interface Dialer2
 mtu 1492
 ip address negotiated
 encapsulation ppp
<output omitted>
```

The **ip tcp adjust-mss** *max-segment-size* interface configuration command helps prevent TCP sessions from being dropped by adjusting the MSS value during the TCP three-way handshake. In most cases, the optimum value for the *max-segment-size* argument is 1452 bytes. Example 3-10 shows this configuration on R1's LAN interface.

Example 3-10 Adjusting the TCP MSS

```
R1(config)# interface g0/0
R1(config-if)# ip tcp adjust-mss 1452
```

The TCP MSS value of 1452 plus the 20-byte IPv4 header, the 20-byte TCP header, and the 8-byte PPPoE header adds up to a 1500-byte MTU, as illustrated previously in Figure 3-15.

Lab 3.2.2.7: Configuring a Router as a PPPoE Client for DSL Connectivity

In this lab, you complete the following objectives:

- Part 1: Build the Network
- Part 2: Configure the ISP Router
- Part 3: Configure the Cust1 Router

Lab 3.2.2.8: Troubleshoot PPPoE

In this lab, you compete the following objectives:

- Part 1: Build the Network
- Part 2: Troubleshoot PPPoE on Cust1

VPNs (3.3)

In this section, you learn how VPNs secure site-to-site and remote-access connectivity.

Fundamentals of VPNs (3.3.1)

In this topic, you learn about the benefits of VPN technology.

Introducing VPNs (3.3.1.1)

Organizations need secure, reliable, and cost-effective ways to interconnect multiple networks, such as allowing branch offices and suppliers to connect to a corporation's headquarter network. Additionally, with the growing number of teleworkers, enterprises have an increasing need for secure, reliable, and cost-effective ways to connect employees working in small office/home office (SOHO) and other remote locations, with resources on corporate sites.

As shown in Figure 3-16, organizations use VPNs to create an end-to-end private network connection over third-party networks, such as the Internet. The tunnel eliminates the distance barrier and enables remote users to access central site network resources.

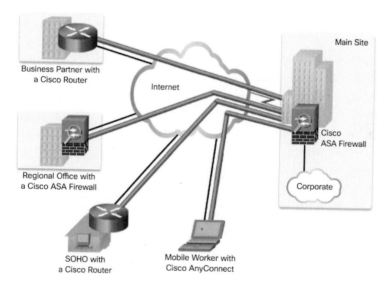

Figure 3-16   VPNs

A VPN is a private network created via tunneling over a public network, usually the Internet. A VPN is a communications environment in which access is strictly controlled to permit peer connections within a defined community of interest.

The first VPNs were strictly IP tunnels that did not include authentication or encryption of the data. For example, Generic Routing Encapsulation (GRE) is a tunneling protocol developed by Cisco that can encapsulate a wide variety of network layer protocol packet types inside IP tunnels. This creates a virtual point-to-point link to Cisco routers at remote points over an IP internetwork. However, GRE does not support encryption.

Today, a secure implementation of VPN with encryption, such as IPsec VPNs, is what is usually meant by virtual private networking.

To implement VPNs, a *VPN gateway* is necessary. The VPN gateway could be a router, a firewall, or a Cisco Adaptive Security Appliance (ASA). An ASA is a stand-alone firewall device that combines firewall, VPN concentrator, and intrusion prevention functionality into one software image.

Benefits of VPNs (3.3.1.2)

As shown in Figure 3-17, a VPN uses virtual connections that are routed through the Internet from the private network of an organization to the remote site or employee host. The information from a private network is securely transported over the public network to form a virtual network.

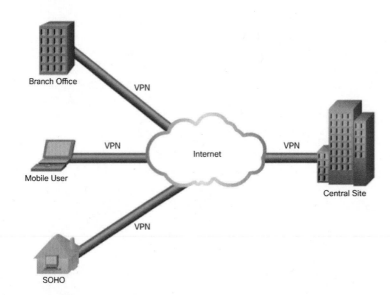

Figure 3-17   VPN Internet Connections

The benefits of a VPN include the following:

■ **Cost savings:** VPNs enable organizations to use cost-effective, third-party Internet transport to connect remote offices and remote users to the main site, thus eliminating expensive, dedicated WAN links and modem banks. Furthermore, with the advent of cost-effective, high-bandwidth technologies, such as DSL, organizations can use VPNs to reduce their connectivity costs while simultaneously increasing remote connection bandwidth.

■ **Scalability:** VPNs enable organizations to use the Internet infrastructure within ISPs and devices, which makes it easy to add new users. Therefore, organizations are able to add large amounts of capacity without adding significant infrastructure.

■ **Compatibility with broadband technology:** VPNs allow mobile workers and teleworkers to take advantage of high-speed, broadband connectivity, such as DSL and cable, to access to their organizations' networks. Broadband connectivity provides flexibility and efficiency. High-speed, broadband connections also provide a cost-effective solution for connecting remote offices.

■ **Security:** VPNs can include security mechanisms that provide the highest level of security by using advanced encryption and authentication protocols that protect data from unauthorized access.

Interactive Graphic

Activity 3.3.1.3: Identify the Benefits of VPNs

Refer to the online course to complete this activity.

Types of VPNs (3.3.2)

In this topic, you learn about site-to-site and remote-access VPNs.

Site-to-Site VPNs (3.3.2.1)

A site-to-site VPN is created when devices on both sides of the VPN connection are aware of the VPN configuration in advance, as shown in Figure 3-18.

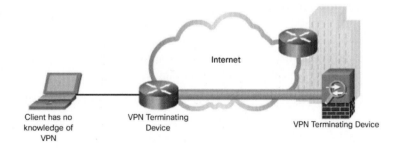

Figure 3-18   Site-to-Site VPNs

The VPN remains static, and internal hosts have no knowledge that a VPN exists. In a site-to-site VPN, end hosts send and receive normal TCP/IP traffic through a VPN "gateway." The VPN gateway is responsible for encapsulating and encrypting outbound traffic for all traffic from a particular site. The VPN gateway then sends it through a VPN tunnel over the Internet to a peer VPN gateway at the target site. Upon receipt, the peer VPN gateway strips the headers, decrypts the content, and relays the packet toward the target host inside its private network.

A site-to-site VPN is an extension of a classic WAN network. Site-to-site VPNs connect entire networks to each other; for example, they can connect a branch office network to a company headquarters network. In the past, a leased-line or Frame Relay connection was required to connect sites, but because most corporations now have Internet access, these connections are commonly replaced with site-to-site VPNs.

Remote-Access VPNs (3.3.2.2)

Where a site-to-site VPN is used to connect entire networks, a remote-access VPN supports the needs of *telecommuters*, mobile users, and extranet, consumer-to-business traffic. A remote-access VPN is created when VPN information is not statically set up, but instead allows for dynamically changing information, and can be enabled and disabled. Remote-access VPNs support a client/server architecture, where the VPN client (remote host) gains secure access to the enterprise network via a VPN server device at the network edge, as shown Figure 3-19.

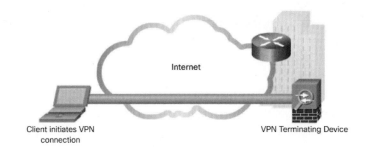

Figure 3-19   Remote-Access VPNs

Remote-access VPNs are used to connect individual hosts that must access their company network securely over the Internet. Internet connectivity used by telecommuters is typically a broadband connection.

VPN client software, such as the *Cisco AnyConnect Secure Mobility Client* software, is installed on the teleworker host. When the host sends traffic, the Cisco AnyConnect VPN Client software encapsulates, encrypts, and sends the traffic over the Internet to the destination VPN gateway. Upon receipt, the VPN gateway behaves as it does for site-to-site VPNs.

Note

The Cisco AnyConnect Secure Mobility Client software builds on prior Cisco AnyConnect VPN Client and Cisco VPN Client offerings to improve the always-on VPN experience across more laptop and smartphone-based mobile devices. This client supports IPv6.

DMVPN (3.3.2.3)

Dynamic Multipoint VPN (DMVPN) is a Cisco software solution for building multiple VPNs in an easy, dynamic, and scalable manner. The goal is to simplify the configuration while easily and flexibly connecting central office sites with branch sites in a hub-and-spoke (or hub-to-spoke) topology, as shown in Figure 3-20.

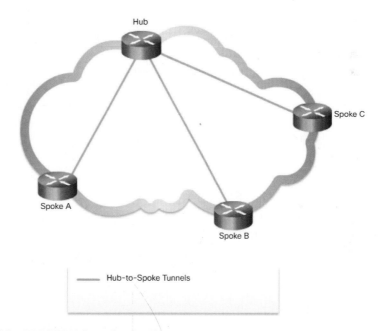

Figure 3-20   DMVPN Hub-to-Spoke Tunnels

With DMVPNs, branch sites can also communicate directly with other branch sites, as shown in Figure 3-21.

DMVPN is built using the following technologies:

- *Next Hop Resolution Protocol (NHRP)*

- Multipoint Generic Routing Encapsulation (mGRE) tunnels

- IP Security (IPsec) encryption

NHRP is a Layer 2 resolution and caching protocol similar to Address Resolution Protocol (ARP). NHRP creates a distributed mapping database of public IP addresses for all tunnel spokes. NHRP is a client/server protocol consisting of the NHRP hub known as the *Next Hop Server (NHS)* and the NHRP spokes known as the *Next Hop Clients (NHCs)*. NHRP supports hub-and-spoke as well as *spoke-to-spoke* configurations.

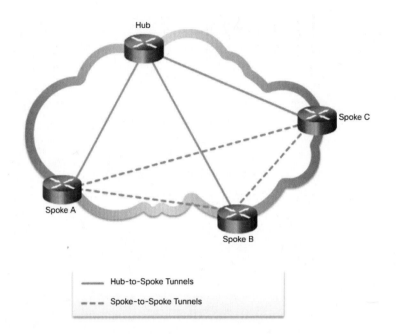

Figure 3-21   DMVPN Hub-to-Spoke and Spoke-to-Spoke Tunnels

Generic Routing Encapsulation (GRE) is a tunneling protocol developed by Cisco that can encapsulate a wide variety of protocol packet types inside IP tunnels. DMVPN makes use of *Multipoint Generic Routing Encapsulation (mGRE)* tunnel. An mGRE tunnel interface allows a single GRE interface to support multiple IPsec tunnels. With mGRE, dynamically allocated tunnels are created through a permanent tunnel source at the hub and dynamically allocated tunnel destinations, created as necessary, at the spokes. This reduces the size and simplifies the complexity of the configuration.

Like other VPN types, DMVPN relies on IPsec to provide secure transport of private information over public networks, such as the Internet.

Interactive Graphic

Activity 3.3.2.4: Compare Types of VPNs

Refer to the online course to complete this activity.

GRE (3.4)

In this section, you implement a GRE tunnel.

GRE Overview (3.4.1)

In this topic, you learn about the purpose and benefits GRE tunnels.

GRE Introduction (3.4.1.1)

Generic Routing Encapsulation (GRE) is one example of a basic, nonsecure, site-to-site VPN tunneling protocol. GRE is a tunneling protocol developed by Cisco that can encapsulate a wide variety of protocol packet types inside IP tunnels. GRE creates a virtual point-to-point link to Cisco routers at remote points, over an IP internetwork.

GRE is designed to manage the transportation of multiprotocol and IP multicast traffic between two or more sites that may have only IP connectivity. It can encapsulate multiple protocol packet types inside an IP tunnel.

As shown in Figure 3-22, a tunnel interface supports a header for each of the following:

■ *Passenger protocol*: This is the original IPv4 or IPv6 packet that will be encapsulated by the carrier protocol. It could also be a legacy AppleTalk, DECnet, or IPX packet.

■ *Carrier protocol*: This is the encapsulation protocol such as GRE that encapsulates the passenger protocol.

■ *Transport protocol*: This is the delivery protocol such as IP that carries the carrier protocol.

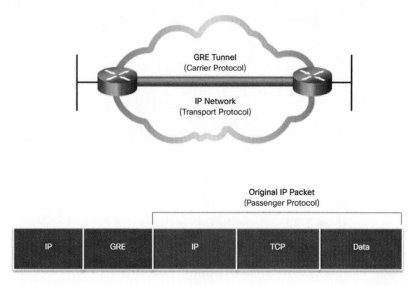

Figure 3-22 Generic Routing Encapsulation

GRE Characteristics (3.4.1.2)

GRE is a tunneling protocol developed by Cisco that can encapsulate a wide variety of protocol packet types inside IP tunnels, creating a virtual point-to-point link to Cisco routers at remote points over an IP internetwork. IP tunneling using GRE enables network expansion across a single-protocol backbone environment. It does this by connecting multiprotocol subnetworks in a single-protocol backbone environment.

GRE has these characteristics:

- GRE is defined as an IETF standard (RFC 2784).

- GRE is identified as IP protocol 47 in the Transport protocol IP protocol field.

- GRE encapsulation includes a protocol type field in its header to provide multi-protocol support. Protocol types are defined in RFC 1700 as "EtherTypes."

- GRE is stateless, which means that, by default, it does not include any flow-control mechanisms.

- GRE does not include any strong security mechanisms to protect its payload.

- The GRE header consumes at least 24 bytes of additional overhead for tunneled packets.

Figure 3-23 illustrates the GRE header components.

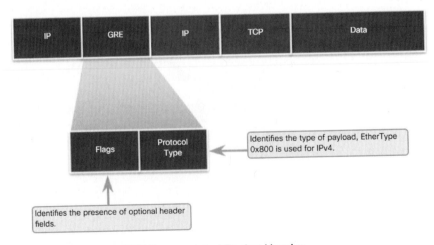

Figure 3-23   Header for GRE Encapsulated Packet Header

Activity 3.4.1.3: Identify GRE Characteristics

Interactive
Graphic

Refer to the online course to complete this activity.

Implement GRE (3.4.2)

In this topic, you learn how to troubleshoot a site-to-site GRE tunnel.

Configure GRE (3.4.2.1)

The topology displayed in Figure 3-24 will be used to create a GRE VPN tunnel between two sites.

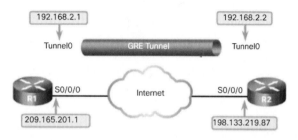

Figure 3-24   GRE Tunnel Configuration Topology

To implement a GRE tunnel, the network administrator must know the reachable IP addresses of the endpoints.

There are five steps to configuring a GRE tunnel:

Step 1.   Create a tunnel interface using the **interface tunnel** *number* global configuration command.

Step 2.   Configure an IP address for the tunnel interface using the **ip address** *ip-address* interface configuration command. This is normally a private IP address.

Step 3.   Specify the tunnel source IP address or source interface using the **tunnel source** {*ip-address* | *interface-name*} interface configuration command.

Step 4.   Specify the tunnel destination IP address using the **tunnel destination** *ip-address* interface configuration command.

Step 5.   (Optional) Specify GRE tunnel mode as the tunnel interface mode using the **tunnel mode gre** *protocol* interface configuration command. GRE tunnel mode is the default tunnel interface mode for Cisco IOS software.

The sample configuration in Example 3-11 illustrates a basic GRE tunnel configuration for R1 and R2.

Example 3-11 R1 and R2 GRE Tunnel Configuration

```
R1(config)# interface Tunnel0
R1(config-if)# ip address 192.168.2.1 255.255.255.0
R1(config-if)# tunnel source 209.165.201.1
R1(config-if)# tunnel destination 209.165.201.2
R1(config-if)# tunnel mode gre ip
R1(config-if)# exit
R1(config)# router ospf 1
R1(config-router)# network 192.168.2.0 0.0.0.255 area 0
```
```
R2(config)# interface Tunnel0
R2(config-if)# ip address 192.168.2.2 255.255.255.0
R2(config-if)# tunnel source 209.165.201.2
R2(config-if)# tunnel destination 209.165.201.1
R2(config-if)# tunnel mode gre ip
R2(config-if)# exit
R2(config)# router ospf 1
R2(config-router)# network 192.168.2.0 0.0.0.255 area 0
```

The minimum configuration requires specification of the tunnel source and destination addresses. The IP subnet must also be configured to provide IP connectivity across the tunnel link. Both tunnel interfaces have the tunnel source set using the IP address of their local serial S0/0/0 interface and the tunnel destination set to the IP address of the peer router serial S0/0/0 interface. The tunnel interface IP address is typically assigned a private IP address. Finally, OSPF is configured to advertise the tunnel network route over the GRE tunnel.

Table 3-1 provides the individual GRE tunnel command descriptions.

Table 3-1   GRE Configuration Command Syntax

Command	Description
ip address *ip_address mask*	Specifies the IP address of the tunnel interface
tunnel source *ip_address*	Specifies the tunnel source IP address, in interface tunnel configuration mode
tunnel destination *ip_address*	Specifies the tunnel destination IP address, in interface tunnel configuration mode
tunnel mode gre ip	Specifies GRE tunnel mode as the tunnel interface mode, in interface tunnel configuration mode •

> **Note**
>
> When you are configuring GRE tunnels, it can be difficult to remember which IP networks are associated with the physical interfaces and which IP networks are associated with the tunnel interfaces. Remember that before a GRE tunnel is created, the physical interfaces have already been configured. The **tunnel source** and **tunnel destination** commands reference the IP addresses of the preconfigured physical interfaces. The **ip address** command on the tunnel interfaces refers to an IP network (usually a private IP network) specifically selected for the purposes of the GRE tunnel.

Verify GRE (3.4.2.2)

Several commands can be used to monitor and troubleshoot GRE tunnels. To determine whether the tunnel interface is up or down, use the **show ip interface brief** and **show interface tunnel** *number* privileged EXEC commands, as demonstrated in Example 3-12.

Example 3-12 Verifying GRE

```
R1# show ip interface brief | include Tunnel

Tunnel0                    192.168.2.1        YES manual up                up
R1#
R1# show interface Tunnel 0
Tunnel0 is up, line protocol is up
  Hardware is Tunnel
  Internet address is 192.168.2.1/24
  MTU 17916 bytes, BW 100 Kbit/sec, DLY 50000 usec,
      reliability 255/255, txload 1/255, rxload 1/255
  Encapsulation TUNNEL, loopback not set
  Keepalive not set
  Tunnel source 209.165.201.1, destination 209.165.201.2
  Tunnel protocol/transport GRE/IP

<output omitted>
```

The first command verifies that the tunnel 0 interface is up and has an IP address assigned to it. The second command verifies the state of a GRE tunnel, the tunnel source and destination addresses, and the GRE mode supported. The line protocol on a GRE tunnel interface is up as long as there is a route to the tunnel destination. Before a GRE tunnel is implemented, IP connectivity must already be in effect between the IP addresses of the physical interfaces on opposite ends of the potential GRE tunnel.

A routing protocol could also be configured to exchange route information over the tunnel interface. For example if OSPF had also been configured to exchange routes over the GRE tunnel, you could verify that an OSPF adjacency had been established using the **show ip ospf neighbor** command.

In Example 3-13, note that the peering address for the OSPF neighbor is on the IP network created for the GRE tunnel.

Example 3-13 Verifying OSPF Adjacency via GRE Tunnel

```
R1# show ip ospf neighbor

Neighbor ID        Pri State       Dead Time  Address       Interface
209.165.201.2        0   FULL/  -    00:00:37   192.168.2.2   Tunnel0
```

GRE is considered a VPN because it is a private network that is created by tunneling over a public network. Using encapsulation, a GRE tunnel creates a virtual point-to-point link to Cisco routers at remote points over an IP internetwork.

The advantages of GRE are that it can be used to tunnel non-IP traffic over an IP network, allowing for network expansion by connecting multiprotocol subnetworks across a single-protocol backbone environment. GRE also supports IP multicast tunneling. This means that routing protocols can be used across the tunnel, enabling dynamic exchange of routing information in the virtual network. Finally, it is common practice to create IPv6 over IPv4 GRE tunnels, where IPv6 is the encapsulated protocol and IPv4 is the transport protocol. In the future, these roles will likely be reversed as IPv6 takes over as the standard IP protocol.

However, GRE does not provide encryption or any other security mechanisms. Therefore, data sent across a GRE tunnel is not secure. If secure data communication is needed, IPsec or *Secure Sockets Layer (SSL)* VPNs should be configured.

Troubleshoot GRE (3.4.2.3)

Issues with GRE are usually due to one or more of the following misconfigurations:

- The tunnel interface IP addresses are not on the same network or the subnet masks do not match.

- The interfaces for the tunnel source and/or tunnel destination are not configured with the correct IP address or are in the down state.

- Static or dynamic routing is not properly configured.

Figure 3-25 shows the GRE configuration topology.

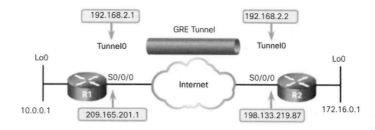

Figure 3-25 GRE Tunnel Configuration Topology

Use the **show ip interface brief** command on both routers to verify that the tunnel interface is up and configured with the correct IP addresses for the physical interface and the tunnel interface. Also, verify that the source interface on each router is up and configured with the correct IP addresses, as shown in Example 3-14.

Example 3-14 Verifying That All Necessary Interfaces Are Up

```
R1# show ip interface brief
<some output omitted>
Interface          IP-Address       OK?  Method   Status    Protocol
Serial0/0/0        209.165.201.1    YES  manual   up        up
Loopback0          10.0.0.1         YES  manual   up        up
Tunnel0            192.168.2.1      YES  manual   up        up
R1#

R2# show ip interface brief
<some output omitted>
Interface          IP-Address       OK?  Method   Status    Protocol
Serial0/0/0        198.133.219.87   YES  manual   up        up
Loopback0          172.16.0.1       YES  manual   up        up
Tunnel0            192.168.2.2      YES  manual   up        up
R2#
```

Routing can cause an issue. Both routers need a default route pointing to the Internet. Also, both routers need the correct dynamic or static routing configured. You can use the **show ip ospf neighbor** command to verify neighbor adjacency. Regardless of the routing used, you can also use **show ip route** to verify that networks are being passed between the two routers, as shown in Example 3-15.

Example 3-15 Verify That Networks Are Being Routed

```
R1# show ip route ospf
      172.16.0.0/32 is subnetted, 1 subnets
O        172.16.0.0 [110/1001] via 192.168.2.2, 00:19:44, Tunnel0
R1#
```
```
R2# show ip route ospf
      10.0.0.0/32 is subnetted, 1 subnets
O        10.0.0.1 [110/1001] via 192.168.2.1, 00:20:35, Tunnel0
R2#
```

Packet Tracer 3.4.2.4: Configuring GRE

You are the network administrator for a company that wants to set up a GRE tunnel to a remote office. Both networks are locally configured and need only the tunnel configured.

Packet Tracer 3.4.2.5: Troubleshooting GRE

A junior network administrator was hired to set up a GRE tunnel between two sites and was unable to complete the task. You have been asked to correct configuration errors in the company network.

Lab 3.4.2.6: Configuring a Point-to-Point GRE VPN Tunnel

In this lab, you complete the following objectives:

- Part 1: Configure Basic Device Settings
- Part 2: Configure a GRE Tunnel
- Part 3: Enable Routing over the GRE Tunnel

eBGP (3.5)

In this section, you implement eBGP in a single-homed remote-access network.

BGP Overview (3.5.1)

In this topic, you learn about the basic BGP features.

IGP and EGP Routing Protocols (3.5.1.1)

RIP, EIGRP, and OSPF are Interior Gateway Protocols (IGPs). ISPs and their customers, such as corporations and other enterprises, usually use an IGP to route traffic within their networks. IGPs are used to exchange routing information within a company network or an autonomous system (AS).

Border Gateway Protocol (BGP) is an Exterior Gateway Protocol (EGP) used for the exchange of routing information between autonomous systems, such as ISPs, companies, and content providers (such as YouTube and Netflix).

In BGP, every AS is assigned a unique 16-bit or 32-bit *AS number (ASN)*, which uniquely identifies it on the Internet. Figure 3-26 shows an example of how IGPs are interconnected using BGP.

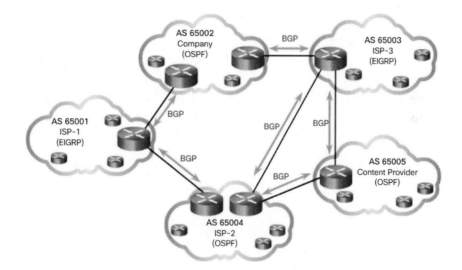

Figure 3-26   IGP and EGP Routing Protocols

Note

Private AS numbers are also available. However, private AS numbers are beyond the scope of this course.

Internal routing protocols use a specific metric, such as OSPF's cost, for determining the best paths to destination networks. BGP does not use a single metric like IGPs. BGP routers exchange several path attributes including a list of AS numbers (hop by hop) necessary to reach a destination network.

For example, in Figure 3-26, AS 65002 may use the AS-path of 65003 and 65005 to reach a network within the content provider AS 65005. BGP is known as a *path vector routing protocol*.

BGP updates are encapsulated over TCP on port 179. Therefore, BGP inherits the connection-oriented properties of TCP, which ensures that BGP updates are transmitted reliably.

IGP routing protocols are used to route traffic within the same organization and administered by a single organization. In contrast, BGP is used to route between networks administered by two different organizations. An AS uses BGP to advertise its networks and, in some cases, networks that it learned about from other autonomous systems, to the rest of the Internet.

eBGP and iBGP (3.5.1.2)

Two routers exchanging BGP routing information are known as BGP peers. As shown in Figure 3-27, there are two types of BGP, as described in the list that follows.

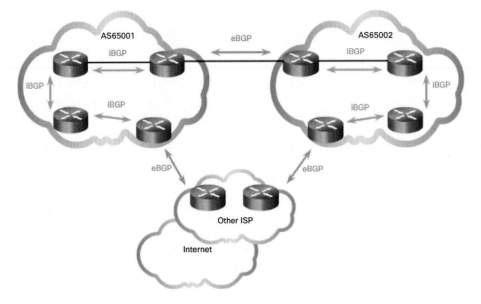

Figure 3-27   eBGP and iBGP Comparison

- *External BGP (eBGP):* External BGP is a BGP configuration between two routers in different autonomous systems. For example, eBGP would be used to connect an enterprise AS to a service provider AS.

- *Internal BGP (iBGP):* Internal BGP is a BGP configuration between two routers in the same autonomous systems. For example, iBGP would be used between routers in a service provider AS.

This course focuses on eBGP only.

Note

There are differences in how eBGP peers and iBGP peers operate; however, these differences are beyond the scope of this course.

BGP Design Considerations (3.5.2)

In this topic, you learn about BGP design considerations.

When to Use BGP (3.5.2.1)

The use of BGP is most appropriate when an AS has connections to multiple autonomous systems. This is known as *multihomed*. Each AS in Figure 3-28 is multihomed because each AS has connections to at least two other autonomous systems or BGP peers.

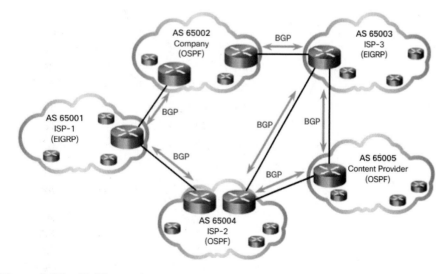

Figure 3-28   Multihomed

When Not to Use BGP (3.5.2.2)

BGP should not be used when at least one of the following conditions exist:

- There is a single connection to the Internet or another AS. This is known as *single-homed*. In this case, Company-A may run an IGP with the ISP, or Company-A and the ISP each use static routes, as shown in Figure 3-29. Although it is recommended only in unusual situations, for the purposes of this course, you will configure single-homed BGP.

- There is a limited understanding of BGP. A misconfiguration of a BGP router can have far-reaching effects beyond the local AS, negatively impacting routers throughout the Internet.

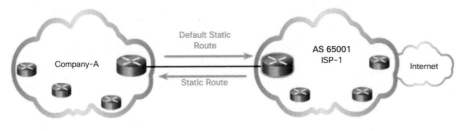

Figure 3-29   Single-Homed

> **Note**
>
> In some single-homed situations, BGP may be appropriate, such as the need for a specific routing policy. However, routing policies are beyond the scope of this course.

BGP Options (3.5.2.3)

BGP is used by autonomous systems to advertise networks that originated within their AS or, in the case of ISPs, the networks that originated from other autonomous systems.

For example, a company connecting to its ISP using BGP would advertise its network addresses to the ISP. The ISP would then advertise these networks to other ISPs (*BGP peers*). Eventually, all other autonomous systems on the Internet would learn about the networks initially originated by the company.

An organization can choose to implement BGP in a multihomed environment in three common ways.

Default Route Only

ISPs advertise a default route to Company-A, as shown in Figure 3-30.

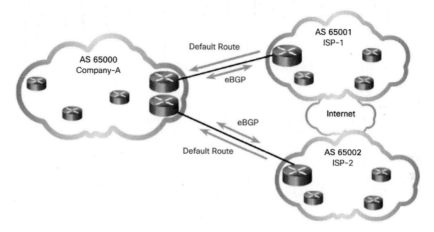

Figure 3-30   Default Route Only

The arrows indicate that the default is configured on the ISPs, not on Company-A. This is the simplest method to implement BGP; however, because the company receives only a default route from both ISPs, suboptimal routing may occur. For example, Company-A may choose to use ISP-1's default route when sending packets to a destination network in ISP-2's AS.

Default Route and ISP Routes

ISPs advertise their default route and their network to Company-A, as shown in Figure 3-31.

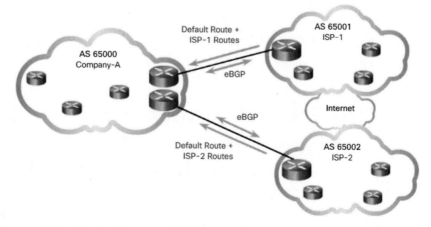

Figure 3-31   Default Route and ISP Routes

This option allows Company-A to forward traffic to the appropriate ISP for networks advertised by that ISP. For example, Company-A would choose ISP-1 for networks advertised by ISP-1. For all other networks, one of the two default routes can be used, which means suboptimal routing may still occur for all other Internet routes.

All Internet Routes

ISPs advertise all Internet routes to Company-A, as shown in Figure 3-32.

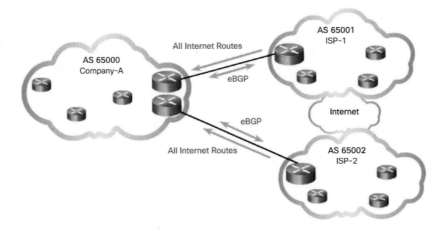

Figure 3-32   All Internet Routes

Because Company-A receives all Internet routes from both ISPs, Company-A can determine which ISP to use as the best path to forward traffic for any network. Although this approach solves the issue of suboptimal routing, the BGP router would require sufficient resources to maintain well over 500,000 Internet networks.

Interactive Graphic

Activity 3.5.2.4: Identify BPG Terminology and Designs

Refer to the online course to complete this activity.

eBGP Branch Configuration (3.5.3)

In this topic, you configure an eBGP branch connection.

Steps to Configure eBGP (3.5.3.1)

To implement eBGP for this course, you need to complete the following tasks:

Step 1.   Enable BGP routing.

Step 2.   Configure BGP neighbor(s) (peering).

Step 3.   Advertise network(s) originating from this AS.

Table 3-2 lists the command syntax and a description for basic eBGP configuration.

Table 3-2   BGP Configuration Commands

Command	Description
Router(config)# **router bgp** *as-number*	Enables a BGP routing process and places the router in router configuration mode.
Router(config-router)# **neighbor** *ip-address* **remote-as** *as-number*	Specifies a BGP neighbor. The *as-number* is the neighbor's AS number.
Router(config-router)# **network** *network-address* [**mask** *network-mask*]	Advertises a network address to an eBGP neighbor as being originated by this AS. The *network-mask* is the subnet mask of the network.

BGP Sample Configuration (3.5.3.2)

In this single-homed BGP topology, Company-A in AS 65000 uses eBGP to advertise its 198.133.219.0/24 network to ISP-1 at AS 65001. ISP-1 advertises a default route in its eBGP updates to Company-A.

Note

BGP is usually not necessary in single-homed AS. It is used here to provide a simple configuration example.

Figure 3-33 shows the BGP configuration topology.

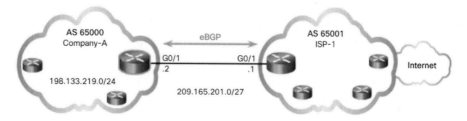

Figure 3-33   BGP Configuration Topology

Example 3-16 shows the BGP configuration for Company-A and ISP-1. Customers typically use private IPv4 address space for internal devices within their own network. Using *Network Address Translation (NAT)*, the Company-A router translates these private IPv4 addresses to one of its public IPv4 addresses, advertised by BGP to the ISP.

Example 3-16 Company-A and ISP BGP Configuration

```
Company-A(config)# router bgp 65000
Company-A(config-router)# neighbor 209.165.201.1 remote-as 65001
Company-A(config-router)# network 198.133.219.0 mask 255.255.255.0

ISP-1(config)# router bgp 65001
ISP-1(config-router)# neighbor 209.165.201.2 remote-as 65000
ISP-1(config-router)# network 0.0.0.0
```

The **router bgp** global configuration command enables BGP and identifies the AS number for Company-A. A router can belong to only a single AS, so only a single BGP process can run on a router.

The **neighbor** router configuration command identifies the BGP peer IP address and AS number. Notice that the ISP AS number is different than the Company-A AS number. This informs the BGP process that the neighbor is in a different AS and is therefore an external BGP neighbor.

The **network** *network-address* [**mask** *network-mask*] router configuration command enters the *network-address* into the local BGP table. The BGP table contains all routes learned via BGP or advertised using BGP. eBGP will then advertise the *network-address* to its eBGP neighbors.

The **mask** *network-mask* command parameter must be used when the network advertised is different from its classful equivalent. In this example, the 198.133.219.0/24 is equivalent to a class C network. Class C networks have a /24 subnet mask, so in this case the **mask** option is not required. If Customer-A were advertising the 198.133.0.0/16 network, the **mask** option would be required. Otherwise, BGP would advertise the network with a /24 classful mask.

Note

In contrast to an IGP protocol, the *network-address* used in the **network** command does not have to be a directly connected network. The router only needs to have a route to this network in its routing table.

The eBGP commands on the ISP-1 router are similar to the configuration on Company-A. Notice how the **network 0.0.0.0** router configuration command is used to advertise a default network to Company-A.

Note

Although the **network 0.0.0.0** command is a valid BGP configuration option, there are better ways to advertise a default route in eBGP. However, these methods are beyond the scope of this course.

Verify eBGP (3.5.3.3)

You can use three commands to verify eBGP, as described in Table 3-3.

Table 3-3 BGP Verification Commands

Command	Description
Router# **show ip route**	Verify routes advertised by the BGP neighbor are present in the IPv4 routing table
Router# **show ip bgp**	Verify that received and advertised IPv4 networks are in the BGP table
Router# **show ip bgp summary**	Verify IPv4 BGP neighbors and other BGP information

Example 3-17 shows the output for Company-A's IPv4 routing table. Notice how the origin code **B** identifies that the route was learned using BGP. Specifically, in this example, Company-A has received a BGP advertised default route from ISP-1.

Example 3-17 Verifying BGP Routes Are in the Table

```
Company-A# show ip route | include Gateway

Gateway of last resort is 209.165.201.1 to network 0.0.0.0

B*    0.0.0.0/0 [20/0] via 209.165.201.1, 00:36:03
      10.0.0.0/8 is variably subnetted, 2 subnets, 2 masks
C        198.133.219.0/24 is directly connected, GigabitEthernet0/0
L        198.133.219.1/32 is directly connected, GigabitEthernet0/0
      209.165.201.0/24 is variably subnetted, 2 subnets, 2 masks
C        209.165.201.0/27 is directly connected, GigabitEthernet0/1
L        209.165.201.2/32 is directly connected, GigabitEthernet0/1
Company-A#
```

Example 3-18 shows the output of Company-A's BGP table.

Example 3-18 Verifying BGP

```
Company-A# show ip bgp
BGP table version is 3, local router ID is 209.165.201.2
Status codes: s suppressed, d damped, h history, * valid, > best, i - internal,
              r RIB-failure, S Stale, m multipath, b backup-path, f RT-Filter,
```

```
              x best-external, a additional-path, c RIB-compressed,
Origin codes: i - IGP, e - EGP, ? - incomplete
RPKI validation codes: V valid, I invalid, N Not found

      Network              Next Hop           Metric LocPrf   Weight Path
 *>   0.0.0.0              209.165.201.1           0               0 65001 i
 *>   198.133.219.0/24 0.0.0.0                     0           32768 i
Company-A#
```

The first entry 0.0.0.0 with a next hop of 209.165.201.1 is the default route advertised by ISP-1. The AS path displays the single AS of 65001 because the 0.0.0.0/0 network advertised by ISP-1 originated from the same AS. Most BGP table entries show multiple autonomous system numbers in the path, listing the sequence of AS numbers required to reach the destination network.

The second entry 198.133.219.0/24 is the network advertised by the Company-A router to ISP-1. The next hop address of 0.0.0.0 indicates that the 198.133.219.0/24 network originated from this router.

Example 3-19 displays the status of BGP connection on Company-A. The first line displays the local IPv4 address used to peer with another BGP neighbor and this router's local AS number. The address and AS number of the remote BGP neighbor are shown at the bottom of the output.

Example 3-19 Verify BGP Summary

```
Company-A# show ip bgp summary
BGP router identifier 209.165.201.2, local AS number 65000
BGP table version is 3, main routing table version 3
2 network entries using 288 bytes of memory
2 path entries using 160 bytes of memory
2/2 BGP path/bestpath attribute entries using 320 bytes of memory
1 BGP AS-PATH entries using 24 bytes of memory
0 BGP route-map cache entries using 0 bytes of memory
0 BGP filter-list cache entries using 0 bytes of memory
BGP using 792 total bytes of memory
BGP activity 2/0 prefixes, 2/0 paths, scan interval 60 secs


Neighbor        V     AS MsgRcvd MsgSent   TblVer  InQ OutQ  Up/Down State/PfxRcd
209.165.201.1   4  65001     66      66        3    0    0 00:56:11             1
Company-A#
```

Packet Tracer 3.5.3.4: Configure and Verify eBGP

In this activity, you configure and verify the operation of eBGP between autonomous systems 65001 and 65002.

Lab 3.5.3.5: Configure and Verify eBGP

In this lab, you complete the following objectives:

- Build the Network and Configure Basic Device Settings

- Configure eBGP on R1

- Verify eBGP Configuration

Summary (3.6)

Class Activity 3.6.1.1: VPN Planning Design

Your small- to medium-sized business has received quite a few new contracts lately. This circumstance has increased the need for teleworkers and workload outsourcing. The new contract vendors and clients will also need access to your network as the projects progress.

As network administrator for the business, you recognize that VPNs must be incorporated as a part of your network strategy to support secure access by the teleworkers, employees, and vendors or clients.

To prepare for implementation of VPNs on the network, you devise a planning checklist to bring to the next department meeting for discussion.

Packet Tracer
□ Activity

Packet Tracer 3.6.1.2: Skills Integration Challenge

In this skills integration challenge, the XYZ Corporation uses a combination of eBGP, PPP, and GRE WAN connections. Other technologies include DHCP, default routing, OSPF for IPv4, and SSH configurations.

Lab 3.6.1.3: Configure a Branch Connection

In this lab, you configure two separate WAN connections: a BGP route over a PPPoE connection and a BGP route over a GRE tunnel. This lab is a test-case scenario and does not represent a realistic BGP implementation.

- Part 1: Build the Network and Load Device Configurations
- Part 2: Configure a PPPoE Client Connection
- Part 3: Configure a GRE Tunnel
- Part 4: Configure BGP over PPPoE and BGP over a GRE Tunnel

Broadband transmission is provided by a wide range of technologies, including DSL, fiber-to-the-home, coaxial cable systems, wireless, and satellite. This transmission requires additional components at the home end and at the corporate end. Broadband wireless solutions include municipal Wi-Fi, cellular/mobile, and satellite Internet. Municipal Wi-Fi mesh networks are not widely deployed. Cellular/mobile coverage can be limited and bandwidth can be an issue. Satellite Internet is relatively expensive and limited, but it may be the only method to provide access.

If multiple broadband connections are available to a particular location, a cost-benefit analysis should be performed to determine the best solution. The best solution may be to connect to multiple service providers to provide redundancy and reliability.

PPPoE is a popular data link protocol for connecting remote networks to their ISPs. PPPoE provides the flexibility of PPP and the convenience of Ethernet.

VPNs are used to create a secure end-to-end private network connection over a third-party network, such as the Internet. GRE is a basic, nonsecure site-to-site VPN tunneling protocol that can encapsulate a wide variety of protocol packet types inside IP tunnels, thus allowing an organization to deliver other protocols through an IP-based WAN. Today it is primarily used to deliver IP multicast traffic or IPv6 traffic over an IPv4 unicast-only connection.

BGP is the routing protocol implemented between autonomous systems. Three basic design options for eBGP are as follows:

- The ISP advertises a default route only to the customer.
- The ISP advertises a default route and all its routes to the customer.
- The ISP advertises all Internet routes to the customer.

Implementing eBGP in a single-homed network requires only a few commands.

Practice

The following activities provide practice with the topics introduced in this chapter. The Labs and Class Activities are available in the companion *Connecting Networks v6 Labs & Study Guide* (ISBN 9781587134296). The Packet Tracer Activity instructions are also in the *Labs & Study Guide*. The PKA files are found in the online course.

Class Activities

Class Activity 3.0.1.2: Broadband Varieties

Class Activity 3.6.1.1: VPN Planning Design

Labs

Lab 3.1.2.2: Researching Broadband Internet Access Technologies

Lab 3.2.2.7: Configuring a Router as a PPPoE Client for DSL Connectivity

Lab 3.2.2.8: Troubleshoot PPPoE

Lab 3.4.2.6: Configuring a Point-to-Point GRE VPN Tunnel

Lab 3.5.3.5: Configure and Verify eBGP

Lab 3.6.1.3: Configure a Branch Connection

Packet Tracer
☐ Activity

Packet Tracer Activities

Packet Tracer 3.4.2.4: Configuring GRE

Packet Tracer 3.4.2.5: Troubleshooting GRE

Packet Tracer 3.5.3.4: Configure and Verify eBGP

Packet Tracer 3.6.1.2: Skills Integration Challenge

Check Your Understanding Questions

Complete all the review questions listed here to test your understanding of the topics and concepts in this chapter. The appendix "Answers to the 'Check Your Understanding' Questions" lists the answers.

1. Which technology provides a secure connection between a SOHO and the headquarters office?

   A. PPPoE

   B. QoS

   C. VPN

   D. WiMax

2. Which two network components does a teleworker require to connect remotely and securely from home to the corporate network? (Choose two.)

   A. Authentication server

   B. Broadband Internet connection

   C. VPN client software or VPN-enabled router

   D. Multifunction security appliance

   E. VPN server or concentrator

3. What advantage does DSL have compared to cable technology?

   A. DSL has no distance limitations.

   B. DSL is faster.

   C. DSL is not a shared medium.

   D. DSL upload and download speeds are always the same.

4. Which medium is used for delivering data via DSL technology through PSTN?

   A. Copper

   B. Fiber

   C. Radio frequency

   D. Wireless

5. What technology provides service providers the capability to use authentication, accounting, and link management features to customers over Ethernet networks?

   A. DSL

   B. ISDN

   C. PPPoE

   D. QoS

6. Why is the MTU for a PPPoE DSL configuration reduced from 1500 bytes to 1492?

   A. To accommodate the PPPoE headers

   B. To enable CHAP authentication

   C. To establish a secure tunnel with less overhead?

   D. To reduce congestion on the DSL link

7. What are two characteristics of a PPPoE configuration on a Cisco customer router? (Choose two.)

   A. An MTU size of 1492 bytes is configured on the Ethernet interface.

   B. The customer router CHAP username and password are independent of what is configured on the ISP router.

   C. The **dialer pool** command is applied to the Ethernet interface to link it to the dialer interface.

   D. The Ethernet interface does not have an IP address.

   E. The PPP configuration is on the dialer interface.

8. When PPPoE is configured on a customer router, which two commands must have the same value for the configuration to work? (Choose two.)

   A. dialer pool 2

   B. interface dialer 2

   C. interface gigabitethernet 0/2

   D. ppp chap hostname 2

   E. ppp chap password 2

   F. pppoe-client dial-pool-number 2

9. A network design engineer is planning the implementation of a cost-effective method to interconnect multiple networks securely over the Internet. Which type of technology is required?

   A. A dedicated ISP

   B. A GRE IP tunnel

   C. A leased line

   D. A VPN gateway

10. Which statement describes a feature of site-to-site VPNs?

    A. Individual hosts can enable and disable the VPN connection.

    B. Internal hosts send normal, unencapsulated packets.

    C. The VPN connection is not statically defined.

    D. VPN client software is installed on each host.

11. Which remote-access implementation scenario will support the use of Generic Routing Encapsulation tunneling?

    A. A branch office that connects securely to a central site

    B. A central site that connects to a SOHO site without encryption

    C. A mobile user who connects to a router at a central site

    D. A mobile user who connects to a SOHO site

12. Which two statements are key characteristics of BGP? (Choose two.)

    A. It provides interdomain routing between autonomous systems.

    B. It is an advanced distance vector routing protocol.

    C. It uses cost as its metric.

    D. It is a link-state routing protocol.

    E. It uses bandwidth and delay as its metric.

    F. It is a policy-based routing protocol.

13. Which BGP routers will become peers and share routing information?

   A. All BGP routers in the same domain share routing information by default

   B. BGP routers that are configured with the same **network** command

   C. BGP routers that are configured with the same **peer** command

   D. BGP routers that are identified with the **neighbor** command

14. Which of the following BGP statements is true?

   A. BGP is an IGP used to exchange routing information with another AS.

   B. BGP updates are encapsulated using TCP port 179.

   C. Every AS is assigned a unique 160-bit AS number (ASN).

   D. Use BGP when there is a single connection to the Internet or another AS.

15. Assume R1 is in AS 5000 and wants to establish an eBGP peer relationship with another router. Which of the following commands would correctly configure an eBGP relationship?

   A. R1(config-router)# **neighbor 209.165.201.1 remote-as 5000**

   B. R1(config-router)# **neighbor 209.165.201.1 remote-as 10000**

   C. R1(config-router)# **peer 209.165.201.1 remote-as 5000**

   D. R1(config-router)# **peer 209.165.201.1 remote-as 10000**

CHAPTER 4

Access Control Lists

Objectives

Upon completion of this chapter, you will be able to answer the following questions:

- What purpose do ACLs serve in small- to medium-sized business networks?

- What are the differences between standard and extended IPv4 ACLs?

- What are the steps to configure standard IPv4 ACLs to filter traffic in a small- to medium-sized business network?

- What is the structure of an extended access control entry (ACE)?

- What are the steps to configure extended IPv4 ACLs to filter traffic according to net-working requirements?

- What are the differences between IPv4 and IPv6 ACL creation?

- What are the steps to configure IPv6 ACLs to filter traffic according to networking requirements?

- How does a router process packets when an ACL is applied?

- What are the steps to troubleshoot common ACL errors using CLI commands?

Key Terms

This chapter uses the following key terms. You can find the definitions in the Glossary.

Introduction (4.0.1.1)

One of the most important skills a network administrator needs is mastery of *access control lists (ACLs)*. ACLs provide packet filtering capabilities to control traffic flow.

Network designers use a *firewall* to protect networks from unauthorized use. Firewalls are hardware or software solutions that enforce network security policies. Consider a lock on a door to a room inside a building. The lock allows only authorized users with a key or access card to pass through the door. Similarly, a firewall filters unauthorized or potentially dangerous packets from entering the network.

On a Cisco router, you can configure a simple firewall that provides basic traffic filtering capabilities using ACLs. Administrators use ACLs to filter traffic, allowing or blocking specified packets on their networks.

This chapter begins with a review of ACLs and standard IPv4 ACL configuration. The chapter then explains how to configure and troubleshoot extended IPv4 ACLs and IPv6 ACLs on a Cisco router as part of a security solution. Included are tips, considerations, recommendations, and general guidelines on how to use ACLs.

Standard ACL Operation and Configuration Review (4.1)

In this section, you review how to configure standard IPv4 ACLs.

ACL Operation Overview (4.1.1)

In this topic, you learn about the purpose and operation of ACLs in small- to medium-sized business networks.

ACLs and the Wildcard Mask (4.1.1.1)

Note

This section includes a brief review of standard IPv4 ACL operation and configuration. If you require additional review, refer to Chapter 7, "Access Control Lists," in the *Routing and Switching Essentials v6* course.

An ACL is a sequential list of **permit** or **deny** statements, known as *access control entries (ACEs)*. ACEs are also commonly called ACL statements. When network traffic passes through an interface configured with an ACL, the router compares the information within the packet against each ACE, in sequential order, to determine if the packet matches one of the ACEs.

IPv4 ACEs include the use of *wildcard masks*. A wildcard mask is a string of 32 binary digits that the router uses to determine which bits of the address to examine for a match.

Figure 4-1 shows how different wildcard masks filter IPv4 addresses. In the example, remember that binary 0 signifies a bit that must match, and binary 1 signifies a bit that can be ignored.

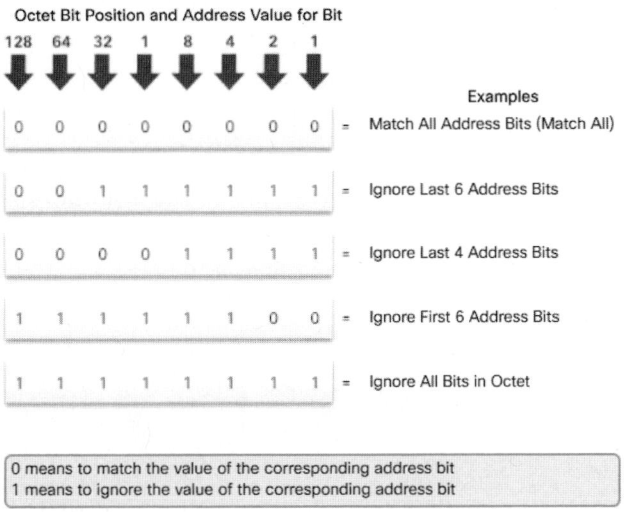

Octet Bit Position and Address Value for Bit

128	64	32	1	8	4	2	1		Examples
0	0	0	0	0	0	0	0	=	Match All Address Bits (Match All)
0	0	1	1	1	1	1	1	=	Ignore Last 6 Address Bits
0	0	0	0	1	1	1	1	=	Ignore Last 4 Address Bits
1	1	1	1	1	1	0	0	=	Ignore First 6 Address Bits
1	1	1	1	1	1	1	1	=	Ignore All Bits in Octet

0 means to match the value of the corresponding address bit
1 means to ignore the value of the corresponding address bit

Figure 4-1   Wildcard Masking

Figure 4-2 provides three examples of wildcard masks that match subnets.

Example 1

	Decimal	Binary
IP Address	192.168.1.1	11000000.10101000.00000001.00000001
Wildcard Mask	0.0.0.0	00000000.00000000.00000000.00000000
Result	192.168.1.1	11000000.10101000.00000001.00000001

Example 2

	Decimal	Binary
IP Address	192.168.1.1	11000000.10101000.00000001.00000001
Wildcard Mask	255.255.255.255	11111111.11111111.11111111.11111111
Result	0.0.0.0	00000000.00000000.00000000.00000000

Example 3

	Decimal	Binary
IP Address	192.168.1.1	11000000.10101000.00000001.00000001
Wildcard Mask	0.0.0.255	00000000.00000000.00000000.11111111
Result	192.168.1.0	11000000.10101000.00000001.00000000

Figure 4-2   Wildcard Mask Examples

In the first example, the wildcard mask stipulates that every bit in the IPv4 192.168.1.1 must match exactly.

In the second example, the wildcard mask stipulates that anything will match.

In the third example, the wildcard mask stipulates that any host within the 192.168.1.0/24 network will match.

Applying ACLs to an Interface (4.1.1.2)

ACLs can be configured to apply to inbound traffic and outbound traffic, as shown in Figure 4-3. The last statement of an ACL is always an implicit deny. This statement is automatically inserted at the end of each ACL even though it is not visible in **show** command output.

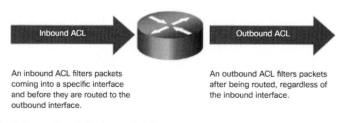

An inbound ACL filters packets coming into a specific interface and before they are routed to the outbound interface.

An outbound ACL filters packets after being routed, regardless of the inbound interface.

Figure 4-3 Inbound and Outbound ACLs

As shown in Figure 4-4 and described in the list that follows, you can configure one ACL per protocol, per direction, and per interface:

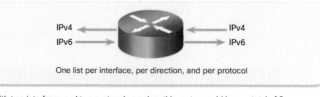

One list per interface, per direction, and per protocol

With two interfaces and two protocols running, this router could have a total of 8 separate ACLs applied.

Figure 4-4 ACL Traffic Filtering on a Router

- **One ACL per protocol:** To control traffic flow on an interface, an ACL must be defined for each protocol enabled on the interface.

- **One ACL per direction:** ACLs control traffic in one direction at a time on an interface. Two separate ACLs must be created to control inbound and outbound traffic.

■ **One ACL per interface:** ACLs control traffic for an interface, for example, GigabitEthernet 0/0.

A TCP Conversation (4.1.1.3)

Administrators can control network traffic based on a number of characteristics, including the TCP port being requested. It is easier to understand how an ACL filters traffic by examining the dialogue that occurs during a TCP conversation, such as when requesting a web page.

When a client requests data from a web server, IP manages the communication between the PC (source) and the server (destination). TCP manages the communication between the web browser (application) and the network server software.

Figure 4-5 illustrates how a TCP/IP conversation takes place.

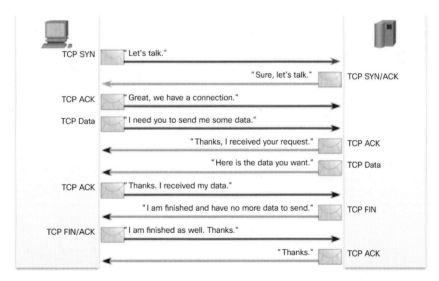

Figure 4-5   A TCP Conversation

TCP segments are marked with flags that denote their purpose: a SYN starts (synchronizes) the session; an ACK is an acknowledgment that an expected segment was received, and a FIN finishes the session. A SYN/ACK acknowledges that the transfer is synchronized. TCP data segments include the higher level protocol needed to direct the application data to the correct application.

The TCP data segment also identifies the port that matches the requested service. Table 4-1 shows ranges of UDP and TCP ports.

Table 4-1   Range of UDP and TCP Port Numbers

Port Number Range	Port Group
0 to 1023	Well-Known Ports
1024 to 49151	Registered Ports
49152 to 65535	Private and/or Dynamic Ports

Table 4-2 shows a listing of well-known port numbers.

Table 4-2   Some Well-Known Port Numbers

Port Number	Protocol	Application	Acronym
20	TCP	File Transfer Protocol (data)	FTP
21	TCP	File Transfer Protocol (control)	FTP
22	TCP	Secure Shell	SSH
23	TCP	Telnet	—
25	TCP	Simple Mail Transfer Protocol	SMTP
53	UDP, TCP	Domain Name Service	DNS
67, 68	UDP	Dynamic Host Configuration Protocol	DHCP
69	UDP	Trivial File Transfer Protocol	TFTP
80	TCP	Hypertext Transfer Protocol	HTTP
110	TCP	Post Office Protocol version 3	POP3
143	TCP	Internet Message Access Protocol	IMAP
161	UDP	Simple Network Management Protocol	SNMP
443	TCP	Hypertext Transfer Protocol Secure	HTTPS

ACL Packet Filtering (4.1.1.4)

Packet filtering controls access to a network by analyzing the incoming and outgoing packets and forwarding them or discarding them based on given criteria. Packet filtering can occur at Layer 3 or Layer 4. Standard ACLs filter only at Layer 3. *Extended ACLs* filter at Layer 3 and Layer 4.

For example, an ACL could be configured to logically "Permit web access to users from network A but deny all other services to network A users. Deny HTTP access to users from network B, but permit network B users to have all other access." Refer to Figure 4-6 to examine the decision path the packet filter uses to accomplish this task.

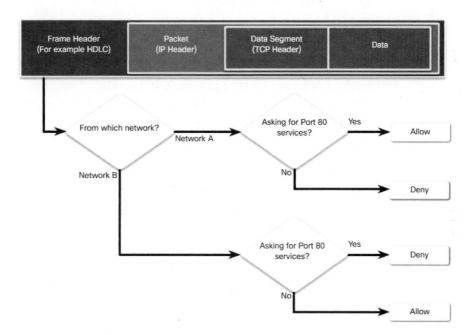

Figure 4-6   Packet Filtering Example

For this scenario, the packet filter looks at each packet as follows:

■ If the packet is a TCP SYN from Network A using Port 80, it is allowed to pass. All other access is denied to those users.

■ If the packet is a TCP SYN from Network B using Port 80, it is blocked. However, all other access is permitted.

This is just a simple example. Multiple rules can be configured to further permit or deny services to specific users.

Interactive Graphic

Activity 4.1.1.5: Determine the Correct Wildcard Mask

Refer to the online course to complete this activity.

Activity 4.1.1.6: ACL Operation

Refer to the online course to complete this activity.

Types of IPv4 ACLs (4.1.2)

In this topic, you compare standard and extended IPv4 ACLs.

Standard and Extended IPv4 ACLs (4.1.2.1)

The two types of Cisco IPv4 ACLs are standard ACLs and extended ACLs.

Standard ACLs can be used to permit or deny traffic only from source IPv4 addresses. The destination of the packet and the ports involved are not evaluated. This standard ACL allows all traffic from the 192.168.30.0/24 network.

```
Router(config)# access-list 10 permit 192.168.30.0 0.0.0.255
```

Because of the implied "deny any" at the end, all traffic except for traffic coming from the 192.168.30.0/24 network is blocked with this ACL. Standard ACLs are created in global configuration mode.

Extended ACLs filter IPv4 packets based on several attributes:

- Protocol type
- Source IPv4 address
- Destination IPv4 address
- Source TCP or UDP ports
- Destination TCP or UDP ports
- Optional protocol type information for finer control

This ACL 103 permits traffic originating from any address on the 192.168.30.0/24 network to any IPv4 network if the destination host port is 80 (HTTP). Extended ACLs are created in global configuration mode.

```
Router(config)# access-list 103 permit tcp 192.168.30.0 0.0.0.255 any eq 80
```

Note

ACL command syntax is discussed in more detail in the section, "Standard IPv4 ACL Implementation (4.1.3)."

Numbered and Named ACLs (4.1.2.2)

Standard and extended ACLs can be created using either a number or a name to identify the ACL and its list of statements.

Using *numbered ACLs* is an effective method for determining the ACL type on smaller networks with more homogeneously defined traffic. However, a number does not provide information about the purpose of the ACL. For this reason, a name can be used to identify a Cisco ACL.

To configure numbered ACLs, assign a number based on the protocol to be filtered. IPv4 ACLs use the following numbers:

- (1 to 99) and (1300 to 1999): Standard IPv4 ACL
- (100 to 199) and (2000 to 2699): Extended IPv4 ACL

Note

IPv6 ACLs do not use numbers.

To configure *named ACLs*, assign a name to identify the ACL:

- Names can contain alphanumeric characters.
- It is suggested that the name be written in CAPITAL LETTERS.
- Names cannot contain spaces or punctuation.
- Entries can be added or deleted within the ACL.

Where to Place ACLs (4.1.2.3)

Every ACL should be placed where it has the greatest impact on efficiency.

The basic rules for placing ACLs are

- **Extended ACLs:** Locate extended ACLs as close as possible to the source of the traffic to be filtered. This way, undesirable traffic is denied close to the source network without crossing the network infrastructure.
- **Standard ACLs:** Because standard ACLs do not specify destination addresses, place them as close to the destination as possible. If a standard ACL was placed at the source of the traffic, the "permit" or "deny" will occur based on the given source address no matter where the traffic is destined.

Figure 4-7 illustrates the basic ACL placement rules if an ACL had to be configured to filter traffic from R1 to R3.

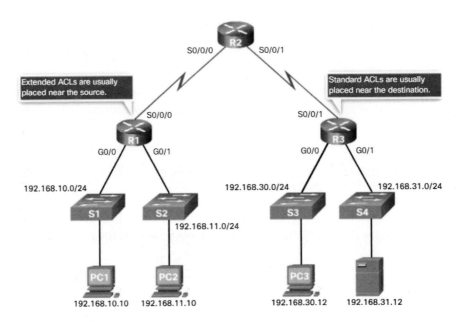

Figure 4-7   ACL Placement

Placement of the ACL and, therefore, the type of ACL used may also depend a variety of factors:

- **The extent of the network administrator's control:** Placement of the ACL can depend on whether or not the network administrator has control of both the source and destination networks.

- **Bandwidth of the networks involved:** Filtering unwanted traffic at the source prevents transmission of the traffic before it consumes bandwidth on the path to a destination. This is especially important in low-bandwidth networks.

- **Ease of configuration:** If a network administrator wants to deny traffic coming from several networks, one option is to use a single standard ACL on the router closest to the destination. The disadvantage is that traffic from these networks will use bandwidth unnecessarily. An extended ACL could be used on each router where the traffic originated. This approach will save bandwidth by filtering the traffic at the source but requires creating extended ACLs on multiple routers.

Note

For CCNA certification, the general rule is that extended ACLs are placed as close as possible to the source and standard ACLs are placed as close as possible to the destination.

Standard ACL Placement Example (4.1.2.4)

In Figure 4-8, the administrator wants to prevent traffic originating in the 192.168.10.0/24 network from reaching the 192.168.30.0/24 network.

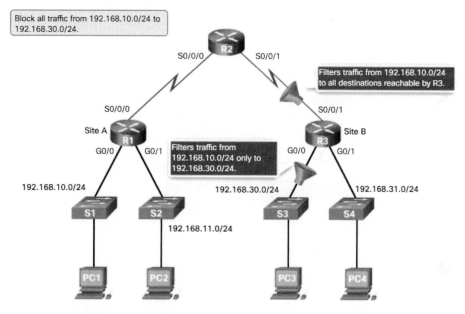

Figure 4-8   Standard ACL Placement

If the standard ACL is placed on the outbound interface of R1 (not shown in Figure 4-8), this would prevent traffic on the 192.168.10.0/24 network from reaching any networks that are reachable through the Serial 0/0/0 interface of R1.

Following the basic placement guidelines of placing the standard ACL close to the destination, Figure 4-8 shows two possible interfaces on R3 to apply the standard ACL:

- **R3 S0/0/1 interface:** Applying a standard ACL to prevent traffic from 192.168.10.0/24 from entering the S0/0/1 interface will prevent this traffic from reaching 192.168.30.0/24 and all other networks that are reachable by R3. This includes the 192.168.31.0/24 network. Because the intent of the ACL is to filter traffic destined only for 192.168.30.0/24, a standard ACL should not be applied to this interface.

- **R3 G0/0 interface:** Applying the standard ACL to traffic exiting the G0/0 interface will filter packets from 192.168.10.0/24 to 192.168.30.0/24. This will not affect other networks that are reachable by R3. Packets from 192.168.10.0/24 will still be able to reach 192.168.31.0/24.

Extended ACL Placement Example (4.1.2.5)

The basic rule for placing an extended ACL is to place it as close to the source as possible. This placement prevents unwanted traffic from being sent across multiple networks only to be denied when it reaches its destination. However, network administrators can place ACLs only on devices that they control. Therefore, placement must be determined in the context of where the control of the network administrator extends.

In Figure 4-9, the administrator of Company A, which includes the 192.168.10.0/24 and 192.168.11.0/24 networks (referred to as .10 and .11 in this example), wants to control traffic to Company B.

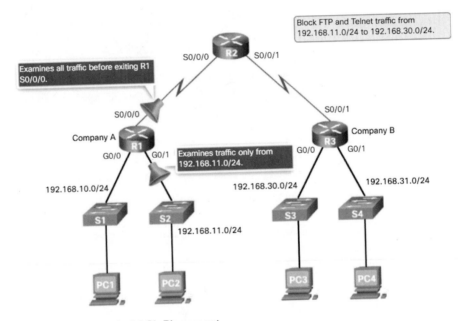

Figure 4-9   Extended ACL Placement

Specifically, the administrator wants to deny Telnet and FTP traffic from the .11 network to Company B's 192.168.30.0/24 (.30, in this example) network. At the same time, all other traffic from the .11 network must be permitted to leave Company A without restriction.

The administrator can accomplish these goals in several ways. An extended ACL on R3 that blocks Telnet and FTP from the .11 network would accomplish the task, but the administrator does not control R3. In addition, this solution also allows unwanted traffic to cross the entire network, only to be blocked at the destination. This affects overall network efficiency.

A better solution is to place an extended ACL on R1 that specifies both source and destination addresses (.11 network and .30 network, respectively) and enforces the rule, "Telnet and FTP traffic from the .11 network is not allowed to go to the .30 network."

Figure 4-9 shows two possible interfaces on R1 to apply the extended ACL:

- **R1 S0/0/0 interface (outbound):** One possibility is to apply an extended ACL outbound on the S0/0/0 interface. Because the extended ACL can examine both source and destination addresses, only FTP and Telnet packets from 192.168.11.0/24 will be denied. Other traffic from 192.168.11.0/24 and other networks will be forwarded by R1. The disadvantage of placing the extended ACL on this interface is that all traffic exiting S0/0/0 must be processed by the ACL, including packets from 192.168.10.0/24.

- **R1 G0/1 interface (inbound):** Applying an extended ACL to traffic entering the G0/1 interface means that only packets from the 192.168.11.0/24 network are subject to ACL processing on R1. Because the filter is to be limited to only those packets leaving the 192.168.11.0/24 network, applying the extended ACL to G0/1 is the best solution.

Interactive Graphic

Activity 4.1.2.6: Placing Standard and Extended ACLs

Refer to the online course to complete this activity.

Standard IPv4 ACL Implementation (4.1.3)

In this topic, you configure standard IPv4 ACLs to filter traffic in a small- to medium-sized business network.

Configure a Standard IPv4 ACL (4.1.3.1)

To create a standard ACL, use the **access-list** *access-list-number* {**remark** *description* | {**deny** | **permit**} *source* [*source-wildcard*][**log**]} global configuration command.

Table 4-3 provides a detailed explanation of the syntax for a standard ACL.

Table 4-3   Standard ACL Command Syntax

Parameter	Description
access-list-number	Identifies the number of an ACL. This is a decimal number from 1 to 99, or 1300 to 1999 (for standard ACL).
remark *description*	Enables you to enter descriptive text in the ACL. Useful to document the ACL.

Parameter	Description
deny	Denies access if the conditions are matched.
permit	Permits access if the conditions are matched.
source	Identifies the number of the network or host from which the packet is being sent.
source-wildcard	(Optional) Specifies the wildcard bits to be applied to the source.
log	(Optional) Causes an informational logging message about the packet that matches the entry to be sent to the console. (The level of messages logged to the console is controlled by the **logging console** command.) The message includes the ACL number, whether the packet was permitted or denied, the source address, and the number of packets. The message is generated for the first packet that matches and then at five-minute intervals, including the number of packets permitted or denied in the prior five-minute interval.

ACEs can permit or deny an individual host or a range of host addresses.

For example, to create numbered ACL 10 that permits a specific host with the IPv4 address 192.168.10.10, you could use **host** keyword and enter

```
R1(config)# access-list 10 permit host 192.168.10.10
```

Example 4-1 enters a numbered ACL 10 that permits all IPv4 addresses in the network 192.168.10.0/24.

Example 4-1 Creating a Standard ACL

```
R1(config)# access-list 10 permit 192.168.10.0 0.0.0.255
R1(config)# exit
R1# show access-lists
Standard IP access list 10
    10 permit 192.168.10.0, wildcard bits 0.0.0.255
R1#
```

To delete an ACL, enter the **no access-list** {*number* | *name*} global configuration command.

Example 4-2 removes ACL 10 and verifies that it is deleted using the **show access-list** privileged EXEC command.

Example 4-2 Removing a Standard ACL

```
R1(config)# no access-list 10
R1(config)# exit
R1#
R1# show access-lists
R1#
```

As shown in Example 4-3, the **remark** *description* keyword is used for documenting the ACL. The **show running-config | include access-list 10** displays the ACEs in ACL 10. Notice how the remark indicates the function of the following ACE, making the ACL easier to understand.

Example 4-3 Adding Remarks to an ACL

```
R1(config)# access-list 10 remark Permit hosts from the 192.168.10.0 LAN
R1(config)# access-list 10 permit 192.168.10.0 0.0.0.255
R1(config)# exit
R1#
R1# show running-config | include access-list 10
access-list 10 remark Permit hosts from the 192.168.10.0 LAN
access-list 10 permit 192.168.10.0 0.0.0.255
R1#
```

Apply a Standard IPv4 ACL (4.1.3.2)

After a standard IPv4 ACL is configured, it is linked to an interface using the **ip access-group** {*access-list-number* | *access-list-name*} {**in** | **out**} interface configuration mode command.

Refer to Figure 4-10 to see an example of how to permit a single network out of an interface.

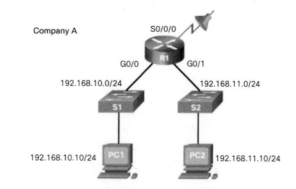

Figure 4-10   Permit a Specific Subnet

Example 4-4 shows a configuration allowing only traffic from the 192.168.10.0/24 network to be permitted out the Serial 0/0/0 interface.

Example 4-4 R1 Configuration to Permit a Specific Subnet

```
R1(config)# access-list 1 permit 192.168.10.0 0.0.0.255
R1(config)#
R1(config)# interface s0/0/0
R1(config-if)# ip access-group 1 out
```

If an ACL must be deleted, you should remove it from the interface using the **no ip access-group** {*access-list-number* | *access-list-name*} command on the interface and then enter the global **no access-list** command to remove the entire ACL.

Standard Named IPv4 ACLs (4.1.3.3)

Use the **ip access-list** [**standard** | **extended**] *acl-name* global configuration command to configure a named ACL.

The steps to create a standard named ACL include the following:

Step 1.   Use the **ip access-list standard** *acl-name* command to create a standard named ACL. ACL names are alphanumeric, case sensitive, and must be unique. After you enter the command, the router prompt changes to standard (std) named ACL (nacl) configuration mode (that is, Router(config-std-nacl)#).

Step 2.   From the named ACL configuration mode, use the [**permit** | **deny** | **remark** *description*] {*source* [*source-wildcard*]} [**log**] command to configure ACEs. Use **permit** or **deny** statements to specify one or more conditions for determining whether a packet is forwarded or dropped. Use the **remark** *description* to add a comment to the ACL.

Step 3.   Apply the ACL to an interface using the **ip access-group** *acl-name* [**in** | **out**] command. Specify whether the ACL should be applied to packets as they enter the interface (**in**) or applied to packets as they exit the interface (**out**).

See Figure 4-11 to see an example of how to configure a standard named ACL.

Example 4-5 configures a standard named ACL named NO_ACCESS on R1. The ACL denies host 192.168.11.10 access to the 192.168.10.0 network. Recall that standard ACLs must be applied as close to the destination as possible; therefore, the named ACL is applied to outgoing traffic on the G0/0 interface.

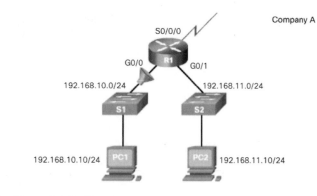

Figure 4-11   Named ACL Topology

Example 4-5   Named ACL Example

```
R1(config)# ip access-list standard NO_ACCESS
R1(config-std-nacl)# deny host 192.168.11.10
R1(config-std-nacl)# permit any
R1(config-std-nacl)# exit
R1(config)#
R1(config)# interface g0/0
R1(config-if)# ip access-group NO_ACCESS out
```

Verify ACLs (4.1.3.4)

As shown in Example 4-6, the **show ip interface** command enables you to verify the ACL on the interface.

Example 4-6   Verifying Standard ACL Interfaces

```
R1# show ip interface s0/0/0
Serial0/0/0 is up, line protocol is up
  Internet address is 10.1.1.1/30
  <output omitted>
  Outgoing access list is 1
  Inbound  access list is not set
 <output omitted>
R1# show ip interface g0/0
GigabitEthernet0/1 is up, line protocol is up
  Internet address is 192.168.10.1/24
  <output omitted>
  Outgoing access list is NO_ACCESS
  Inbound  access list is not set
  <output omitted>
```

The output from this command includes the number or name of the access list and the direction in which the ACL was applied. The output shows router R1 has the access list 1 applied to its S0/0/0 outbound interface and the access list NO_ACCESS applied to its g0/0 interface also in the outbound direction.

Example 4-7 shows the result of issuing the **show access-lists** command on router R1.

Example 4-7 Verifying Standard ACL Statements

```
R1# show access-lists
Standard IP access list 1
    10 deny   192.168.10.10
    20 permit 192.168.0.0, wildcard bits 0.0.255.255
Standard IP access list NO_ACCESS
    15 deny   192.168.11.11
    10 deny   192.168.11.10
    20 permit 192.168.11.0, wildcard bits 0.0.0.255
R1#
```

Notice that the NO_ACCESS statements are out of order and that sequence number 15 is displayed prior to sequence number 10. The reason for this is that Cisco IOS uses a special hashing function for standard ACLs and reorders host ACEs so they are processed first, optimizing the search for a host ACL entry. Standard ACLs process network ACEs in the order in which they were entered. Therefore, standard ACLs process ACEs in order by the ACE number and not by the order in which they are displayed on the screen.

Note

The details of the IOS standard ACL hashing function are beyond the scope of this course.

To view an individual access list, use the **show access-lists** command followed by the access list number or name.

Packet Tracer
☐ Activity

Packet Tracer 4.1.3.5: Configure Standard IPv4 ACLs

In this activity, you practice configuring standard IPv4 ACLs to restrict traffic on the network. The next two pages include video demonstrations of this activity.

Video

Video Demonstration 4.1.3.6: Standard ACL Configuration Part 1

Refer to the online course to view this video.

Video

Video Demonstration 4.1.3.7: Standard ACL Configuration Part 2

Refer to the online course to view this video.

Extended IPv4 ACLs (4.2)

In this section, you configure extended IPv4 ACLs.

Structure of an Extended IPv4 ACLs (4.2.1)

In this topic, you configure extended IPv4 ACLs.

Extended ACLs (4.2.1.1)

For more precise traffic-filtering control, extended IPv4 ACLs can be created. Extended ACLs are numbered 100 to 199 and 2000 to 2699, providing a total of 799 possible extended numbered ACLs. Like standard ACLs, extended ACLs can also be named.

Extended ACLs are used more often than standard ACLs because they provide a greater degree of control. Like standard ACLs, extended ACLs have the capability to check source addresses of packets, but they also have the capability to check the destination address, protocols, and port numbers (or services). This provides a greater range of criteria on which to base the ACL. For example, one extended ACL can allow email traffic from a network to a specific destination while denying file transfers and web browsing.

Filtering Ports and Services (4.2.1.2)

The ability to filter on protocol and port number enables network administrators to build specific extended ACLs. An application can be specified by configuring either the port number or the name of a well-known port.

Example 4-8 shows some examples of how an administrator specifies a TCP or UDP port number by placing it at the end of the extended ACL statement. Logical operations can be used, such as equal (**eq**), not equal (**neq**), greater than (**gt**), and less than (**lt**).

Example 4-8 Using Port Numbers or Keywords to Configure an Extended ACL

```
Router(config)# access-list 114 permit tcp 192.168.20.0 0.0.0.255 any eq 23
Router(config)# access-list 114 permit tcp 192.168.20.0 0.0.0.255 any eq 21
Router(config)# access-list 114 permit tcp 192.168.20.0 0.0.0.255 any eq 20
Router(config)# !Using Keywords
Router(config)# access-list 114 permit tcp 192.168.20.0 0.0.0.255 any eq telnet
Router(config)# access-list 114 permit tcp 192.168.20.0 0.0.0.255 any eq ftp
Router(config)# access-list 114 permit tcp 192.168.20.0 0.0.0.255 any eq ftp-data
```

Example 4-9 shows how to display a list of port numbers and keywords that can be used when building an ACL using the command.

Example 4-9 Displaying a List of Port Numbers and Keywords

```
Router(config)# access-list 101 permit tcp any any eq ?
  <0-65535>    Port number
  bgp          Border Gateway Protocol (179)
  chargen      Character generator (19)
  cmd          Remote commands (rcmd, 514)
  daytime      Daytime (13)
  discard      Discard (9)
  domain       Domain Name Service (53)
  drip         Dynamic Routing Information Protocol (3949)
  echo         Echo (7)
  exec         Exec (rsh, 512)
  finger       Finger (79)
  ftp          File Transfer Protocol (21)
  ftp-data     FTP data connections (20)
  gopher       Gopher (70)
  hostname     NIC hostname server (101)
  ident        Ident Protocol (113)
  irc          Internet Relay Chat (194)
  klogin       Kerberos login (543)
  kshell       Kerberos shell (544)
  login        Login (rlogin, 513)
  lpd          Printer service (515)
  nntp         Network News Transport Protocol (119)
  onep-plain   ONEP Cleartext (15001)
  onep-tls     ONEP TLS (15002)
  pim-auto-rp  PIM Auto-RP (496)
  pop2         Post Office Protocol v2 (109)
  pop3         Post Office Protocol v3 (110)
  smtp         Simple Mail Transport Protocol (25)
```

```
    sunrpc         Sun Remote Procedure Call (111)
    tacacs         TAC Access Control System (49)
    talk           Talk (517)
    telnet         Telnet (23)
    time           Time (37)
    uucp           Unix-to-Unix Copy Program (540)
    whois          Nicname (43)
    www            World Wide Web (HTTP, 80)
Router(config)# access-list 101 permit tcp any any eq
```

Configure Extended IPv4 ACLs (4.2.2)

In this topic, you configure extended IPv4 ACLs to filter traffic according to networking requirements.

Configuring Extended ACLs (4.2.2.1)

The procedural steps for configuring extended ACLs are the same as for standard ACLs. The extended ACL is first configured, and then it is applied on an interface. However, the command syntax and parameters are more complex to support the additional features provided by extended ACLs.

Note

The internal logic applied to the ordering of standard ACL statements does not apply to extended ACLs. The order in which extended ACL statements are entered during configuration is the order they are displayed and processed.

The common command syntax for extended IPv4 ACLs is as follows:

```
Router(config)# access-list access-list-number {deny | permit | remark description}
    protocol {source source-wildcard} [operator port [port-number | acl-name]]
    {destination destination-wildcard} [operator port [port-number | acl-name]]
```

Note that there are many keywords and parameters for extended ACLs. It is not necessary to use all the keywords and parameters when configuring an extended ACL. Recall that you can use the ? to get help when entering complex commands.

Table 4-4 shows the description for each part of the common extended IPv4 ACL syntax.

Table 4-4   Extended ACL Command Syntax

Parameter	Description
access-list-number	Identifies the access list using a number in the range 100 to 199 (for an extended IP ACL) and 2000 to 2699 (expanded IP ACLs).
deny	Denies access if the conditions are matched.
permit	Permits access if the conditions are matched.
remark *description*	Enables you to enter descriptive text in the ACL. Useful to document the ACL.
protocol	Specifies the name or number of an IP protocol. Common keywords include **ip**, **tcp**, **udp**, or **icmp**. To match all IP protocols (including ICMP, TCP, and UDP), use the **ip** keyword.
source	Identifies the number of the network or host from which the packet is being sent.
source-wildcard	Specifies the wildcard bits to be applied to the source.
destination	Identifies the number of the network or host to which the packet is being sent.
destination-wildcard	Specifies the wildcard bits to be applied to the destination.
operator	(Optional) Compares source or destination ports. Possible operands include **lt** (less than), **gt** (greater than), **eq** (equal), **neq** (not equal), and **range** (inclusive range).
port	(Optional) Specifies the number or name of a TCP or UDP port.
established	(Optional) For the TCP protocol only, indicates an established connection.

See Figure 4-12 to see an example of how to configure an extended ACL.

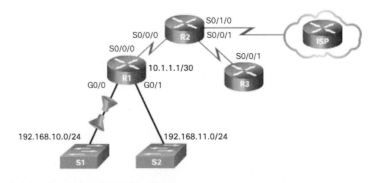

Figure 4-12   Extended ACL Topology

Example 4-10 shows the configuration of an extended ACL for the topology in Figure 4-12.

Example 4-10 Configuring an Extended ACL

```
R1(config)# access-list 103 permit tcp 192.168.10.0 0.0.0.255 any eq 80
R1(config)# access-list 103 permit tcp 192.168.10.0 0.0.0.255 any eq 443
R1(config)#
R1(config)# access-list 104 permit tcp any 192.168.10.0 0.0.0.255 established
R1(config)#
R1(config)# interface S0/0/0
R1(config-if)# ip access-group 103 out
R1(config-if)# ip access-group 104 in
```

In this example, the network administrator has configured two ACLs to restrict network access to allow website browsing only from the LAN attached to interface G0/0 to any external network. ACL 103 allows traffic coming from any address on the 192.168.10.0 network to go to any destination, subject to the limitation that the traffic is using ports 80 (HTTP) and 443 (HTTPS) only.

The nature of HTTP requires that traffic flows back into the network from websites accessed from internal clients. The network administrator wants to restrict that return traffic to HTTP exchanges from requested websites, while denying all other traffic. ACL 104 does that by blocking all incoming traffic, except for previously established connections. The **permit** statement in ACL 104 allows inbound traffic using the **established** parameter.

The **established** parameter allows only responses to traffic that originates from the 192.168.10.0/24 network to return to that network. A match occurs if the returning TCP segment has the ACK or reset (RST) flags set, which indicates that the packet belongs to an existing connection. Without the **established** parameter in the ACL statement, clients could send traffic to a web server but not receive traffic returning from the web server.

In Example 4-10, the network administrator configured an ACL to allow users from the 192.168.10.0/24 network to browse both insecure and secure websites. Even though it has been configured, the ACL will not filter traffic until it is applied to an interface.

Applying Extended ACLs to Interfaces (4.2.2.2)

To apply an ACL to an interface, first consider whether the traffic to be filtered is going in or out. When a user on the internal LAN accesses a website on the Internet, traffic is traffic going out to the Internet. When an internal user receives an email from the Internet, traffic is coming into the local router; however, when an ACL is applied to an interface, **in** and **out** take on different meanings. From an ACL aspect, **in** and **out** are in reference to the router interface.

In the topology in Figure 4-12, R1 has a serial interface, S0/0/0, and two Gigabit Ethernet interfaces, G0/0 and G0/1. Recall that an extended ACL should typically be applied as close to the source as possible. In this topology, the interface closest to the source of the target traffic is the G0/0 interface.

Web request traffic from users on the 192.168.10.0/24 LAN is inbound to the G0/0 interface. Return traffic from established connections to users on the LAN is outbound from the G0/0 interface.

Example 4-11 shows the commands to apply the ACLs to the G0/0 interface in both directions. The inbound ACL 103 checks for the type of traffic while the outbound ACL 104 checks for return traffic from established connections. This will restrict 192.168.10.0 Internet access to allow only website browsing.

Example 4-11 Applying an Extended ACL

```
R1(config)# interface S0/0/0
R1(config-if)# ip access-group 103 out
R1(config-if)# ip access-group 104 in
```

Note

The access lists could have been applied to the S0/0/0 interface, but in that case, the router's ACL process would have to examine all packets entering the router, not only traffic to and from 192.168.11.0. This would cause unnecessary processing by the router.

Filtering Traffic with Extended ACLs (4.2.2.3)

See Figure 4-13 to see another extended ACL example.

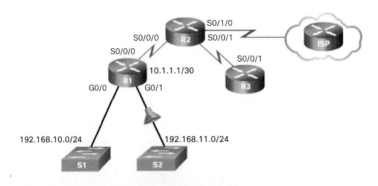

Figure 4-13 Extended ACL to Deny FTP Topology

Example 4-12 shows an extended ACL configuration that denies FTP traffic from subnet 192.168.11.0 going to subnet 192.168.10.0 but permits all other traffic.

Example 4-12 Configuring and Applying an Extended ACL to Deny FTP

```
R1(config)# access-list 101 deny tcp 192.168.11.0 0.0.0.255 192.168.10.0 0.0.0.255
  eq ftp
R1(config)# access-list 101 deny tcp 192.168.11.0 0.0.0.255 192.168.10.0 0.0.0.255
  eq ftp-data
R1(config)# access-list 101 permit ip any any
R1(config)#
R1(config)# interface g0/1
R1(config-if)# ip access-group 101 in
```

Remember that FTP uses TCP ports 20 and 21. Therefore, the ACL requires both port name keywords **ftp** and **ftp-data**. Alternatively, the port numbers could have been specified.

Example 4-13 removes the previously configured ACL 101 and configures the ACL using port numbers instead of port names.

Example 4-13 Configuring and Applying an Extended ACL Using Port Numbers

```
R1(config)# no access-list 101
R1(config)# access-list 101 deny tcp 192.168.11.0 0.0.0.255 192.168.10.0 0.0.0.255
  eq 20
R1(config)# access-list 101 deny tcp 192.168.11.0 0.0.0.255 192.168.10.0 0.0.0.255
  eq 21
R1(config)# access-list 101 permit ip any any
R1(config)#
```

To prevent the implied **deny any** statement at the end of the ACL from blocking all traffic, you add the **permit ip any any** statement. Without at least one **permit** statement in an ACL, all traffic on the interface where that ACL was applied would be dropped. The ACL should be applied inbound on the G0/1 interface so that traffic from the 192.168.11.0/24 LAN is filtered as it enters the router interface.

See Figure 4-14 to see another extended ACL example.

Example 4-14 shows an extended ACL configuration that denies Telnet (TCP 23) traffic from any source to the 192.168.11.0/24 LAN but allows all other IP traffic.

Because traffic destined for the 192.168.11.0/24 LAN is outbound on interface G0/1, the ACL would be applied to G0/1 using the **out** keyword. Note the use of the **any** keywords in the **permit** statement. This **permit** statement is added to ensure that no other traffic is blocked.

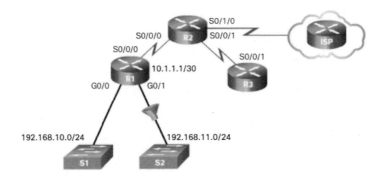

Figure 4-14 Extended ACL to Deny Telnet Topology

Example 4-14 Configuring and Applying an Extend ACL to Deny Telnet

```
R1(config)# access-list 102 deny tcp 192.168.11.0 0.0.0.255 any eq 23
R1(config)# access-list 102 permit ip any any
R1(config)#
R1(config)# interface g0/1
R1(config-if)# ip access-group 102 out
```

Note

The configurations in Examples 4-13 and 4-14 both use the **permit ip any any** statement at the end of the ACL. For greater security, the **permit 192.168.11.0 0.0.0.255 any** command may be used.

Creating Extended Named ACLs (4.2.2.4)

Extended named ACLs are created in essentially the same way that standard named ACLs are created. Follow these steps to create an extended ACL using names:

Step 1.   From global configuration mode, use the **ip access-list extended** *acl-name* command to define a name for the extended ACL.

Step 2.   In named ACL configuration mode, specify the conditions to permit or deny.

Step 3.   From interface configuration mode, apply the named ACL using **ip access-group** *acl-name* [**in** | **out**] command.

To remove an extended named ACL, use the **no ip access-list extended** *acl-name* global configuration command.

See Figure 4-15 to see an extended named ACL example.

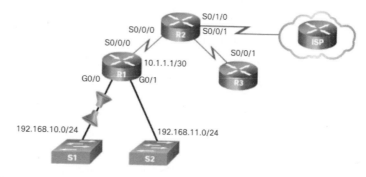

Figure 4-15   Extended Named ACLs Topology

Example 4-15 shows the named versions of the ACLs created in previous examples.

Example 4-15 Configuring and Applying Named ACLs

```
R1(config)# access-list extended SURFING
R1(config-ext-nacl)# permit tcp 192.168.10.0 0.0.0.255 any eq 80
R1(config-ext-nacl)# permit tcp 192.168.10.0 0.0.0.255 any eq 443
R1(config-ext-nacl)# exit
R1(config)#
R1(config)# access-list extended BROWSING
R1(config-ext-nacl)# permit tcp any 192.168.10.0 0.0.0.255 established
R1(config-ext-nacl)# exit
R1(config)#
R1(config)# interface g0/0
R1(config-if)# ip access-group SURFING in
R1(config-if)# ip access-group BROWSING out
```

The named ACL SURFING permits the users on the 192.168.10.0/24 LAN to access websites. The named ACL BROWSING allows the return traffic from established connections. Using the ACL names, the rules are applied inbound and outbound on the G0/0 interface.

Verifying Extended ACLs (4.2.2.5)

After an ACL has been configured and applied to an interface, use Cisco IOS **show** commands to verify the configuration, as shown in Example 4-16.

The **show access-lists** command is used to display the contents of all ACLs. Unlike standard ACLs, extended ACLs do not implement the same internal logic and hashing function. The output and sequence numbers displayed in the **show access-lists** command output are shown in the order in which the extended ACL statements were entered. Host entries are not automatically listed prior to range entries.

Example 4-16 Verifying Extended ACLs

```
R1# show access-lists
Extended IP access list BROWSING
    10 permit tcp any 192.168.10.0 0.0.0.255 established
Extended IP access list SURFING
    10 permit tcp 192.168.10.0 0.0.0.255 any eq www
    20 permit tcp 192.168.10.0 0.0.0.255 any eq 443
R1#
R1# show ip interface g0/0 | include access list
  Outgoing access list is BROWSING
  Inbound  access list is SURFING
```

The **show ip interface g0/0** command is used to verify if any ACLs are applied to the interface. The output from the command includes the number or name of the access list and the direction in which the ACL was applied. Using uppercase letters when naming named ACLs helps them stand out in the output of the configuration.

After an ACL configuration has been verified, the next step is to confirm that the ACLs work as planned: blocking and permitting traffic as expected.

The guidelines discussed earlier in this section suggest that ACLs should be configured on a test network and then implemented on the production network.

Editing Extended ACLs (4.2.2.6)

An extended ACL can be edited in one of two ways:

- **Method 1 Text editor:** Using this method, the ACL is copied and pasted into the text editor where the changes are made. The current access list is removed using the **no access-list** command. The modified ACL is then pasted back into the configuration.

- **Method 2 Sequence numbers:** Sequence numbers can be used to delete or insert an ACL statement. The **ip access-list extended** *acl-name* command is used to enter named-ACL configuration mode. If the ACL is numbered instead of named, the ACL number is used in the *acl-name* parameter. ACEs can be inserted or removed.

In the following example, the wrong network address was specified to filter HTTP traffic. Specifically, network 192.168.11.0 was incorrectly permitted HTTP access instead of network 192.168.10.0

Example 4-17 displays the line numbers associated with each ACE in the ACL, corrects the incorrect ACE, and verifies the resulting ACL ACEs.

Example 4-17 Editing an ACL

```
R1# show access-lists
Extended IP access list BROWSING
    10 permit tcp any 192.168.10.0 0.0.0.255 established
Extended IP access list SURFING
    10 permit tcp 192.168.11.0 0.0.0.255 any eq www
    20 permit tcp 192.168.10.0 0.0.0.255 any eq 443
R1#
R1# configure terminal
R1(config)# ip access-list extended SURFING
R1(config-ext-nacl)# no 10
R1(config-ext-nacl)# 10 permit tcp 192.168.10.0 0.0.0.255 any eq www
R1(config-ext-nacl)# exit
R1#
R1# show access-lists
Extended IP access list BROWSING
    10 permit tcp any 192.168.10.0 0.0.0.255 established
Extended IP access list SURFING
    10 permit tcp 192.168.10.0 0.0.0.255 any eq www
    20 permit tcp 192.168.10.0 0.0.0.255 any eq 443
```

The **show access-lists** command is useful to identify the sequence numbers in an ACL. In this example, the incorrect statement that needs to correct is identified as statement 10.

Notice how the original statement is removed using the **no** *sequence_#* command and the corrected statement is entered, thereby replacing the original statement. Finally, **show access-list** is used again to verify that the desired ACE is entered.

Interactive Graphic

Activity 4.2.2.7: Creating an Extended ACL Statement

Refer to the online course to complete this activity.

Interactive Graphic

Activity 4.2.2.8: Evaluating Extended ACEs

Refer to the online course to complete this activity.

Interactive Graphic

Activity 4.2.2.9: ACL Testlet

Refer to the online course to complete this activity.

Packet Tracer 4.2.2.10: Configuring Extended ACLs—Scenario 1

Two employees need access to services provided by the server. PC1 needs only FTP access, whereas PC2 needs only web access. Both computers will be able to ping the server but not each other.

Packet Tracer 4.2.2.11: Configuring Extended ACLs—Scenario 2

In this scenario, devices on one LAN are allowed to remotely access devices in another LAN using the Telnet protocol. Besides ICMP, all traffic from other networks is denied.

Packet Tracer 4.2.2.12: Configuring Extended ACLs—Scenario 3

In this scenario, specific devices on the LAN are allowed to access various services on servers that are located on the Internet.

Lab 4.2.2.13: Configuring and Verifying Extended ACLs

In this lab, you complete the following objectives :

- Part 1: Set Up the Topology and Initialize Devices
- Part 2: Configure Devices and Verify Connectivity
- Part 3: Configure and Verify Extended Numbered and Named ACLs
- Part 4: Modify and Verify Extended ACLs

IPv6 ACLs (4.3)

In this section, you configure IPv6 ACLs.

IPv6 ACL Creation (4.3.1)

In this topic, you compare IPv4 and IPv6 ACL creation.

Types of IPv6 ACLs (4.3.1.1)

IPv6 ACLs are similar to IPv4 ACLs in both operation and configuration. Being familiar with IPv4 access lists makes IPv6 ACLs easy to understand and configure.

In IPv4, there are two types of ACLs, standard and extended. Both types of ACLs can be either numbered or named ACLs.

With IPv6, there is only one type of ACL, which is equivalent to an IPv4 extended named ACL. There are no numbered ACLs in IPv6.

An IPv4 named ACL and an IPv6 ACL cannot share the same name.

Comparing IPv4 and IPv6 ACLs (4.3.1.2)

Although IPv4 and IPv6 ACLs are similar, there are three significant differences between them:

- IPv4 ACLs use the **ip access-group** {*access-list-number* | *acl-name*} {**in** | **out**} interface configuration command to apply an IPv4 ACL to an interface. IPv6 uses the **ipv6 traffic-filter** *acl-name* {**in** | **out**} interface configuration command.

- IPv4 ACLs use wildcard masks. IPv6 ACLs use the prefix-length to indicate how much of an IPv6 source or destination address should be matched.

- IPv4 ACLs end with an implicit **deny any** or **deny ip any any**. IPv6 ACLs end with a similar **deny ipv6 any any** statement but also adds two other implicit statements. Specifically, it adds the **permit icmp any any nd-na** and **permit icmp any any nd-ns** statements.

The two new implicit statements added to an IPv6 ACL allow the router to participate in the IPv6 equivalent of ARP for IPv4. Recall that ARP is used in IPv4 to resolve Layer 3 addresses to Layer 2 MAC addresses. As illustrated in Figure 4-16, IPv6 uses ICMPv6 *Neighbor Discovery (ND)* messages to accomplish the same thing. ND uses ICMPv6 *Neighbor Solicitation (NS)* and ICMPv6 *Neighbor Advertisement (NA)* messages.

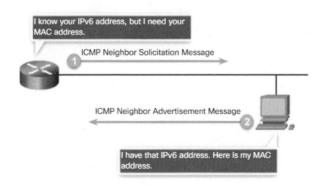

Figure 4-16   IPv6 Neighbor Discovery

ND messages are encapsulated in IPv6 packets and require the services of the IPv6 network layer while ARP for IPv4 does not use Layer 3. Because IPv6 uses the Layer 3 service for neighbor discovery, IPv6 ACLs need to implicitly permit

ND packets to be sent and received on an interface. Specifically, both *Neighbor Discovery-Neighbor Advertisement (nd-na)* and *Neighbor Discovery-Neighbor Solicitation (nd-ns)* messages are permitted.

Configuring IPv6 ACLs (4.3.2)

In this topic, you configure IPv6 ACLs to filter traffic according to networking requirements.

Configuring IPv6 Topology (4.3.2.1)

Figure 4-17 shows the topology that will be used for configuring IPv6 ACLs.

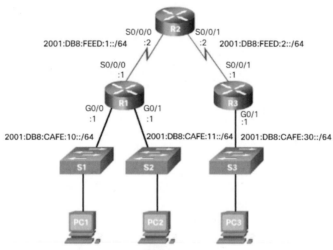

Figure 4-17   IPv6 Configuration Topology

The topology is similar to the previous IPv4 topology except for the IPv6 addressing scheme. It has three 2001:DB8:CAFE::/64 subnets:

- 2001:DB8:CAFE:10::/64

- 2001:DB8:CAFE:11::/64

- 2001:DB8:CAFE:30::/64

Two serial networks connect the three routers:

- 2001:DB8:FEED:1::/64

- 2001:DB8:FEED:2::/64

Examples 4-18–20 show the IPv6 address configuration for each router.

Example 4-18 R1 Configuration

```
R1(config)# interface g0/0
R1(config-if)# ipv6 address 2001:db8:cafe:10::1/64
R1(config-if)# exit
R1(config)#
R1(config)# interface s0/0/0
R1(config-if)# ipv6 address 2001:db8:feed:1::1/64
R1(config-if)# exit
R1(config)#
R1(config)# interface g0/1
R1(config-if)# ipv6 address 2001:db8:cafe:11::1/64
R1(config-if)# end
R1#
```

Example 4-19 R2 Configuration

```
R2(config)# interface s0/0/0
R2(config-if)# ipv6 address 2001:db8:feed:1::2/64
R2(config-if)# exit
R2(config)#
R2(config)# interface s0/0/1
R2(config-if)# ipv6 address 2001:db8:feed:2::2/64
R2(config-if)# end
R2#
```

Example 4-20 R3 Configuration

```
R3(config)# interface s0/0/1
R3(config-if)# ipv6 address 2001:db8:feed:2::1/64
R3(config-if)# exit
R3(config)#
R3(config)# interface g0/0
R3(config-if)# ipv6 address 2001:db8:cafe:30::1/64
R3(config-if)# end
R3#
```

Note

The **no shutdown** command and the **clock rate** command are not shown.

After interfaces have been configured, you should use the **show ipv6 interface brief** command to verify the address and the state of the configured interfaces.

Configuring IPv6 ACLs (4.3.2.2)

IPv6 has only named ACLs. The configuration is similar to that of an IPv4 extended named ACL.

The three basic steps to configure an IPv6 ACL are as follows:

Step 1.   From global configuration mode, use the **ipv6 access-list** *acl-name* command to create an IPv6 ACL. Like IPv4 named ACLs, IPv6 names are alphanumeric, case sensitive, and must be unique. Unlike IPv4, there is no need for a standard or extended option.

Step 2.   From the named ACL configuration mode, use the **permit** or **deny** statements to specify one or more conditions to determine if a packet is forwarded or dropped.

Step 3.   Apply the ACL to an interface.

The specific syntax of the **permit** and **deny** is similar to the syntax used for an IPv4 extended ACL with the exception that it uses the IPv6 prefix-length instead of an IPv4 wildcard mask.

Specifically, the syntax is

```
R1(config-ipv6-acl)# deny | permit protocol {source-ipv6-prefix/prefix-length | any
    | host source-ipv6-address} [operator [port-number]] {destination-ipv6-prefix/
    prefix-length | any | host destination-ipv6-address} [operator [port-number]]
```

Table 4-5 summarizes the function of the IPv6 **permit** and **deny** ACL commands.

Table 4-5   IPv6 ACL **permit** and **deny** Command Syntax

Parameter	Description
**deny	permit**	Specifies whether to deny or permit the packet.
protocol	Enables you to enter the name or number of an Internet protocol, or an integer representing an IPv6 protocol number.
source-ipv6-prefix/prefix-length *destination-ipv6-address*	Identifies the source or destination IPv6 network or class of networks for which to set deny or permit conditions.
any	Allows you to enter **any** as an abbreviation for the IPv6 prefix ::/0. This matches all addresses.

Parameter	Description
host	For **host** *source-ipv6-address* or *destination-ipv6-address*, allows you to enter the source or destination IPv6 host address for which to set deny or permit conditions.
operator	(Optional) Specifies an operand that compares the source or destination ports of the specified protocol. Operands are **lt** (less than), **gt** (greater than), **eq** (equal), **neq** (not equal), and **range**.
port-number	(Optional) Specifies a decimal number or the name of a TCP or UDP port for filtering TCP or UDP, respectively.

Example 4-21 displays the commands to create a simple IPv6 ACL based on the topology in Figure 4-17.

Example 4-21 Configuring an IPv6 ACL

```
R1(config)# ipv6 access-list NO-R3-LAN-ACCESS
R1(config-ipv6-acl)# deny ipv6 2001:db8:cafe:30::/64 any
R1(config-ipv6-acl)# permit ipv6 any any
R1(config-ipv6-acl)# end
R1#
```

The first statement names the IPv6 access list NO-R3-LAN-ACCESS. Similar to IPv4 named ACLs, capitalizing IPv6 ACL names is not required but makes them stand out when viewing the running-config output.

The second statement denies all IPv6 packets from the 2001:DB8:CAFE:30::/64 destined for any IPv6 network. The third statement allows all other IPv6 packets.

Applying an IPv6 ACL to an Interface (4.3.2.3)

After an IPv6 ACL is configured, you apply it to an interface using the **ipv6 traffic-filter** *acl-name* {**in** | **out**} interface configuration command.

Example 4-22 shows the NO-R3-LAN-ACCESS ACL applied inbound to the S0/0/0 interface. Applying the ACL to the inbound S0/0/0 interface will deny packets from 2001:DB8:CAFE:30::/64 to both of the LANs on R1.

Example 4-22 Applying an IPv6 ACL

```
R1(config)# interface s0/0/0
R1(config-if)# ipv6 traffic-filter NO-R3-LAN-ACCESS in
```

To remove an ACL from an interface, first enter the **no ipv6 traffic-filter** command on the interface and then enter the global **no ipv6 access-list** command to remove the access list.

> **Note**
>
> IPv4 and IPv6 both use the **access-class** command to apply an access list to VTY ports.

IPv6 ACL Examples (4.3.2.4)

To help understand how to configure IPv6 ACLs, refer to the following two examples.

Deny FTP

In Example 4-23, router R1 is configured with an IPv6 access list to deny FTP traffic to 2001:DB8:CAFE:11::/64. Ports for both FTP data (port 20) and FTP control (port 21) need to be blocked. Because the filter is applied inbound on the G0/0 interface on R1, only traffic from the 2001:DB8:CAFE:10::/64 network will be denied.

Example 4-23 Configuring an IPv6 ACL to Deny FTP

```
R1(config)# ipv6 access-list NO-FTP-TO-11
R1(config-ipv6-acl)# deny tcp any 2001:db8:cafe:11::/64 eq ftp
R1(config-ipv6-acl)# deny tcp any 2001:db8:cafe:11::/64 eq ftp-data
R1(config-ipv6-acl)# permit ipv6 any any
R1(config-ipv6-acl)# exit
R1(config)#
R1(config)# interface g0/0
R1(config-if)# ipv6 traffic-filter NO-FTP-TO-11 in
R1(config-if)#
```

Restricted Access

In Example 4-24, an IPv6 ACL is configured to give the LAN on R3 limited access to the LANs on R1.

Example 4-24 Configuring an IPv6 ACL to Restrict Access

```
R3(config)# ipv6 access-list RESTRICTED-ACCESS
R3(config-ipv6-acl)# remark Permit access only HTTP and HTTPS to Network 10
R3(config-ipv6-acl)# permit tcp any host 2001:db8:cafe:10::10 eq 80
R3(config-ipv6-acl)# permit tcp any host 2001:db8:cafe:10::10 eq 443
R3(config-ipv6-acl)#
R3(config-ipv6-acl)# remark Deny all other traffic to Network 10
R3(config-ipv6-acl)# deny ipv6 any 2001:db8:cafe:10::/64
R3(config-ipv6-acl)#
R3(config-ipv6-acl)# remark Permit PC3 telnet access to PC2
R3(config-ipv6-acl)# permit tcp host 2001:DB8:CAFE:30::12 host 2001:DB8:CAFE:11::11
  eq 23
R3(config-ipv6-acl)#
R3(config-ipv6-acl)# remark Deny telnet access to PC2 for all other devices
R3(config-ipv6-acl)# deny tcp any host 2001:db8:cafe:11::11 eq 23
R3(config-ipv6-acl)#
R3(config-ipv6-acl)# remark Permit access to everything else
R3(config-ipv6-acl)# permit ipv6 any any
R3(config-ipv6-acl)# exit
R3(config)#
R3(config)# interface g0/0
R3(config-if)# ipv6 traffic-filter RESTRICTED-ACCESS in
R3(config-if)#
```

Notice how the inline remarks in the configuration help document the function of the ACL.

The following summarizes the configuration of the ACL in the example:

- The first two **permit** statements allow access from any device to the web server at 2001:DB8:CAFE:10::10.

- The next **deny** statement denies access to all other devices to the 2001:DB8:CAFE:10::/64 network.

- The next **permit** statement provides PC3 at 2001:DB8:CAFE:30::12 Telnet access to PC2 at 2001:DB8:CAFE:11::11.

- The next **deny** statement denies Telnet access to all other devices.

- The last **permit** statement permits all other IPv6 traffic to all other destinations.

The IPv6 access list is applied to interface G0/0 in the inbound direction, so only the 2001:DB8:CAFE:30::/64 network is affected.

Verifying IPv6 ACLs (4.3.2.5)

The commands used to verify an IPv6 access list are similar to those used for IPv4 ACLs. Using these commands, you can verify the IPv6 access list RESTRICTED-ACCESS that was configured previously.

Example 4-25 shows the output of the **show ipv6 interface** command.

Example 4-25 Verifying IPv6 ACL on an Interface

```
R3# show ipv6 interface g0/0
GigabitEthernet0/0 is up, line protocol is up
  Global unicast address(es):
    2001:DB8:CAFE:30::1, subnet is 2001:DB8:CAFE:30::/64
    Input features: Access List
    Inbound access list RESTRICTED-ACCESS
<output omitted>
```

The output confirms that RESTRICTED-ACCESS ACL is configured inbound on the G0/0 interface.

As shown in Example 4-26, the same **show access-list** command that you used to verify which IPv4 ACLs were configured on a router is used to display the IPv6 ACLs.

Example 4-26 Verifying IPv6 ACL Statements

```
R3# show access-lists
IPv6 access list RESTRICTED-ACCESS
    permit tcp any host 2001:DB8:CAFE:10::10 eq www sequence 20
    permit tcp any host 2001:DB8:CAFE:10::10 eq 443 sequence 30
    deny ipv6 any 2001:DB8:CAFE:10::/64 sequence 50
    permit tcp host 2001:DB8:CAFE:30::12 host 2001:DB8:CAFE:11::11 eq telnet
  sequence 70
    deny tcp any host 2001:DB8:CAFE:11::11 eq telnet sequence 90
    permit ipv6 any any sequence 110
R3#
```

Similar to extended ACLs for IPv4, IPv6 access lists are processed in the order the statements are entered. However, notice that IPv6 ACLs sequence numbers are displayed at the end of the statement and not the beginning as with IPv4 access lists.

Although the statements appear in the order they were entered, they are not always incremented by 10. The reason is that the remark statements that were entered also use a sequence number but are not displayed in the output of the **show access-lists** command.

As shown in Example 4-27, the output from the **show running-config** command includes all the ACEs and remark statements. Remark statements can come before or after **permit** or **deny** statements but should be consistent in their placement.

Example 4-27 Verifying IPv6 ACL Configuration

```
R3# show running-config
<output omitted>
ipv6 access-list RESTRICTED-ACCESS
 remark Permit access only HTTP and HTTPS to Network 10
 permit tcp any host 2001:DB8:CAFE:10::10 eq www
 permit tcp any host 2001:DB8:CAFE:10::10 eq 443
 remark Deny all other traffic to Network 10
 deny ipv6 any 2001:DB8:CAFE:10::/64
 remark Permit PC3 telnet access to PC2
 permit tcp host 2001:DB8:CAFE:30::12 host 2001:DB8:CAFE:11::11 eq telnet
 remark Deny telnet access to PC2 for all other devices
 deny tcp any host 2001:DB8:CAFE:11::11 eq telnet
 remark Permit access to everything else
 permit ipv6 any any
```

Packet Tracer 4.3.2.6: Configuring IPv6 ACLs

In this Packet Tracer, you complete the following objectives:

- Part 1: Configure, Apply, and Verify an IPv6 ACL

- Part 2: Configure, Apply, and Verify a Second IPv6 ACL

Lab 4.3.2.7: Configuring and Verifying IPv6 ACLs

In this lab, you complete the following objectives:

- Part 1: Set Up the Topology and Initialize Devices

- Part 2: Configure Devices and Verify Connectivity

- Part 3: Configure and Verify IPv6 ACLs

- Part 4: Edit IPv6 ACLs

Troubleshoot ACLs (4.4)

In this section, you troubleshoot IPv4 and IPv6 ACLs.

Processing Packets with ACLs (4.4.1)

In this topic, you learn how a router processes packets when an ACL is applied.

Inbound and Outbound ACL Logic (4.4.1.1)

When you want to troubleshoot IPv6 ACLs, it is helpful to understand how inbound and outbound IPv6 ACLs operate. The following sections describe the logic applied to inbound and outbound IPv6 ACLs.

Inbound ACL Logic

Figure 4-18 shows a logic diagram for an inbound ACL.

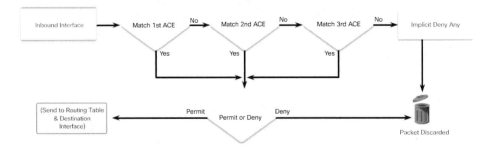

Figure 4-18   Inbound ACL Process

As indicated in the diagram in Figure 4-18, if the information in a packet header and an ACL statement match, the rest of the statements in the list are skipped, and the packet is permitted or denied as specified by the matched statement. If a packet header does not match an ACL statement, the packet is tested against the next statement in the list. This matching process continues until the end of the list is reached.

At the end of every ACL is a statement is an implicit **deny any** statement. This statement is not shown in output. This final implied statement applied to all packets for which conditions did not test true. This final test condition matches all other packets and results in a "deny" action. Instead of proceeding into or out of an interface, the router drops all of these remaining packets. This final statement is often referred to as the "implicit deny any statement" or the "deny all traffic" statement. Because of this statement, an ACL should have at least one **permit** statement in it; otherwise, the ACL blocks all traffic.

Outbound ACL Logic

Figure 4-19 shows the logic diagram for an outbound ACL.

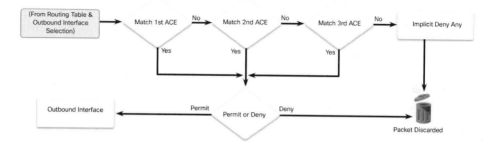

Figure 4-19   Outbound ACL Process

Before a packet is forwarded to an outbound interface, the router checks the routing table to see if the packet is routable. If the packet is not routable, it is dropped and is not tested against the ACEs.

Next, the router checks to see whether the outbound interface is associated with an ACL. If the outbound interface is not associated with an ACL, the packet can be sent to the output buffer.

Examples of outbound ACL operation are as follows:

- **No ACL applied to the interface:** If the outbound interface is not associated with an outbound ACL, the packet is sent directly to the outbound interface.

- **ACL applied to the interface:** If the outbound interface is associated with an outbound ACL, the packet is not sent out on the outbound interface until it is tested by the combination of ACEs that are associated with that interface. Based on the ACL tests, the packet is permitted or denied.

For outbound lists, "permit" means to send the packet to the output buffer, and "deny" means to discard the packet.

ACL Logic Operations (4.4.1.2)

Figure 4-20 shows the logic diagram of routing and ACL processes.

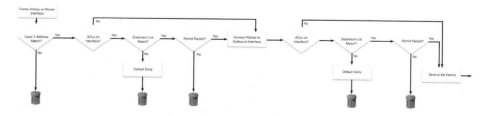

Figure 4-20   ACL and Routing Processes in a Router

When a packet arrives at a router interface, the router process is the same, whether or not ACLs are used. As a frame enters an interface, the router checks to see whether the destination Layer 2 address matches its interface Layer 2 address, or whether the frame is a broadcast frame.

If the frame address is accepted, the frame information is stripped off and the router checks for an ACL on the inbound interface. If an ACL exists, the packet is tested against the statements in the list.

If the packet matches a statement, the packet is either permitted or denied. If the packet is accepted, it is then checked against routing table entries to determine the destination interface. If a routing table entry exists for the destination, the packet is then switched to the outgoing interface; otherwise, the packet is dropped.

Next, the router checks whether the outgoing interface has an ACL. If an ACL exists, the packet is tested against the statements in the list.

If the packet matches a statement, it is either permitted or denied.

If there is no ACL or the packet is permitted, the packet is encapsulated in the new Layer 2 protocol and forwarded out the interface to the next device.

Standard ACL Decision Process (4.4.1.3)

Standard ACLs examine only the source IPv4 address. The destination of the packet and the ports involved are not considered.

The decision process for a standard ACL is mapped in Figure 4-21.

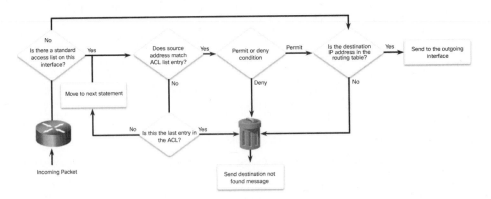

Figure 4-21   How a Standard ACL Works

Cisco IOS Software tests addresses against the conditions in the ACL one by one. The first match determines whether the software accepts or rejects the address.

Because the software stops testing conditions after the first match, the order of the conditions is critical. If no conditions match, the address is rejected.

Extended ACL Decision Process (4.4.1.4)

Figure 4-22 shows the logical decision path used by an extended ACL built to filter on source and destination addresses, and protocol and port numbers.

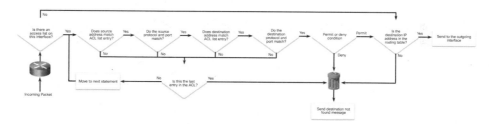

Figure 4-22   Testing Packets with Extended ACLs

In this example, the ACL first filters on the source address, then on the port and protocol of the source. It then filters on the destination address, then on the port and protocol of the destination, and makes a final permit or deny decision.

Recall that entries in ACLs are processed one after the other, so a "No" decision does not necessarily equal a "Deny." As you go through the logical decision path, note that a "No" means go to the next entry until a condition is matched.

Interactive Graphic

Activity 4.4.1.5: Place in Order the Steps of the ACL Decision-Making Process

Refer to the online course to complete this activity.

Common ACL Errors (4.4.2)

In this topic, you learn how to troubleshoot common ACL errors using CLI commands.

Troubleshooting IPv4 ACLs: Example 1 (4.4.2.1)

Using the **show** commands described earlier reveals most of the common ACL errors. The most common errors are entering ACEs in the wrong order and not applying adequate criteria to the ACL rules.

This scenario uses the topology in Figure 4-23 and the configuration in Example 4-28.

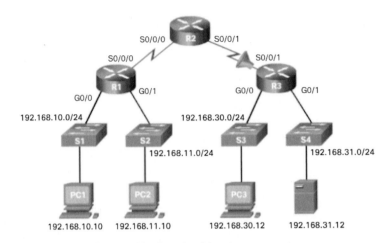

Figure 4-23 IPv4 ACL Troubleshooting Topology

Example 4-28 Troubleshooting IPv4 ACLs: Scenario 1

```
R3# show access-lists
Extended IP access list 110
    10 deny tcp 192.168.10.0 0.0.0.255 any (12 match(es))
    20 permit tcp 192.168.10.0 0.0.0.255 any eq telnet
    30 permit ip any any
```

In this example, ACL 110 is applied inbound on the S0/0/1 interface of R3. Host 192.168.10.10 has no Telnet connectivity with 192.168.30.12. When you are viewing the output of the **show access-lists** command, matches are shown for the first **deny** statement. This is an indicator that this statement has been matched by traffic.

Solution: Look at the order of the ACEs. Host 192.168.10.10 has no connectivity with 192.168.30.12 because of the order of rule 10 in the access list. Because the router processes ACLs from the top down, statement 10 denies host 192.168.10.10, so statement 20 can never be matched. Statements 10 and 20 should be reversed. The last line allows all other non-TCP traffic that falls under IP (ICMP, UDP, and so on).

Troubleshooting IPv4 ACLs: Example 2 (4.4.2.2)

This scenario is based on the topology shown previously in Figure 4-23 and the configuration in Example 4-29. However, in this example, ACL 120 is applied inbound on the Gigabit Ethernet 0/0 interface of R1.

Example 4-29 Troubleshooting IPv4 ACLs: Scenario 2

```
R1# show access-lists 120
Extended IP access list 120
    10 deny tcp 192.168.10.0 0.0.0.255 any eq telnet
    20 deny tcp 192.168.10.0 0.0.0.255 host 192.168.31.12 eq smtp
    30 permit tcp any any
```

The 192.168.10.0/24 network cannot use TFTP to connect to the 192.168.30.0/24 network.

Solution: The 192.168.10.0/24 network cannot use TFTP to connect to the 192.168.30.0/24 network because TFTP uses the transport protocol UDP. Statement 30 in access list 120 allows all other TCP traffic; however, because TFTP uses UDP instead of TCP, it is implicitly denied. Recall that the implied **deny any** statement does not appear in **show access-lists** output, and therefore, matches are not shown.

Statement 30 should be **ip any any**.

This ACL works whether it is applied to G0/0 of R1, or S0/0/1 of R3, or S0/0/0 of R2 in the incoming direction; however, based on the rule about placing extended ACLs closest to the source, the best option is to place it inbound on G0/0 of R1 because it allows undesirable traffic to be filtered without crossing the network infrastructure.

Troubleshooting IPv4 ACLs: Example 3 (4.4.2.3)

This scenario is based on the topology shown previously in Figure 4-23 and the configuration in Example 4-30. However, in this example, ACL 130 is applied inbound on the Gigabit Ethernet 0/1 interface of R1.

Example 4-30 Troubleshooting IPv4 ACLs: Scenario 3

```
R1# show access-lists 130
Extended IP access list 130
    10 deny tcp any eq telnet any
    20 deny tcp 192.168.11.0 0.0.0.255 host 192.168.31.12 eq smtp
    30 permit tcp any any (12 match(es))
```

The 192.168.11.0/24 network can use Telnet to connect to 192.168.30.0/24, but according to company policy, this connection should not be allowed. The results of the **show access-lists 130** command indicate that the **permit** statement has been matched.

Solution: The 192.168.11.0/24 network can use Telnet to connect to the 192.168.30.0/24 network because the Telnet port number in statement 10 of access list 130 is listed in the wrong position in the ACL statement. Statement 10 currently denies any source packet with a port number that is equal to Telnet. To deny Telnet traffic inbound on G0/1, deny the destination port number that is equal to Telnet, for example, **10 deny tcp 192.168.11.0 0.0.0.255 192.168.30.0 0.0.0.255 eq telnet.**

Troubleshooting IPv4 ACLs: Example 4 (4.4.2.4)

This scenario is based on the topology shown previously in Figure 4-23 and the configuration in Example 4-31. However, in this example, ACL 140 is applied inbound on the Gigabit Ethernet 0/0 interface of R3.

Example 4-31   Troubleshooting IPv4 ACLs: Scenario 4

```
R3# show access-lists 140
Extended IP access list 140
    10 deny tcp host 192.168.30.1 any eq telnet
    20 permit ip any any (5 match(es))
```

Host 192.168.30.12 is able to Telnet to connect to 192.168.31.12, but company policy states that this connection should not be allowed. Output from the **show access-lists 140** command indicates that the **permit** statement has been matched.

Solution: Host 192.168.30.12 can use Telnet to connect to 192.168.31.12 because there are no rules that deny host 192.168.30.12 or its network as the source. Statement 10 of access list 140 denies the router interface on which traffic enters the router. The host IPv4 address in statement 10 should be 192.168.30.12.

Troubleshooting IPv4 ACLs: Example 5 (4.4.2.5)

This scenario is based on the topology shown previously in Figure 4-23. However, in this example, ACL 150 is applied inbound on the Gigabit Ethernet 0/1 interface of R3.

In this example, the security policy explicitly states that Telnet access should not be permitted to the server at IP 192.168.31.12. However, a quick test from PC3 permits Telnet access to the server.

Example 4-32 displays the ACEs for ACL 150 configured on R3.

Example 4-32 Troubleshooting IPv4 ACLs: Scenario 5

```
R3# show access-lists 150
Extended IP access list 150
    10 deny tcp any host 192.168.31.12 eq telnet
    20 permit ip any any
```

Solution: Statement 10 appears to be correct because it denies any source address to Telnet to host 192.168.31.12. However, the output does not list any matches. The reason is the direction of the ACL. Notice in the example that the ACL is applied inbound on G0/1. However, to filter correctly, the ACL should be applied outbound on G0/1.

Troubleshooting IPv6 ACLs: Example 1 (4.4.2.6)

Similar to IPv4 ACLs, the **show ipv6 access-list** and **show running-config** commands reveal typical IPv6 ACL errors.

This scenario uses the topology in Figure 4-24. R1 is configured with an IPv6 ACL to deny FTP access from the :10 network to the :11 network. After the ACL is configured, however, PC1 is still able to connect to the FTP server running on PC2.

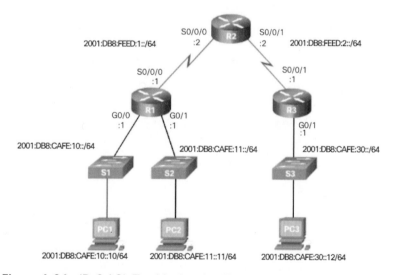

Figure 4-24   IPv6 ACL Troubleshooting Topology

Referring to the output for the **show ipv6 access-list** command in Example 4-33, you can see that matches are shown for the **permit** statement but not the **deny** statements.

Example 4-33 Verify the IPv6 ACL Configuration and Application: Scenario 1

```
R1# show ipv6 access-list
IPv6 access list NO-FTP-TO-11
    deny tcp any 2001:DB8:CAFE:11::/64 eq ftp sequence 10
    deny tcp any 2001:DB8:CAFE:11::/64 eq ftp-data sequence 20
    permit ipv6 any any (11 matches) sequence 30
R1# show running-config | begin interface G
interface GigabitEthernet0/0
 no ip address
 ipv6 traffic-filter NO-FTP-TO-11 out
 duplex auto
 speed auto
 ipv6 address FE80::1 link-local
 ipv6 address 2001:DB8:1:10::1/64
 ipv6 eigrp 1
<output omitted>
R1#
```

Solution: The ACEs in the ACL reveal no problems in their order or in the criteria of their rules. The next step is to consider how the ACL is applied at the interface using the **ipv6 traffic-filter** command. Did the ACL get applied using the correct name, the correct interface, and in the correct direction? To check for interface configuration errors, display the running configuration, as shown in Example 4-34.

Example 4-34 Correct and Verify the IPv6 ACL: Scenario 1

```
R1(config)# interface g0/0
R1(config-if)# no ipv6 traffic-filter NO-FTP-TO-11 out
R1(config-if)# ipv6 traffic-filter NO-FTP-TO-11 in
R1(config-if)# end
R1#

<PC1 attempts to access the FTP server again.>

R1# show ipv6 access-list
IPv6 access list NO-FTP-TO-11
    deny tcp any 2001:DB8:CAFE:11::/64 eq ftp (37 matches) sequence 10
    deny tcp any 2001:DB8:CAFE:11::/64 eq ftp-data sequence 20
    permit ipv6 any any (11 matches) sequence 30
```

The ACL was applied using the correct name, but not the correct direction. The **in** or **out** direction is from the perspective of the router, meaning the ACL is currently applied to traffic before it is forwarded out the G0/0 interface and enters the :10 network.

To correct the issue, remove the **ipv6 traffic-filter NO-FTP-TO-11 out** statement and replace it with **ipv6 traffic-filter NO-FTP-TO-11 in**, as shown in Example 4-34. Now PC1's attempts to access the FTP server are denied, as verified with the **show ipv6 access-list** command.

Troubleshooting IPv6 ACLs: Example 2 (4.4.2.7)

For this scenario, R3 is configured with an IPv6 ACL named RESTRICTED-ACCESS that should enforce the following policy for the R3 LAN:

- Permit access to the :10 network
- Deny access to the :11 network
- Permit SSH access to the PC at 2001:DB8:CAFE:11::11

After configuring the ACL, however, PC3 cannot reach the 10 network or the 11 network, and it cannot SSH into the host at 2001:DB8:CAFE:11::11.

Solution: In this situation, the problem is not with how the ACL was applied. At the interface, the ACL is not misspelled and the direction and location are correct, as shown in Example 4-35.

Example 4-35 Verify the IPv6 ACL Configuration and Application: Scenario 2

```
R3# show running-config | section interface GigabitEthernet0/0
interface GigabitEthernet0/0
 no ip address
 duplex auto
 speed auto
 ipv6 address FE80::3 link-local
 ipv6 address 2001:DB8:1:30::1/64
 ipv6 eigrp 1
 ipv6 traffic-filter RESTRICTED-ACCESS in
R3#
R3# show ipv6 access-list
IPv6 access list RESTRICTED-ACCESS
    permit ipv6 any host 2001:DB8:CAFE:10:: sequence 10
    deny ipv6 any 2001:DB8:CAFE:11::/64 sequence 20
    permit tcp any host 2001:DB8:CAFE:11::11 eq 22 sequence 30
R3#
```

A close look at the IPv6 ACL reveals that the problem is with the order and criteria of the ACE rules. The first **permit** statement should allow access to the :10 network; however, the administrator configured a host statement and did not specify a prefix. In this case, only access to the 2001:DB8:CAFE:10:: host is allowed.

To correct this issue, remove the host argument and change the prefix to /64. You can do this without removing the ACL by replacing the ACE using the sequence number 10, as shown in Example 4-36.

Example 4-36 Replace the IPv6 ACL Host Statement

```
R3(config)# ipv6 access-list RESTRICTED-ACCESS
R3(config-ipv6-acl)# permit ipv6 any 2001:db8:cafe:10::/64 sequence 10
R3(config-ipv6-acl)# end
R3#
R3# show access-list
IPv6 access list RESTRICTED-ACCESS
    permit ipv6 any 2001:DB8:CAFE:10::/64 sequence 10
    deny ipv6 any 2001:DB8:CAFE:11::/64 sequence 20
    permit tcp any host 2001:DB8:CAFE:11::11 eq 22 sequence 30
R3#
```

The second error in the ACL is the order of the next two statements. The policy specifies that hosts on the R3 LAN should be able to SSH into host 2001:DB8:CAFE:11::11. However, the **deny** statement for :11 network is listed before the **permit** statement. Therefore, all attempts to access the :11 network are denied before the statement permitting SSH access can be evaluated. After a match is made, no further statements are analyzed.

To correct this issue, you need to remove the statements first and then enter them in the correct order, as shown in Example 4-37.

Example 4-37 Reorder the IPv6 ACL Statements

```
R3(config)# ipv6 access-list RESTRICTED-ACCESS
R3(config-ipv6-acl)# no deny ipv6 any 2001:DB8:CAFE:11::/64
R3(config-ipv6-acl)# no permit tcp any host 2001:DB8:CAFE:11::11 eq 22
R3(config-ipv6-acl)# permit tcp any host 2001:DB8:CAFE:11::11 eq 22
R3(config-ipv6-acl)# deny ipv6 any 2001:DB8:CAFE:11::/64
R3(config-ipv6-acl)# end
R3#
R3# show access-list
IPv6 access list RESTRICTED-ACCESS
    permit ipv6 any 2001:DB8:CAFE:10::/64 sequence 10
    permit tcp any host 2001:DB8:CAFE:11::11 eq 22 sequence 20
    deny ipv6 any 2001:DB8:CAFE:11::/64 sequence 30
R3#
```

Troubleshooting IPv6 ACLs: Example 3 (4.4.2.8)

For this scenario, R1 is configured with an IPv6 ACL named DENY-ACCESS that should enforce the following policy for the R3 LAN:

- Permit access to the :11 network from the :30 network
- Deny access to the :10 network

Example 4-38 shows the configuration and application of the IPv6 ACL.

Example 4-38 Verify the IPv6 ACL Configuration and Application: Scenario 3

```
R1# show access-list
IPv6 access list DENY-ACCESS
    permit ipv6 any 2001:DB8:CAFE:11::/64 sequence 10
    deny ipv6 any 2001:DB8:CAFE:10::/64 sequence 20
R1#
R1# show running-config interface GigabitEthernet0/1
interface GigabitEthernet0/1
 no ip address
 duplex auto
 speed auto
 ipv6 address FE80::1 link-local
 ipv6 address 2001:DB8:CAFE:11::1/64
 ipv6 eigrp 1
 ipv6 traffic-filter DENY-ACCESS out
R1#
```

The DENY-ACCESS ACL is supposed to permit access to the :11 network from the :30 network while denying access to the :10 network. However, after the ACL is applied to the interface, the :10 network is still reachable from the :30 network.

Solution: In this situation, the problem is not with how the ACL statements were written but with the location of the ACL. Because IPv6 ACLs must be configured with both a source and a destination, they should be applied closest to the source of the traffic. The DENY-ACCESS ACL was applied in the outbound direction on the R1 G0/1 interface, which is closest to the destination. As a result, traffic to the :10 network is completely unaffected because it reaches the :10 network through the other LAN interface, G0/0. You could apply the ACL inbound on the R1 S0/0/0 interface. However, because we have control over R3, the best location would be to configure and apply the ACL closest to the source of the traffic.

Example 4-39 shows the removal of the ACL on R1 and the correct configuration and application of the ACL on R3.

Example 4-39 Remove ACL on R1, then Configure and Apply ACL on R2

```
R1(config)# no ipv6 access-list DENY-ACCESS
R1(config)#
R1(config)# interface g0/1
R1(config-if)# no ipv6 traffic-filter DENY-ACCESS out
R1(config-if)#
!-------------------------------------------------------
R3(config)# ipv6 access-list DENY-ACCESS
R3(config-ipv6-acl)# permit ipv6 any 2001:DB8:CAFE:11::/64
R3(config-ipv6-acl)# deny ipv6 any 2001:DB8:CAFE:10::/64
R3(config-ipv6-acl)# exit
R3(config)#
R3(config)# interface g0/0
R3(config-if)# ipv6 traffic-filter DENY-ACCESS in
R3(config-if)#
```

Packet Tracer
☐ Activity

Packet Tracer 4.4.2.9: Troubleshooting IPv4 ACLs

Create a network that has the following three policies implemented:

- Hosts from the 192.168.0.0/24 network are unable to access any TCP service of Server3.

- Hosts from the 10.0.0.0/8 network are unable to access the HTTP service of Server1.

- Hosts from the 172.16.0.0/16 network are unable to access the FTP service of Server2.

Packet Tracer
☐ Activity·

Packet Tracer 4.4.2.10: Troubleshooting IPv6 ACLs

The following three policies have been implemented on the network:

- Hosts from the 2001:DB8:CAFE::/64 network do not have HTTP access to the other networks.

- Hosts from the 2001:DB8:CAFE:1::/64 network are prevented from access to the FTP service on Server2.

- Hosts from the 2001:DB8:CAFE:1::/64 and 2001:DB8:CAFE:2::/64 networks are prevented from accessing R1 via SSH.

No other restrictions should be in place. Unfortunately, the rules that have been implemented are not working correctly. Your task is to find and fix the errors related to the access lists on R1.

Lab 4.4.2.11: Troubleshooting ACL Configuration and Placement

In this lab, you complete the following objectives:

- Part 1: Build the Network and Configure Basic Device Settings

- Part 2: Troubleshoot Internal Access

- Part 3: Troubleshoot Remote Access

Summary (4.5)

Packet Tracer
☐ Activity

Packet Tracer 4.5.1.1: Skills Integration Challenge

In this challenge activity, you finish the addressing scheme, configure routing, and implement named access control lists.

By default, a router does not filter traffic. Traffic that enters the router is routed solely based on information within the routing table.

Packet filtering controls access to a network by analyzing the incoming and outgoing packets and passing or dropping them based on criteria such as the source IP address, destination IP addresses, and the protocol carried within the packet. A packet-filtering router uses rules to determine whether to permit or deny traffic. A router can also perform packet filtering at Layer 4, the transport layer.

An ACL is a sequential list of **permit** or **deny** statements. The last statement of an ACL is always an implicit **deny any** statement that blocks all traffic. To prevent the implied **deny any** statement at the end of the ACL from blocking all traffic, you can add the **permit ip any any** statement.

When network traffic passes through an interface configured with an ACL, the router compares the information within the packet against each entry, in sequential order, to determine if the packet matches one of the statements. If a match is found, the packet is processed accordingly.

ACLs are configured to apply to inbound traffic or to apply to outbound traffic.

Standard ACLs can be used to permit or deny traffic only from a source IPv4 addresses. The destination of the packet and the ports involved are not evaluated. The basic rule for placing a standard ACL is to place it close to the destination.

Extended ACLs filter packets based on several attributes: protocol type, source or destination IPv4 address, and source or destination ports. The basic rule for placing an extended ACL is to place it as close to the source as possible.

The **access-list** global configuration command defines a standard ACL with a number in the range of 1 through 99 or an extended ACL with numbers in the range of 100 to 199 and 2000 to 2699. Both standard and extended ACLs can be named instead of numbered. The **ip access-list standard** *acl-name* is used to create a standard named ACL, whereas the command **ip access-list extended** *acl-name* is for an extended access list. IPv4 ACEs include the use of wildcard masks.

After an ACL is configured, it is linked to an interface using the **ip access-group** command in interface configuration mode. A device can have only one ACL per protocol, per direction, per interface.

To remove an ACL from an interface, first enter the **no ip access-group** command on the interface, and then enter the global **no access-list** command to remove the entire ACL.

The **show running-config** and **show access-lists** commands are used to verify ACL configuration. The **show ip interface** command is used to verify the ACL on the interface and the direction in which it was applied.

The **access-class** command configured in line configuration mode restricts incoming and outgoing connections between a particular VTY and the addresses in an access list.

Like IPv4 named ACLs, IPv6 names are alphanumeric, case sensitive, and must be unique. Unlike IPv4, there is no need for a standard or extended option.

From global configuration mode, use the **ipv6 access-list** *acl-name* command to create an IPv6 ACL. Unlike IPv4 ACLs, IPv6 ACLs do not use wildcard masks. Instead, the prefix-length is used to indicate how much of an IPv6 source or destination address should be matched.

After an IPv6 ACL is configured, it is linked to an interface using the **ipv6 traffic-filter** command.

Practice

The following activities provide practice with the topics introduced in this chapter. The Labs and Class Activities are available in the companion *Connecting Networks v6 Labs & Study Guide* (ISBN 9781587134296). The Packet Tracer Activity instructions are also in the *Labs & Study Guide*. The PKA files are found in the online course.

Labs

Lab 4.2.2.13: Configuring and Verifying Extended ACLs

Lab 4.3.2.7: Configuring and Verifying IPv6 ACLs

Lab 4.4.2.11: Troubleshooting ACL Configuration and Placement

Packet Tracer
☐ **Activity**

Packet Tracer Activities

Packet Tracer 4.1.3.5: Configure Standard IPv4 ACLs

Packet Tracer 4.2.2.10: Configuring Extended ACLs: Scenario 1

Packet Tracer 4.2.2.11: Configuring Extended ACLs: Scenario 2

Packet Tracer 4.2.2.12: Configuring Extended ACLs: Scenario 3

Packet Tracer 4.3.2.6: Configuring IPv6 ACLs

Packet Tracer 4.4.2.9: Troubleshooting IPv4 ACLs

Packet Tracer 4.4.2.10: Troubleshooting IPv6 ACLs

Packet Tracer 4.5.1.1: Skills Integration Challenge

Check Your Understanding Questions

Complete all the review questions listed here to test your understanding of the topics and concepts in this chapter. The appendix "Answers to the 'Check Your Understanding' Questions" lists the answers.

1. Which three statements describe ACL processing of packets? (Choose three.)

   A. A packet can either be rejected or forwarded as directed by the ACE that is matched.

   B. A packet that does not match the conditions of any ACE will be forwarded by default.

   C. A packet that has been denied by one ACE can be permitted by a subsequent ACE.

   D. An implicit **deny any** rejects any packet that does not match any ACE.

   E. Each statement is checked only until a match is detected or until the end of the ACE list.

   F. Each packet is compared to the conditions of every ACE in the ACL before a forwarding decision is made.

2. What two functions describe uses of an access control list? (Choose two.)

   A. ACLs assist the router in determining the best path to a destination.

   B. ACLs can control which areas a host can access on a network.

   C. ACLs can permit or deny traffic based on the MAC address originating on the router.

D. ACLs provide a basic level of security for network access.

E. Standard ACLs can restrict access to specific applications and ports.

3. In which configuration would an outbound ACL placement be preferred over an inbound ACL placement?

A. When a router has more than one ACL

B. When an interface is filtered by an outbound ACL and the network attached to the interface is the source network being filtered within the ACL

C. When an outbound ACL is closer to the source of the traffic flow

D. When the ACL is applied to an outbound interface to filter packets coming from multiple inbound interfaces before the packets exit the interface

4. Which two characteristics are shared by both standard and extended ACLs? (Choose two.)

A. Both kinds of ACLs can filter based on protocol type.

B. Both can permit or deny specific services by port number.

C. Both include an implicit deny as a final entry.

D. Both filter packets for a specific destination host IP address.

E. Both can be created by using either a descriptive name or number.

5. A network administrator needs to configure a standard ACL so that only the workstation of the administrator with the IP address 192.168.15.23 can access the virtual terminal of the main router. Which two configuration commands can achieve the task? (Choose two.)

A. R1(config)# access-list 10 permit host 192.168.15.23

B. R1(config)# access-list 10 permit 192.168.15.23 0.0.0.0

C. R1(config)# access-list 10 permit 192.168.15.23 0.0.0.255

D. R1(config)# access-list 10 permit 192.168.15.23 255.255.255.0

E. R1(config)# access-list 10 permit 192.168.15.23 255.255.255.255

6. Which three statements are generally considered to be best practices in the place-ment of ACLs? (Choose three.)

A. Filter unwanted traffic before it travels onto a low-bandwidth link.

B. For every inbound ACL placed on an interface, there should be a matching outbound ACL.

C. Place extended ACLs close to the destination IP address of the traffic.

D. Place extended ACLs close to the source IP address of the traffic.

E. Place standard ACLs close to the destination IP address of the traffic.

F. Place standard ACLs close to the source IP address of the traffic.

7. What packets match **access-list 110 permit tcp 172.16.0.0 0.0.0.255 any eq 22?**

A. Any TCP traffic from any host to the 172.16.0.0 network

B. Any TCP traffic from the 172.16.0.0 network to any destination network

C. SSH traffic from any source network to the 172.16.0.0 network

D. SSH traffic from the 172.16.0.0 network to any destination network

8. Which statement describes a difference between the operation of inbound and outbound ACLs?

A. In contrast to outbound ACLs, inbound ACLs can be used to filter packets with multiple criteria.

B. Inbound ACLs are processed before the packets are routed, whereas outbound ACLs are processed after the routing is completed.

C. Inbound ACLs can be used in both routers and switches, but outbound ACLs can be used only on routers.

D. On a network interface, more than one inbound ACL can be configured, but only one outbound ACL can be configured.

9. What is a limitation when utilizing both IPv4 and IPv6 ACLs on a router?

A. A device can run only IPv4 ACLs or IPv6 ACLs.

B. Both IPv4 and IPv6 ACLs can be configured on a single device but cannot share the same name.

C. IPv4 ACLs can be numbered or named, whereas IPv6 ACLs must be numbered.

D. IPv6 ACLs perform the same functions as standard IPv4 ACLs.

10. What method is used to apply an IPv6 ACL to a router interface?

A. The use of the **access-class** command

B. The use of the **ip access-group** command

C. The use of the **ipv6 access-list** command

D. The use of the **ipv6 traffic-filter** command

11. Which IPv6 ACL command entry will permit traffic from any host to an SMTP server on network 2001:DB8:10:10::/64?

    A. **permit tcp any host 2001:DB8:10:10::100 eq 23**

    B. **permit tcp any host 2001:DB8:10:10::100 eq 25**

    C. **permit tcp host 2001:DB8:10:10::100 any eq 23**

    D. **permit tcp host 2001:DB8:10:10::100 any eq 25**

12. Which feature is unique to IPv6 ACLs when compared to those of IPv4 ACLs?

    A. An implicit **deny any any** ACE

    B. An implicit permit of neighbor discovery packets

    C. The use of named ACL entries

    D. The use of wildcard masks

13. Which three implicit access control entries are automatically added to the end of an IPv6 ACL? (Choose three.)

    A. **deny icmp any any**

    B. **deny ip any any**

    C. **deny ipv6 any any**

    D. **permit icmp any any nd-na**

    E. **permit icmp any any nd-ns**

    F. **permit ipv6 any any**

14. What is the only type of ACL available for IPv6?

    A. Named extended

    B. Named standard

    C. Numbered extended

    D. Numbered standard

CHAPTER 5

Network Security and Monitoring

Objectives

Upon completion of this chapter, you will be able to answer the following questions:

- What are common LAN security attacks?

- How do you use security best practices to mitigate LAN attacks?

- How does SNMP operate?

- How do you configure SNMP to compile network performance data?

- What are the features and characteristics of SPAN?

- How do you configure local SPAN?

- How can you use SPAN to troubleshoot suspicious LAN traffic.

Key Terms

This chapter uses the following key terms. You can find the definitions in the Glossary.

Introduction (5.0.1.1)

A secure network is only as strong as its weakest link, and Layer 2 is potentially the weakest link. Common Layer 2 attacks include *CDP reconnaissance attacks*, *Telnet attacks*, *MAC address table flooding attacks*, VLAN attacks, *DHCP spoofing attacks*, and VLAN attacks. Network administrators must know how to mitigate these attacks and secure administrative access using *Authentication, Authorization, and Accounting (AAA)* and secure port access using *IEEE 802.1X*.

Monitoring an operational network can provide a network administrator with information to proactively manage the network and to report network usage statistics to others. Link activity, error rates, and link status are a few of the factors that help a network administrator determine the health and usage of a network. Collecting and reviewing this information over time enable a network administrator to see and project growth, and may enable the administrator to detect and replace a failing part before it completely fails. *Simple Network Management Protocol (SNMP)* is commonly used to collect device information.

Network traffic must be monitored for malicious traffic. Network administrators use port analyzers and *intrusion prevention system (IPS)* devices to help with this task; however, the switched infrastructure does not enable port mirroring by default. Cisco *Switched Port Analyzer (SPAN)* must be implemented to enable port mirroring. SPAN enables the switch to send duplicate traffic to port analyzers or IPS devices for monitoring of malicious or questionable traffic.

This chapter covers common LAN security threats and how to mitigate them. It then covers SNMP and how to enable it to monitor a network, and how to implement local SPAN to capture and monitor traffic with port analyzers or IPS devices.

Class Activity 5.0.1.2: Network Maintenance Development

Currently, there are no formal policies or procedures for recording problems experienced on your company's network. Furthermore, when network problems occur, you must try many methods to find the causes, and this approach takes time.

You know there must be a better way to resolve these issues. You decide to create a network maintenance plan to keep repair records and pinpoint the causes of errors on the network.

LAN Security (5.1)

In this section, you learn how to mitigate common LAN security attacks.

LAN Security Attacks (5.1.1)

In this topic, you learn about common LAN security attacks.

Common LAN Attacks (5.1.1.1)

Organizations commonly implement security solutions using routers, firewalls, intrusion prevention system (IPSs), and VPN devices. They protect the elements in Layer 3 up through Layer 7.

Layer 2 LANs are often considered to be safe and secure environments. However, as shown in Figure 5-1, if Layer 2 is compromised, all layers above it are also affected. Today, with BYOD and more sophisticated attacks, LANs have become more vulnerable.

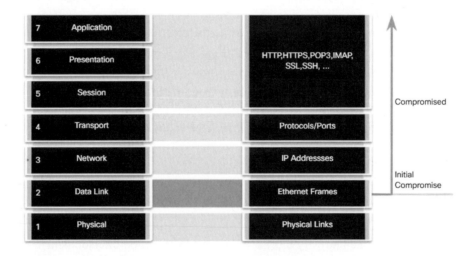

Figure 5-1   Layer 2 Compromise Affects Upper Layers

For example, a disgruntled employee with internal network access could capture Layer 2 frames. The attacker could also wreak havoc on the Layer 2 LAN networking infrastructure and create DoS situations rendering all the security implemented in Layers 3 and above useless. Therefore, in addition to protecting Layer 3 to Layer 7, network security professionals must also mitigate threats against the Layer 2 LAN infrastructure.

The first step in mitigating attacks on the Layer 2 infrastructure is to understand the underlying operation of Layer 2 and the threats posed by the Layer 2 infrastructure.

Common attacks against the Layer 2 LAN infrastructure include

- CDP reconnaissance attacks

- Telnet attacks

- MAC address table flooding attacks

- VLAN attacks

- DHCP attacks

The first two attacks are focused on gaining administrative access to the network device. The remaining attacks are focused on disrupting the network operation. Other more sophisticated attacks exist; however, the focus of this section is on common Layer 2 attacks.

Note

For more information on Layer 2 attacks, refer to the CCNA Security course.

CDP Reconnaissance Attack (5.1.1.2)

The *Cisco Discovery Protocol (CDP)* is a proprietary Layer 2 link discovery protocol. It is enabled on all Cisco devices by default. CDP can automatically discover other CDP-enabled devices and help autoconfigure their connection. Network administrators also use CDP to help configure and troubleshoot network devices.

CDP information is sent out CDP-enabled ports in periodic, unencrypted broadcasts. CDP information includes the IP address of the device, IOS software version, platform, capabilities, and the native VLAN. The device receiving the CDP message updates its CDP database.

CDP information is extremely useful in network troubleshooting. For example, CDP can be used to verify Layer 1 and Layer 2 connectivity. If an administrator cannot ping a directly connected interface but still receives CDP information, the problem is most likely related to the Layer 3 configuration.

However, CDP can also be used for nefarious reasons. For example, a cybercriminal can use the information provided by CDP to perform reconnaissance and attempt to discover network infrastructure vulnerabilities.

In Figure 5-2, a sample Wireshark capture displays the contents of a CDP packet. Notice that an attacker could identify the Cisco IOS software version used by the device to determine whether there are any security vulnerabilities specific to that particular version of IOS.

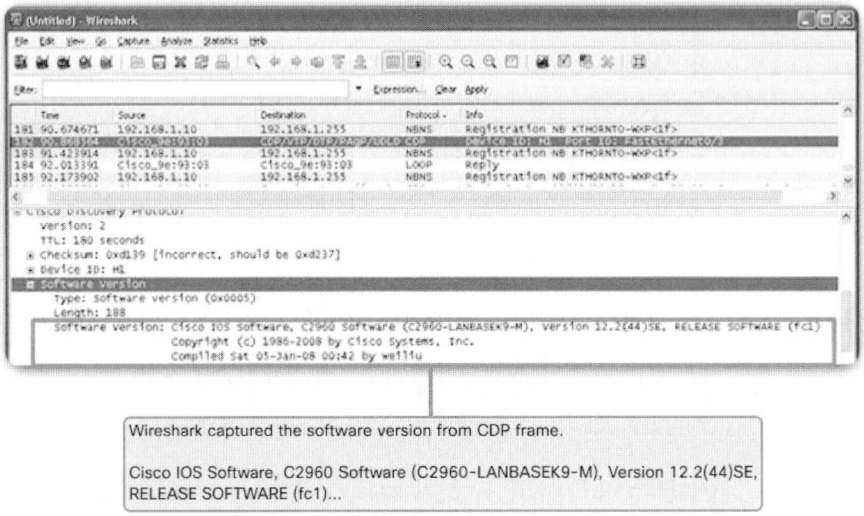

Wireshark captured the software version from CDP frame.

Cisco IOS Software, C2960 Software (C2960-LANBASEK9-M), Version 12.2(44)SE, RELEASE SOFTWARE (fc1)...

Figure 5-2 Wireshark Capture of CDP Packet

CDP broadcasts are sent unencrypted and unauthenticated. Therefore, an attacker could interfere with the network infrastructure by sending crafted CDP frames containing bogus device information to directly connected Cisco devices.

To mitigate the exploitation of CDP, limit the use of CDP on devices or ports. For example, disable CDP on edge ports that connect to untrusted devices.

To disable CDP globally on a device, use the **no cdp run** global configuration mode command. To enable CDP globally, use the **cdp run** global configuration command.

To disable CDP on a port, use the **no cdp enable** interface configuration command. To enable CDP on a port, use the **cdp enable** interface configuration command.

Note

Link Layer Discovery Protocol (LLDP) in also vulnerable to reconnaissance attacks. Configure **no lldp run** to disable LLDP globally. To disable LLDP on the interface, configure **no lldp transmit** and **no lldp receive**.

Telnet Attacks (5.1.1.3)

The ability to remotely manage a switched LAN infrastructure is an operational requirement; therefore, it must be supported. However, the Telnet protocol is inherently insecure and can be leveraged by an attacker to gain remote access to a Cisco network device. Some available tools allow an attacker to launch attacks against the vty lines on the switch.

There are two types of Telnet attacks:

- **Telnet DoS attack:** The attacker continuously requests Telnet connections in an attempt to render the Telnet service unavailable when an administrator tries to remotely access the device. This technique can be combined with other direct attacks on the network as part of a coordinated attempt to prevent the network administrator from accessing core devices during the breach.

- **Brute-force password attack:** The attacker may use a list of common passwords, dictionary words, and variations of words to discover the administrative password. If the password is not discovered by the first phase, a second phase begins. The attacker uses specialized password auditing tools. The software creates sequential character combinations in an attempt to guess the password. Given enough time and the right conditions, a brute-force password attack can crack almost all passwords.

Figure 5-3 displays a sample screen of the brute-force attack tool L0phtCrack attempting to discover passwords.

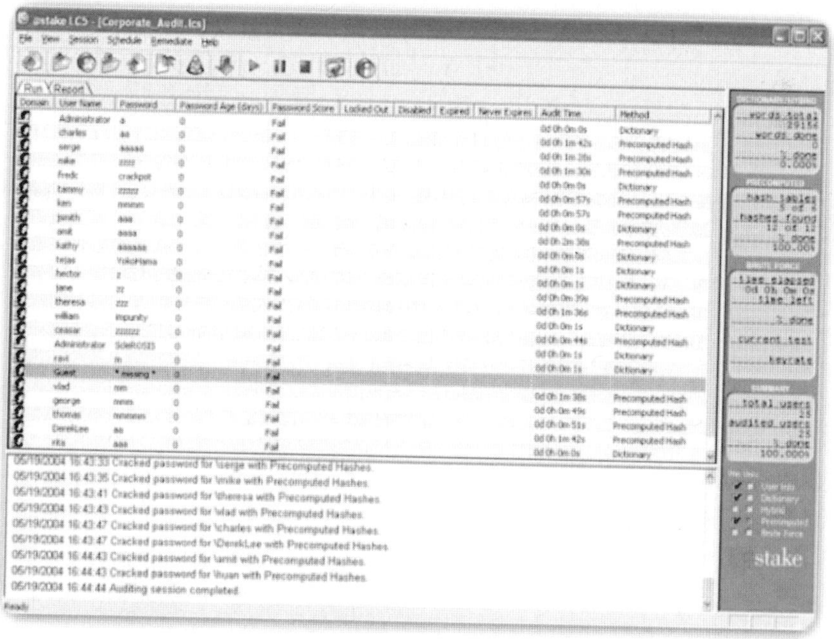

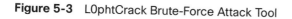

Figure 5-3 L0phtCrack Brute-Force Attack Tool

You can mitigate against Telnet attacks in several ways:

- Use SSH rather than Telnet for remote management connections.

- Use strong passwords that are changed frequently. A strong password should have a mix of upper- and lowercase letters and should include numerals and symbols (special characters).

- Limit access to the vty lines using an access control list (ACL) permitting only administrator devices and denying all other devices.

- Authenticate and authorize administrative access to the device using AAA with either *Terminal Access Controller Access Control System (TACACS+)* protocol or the *Remote Authentication Dial-In User Service (RADIUS)* protocol.

MAC Address Table Flooding Attack (5.1.1.4)

One of the most basic and common LAN switch attacks is the MAC address flooding attack. This attack is also known as a MAC address table overflow attack or a CAM table overflow attack.

Consider what happens when a switch receives incoming frames. The MAC address table in a switch contains the MAC addresses associated with each physical port, and the associated VLAN for each port. When a Layer 2 switch receives a frame, the switch looks in the MAC address table for the destination MAC address. All Catalyst switch models use a MAC address table for Layer 2 switching. As frames arrive on switch ports, the source MAC addresses are recorded in the MAC address table. If an entry exists for the MAC address, the switch forwards the frame to the correct port. If the MAC address does not exist in the MAC address table, the switch floods the frame out of every port on the switch, except the port where the frame was received.

Figures 5-4 through 5-6 illustrate this default switch behavior.

In Figure 5-4, host A sends traffic to host B. The switch receives the frames and adds the source MAC address of host A to its MAC address table. The switch then looks up the destination MAC address in its MAC address table. If the switch does not find the destination MAC in the MAC address table, it copies the frame and floods (broadcasts) it out of every switch port, except the port where it was received.

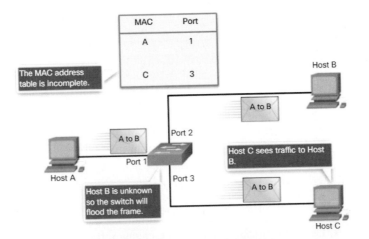

Figure 5-4   Switch Floods Frame for Unknown MAC

In Figure 5-5, host B receives and processes the frame. It then sends a reply to host A. The switch receives the incoming frame from host B. The switch then adds the source MAC address and port assignment for host B to its MAC address table. The switch then looks for the destination MAC address in its MAC address table and forwards the frames out of Port 1 toward host A.

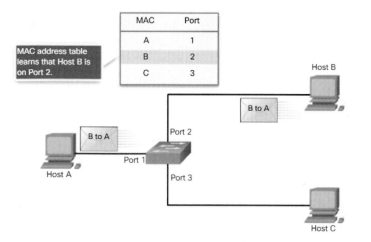

Figure 5-5   Switch Records MAC Address

The MAC address table of the switch eventually learns all MAC addresses connected to it and forwards frames between communicating ports only. In Figure 5-6, for example, any frame sent by host A (or any other host) to host B is forwarded out port 2 of the switch. It is not broadcasted out every port because the switch knows the location of the destination MAC address.

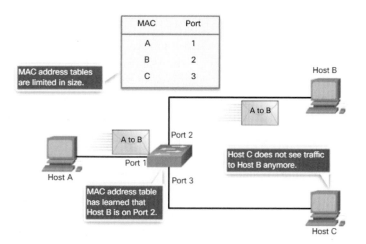

Figure 5-6   Switch Uses MAC Address Table to Forward Traffic

An attacker can exploit this default switch behavior to create a MAC address flooding attack. MAC address tables are limited in size. MAC flooding attacks exploit this limitation with fake source MAC addresses until the switch MAC address table is full and the switch is overwhelmed.

Figures 5-7 and 5-8 illustrate how a MAC address table flooding attack is generated.

In Figure 5-7, an attacker uses a network attack tool and continuously sends frames with fake, randomly generated source and destination MAC addresses to the switch. The switch keeps updating its MAC address table with the information in the fake frames.

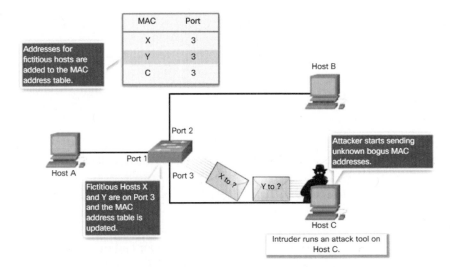

Figure 5-7   Attacker Initiates MAC Address Flooding Attack

Eventually, the MAC address table becomes full of fake MAC addresses and enters into what is known as fail-open mode. In this mode, the switch broadcasts all frames to all machines on the network. As a result, the attacker can capture all the frames, even frames that are not addressed to its MAC address table.

In Figure 5-8, the switch is in fail-open mode and broadcasts all received frames out of every port. Therefore, frames sent from host A to host B are also broadcast out of port 3 on the switch and seen by the attacker.

Configure port security on the switch to mitigate MAC address table overflow attacks. Mitigation techniques are discussed in more detail in the section "LAN Security Best Practices (5.1.2)."

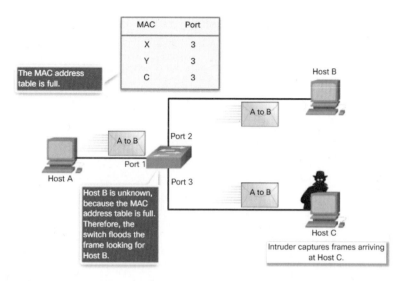

Figure 5-8 Switch Is Compromised

VLAN Attacks (5.1.1.5)

The VLAN architecture simplifies network maintenance and improves performance, but it also opens the door to abuse. A variety of VLAN-related attacks exist. Figure 5-9 illustrates one type of VLAN threat, which is the switch spoofing attack.

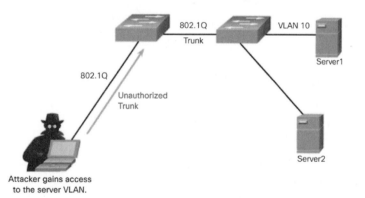

Figure 5-9 Switch Spoofing Attack

The attacker attempts to gain VLAN access by configuring a host to spoof a switch and use the 802.1Q trunking protocol and the Cisco-proprietary *Dynamic Trunking Protocol (DTP)* feature to trunk with the connecting switch. If successful and the switch establishes a trunk link with the host, the attacker can then access all the VLANS on the switch and hop (that is, send and receive) traffic on all the VLANs.

You can mitigate VLAN attacks in several ways:

- Explicitly configure access links

- Explicitly disable auto trunking

- Manually enable trunk links

- Disable unused ports, make them access ports, and assign them to a black-hole VLAN

- Change the default native VLAN

- Implement *port security*

VLAN attack mitigation techniques are discussed in more detail in the section "LAN Security Best Practices (5.1.2)."

DHCP Attacks (5.1.1.6)

DHCP is the protocol that automatically assigns a host a valid IP address out of a DHCP pool. Figure 5-10 shows a DHCP topology with a DHCP attacker.

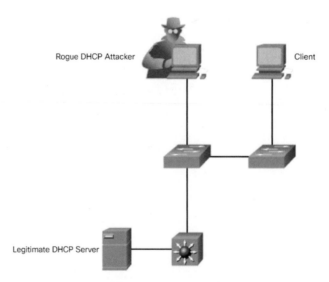

Figure 5-10 DHCP Spoofing and Starvation Attack

Two types of DHCP attacks can be performed against a switched network:

- **DHCP spoofing attack:** An attacker configures a fake DHCP server on the network to issue IP addresses to clients. This type of attack forces the clients to use both a false Domain Name System (DNS) server and a computer that is under the control of the attacker as their default gateway.

■ *DHCP starvation attack*: An attacker floods the DHCP server with bogus DHCP requests and eventually leases all the available IP addresses in the DHCP server pool. After these IP addresses are issued, the server cannot issue any more addresses, and this situation produces a *denial-of-service (DoS) attack* because new clients cannot obtain network access.

Note

A DoS attack is any attack that is used to overload specific devices and network services with illegitimate traffic, thereby preventing legitimate traffic from reaching those resources.

DHCP starvation is often used before a DHCP spoofing attack to deny service to the legitimate DHCP server. This makes it easier to introduce a fake DHCP server into the network.

To mitigate DHCP attacks, configure *DHCP snooping* and port security on the switch. DHCP attack mitigation techniques are discussed in more detail in the section "LAN Security Best Practices (5.1.2)."

Interactive Graphic

Activity 5.1.1.7: Identify Common Security Attacks

Refer to the online course to complete this activity.

LAN Security Best Practices (5.1.2)

In this topic, you learn how to use security best practices to mitigate LAN attacks.

Secure the LAN (5.1.2.1)

As noted at the beginning of this chapter, security is only as strong as the weakest link in the system, and Layer 2 is considered to be that weakest link. Therefore, Layer 2 security solutions must be implemented to help secure a network.

Many network management protocols including Telnet, Syslog, SNMP, TFTP, and FTP are insecure. There are several strategies to help secure Layer 2 of a network:

■ Always use secure variants of these protocols such as SSH, SCP, SSL, SNMPv3, and SFTP.

■ Always use strong passwords and change them often.

■ Enable CDP on select ports only.

- Secure Telnet access.

- Use a dedicated management VLAN where nothing but management traffic resides.

- Use ACLs to filter unwanted access.

The following four Cisco switch security solutions help mitigate Layer 2 attacks:

- Port security prevents many types of attacks, including CAM table overflow attacks and DHCP starvation attacks.

- DHCP snooping prevents DHCP starvation and DHCP spoofing attacks.

- *Dynamic ARP inspection* prevents ARP spoofing and ARP poisoning attacks.

- *IP Source Guard* prevents MAC and IP address spoofing attacks.

The sections that follow cover several Layer 2 security solutions:

- Mitigating MAC address table flooding attacks using port security

- Mitigating VLAN attacks

- Mitigating DHCP attacks using DHCP snooping

- Securing administrative access using AAA

- Securing device access using 802.1X port authentication

Note

IP Source Guard (IPSG) and Dynamic ARP Inspection (DAI) are advanced switch security solutions discussed in the CCNA Security course.

Mitigate MAC Address Flooding Table Attacks (5.1.2.2)

The simplest and most effective method to prevent MAC table flooding attacks is to enable port security.

Port security allows an administrator to statically specify MAC addresses for a port or to permit the switch to dynamically learn a limited number of MAC addresses. By limiting the number of permitted MAC addresses on a port to one, the administrator can use port security to control unauthorized expansion of the network, as shown in Figure 5-11.

When MAC addresses are assigned to a secure port, the port does not forward frames with source MAC addresses outside the group of defined addresses. When a port configured with port security receives a frame, the source MAC address of the frame is compared to the list of secure source addresses that were manually configured or autoconfigured (learned) on the port.

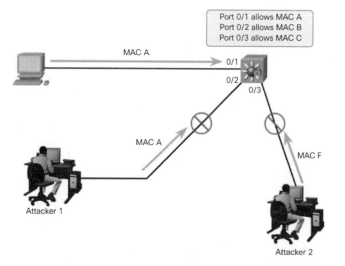

Figure 5-11 Port Security Operation

If a port is configured as a secure port and the maximum number of MAC addresses is reached, any additional attempts to connect by unknown MAC addresses will generate a security violation. Figure 5-11 summarizes these points.

Mitigate VLAN Attacks (5.1.2.3)

Figure 5-12 and the list that follows explain the best method to prevent basic VLAN attacks.

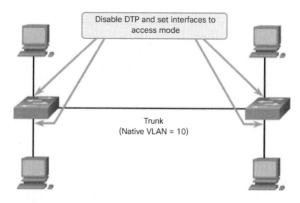

Figure 5-12 Secure VLANs

- Disable DTP (auto trunking) negotiations on nontrunking ports by using the **switchport mode access** interface configuration command.

- Manually enable the trunk link on a trunking port using the **switchport mode trunk** interface configuration command.

- Disable DTP (auto trunking) negotiations on trunking ports using the **switchport non-negotiate** interface configuration command.

- Set the native VLAN to be something other than VLAN 1. Set it on an unused VLAN using the **switchport trunk native vlan** *vlan_number* interface configuration mode command.

- Disable unused ports and assign them to an unused VLAN.

Mitigate DHCP Attacks (5.1.2.4)

A DHCP spoofing attack occurs when a rogue DHCP server is connected to the network and provides false IP configuration parameters to legitimate clients. DHCP spoofing is dangerous because clients can be leased IP information for malicious DNS server addresses, malicious default gateways, and malicious IP assignments.

Security best practices recommend using DHCP snooping to mitigate DHCP spoofing attacks.

When DHCP snooping is enabled on an interface or VLAN and a switch receives a DHCP packet on an untrusted port, the switch compares the source packet information with that held in the DHCP Snooping Binding Database. The switch will deny packets containing any of the following information:

- Unauthorized DHCP server messages coming from an untrusted port

- Unauthorized DHCP client messages not adhering to the DHCP Snooping Binding Database or rate limits

In a large network, the *DHCP Snooping Binding Database* may take time to build after it is enabled. For example, it could take two days for DHCP snooping to complete the database if DHCP lease time is four days.

DHCP snooping recognizes two types of ports:

- **Trusted DHCP ports:** Only ports connecting to upstream DHCP servers should be trusted. These ports should lead to legitimate DHCP servers replying with DHCP Offer and DHCP Ack messages. Trusted ports must be explicitly identified in the configuration.

- **Untrusted ports:** These ports connect to hosts that should not be providing DHCP server messages. By default, all switch ports are untrusted.

Figure 5-13 provides a visual example of how DHCP snooping ports should be assigned on a network. Notice how the trusted ports always lead to the legitimate DHCP server while all other ports (that is, access ports connecting to endpoints) are untrusted by default.

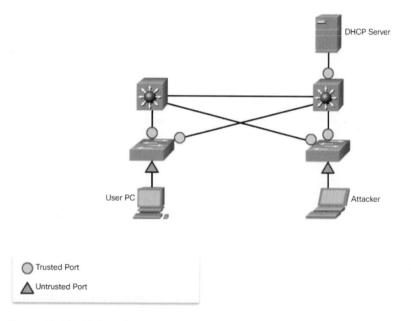

Figure 5-13   DCHP Snooping Trusted and Untrusted Port Assignments

Note

For more information on DHCP snooping, refer to the CCNA Security course.

Secure Administrative Access Using AAA (5.1.2.5)

To keep malicious users from gaining access to sensitive network equipment and services, administrators must enable access control. Access control limits who or what can use specific resources. It also limits the services or options that are available after access is granted.

Authentication on a Cisco device can be implemented using different methods, and each method offers varying levels of security. The Authentication, Authorization, and Accounting (AAA) framework is used to help secure device access. AAA authentication can be used to authenticate users for administrative access, or it can be used to authenticate users for remote network access.

Cisco provides two common methods of implementing AAA services:

- *Local AAA Authentication*: Local AAA uses a local database for authentication. This method is sometimes known as self-contained authentication. It stores usernames and passwords locally in the Cisco router, and users authenticate against the local database. Local AAA is ideal for small networks.

- *Server-Based AAA Authentication*: Server-based AAA authentication is a much more scalable solution. With this method, the router accesses a central AAA server that contains the usernames and passwords for all users. The AAA server functions as a central authentication system for all infrastructure devices.

Figure 5-14 and the list that follows illustrate how local AAA authentication works.

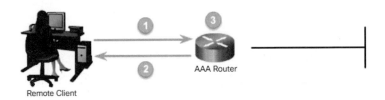

Figure 5-14   Local AAA Authentication

1. The client establishes a connection with the router.

2. The AAA router prompts the user for a username and password.

3. The router authenticates the username and password using the local database, and the user is provided access to the network based on the information in the local database.

Figure 5-15 and the list that follows illustrate how server-based AAA authentication works.

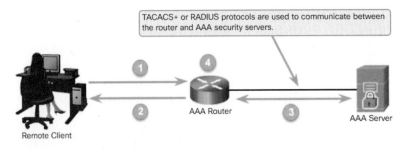

Figure 5-15   Server-Based AAA Authentication

1. The client establishes a connection with the router.

2. The AAA router prompts the user for a username and password.

3. The router authenticates the username and password using a remote AAA server.

As shown in Figure 5-15, the AAA-enabled router uses either the TACACS+ protocol or the RADIUS protocol to communicate with the AAA server. While both protocols can be used to communicate between a router and AAA servers, TACACS+ is considered the more secure protocol. The reason is that all TACACS+ protocol exchanges are encrypted, while RADIUS only encrypts the user's password. RADIUS does not encrypt usernames, accounting information, or any other information carried in the RADIUS message.

Note

For more information on AAA, refer to the CCNA Security course.

Secure Device Access Using 802.1X (5.1.2.6)

Network user authentication can be provided with AAA server-based authentication. The 802.1X protocol/standard can be used to authenticate network devices on the corporate network. There is another protocol used to secure computers connecting to a LAN.

The IEEE 802.1X standard defines a port-based access control and authentication protocol. IEEE 802.1X restricts unauthorized workstations from connecting to a LAN through publicly accessible switch ports. The authentication server authenticates each workstation that is connected to a switch port before making available any services offered by the switch or the LAN.

With 802.1X port-based authentication, the devices in the network have specific roles, as shown in Figure 5-16 and described in the list that follows.

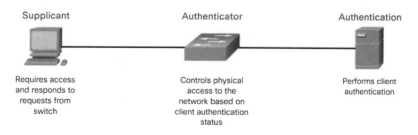

Supplicant

Requires access
and responds to
requests from
switch

Authenticator

Controls physical
access to the
network based on
client authentication
status

Authentication

Performs client
authentication

Figure 5-16   802.1X Roles

- *Supplicant*: This is usually the 802.1X-enabled port on the client device. The device requests access to LAN and switch services and then responds to requests from the switch. In Figure 5-16, the device is a PC running 802.1X-compliant client software. Another client supplicant is the 802.1X-compliant wireless device such as a laptop or tablet.

- *Authenticator*: This is usually a switch that controls physical access to the network based on the authentication status of the client. The switch acts as an intermediary (proxy) between the client and the authentication server. It requests identifying information from the client, verifies that information with the authentication server, and relays a response to the client. The switch uses a RADIUS software agent, which is responsible for encapsulating and de-encapsulating the *Extensible Authentication Protocol (EAP)* frames and interacting with the authentication server. Another device that could act as authenticator is a wireless access point acting as the intermediary between the wireless client and the authentication server.

- **Authentication server:** This server performs the actual authentication of the client. The authentication server validates the identity of the client and notifies the switch or other authenticator such as a wireless access point whether the client is authorized to access the LAN and switch services. Because the switch acts as the proxy, the authentication service is transparent to the client. The RADIUS security system with EAP extensions is the only supported authentication server.

Note

For more information on 802.1X, refer to the CCNA Security course.

Interactive Graphic

Activity 5.1.2.7: Identify the Security Best Practice

Refer to the online course to complete this activity.

SNMP (5.2)

In this section, you configure SNMP to monitor network operations in a small- to medium-sized business network.

SNMP Operation (5.2.1)

In this topic, you learn how SNMP operates.

Introduction to SNMP (5.2.1.1)

Simple Network Management Protocol (SNMP) was developed to allow administrators to manage nodes such as servers, workstations, routers, switches, and security appliances on an IP network. It enables network administrators to monitor and manage network performance, find and solve network problems, and plan for network growth.

SNMP is an application layer protocol that provides a message format for communication between managers and agents. The SNMP system consists of three elements:

- *SNMP manager*
- *SNMP agents* (managed node)
- *Management Information Base (MIB)*

To configure SNMP on a networking device, you first need to define the relationship between the manager and the agent.

The SNMP manager is part of a *network management system (NMS).* The SNMP manager runs SNMP management software. As shown in Figure 5-17, the SNMP manager can collect information from an SNMP agent using the "get" action and can change configurations on an agent using the "set" action. In addition, SNMP agents can forward information directly to a network manager using *SNMP traps*.

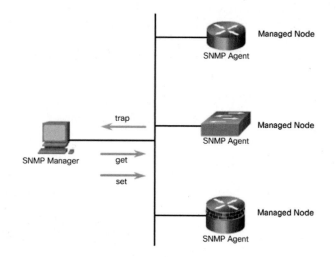

Figure 5-17   SNMP Elements

The SNMP agent and MIB reside on SNMP client devices. Network devices that must be managed such as switches, routers, servers, firewalls, and workstations are equipped with an SMNP agent software module. MIBs store data about the device and operational statistics and are meant to be available to authenticated remote users. The SNMP agent is responsible for providing access to the local MIB.

SNMP defines how management information is exchanged between network management applications and management agents. The SNMP manager polls the agents and queries the MIB for SNMP agents on UDP port 161. SNMP agents send any SNMP traps to the SNMP manager on UDP port 162.

SNMP Operation (5.2.1.2)

SNMP agents that reside on managed devices collect and store information about the device and its operation. This information is stored by the agent locally in the MIB. The SNMP manager then uses the SNMP agent to access information within the MIB.

Ther two primary SNMP manager requests are

- *get request*: Used by the NMS to query the device for data.

- *set request*: Used by the NMS to change the configuration in the agent device. A set request can also initiate actions within a device.

For example, a set can cause a router to reboot, send a configuration file, or receive a configuration file. The SNMP manager uses the get and set actions to perform the operations described in Table 5-1.

Table 5-1   SNMP Operations

Operation	Description
get-request	Retrieves a value from a specific variable
get-next-request	Retrieves a value from a variable within a table; the SNMP manager does not need to know the exact variable name; a sequential search is performed to find the needed variable from within a table
get-bulk-request	Retrieves large blocks of data, such as multiple rows in a table, that would otherwise require the transmission of many small blocks of data; only works with SNMPv2 or later
get-response	Replies to a get-request, get-next-request, and set-request sent by an NMS
set-request	Stores a value in a specific variable

The SNMP agent responds to SNMP manager requests as follows:

- **Get an MIB variable:** The SNMP agent performs this function in response to a GetRequest-PDU from the network manager. The agent retrieves the value of the requested MIB variable and responds to the network manager with that value.

- **Set an MIB variable:** The SNMP agent performs this function in response to a SetRequest-PDU from the network manager. The SNMP agent changes the value of the MIB variable to the value specified by the network manager. An SNMP agent reply to a set request includes the new settings in the device.

Figure 5-18 illustrates the use of an SNMP GetRequest to determine if interface G0/0 is up/up.

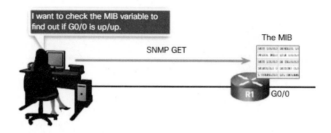

Figure 5-18   SNMP Get Request

SNMP Agent Traps (5.2.1.3)

An NMS periodically polls the SNMP agents residing on managed devices, by querying the device for data using the get request. Using this process, a network management application can collect information to monitor traffic loads and to verify device configurations of managed devices. The information can be displayed via a GUI on the NMS. Averages, minimums, or maximums can be calculated, the data can be graphed, or thresholds can be set to trigger a notification process when the thresholds are exceeded. For example, an NMS can monitor CPU utilization of a Cisco router. The SNMP manager samples the value periodically and presents this information in a graph for the network administrator to use in creating a *network baseline*, creating a report, or viewing real-time information.

Periodic SNMP polling does have disadvantages. First, there is a delay between the time that an event occurs and the time that it is noticed (via polling) by the NMS. Second, there is a trade-off between polling frequency and bandwidth usage.

To mitigate these disadvantages, it is possible for SNMP agents to generate and send traps to inform the NMS immediately of certain events. Traps are unsolicited messages alerting the SNMP manager to a condition or event on the network. Examples of trap conditions include, but are not limited to, improper user authentication, restarts, link status (up or down), MAC address tracking, closing of a TCP connection, loss of connection to a neighbor, or other significant events. Trap-directed notifications reduce network and agent resources by eliminating the need for some SNMP polling requests.

Figure 5-19 illustrates the use of an SNMP trap to alert the network administrator that interface G0/0 has failed. The NMS software can send the network administrator a text message, pop up a window on the NMS software, or turn the router icon red in the NMS GUI.

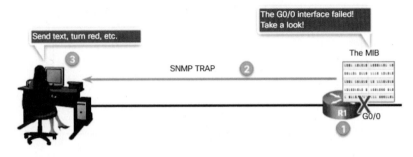
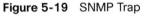

Figure 5-19   SNMP Trap

Figure 5-20 illustrates the exchange of all SNMP messages.

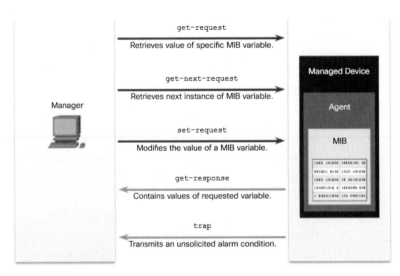

Figure 5-20   SNMP Operations

SNMP Versions (5.2.1.4)

SNMP is available in several versions:

- **SNMPv1:** This is the Simple Network Management Protocol, a Full Internet Standard, defined in RFC 1157.

- **SNMPv2c:** Defined in RFCs 1901 to 1908, this version utilizes community-string-based Administrative Framework.

- **SNMPv3:** This interoperable standards-based protocol was originally defined in RFCs 2273 to 2275; it provides secure access to devices by authenticating and encrypting packets over the network. It includes these security features: message integrity to ensure that a packet was not tampered with in transit; authentication to determine that the message is from a valid source, and encryption to prevent an unauthorized source from reading the contents of a message.

All versions use SNMP managers, agents, and MIBs. Cisco IOS software supports the preceding three versions. Version 1 is a legacy solution and not often encountered in networks today; therefore, this course focuses on versions 2c and 3.

Both SNMPv1 and SNMPv2c use a community-based form of security. The community of managers able to access the agent's MIB is defined by an ACL and password.

Unlike SNMPv1, SNMPv2c includes a bulk retrieval mechanism and more detailed error message reporting to management stations. The bulk retrieval mechanism retrieves tables and large quantities of information, minimizing the number of round trips required. The SNMPv2c improved error-handling includes expanded error codes that distinguish different kinds of error conditions. These conditions are reported through a single error code in SNMPv1. Error return codes in SNMPv2c include the error type.

Note

SNMPv1 and SNMPv2c offer minimal security features. Specifically, SNMPv1 and SNMPv2c can neither authenticate the source of a management message nor provide encryption. SNMPv3 is most currently described in RFCs 3410 to 3415. It adds methods to ensure the secure transmission of critical data between managed devices.

SNMPv3 provides for both security models and security levels. A security model is an authentication strategy set up for a user and the group within which the user resides. A security level is the permitted level of security within a security model. A combination of the security level and the security model determine which security mechanism is used when handling an SNMP packet. Available security models are SNMPv1, SNMPv2c, and SNMPv3.

Table 5-2 identifies the characteristics of the different combinations of security models and levels.

Table 5-2   SNMP Security Models and Levels

Model	Level	Authentication	Encryption	Result
SNMPv1	noAuthNoPriv	Community string	No	Uses a community string match for authentication
SNMPv2c	noAuthNoPriv	Community string	No	Uses a community string match for authentication
SNMPv3	noAuthNoPriv	Username	No	Uses a username match for authentication (an improvement over SNMPv2c)
SNMPv3	authNoPriv	Message Digest 5 (MD5) or Secure Hash Algorithm (SHA)	No	Provides authentication based on the HMAC-MD5 or HMAC-SHA algorithms
SNMPv3	authPriv (requires the cryptographic software image)	MD5 or SHA	Data Encryption Standard (DES) or Advanced Encryption Standard (AES)	Provides authentication based on the HMAC-MD5 or HMAC-SHA algorithms. Allows specifying the User-based Security Model (USM) with these encryption algorithms: ■ DES 56-bit encryption in addition to authentication based on the CBC-DES (DES-56) standard. ■ 3DES 168-bit encryption ■ AES 128-bit, 192-bit, or 256-bit encryption

A network administrator must configure the SNMP agent to use the SNMP version supported by the NMS. Because an agent can communicate with multiple SNMP managers, it is possible to configure the software to support communications using SNMPv1, SNMPv2c, or SNMPv3.

Community Strings (5.2.1.5)

For SNMP to operate, the NMS must have access to the MIB. To ensure that access requests are valid, some form of authentication must be in place.

SNMPv1 and SNMPv2c use *community strings* that control access to the MIB. Community strings are plaintext passwords. SNMP community strings authenticate access to MIB objects.

The two types of community strings are

■ **Read-only (ro):** Provides access to the MIB variables but does not allow these variables to be changed, only read. Because security is minimal in version 2c, many organizations use SNMPv2c in read-only mode.

■ **Read-write (rw):** Provides read and write access to all objects in the MIB.

To view or set MIB variables, the user must specify the appropriate community string for read or write access.

Figures 5-21 through 5-24 demonstrate how SNMP operates with the community string.

Step 1.   A customer has called to report a problem that access to her web server is slow (see Figure 5-21).

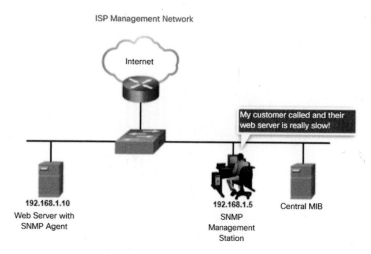

Figure 5-21   Community String Example: Step 1

Step 2.   The administrator uses the NMS to send a get request to the web server SNMP agent (get 192.168.1.10) for its connection statistics. The get request also includes the community string (2#B7!9). See Figure 5-22.

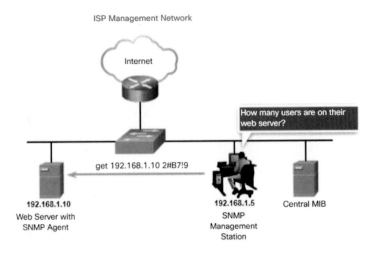

Figure 5-22   Community String Example: Step 2

Step 3.   The SNMP agent verifies the received community string and IP address before replying to the get request (see Figure 5-23).

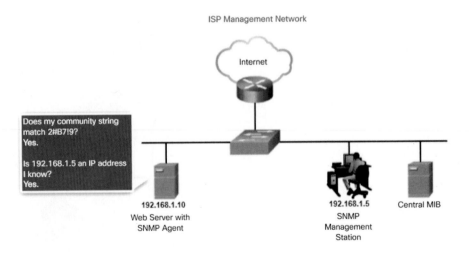

Figure 5-23   Community String Example: Step 3

Step 4.   The SNMP agent sends the requested statistics to the NMS with the connection variable reporting 10,000 users are currently connected to the web server (see Figure 5-24).

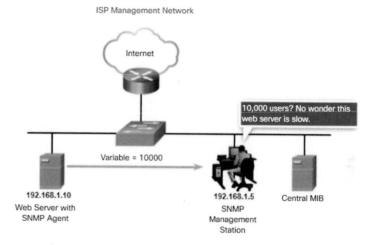

Figure 5-24   Community String Example: Step 4

Note

Plaintext passwords are not considered a security mechanism. The reason is that plaintext passwords are highly vulnerable to man-in-the-middle attacks, in which they are compromised through the capture of packets.

Management Information Base Object ID (5.2.1.6)

The MIB organizes variables hierarchically. MIB variables enable the management software to monitor and control the network device. Formally, the MIB defines each variable as an *object ID (OID)*. OIDs uniquely identify managed objects in the MIB hierarchy. The MIB organizes the OIDs based on RFC standards into a hierarchy of OIDs, usually shown as a tree.

The MIB tree for any given device includes some branches with variables common to many networking devices and some branches with variables specific to that device or vendor.

RFCs define some common public variables. Most devices implement these MIB variables. In addition, networking equipment vendors, like Cisco, can define their own private branches of the tree to accommodate new variables specific to their devices. Figure 5-25 shows portions of the MIB structure defined by Cisco Systems, Inc.

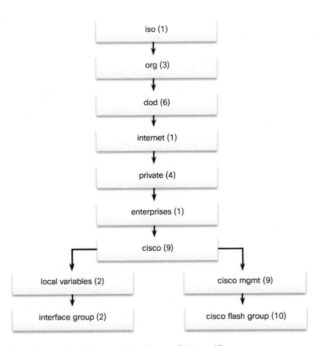

Figure 5-25   Management Information Base Object ID

Note how the OID can be described in words or numbers to help locate a particular variable in the tree. OIDs belonging to Cisco are numbered as follows: .iso (1). org (3).dod (6).internet (1).private (4).enterprises (1).cisco (9). Therefore, the OID is 1.3.6.1.4.1.9.

Because the CPU is one of the key resources, it should be measured continuously. CPU statistics should be compiled on the NMS and graphed. Observing CPU utilization over an extended time period allows the administrator to establish a baseline estimate for CPU utilization. Threshold values can then be set relative to this baseline. When CPU utilization exceeds this threshold, notifications are sent. An SNMP graphing tool can periodically poll SNMP agents (such as a router) and graph the gathered values. Figure 5-26 illustrates 5-minute samples of router CPU utilization over the period of a few weeks.

The data is retrieved via the snmpget utility, issued on the NMS. Using the *snmpget* utility, you can manually retrieve real-time data or have the NMS run a report that would give you a period of time that you could use the data to get the average. The snmpget utility requires that the SNMP version, the correct community, the IP address of the network device to query, and the OID number are set.

Figure 5-27 demonstrates the use of the freeware snmpget utility, which allows quick retrieval of information from the MIB.

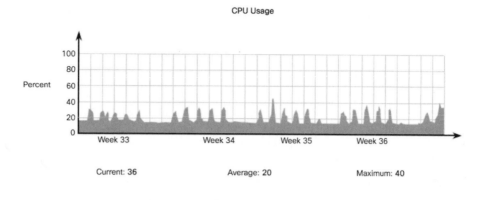

CPU Usage

Figure 5-26 SNMP Graphing Tool

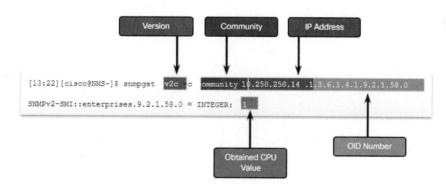

Figure 5-27 The snmpget Utility

Figure 5-27 shows a sample **snmpget** utility command with several parameters, including

- **-v2c:** Version of SNMP

- **-c community:** SNMP password, called a community string

- **10.250.250.14:** IP address of monitored device

- **1.3.6.1.4.1.9.2.1.58.0:** OID of MIB variable

The last line shows the response. The output shows a shortened version of the MIB variable. It then lists the actual value in the MIB location. In this case, the 5-minute exponential moving average of the CPU busy percentage is 11 percent. The utility gives some insight into the basic mechanics of how SNMP works. However, working with long MIB variable names like 1.3.6.1.4.1.9.2.1.58.0 can be problematic for the average user. More commonly, the network operations staff uses a network management product with an easy-to-use GUI, with the entire MIB data variable naming transparent to the user.

Many NMSs use simple GUI dashboards that make the entire MIB data variable naming transparent to the user.

The Cisco SNMP Navigator on the Cisco.com website allows a network administrator to research details about a particular OID. Figure 5-28 displays an example associated with a configuration change on a Cisco 2960 switch.

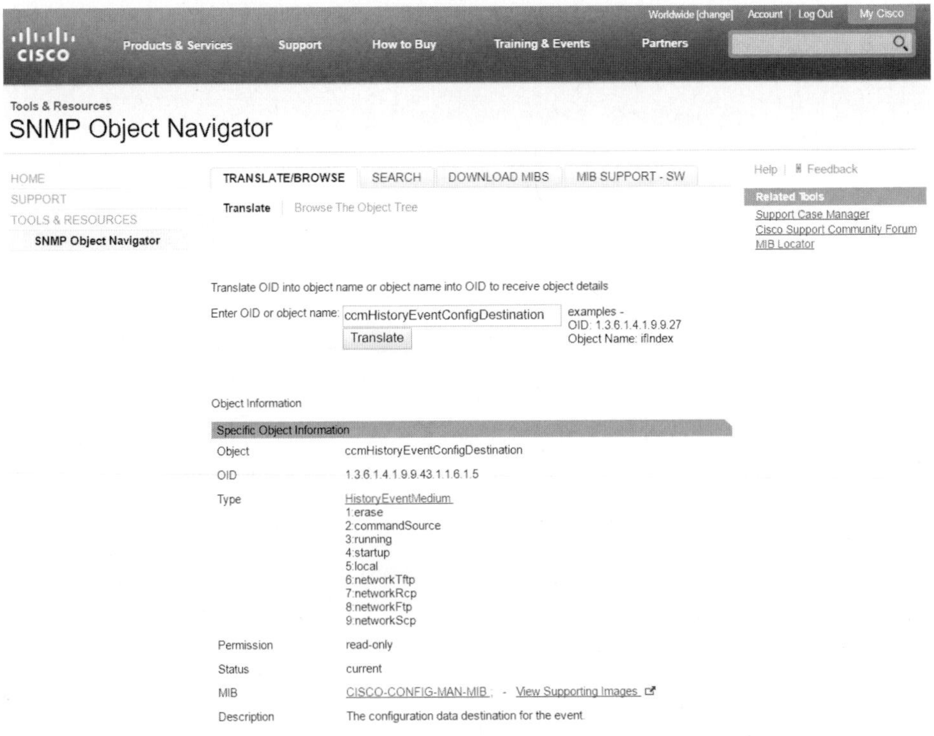

Figure 5-28   SNMP Object Navigator

SNMPv3 (5.2.1.7)

Simple Network Management Protocol version 3 (SNMPv3) authenticates and encrypts packets over the network to provide secure access to devices. Adding authentication and encryption to SNMPv3 addresses the vulnerabilities of earlier versions of SNMP.

SNMPv3 authenticates and encrypts packets over the network to provide secure access to devices, as shown in Figure 5-29. This version addresses the vulnerabilities of earlier versions of SNMP.

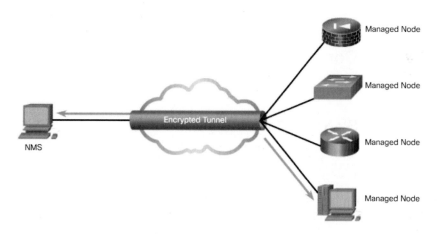

Figure 5-29   SNMPv3 Message Encryption and Authentication

SNMPv3 provides three security features:

- **Message integrity and authentication:** Transmissions from the SNMP manager (NMS) to agents (managed nodes) can be authenticated to guarantee the identity of the sender and the integrity and timeliness of a message. This ensures that a packet has not been tampered with in transit and is from a valid source.

- **Encryption:** SNMPv3 messages may be encrypted to ensure privacy. Encryption scrambles the contents of a packet to prevent an unauthorized source from seeing it.

- **Access control:** Restricts SNMP managers to certain actions on specific portions of data. For example, you may not want the NMS to have full access to your firewall device.

Interactive Graphic

Activity 5.2.1.8: Identify Characteristics of SNMP Versions

Refer to the online course to complete this activity.

Lab 5.2.1.9: Researching Network Monitoring Software

In this lab, you complete the following objectives:

- Part 1: Survey Your Understanding of Network Monitoring
- Part 2: Research Network Monitoring Tools
- Part 3: Select a Network Monitoring Tool

Configuring SNMP (5.2.2)

In this topic, you configure SNMP to compile network performance data.

Steps for Configuring SNMP (5.2.2.1)

A network administrator can configure SNMPv2 to obtain network information from network devices. The basic steps to configuring SNMP are all in global configuration mode.

Step 1.   (Required) Configure the community string and access level (read-only or read-write) with the **snmp-server community** *string* **ro | rw** global configuration command.

Step 2.   (Optional) Document the location of the device using the **snmp-server location** *text* global configuration command.

Step 3.   (Optional) Document the system contact using the **snmp-server contact** *text* global configuration command.

Step 4.   (Optional) Restrict SNMP access to NMS hosts (SNMP managers) that are permitted by an ACL: define the ACL and then reference the ACL with the **snmp-server community** *string access-list-number-or-name* global configuration command. This command can be used both to specify a community string and to restrict SNMP access via ACLs. Step 1 and Step 4 can be combined into one step, if desired; the Cisco networking device combines the two commands into one if they are entered separately.

Step 5.   (Optional) Specify the recipient of the SNMP trap operations (that is, trap manager) with the **snmp-server host** *host-id* [**version** {1| 2c | 3 [**auth** | **noauth** | **priv**]}] *community-string* global configuration command. By default, no trap manager is defined.

Step 6.   (Optional) Enable traps on an SNMP agent with the **snmp-server enable traps** *notification-types* global configuration command. If no trap notification types are specified in this command, all trap types are sent. Repeated use of this command is required if a particular subset of trap types is desired.

Example 5-1 shows the SNMP v2c configuration for the router, R1, in Figure 5-30.

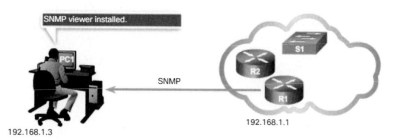

Figure 5-30   Configuration Supports the SNMP Manager

Example 5-1 SNMP Configuration

```
R1(config)# snmp-server community batonaug ro SNMP_ACL
R1(config)# snmp-server location NOC_SNMP_MANAGER
R1(config)# snmp-server contact Wayne World
R1(config)# snmp-server host 192.168.1.3 version 2c batonaug
R1(config)# snmp-server enable traps
R1(config)# ip access-list standard SNMP_ACL
R1(config-std-nacl)# permit 192.168.1.3
```

Note

By default, SNMP does not have any traps set. Without the **snmp-server enable traps** *notification-types* command, SNMP managers must poll for all relevant information.

Verifying SNMP Configuration (5.2.2.2)

Several software solutions are available for viewing SNMP output. For our purposes, the *Kiwi Syslog Server* displays SNMP messages associated with SNMP traps.

PC1 and R1 are configured to demonstrate output on an SNMP manager as related to SNMP traps.

As shown previously in Figure 5-30, PC1 is assigned the IP address 192.168.1.3/24. The Kiwi Syslog Server is installed on PC1.

After R1 is configured, whenever an event triggers a trap, the SNMP trap is sent to the SNMP manager. For instance, if an interface comes up, a trap is sent to the server. Configuration changes on the router also trigger SNMP traps to be sent to the SNMP manager. A list of over 60 trap notification types can be seen with the **snmp-server enable traps ?** command. In the configuration of R1, no trap notification types are specified in the **snmp-server enable traps** *notification-types* command; therefore, all traps are sent.

In Figure 5-31, a check box is checked in the **Setup** menu to indicate that the network administrator wants SNMP manager software to listen for SNMP traps on UDP port 162.

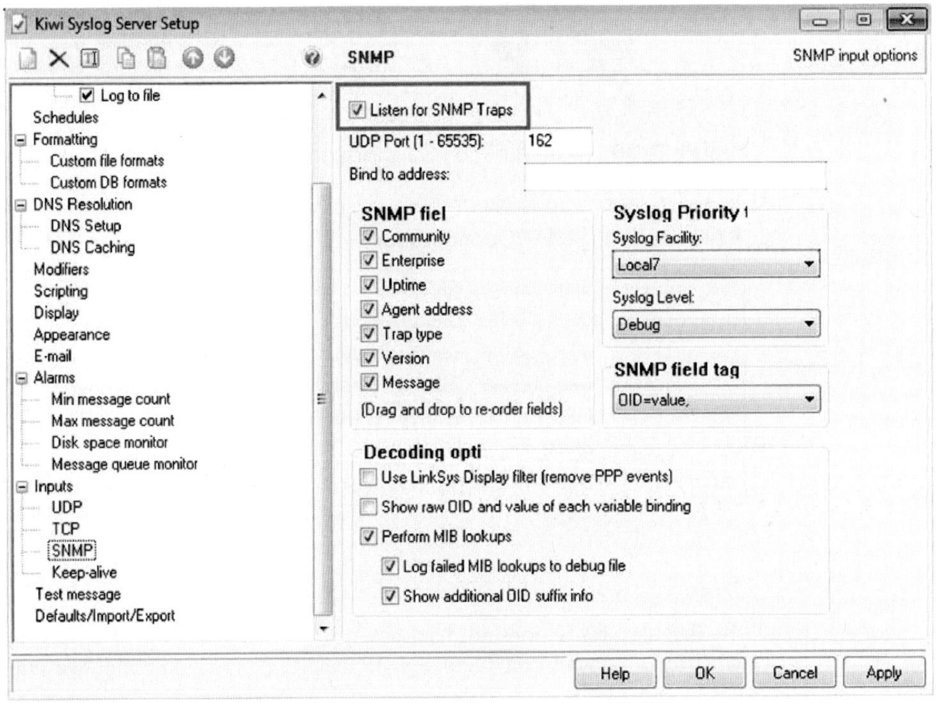

Figure 5-31   Setting Syslog to Listen for SNMP

In Figure 5-32, the top row of the displayed SNMP trap output indicates that interface GigabitEthernet0/0 changed state to up. Also, each time the global configuration mode is entered from privileged EXEC mode, the SNMP manager receives a trap, as shown in the highlighted row.

To verify the SNMP configuration, use any of the variations of the **show snmp** privileged EXEC mode command. The most useful command is simply the **show snmp** command because it displays the information that is commonly of interest when examining the SNMP configuration. Unless there is an involved SNMPv3 configuration, for the most part the other command options display only selected portions of the output of the **show snmp** command. Example 5-2 provides an example of **show snmp** output.

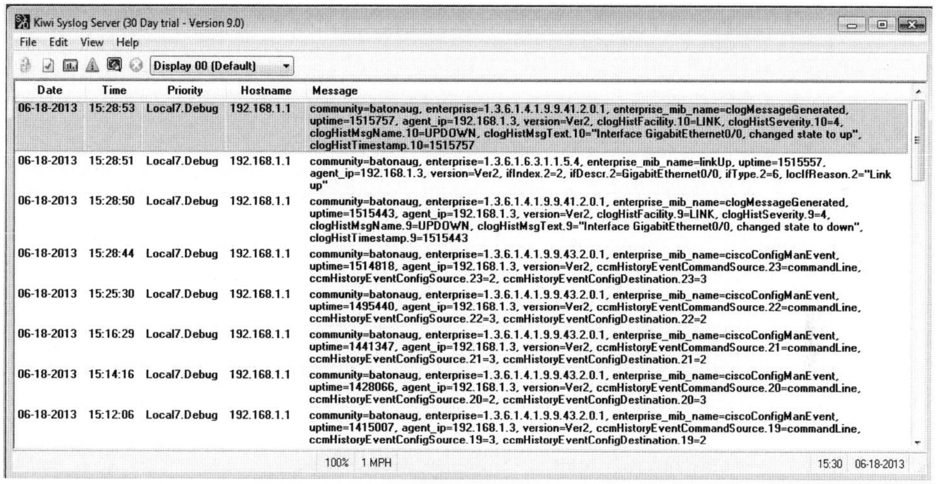

Figure 5-32   Viewing the SNMP Trap Logs

Example 5-2   Verifying SNMP Configuration

```
R1# show snmp
Chassis: FTX1636848Z
Contact: Wayne World
Location: NOC_SNMP_MANAGER
0 SNMP packets input
    0 Bad SNMP version errors
    0 Unknown community name
    0 Illegal operation for community name supplied
    0 Encoding errors
    0 Number of requested variables
    0 Number of altered variables
    0 Get-request PDUs
    0 Get-next PDUs
    0 Set-request PDUs
    0 Input queue packet drops (Maximum queue size 1000)
19 SNMP packets output
    0 Too big errors (Maximum packet size 1500)
    0 No such name errors
    0 Bad values errors
    0 General errors
    0 Response PDUs
    19 Trap PDUs
```

```
SNMP Dispatcher:
    queue 0/75 (current/max), 0 dropped
SNMP Engine:
    queue 0/1000 (current/max), 0 dropped

SNMP logging: enabled
    Logging to 192.168.1.3.162, 0/10, 19 sent, 0 dropped.
```

The **show snmp** command output does not display information relating to the SNMP community string or, if applicable, the associated ACL. Example 5-3 displays the SNMP community string and ACL information, using the **show snmp community** command.

Example 5-3 SNMP Community Service

```
R1# show snmp community

Community name: ILMI
Community Index: cisco0
Community SecurityName: ILMI
storage-type: read-only          active

Community name: batonaug
Community Index: cisco7
Community SecurityName: batonaug
storage-type: nonvolatile        active       access-list: SNMP_ACL

Community name: batonaug@1
Community Index: cisco8
Community SecurityName: batonaug@1
storage-type: nonvolatile        active       access-list: SNMP_ACL
```

SNMP Best Practices (5.2.2.3)

SNMP is useful for monitoring and troubleshooting. For example, as illustrated in Figure 5-33, the NMS manager can manage the router and switch infrastructure using SNMP and Syslog.

SNMP can also create security vulnerabilities. For this reason, prior to implementing SNMP, be mindful of security best practices.

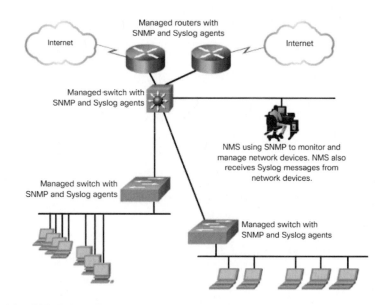

Figure 5-33   SNMP Best Practices

Both SNMPv1 and SNMPv2c rely on SNMP community strings in plaintext to authenticate access to MIB objects. These community strings, as with all passwords, should be carefully chosen to ensure that they are not too easy to crack. Additionally, community strings should be changed at regular intervals and in accordance with network security policies. For example, the strings should be changed when a network administrator changes roles or leaves the company. If SNMP is used only to monitor devices, use read-only communities.

Ensure that SNMP messages do not spread beyond the management consoles. ACLs should be used to prevent SNMP messages from going beyond the required devices. ACLs should also be used on the monitored devices to limit access for management systems only.

SNMPv3 is recommended because it provides security authentication and encryption. A network administrator can implement a number of other global configuration mode commands to take advantage of the authentication and encryption support in SNMPv3:

- The **snmp-server group** *groupname* {**v1** | **v2c** | **v3** {**auth** | **noauth** | **priv**}} command creates a new SNMP group on the device.

- The **snmp-server user** *username groupname* **v3** [**encrypted**] [**auth** {**md5** | **sha**} *auth-password*] [**priv** {**des** | **3des** | **aes** {**128** | **192** | **256**}} *priv-password*] command is used to add a new user to the SNMP group specified in the **snmp-server group** *groupname* command.

Steps for Configuring SNMPv3 (5.2.2.4)

SNMPv3 can be secured with the following four steps:

Step 1. Configure a standard ACL that will be used to permit access for authorized SNMP managers.

Step 2. Configure an SNMP view with the **snmp-server view** *view-name oid-tree* global configuration command to identify which OIDs the SNMP manager will be able to read. Configuring a view is required to limit SNMP messages to read-only access.

Step 3. Configure the SNMP group features with the **snmp-server group** *group-name* **v3 priv read** *view-name* **access** [*acl-number* | *acl-name*] global configuration command.

This command has the following parameters:

- Configure a name for the group.
- Set the SNMP version.
- Specify the required authentication and encryption.
- Associate the view from Step 2 to the group.
- Specify read or read-write access.
- Filter the group with the ACL configured in Step 1.

Step 4. Configure the SNMP group user features with the **snmp-server user** *username group-name* **v3 auth** {**md5** | **sha**} *auth-password* **priv** {**des** | **3des** | **aes** {**128** | **192** | **256**}} *priv-password* global configuration command.

The command has the following parameters:

- Configure a username.
- Associate the user with the group name that was configured in Step 3.
- Set the SNMP version.
- Set the authentication type. SHA is preferred and should be supported by the SNMP management software.
- Set the encryption type.
- Configure an encryption password.

Verifying SNMPv3 Configuration (5.2.2.5)

Example 5-4 displays a sample SNMPv3 configuration.

Example 5-4 SNMPv3 Configuration

```
R1(config)# ip access-list standard PERMIT-ADMIN
R1(config-std-nacl)# permit 192.168.1.0 0.0.0.255
R1(config-std-nacl)# exit
R1(config)#
R1(config)# snmp-server view SNMP-RO iso included
R1(config)# snmp-server group ADMIN v3 priv read SNMP-RO access PERMIT-ADMIN
R1(config)# snmp-server user BOB ADMIN v3 auth sha cisco12345 priv aes 128
  cisco54321
R1(config)# end
R1#
```

The example first configures a standard ACL named PERMIT-ADMIN permitting only the 192.168.1.0/24 network. All hosts attached to this network will be allowed to access the SNMP agent running on R1.

The example then creates an SNMP view named SNMP-RO that is configured to include the entire ISO tree from the MIB. On a production network, the network administrator would probably configure this view to include only the MIB OIDs that were necessary for monitoring and managing the network.

The example then creates an SNMP group with the name ADMIN. SNMP is set to version 3 with authentication and encryption required. The group is allowed read-only access to the view (SNMP-RO). Access for the group is limited by the PERMIT-ADMIN ACL.

Finally, an SNMP user (that is, BOB) is configured as a member of the group ADMIN. SNMP is set to version 3. Authentication is set to use SHA, and an authentication password is configured. Although R1 supports up to AES 256 encryption, the SNMP management software supports only AES 128. Therefore, the encryption is set to AES 128, and an encryption password is configured.

Lab 5.2.2.6: Configuring SNMP

In this lab, you complete the following objectives:

- Part 1: Build the Network and Configure Basic Device Settings
- Part 2: Configure an SNMP Manager and Agents
- Part 3: Convert OID Codes with the Cisco SNMP Object Navigator

Cisco Switch Port Analyzer (5.3)

In this section, you learn how to troubleshoot a network problem using SPAN.

SPAN Overview (5.3.1)

In this topic, you learn about the features and characteristics of SPAN.

Port Mirroring (5.3.1.1)

A *packet analyzer* (also known as a sniffer, packet sniffer, or traffic sniffer) is a valuable tool to help monitor and troubleshoot a network. A packet analyzer is typically software that captures packets entering and exiting a network interface card (NIC). For example, Wireshark is a packet analyzer that is commonly used to capture and analyze packets on a local computer.

What if a network administrator wanted to capture packets from many other key devices and not just the local NIC? A solution is to configure networking devices to copy and send traffic going to ports of interest to a port connected to a packet analyzer. The administrator could then analyze network traffic from various sources in the network.

However, the basic operation of a modern switched network disables the packet analyzer's capability to capture traffic from other sources. For instance, a user running Wireshark can only capture traffic going to his or her NIC. That user cannot capture traffic between another host and a server. The reason is that a Layer 2 switch populates its MAC address table based on the source MAC address and the ingress port of the Ethernet frame. After the table is built, the switch forwards only traffic destined for a MAC address directly to the corresponding port. This prevents a packet analyzer connected to another port on the switch from "hearing" other switch traffic.

The solution to this dilemma is to enable *port mirroring*. The port mirroring feature allows a switch to copy and send Ethernet frames from specific ports to the destination port connected to a packet analyzer. The original frame is still forwarded in the usual manner.

Figure 5-34 shows an example of port mirroring. Notice how traffic between PC1 and PC2 is also being sent to the laptop that has a packet analyzer installed.

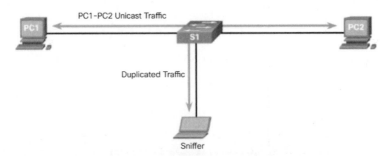

Figure 5-34   Switch Frame Duplication for Packet Capture

Analyzing Suspicious Traffic (5.3.1.2)

The Switched Port Analyzer (SPAN) feature on Cisco switches is a type of port mirroring that sends copies of the frame entering a port, out another port on the same switch. SPAN allows administrators or devices to collect and analyze traffic.

As shown in Figure 5-35, SPAN is commonly implemented to deliver traffic to specialized devices, including

■ **Packet analyzers:** Using software such as Wireshark, administrators can capture and analyze traffic for troubleshooting purposes. For example, an administrator can capture traffic destined to a server to troubleshoot the suboptimal operation of a network application.

■ **Intrusion prevention systems (IPSs):** IPSs are focused on the security aspect of traffic and are implemented to detect network attacks as they happen, issuing alerts or even blocking the malicious packets as the attack takes place. IPSs are typically deployed as a service on an ISR G2 router or using a dedicated device such as an IPS sensor.

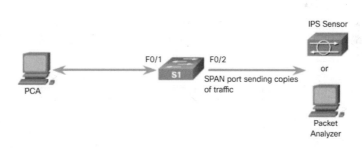

Figure 5-35 Implementing Cisco SPAN

While packet analyzers are commonly used for troubleshooting purposes, an IPS looks for specific patterns in traffic. As the traffic flows through the IPS, it analyzes traffic in real time and takes action on the discovery of malicious traffic patterns.

Modern networks are switched environments. Therefore, SPAN is crucial for effective IPS operation. SPAN can be implemented as either *local SPAN* or *remote SPAN (RSPAN)*.

Local SPAN (5.3.1.3)

In a local SPAN implementation, traffic on a switch is mirrored to another port on that switch. As described in Table 5-3, various terms are used to identify incoming and outgoing ports.

Table 5-3   SPAN Terminology

Term	Definition
Ingress traffic	This is traffic that enters the switch.
Egress traffic	This is traffic that leaves the switch.
Source (SPAN) port	This is a port that is monitored with use of the SPAN feature.
Destination (SPAN) port	This is a port that monitors source ports, usually where a packet analyzer, IDS, or IPS is connected. This port is also called the monitor port.
SPAN session	This is an association of a destination port with one or more source ports.
Source VLAN	This is the VLAN monitored for traffic analysis.

Figure 5-36 identifies the SPAN ports.

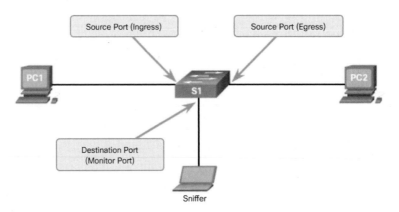

Figure 5-36   SPAN Ports

A SPAN session is the association between source ports (or VLANs) and a destination port.

Traffic entering or leaving the source port (or VLAN) is replicated by the switch on the destination port. Although SPAN can support multiple source ports under the same session or an entire VLAN as the traffic source, a SPAN session does not support both. Both Layer 2 and Layer 3 ports can be configured as source ports.

When configuring SPAN, consider these three important things:

- The destination port cannot be a source port, and the source port cannot be a destination port.

- The number of destination ports is platform-dependent. Some platforms allow for more than one destination port.

- The destination port is no longer a normal switch port. Only monitored traffic passes through that port.

The SPAN feature is said to be local when the monitored ports are all located on the same switch as the destination port. This feature is in contrast to remote SPAN (RSPAN).

Remote SPAN (5.3.1.4)

Remote SPAN (RSPAN) allows source and destination ports to be in different switches. RSPAN is useful when the packet analyzer or IPS is on a different switch than the traffic being monitored.

Table 5-4 describes RSPAN terms.

Table 5-4   RSPAN Terminology

Term	Definition
RSPAN source session	This is the source port or VLAN to copy traffic from.
RSPAN destination session	This is the destination VLAN or port to send the traffic to.
RSPAN VLAN	- A unique VLAN is required to transport the traffic from one switch to another. - VLAN is configured with the remote-span VLAN configuration command. - This VLAN must be defined on all switches in the path and must also be allowed on trunk ports between the source and destination.

Figure 5-37 illustrates how RSPAN is forwarded between two switches. Notice how RSPAN extends SPAN by enabling remote monitoring of multiple switches across the network.

RSPAN uses two sessions. One session is used as the source, and one session is used to copy or receive the traffic from a VLAN. The traffic for each RSPAN session is carried over trunk links in a user-specified RSPAN VLAN that is dedicated (for that RSPAN session) in all participating switches.

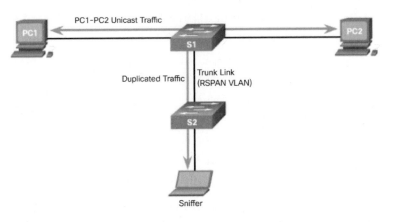

Figure 5-37   RSPAN Ports

Interactive Graphic

Activity 5.3.1.5: Identify SPAN Terminology

Refer to the online course to complete this activity.

SPAN Configuration (5.3.2)

In this topic, you configure local SPAN.

Configuring Local SPAN (5.3.2.1)

The SPAN feature on Cisco switches sends a copy of each frame that is entering the source port out the destination port and toward the packet analyzer or IPS. A session number is used to identify a local SPAN session.

SPAN is configured with the **monitor session** global configuration command. This command is used to associate a source port and a destination port with a SPAN session. A separate **monitor session** command is used for each session. A VLAN can be specified instead of a physical port.

To associate a SPAN session with a source port, use the **monitor session** *number* **source** [**interface** *interface* | **vlan** *vlan*] global configuration command.

To associate a SPAN session with a destination port, use the **monitor session** *number* **destination** [**interface** *interface* | **vlan** *vlan*] global configuration command.

For example, in Figure 5-38, PCA is connected to F0/1, and a computer with a packet analyzer application is connected to F0/2.

Figure 5-38 SPAN Configuration Topology

The objective is to capture all the traffic that is sent or received by PCA on port F0/1 and send a copy of those frames to the packet analyzer (or IPS) on port F0/2. The SPAN session on the switch will copy all the traffic that it sends and receives on source port F0/1 to the destination port F0/2. Example 5-5 shows the SPAN configuration.

Example 5-5 SPAN Configuration

```
S1(config)# monitor session 1 source interface fastethernet 0/1
S1(config)# monitor session 1 destination interface fastethernet 0/2
```

Verifying Local SPAN (5.3.2.2)

The **show monitor** command is used to verify the SPAN session. As shown in Example 5-6, the command displays the type of the session, the source ports for each traffic direction, and the destination port.

Example 5-6 Verifying SPAN

```
S1# show monitor
Session 1
---------
Type                    : Local Session
Source Ports            :
    Both                : Fa0/1
Destination Ports       : Fa0/2
    Encapsulation       : Native
            Ingress     : Disabled


S1#
```

In this example, the session number is 1, and the source port (F0/1) is mirroring incoming and outgoing traffic (both) to the destination port. The destination port (F0/2) will only forward egress traffic (Ingress = Disabled) to connected devices.

Lab 5.3.2.3: Implement a Local SPAN

In this lab, you complete the following objectives:

- Part 1: Build the Network and Verify Connectivity
- Part 2: Configure Local SPAN and Capture Copied Traffic with Wireshark

SPAN as a Troubleshooting Tool (5.3.3)

In this topic, you learn how to troubleshoot suspicious LAN traffic using SPAN.

Troubleshooting with SPAN Overview (5.3.3.1)

SPAN allows administrators to troubleshoot network issues. For example, a network application may be taking too long to execute tasks. To investigate, a network administrator may use SPAN to duplicate and redirect traffic to a packet analyzer such as Wireshark. The administrator can then analyze the traffic from all devices to troubleshoot suboptimal operation of the network application.

Older systems with faulty NICs can also cause issues. If SPAN is enabled on a switch to send traffic to a packet analyzer, a network technician can detect and isolate the end device causing the excess traffic, as shown Figure 5-39.

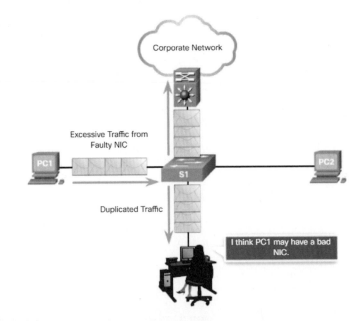

Figure 5-39   SPAN Troubleshooting Scenario

Lab 5.3.3.2: Troubleshoot LAN Traffic Using SPAN

In this lab, you complete the following objectives:

- Part 1: Build the Network and Verify Connectivity

- Part 2: Configure Local SPAN and Capture Copied Traffic with Wireshark

Summary (5.4)

At Layer 2, a number of vulnerabilities exist that require specialized mitigation techniques:

- MAC address table flooding attacks are addressed with port security.
- VLAN attacks are controlled by disabling DTP and following basic guidelines for configuring trunk ports.
- DHCP attacks are addressed with DHCP snooping.

The SNMP protocol has three elements: the manager, the agent, and the MIB. The SNMP manager resides on the NMS, and the agent and the MIB are on the client devices. The SNMP Manager can poll the client devices for information, or it can use a TRAP message that tells a client to report immediately if the client reaches a particular threshold. SNMP can also be used to change the configuration of a device. SNMPv3 is the recommended version because it provides security. SNMP is a comprehensive and powerful remote management tool. Nearly every item available in a **show** command is available through SNMP.

Switched Port Analyzer (SPAN) is used to mirror the traffic going to and/or coming from the host. It is commonly implemented to support traffic analyzers or IPS devices.

Practice

The following activities provide practice with the topics introduced in this chapter. The Labs and Class Activities are available in the companion *Connecting Networks v6 Labs & Study Guide* (ISBN 9781587134296). The Packet Tracer Activity instructions are also in the *Labs & Study Guide*. The PKA files are found in the online course.

Class Activities

Class Activity 5.0.1.2: Network Maintenance Development

Labs

Lab 5.2.1.9: Researching Network Monitoring Software

Lab 5.2.2.6: Configuring SNMP

Lab 5.3.2.3: Implement a Local SPAN

Lab 5.3.3.2: Troubleshoot LAN Traffic Using SPAN

Check Your Understanding Questions

Complete all the review questions listed here to test your understanding of the topics and concepts in this chapter. The appendix "Answers to the 'Check Your Understanding' Questions" lists the answers.

1. Which statement describes SNMP operation?

   A. A get request is used by the SNMP agent to query the device for data.

   B. A set request is used by the NMS to change configuration variables in the agent device.

   C. An NMS periodically polls the SNMP agents that are residing on managed devices by using traps to query the devices for data.

   D. An SNMP agent that resides on a managed device collects information about the device and stores that information remotely in the MIB that is located on the NMS.

2. Which SNMP feature provides a solution to the main disadvantage of SNMP polling?

   A. SNMP community strings

   B. SNMP get messages

   C. SNMP set messages

   D. SNMP trap messages

3. When SNMPv1 or SNMPv2 is being used, which feature provides secure access to MIB objects?

   A. Community strings

   B. Message integrity

   C. Packet encryption

   D. Source validation

4. Which SNMP version uses weak community string-based access control and supports bulk retrieval?

   A. SNMPv1

   B. SNMPv2c

   C. SNMPv3

   D. SNMPv2Classic

5. A network administrator has issued the **snmp-server user admin1 admin v3 encrypted auth md5 abc789 priv des 256 key99** command. What are two features of this command? (Choose two.)

    A. It adds a new user to the SNMP group.

    B. It allows a network administrator to configure a secret encrypted password on the SNMP server.

    C. It forces the network manager to log in to the agent to retrieve the SNMP messages.

    D. It restricts SNMP access to defined SNMP managers.

    E. It uses the MD5 authentication of the SNMP messages.

6. A network administrator issues two commands on a router:

    ```
    R1(config)# snmp-server host 10.10.50.25 version 2c campus
    R1(config)# snmp-server enable traps
    ```

    What can be concluded after the commands are entered?

    A. If an interface comes up, a trap is sent to the server.

    B. No traps are sent because the *notification-types* argument was not specified yet.

    C. The **snmp-server enable traps** command needs to be used repeatedly if a particular subset of trap types is desired.

    D. Traps are sent using the source IP address 10.10.50.25.

7. Which security feature should be enabled to prevent an attacker from overflowing the MAC address table of a switch?

    A. BPDU filter

    B. Port security .

    C. Root guard

    D. Storm control

8. What protocol should be disabled to help mitigate VLAN hopping attacks?

    A. ARP

    B. CDP

    C. DTP

    D. STP

9. What network attack seeks to create a DoS for clients by preventing them from being able to obtain a DHCP lease?

   A. CAM table attack

   B. DHCP spoofing attack

   C. DHCP starvation attack

   D. IP address spoofing

10. What represents a best practice concerning discovery protocols such as CDP and LLDP on network devices?

   A. Disable both protocols on all interfaces where they are not required.

   B. Enable CDP on edge devices and enable LLDP on interior devices.

   C. Use the default router settings for CDP and LLDP.

   D. Use the open standard LLDP rather than CDP.

11. Why is the SPAN feature necessary on today's switches?

   A. Switches do not flood traffic on all ports; they switch traffic based on destination MAC address.

   B. Switches flood data traffic on all ports, overloading probes and traffic sniffers.

   C. Switches flood control traffic on all ports, overloading probes and traffic sniffers.

12. Which command should you use to verify the SPAN session?

   A. show monitor

   B. show monitor span

   C. show monitor span session

   D. show session

CHAPTER 6

Quality of Service

Objectives

Upon completion of this chapter, you will be able to answer the following questions:

- How do network transmission characteristics impact quality?

- What are the minimum network requirements for voice, video, and data traffic?

- What are the queuing algorithms used by networking devices?

- What are the different QoS models?

- How does QoS use mechanisms to ensure transmission quality?

Key Terms

This chapter uses the following key terms. You can find the definitions in the Glossary.

delay   Page 272

packet loss   Page 274

playout delay buffer   Page 274

digital signal processor (DSP)   Page 274

Cisco Visual Networking Index (VNI)   Page 275

Real-Time Streaming Protocol (RSTP)   Page 277

first-in, first-out (FIFO)   Page 279

Weighted Fair Queuing (WFQ)   Page 279

Class-Based Weighted Fair Queuing (CBWFQ)   Page 279

Low Latency Queuing (LLQ)   Page 279

Classification   Page 279

type of service (ToS)   Page 281

best-effort model   Page 284

integrated services (IntServ)   Page 284

differentiated services (DiffServ)   Page 284

Resource Reservation Protocol (RSVP)   Page 286

Weighted Random Early Detection (WRED)   Page 289

congestion avoidance   Page 289

marking   Page 290

Network-Based Application Recognition (NBAR)   Page 290

class of service (CoS)   Page 290

differentiated services code point (DSCP)   Page 290

IEEE 802.1p   Page 291

Tag Control Information (TCI) field   Page 291

Introduction (6.0.1.1)

In today's networks, users expect content to be immediately available. But if the traffic exceeds the bandwidth of the links between the source of the content and the user, how do network administrators ensure a quality experience?

Quality-of-service (QoS) tools can be designed into the network to guarantee that certain traffic types, such as voice and video, are prioritized over traffic that is not as time-sensitive, such as email and web browsing.

This chapter describes network transmission quality, traffic characteristics, queueing algorithms, QoS models, and QoS implementation techniques.

QoS Overview (6.1)

In this section, you learn about the purpose and characteristics of QoS.

Network Transmission Quality (6.1.1)

In this topic, you learn how network transmission characteristics impact quality.

Video

Video Tutorial 6.1.1.1: The Purpose of QoS

Refer to the online course to view this video.

Prioritizing Traffic (6.1.1.1)

Quality of service (QoS) is an ever-increasing requirement of networks today. New applications available to users, such as voice and live video transmissions, create higher expectations for quality delivery.

Congestion occurs when multiple communication lines aggregate onto a single device such as a router, and then much of that data is placed on fewer outbound interfaces or onto a slower interface. Congestion can also occur when large data packets prevent smaller packets from being transmitted in a timely manner.

When the volume of traffic is greater than what can be transported across the network, devices queue, or hold, the packets in memory until resources become available to transmit them. Queuing packets causes delay because new packets cannot be transmitted until previous packets have been processed. If the number of packets to be queued continues to increase, the memory within the device fills up and packets are dropped. One QoS technique that can help with this problem is to classify data into multiple queues, as shown in Figure 6-1.

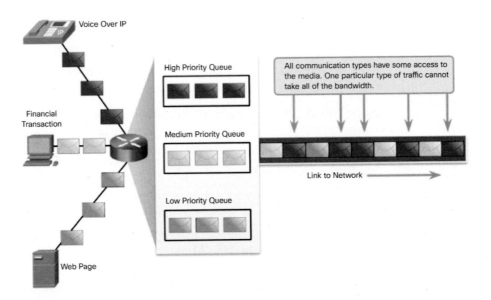

Figure 6-1   Using Queues to Prioritize Communications

Bandwidth, Congestion, Delay, and Jitter (6.1.1.2)

Network bandwidth is measured in the number of bits that can be transmitted in a single second, or bits per second (bps or b/s). For example, a network device may be described as having the capability to perform at 10 gigabits per second (Gbps or Gb/s).

Network congestion causes delay. An interface experiences congestion when it is presented with more traffic than it can handle. Network congestion points are strong candidates for QoS mechanisms. Figure 6-2 shows three examples of typical congestion points.

Delay or latency refers to the time it takes for a packet to travel from the source to the destination. Two types of delays are as follows:

- **Fixed delay:** A specific amount of time a specific process takes, such as how long it takes to place a bit on the transmission media.

- **Variable delay:** An unspecified amount of time a process takes; it is affected by factors such as how much traffic is being processed.

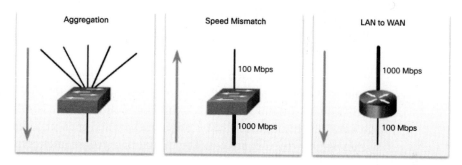

Figure 6-2   Examples of Congestion Points

Table 6-1 summarizes the sources of delay.

Table 6-1   Source of Delay

Delay	Description
Code delay	The fixed amount of time it takes to compress data at the source before transmitting to the first internetworking device, usually a switch.
Packetization delay	The fixed time it takes to encapsulate a packet with all the necessary header information.
Queuing delay	The variable amount of time a frame or packet waits to be transmitted on the link.
Serialization delay	The fixed amount of time it takes to transmit a frame from the NIC to the wire.
Propagation delay	The variable amount of time it takes for the frame to traverse the links between the source and destination.
De-jitter delay	The fixed amount of time it takes to buffer a flow of packets and then send them out in evenly spaced intervals.

Jitter is the variation in the delay of received packets. At the sending side, packets are sent in a continuous stream with the packets spaced evenly apart. Due to network congestion, improper queuing, or configuration errors, the delay between each packet can vary instead of remaining constant. Both delay and jitter need to be controlled and minimized to support real-time and interactive traffic.

Packet Loss (6.1.1.3)

Without any QoS mechanisms in place, packets are processed in the order in which they are received. When congestion occurs, network devices such as routers and switches can drop packets. *Packet loss* means that time-sensitive packets, such as real-time video and voice, will be dropped with the same frequency as data that is not time-sensitive, such as email and web browsing.

For example, when a router receives a Real-Time Protocol (RTP) digital audio stream for voice over IP (VoIP), it must compensate for the jitter that is encountered. The mechanism that handles this function is the *playout delay buffer*. The playout delay buffer must buffer these packets and then play them out in a steady stream, as shown in Figure 6-3. The digital packets are later converted back to an analog audio stream.

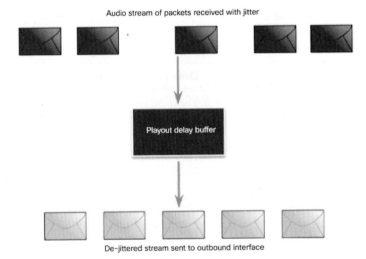

Figure 6-3   Playout Delay Buffer Compensates for Jitter

If the jitter is so large that it causes packets to be received out of the range of this buffer, the out-of-range packets are discarded and dropouts are heard in the audio, as shown in Figure 6-4.

For losses as small as one packet, the *digital signal processor (DSP)* interpolates what it thinks the audio should be and no problem is audible to the user. However, when jitter exceeds what the DSP can do to make up for the missing packets, audio problems are heard.

Packet loss is a common cause of voice quality problems on an IP network. In a properly designed network, packet loss should be near zero. The voice codecs used by the DSP can tolerate some degree of packet loss without a dramatic effect on voice quality. Network engineers use QoS mechanisms to classify voice packets for zero packet loss. Bandwidth is guaranteed for the voice calls by giving priority to voice traffic over traffic that is not time-sensitive.

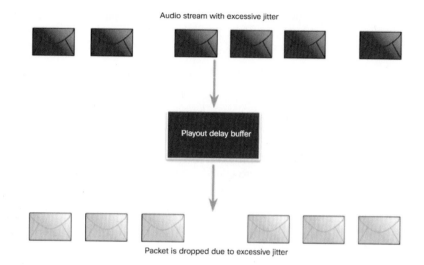

Figure 6-4   Packet Dropped Due to Excessive Jitter

Interactive
Graphic

Activity 6.1.1.5: Identify Network Transmission Quality Terminology

Refer to the online course to complete this activity.

Traffic Characteristics (6.1.2)

In this topic, you learn about the minimum network requirements to support voice, video, and data traffic.

Video

Video Tutorial 6.1.2.1: Traffic Characteristics

Refer to the online course to view this video.

Network Traffic Trends (6.1.2.1)

In the early 2000s, the predominant types of IP traffic were voice and data. Voice traffic has a predictable bandwidth need and known packet arrival times. Data traffic is not real time and has unpredictable bandwidth needs. Data traffic can temporarily burst, such as when a large file is being downloaded. This bursting can consume the entire bandwidth of a link.

More recently, video traffic has become the increasingly important to business communications and operations. According to the *Cisco Visual Networking Index (VNI)*, video traffic represented 67 percent of all traffic in 2014. By 2019, video will represent 80 percent of all traffic. In addition, mobile video traffic will increase over 600 percent from 113,672 TB to 768,334 TB.

The types of demands voice, video, and data traffic place on the network are very different.

Voice (6.1.2.2)

Voice traffic is predictable and smooth; however, voice is sensitive to delays and packet loss and there is no reason to retransmit voice if packets are lost. Therefore, voice packets must receive a higher priority than other types of traffic.

For example, Cisco products use the RTP port range 16384 to 32767 to prioritize voice traffic. Voice can tolerate a certain amount of latency, jitter, and loss without any noticeable effects. Latency should be no more than 150 milliseconds (ms). Jitter should be no more than 30 ms, and voice packet loss should be no more than 1 percent. Voice traffic requires at least 30 kb/s of bandwidth.

The following summarizes voice one-way requirements:

- Bandwidth (30–128 kb/s)

- Latency ≤ 150 ms

- Jitter ≤ 30 ms

- Loss ≤ 1%

Video (6.1.2.3)

Without QoS and a significant amount of extra bandwidth capacity, video quality typically degrades. The picture appears blurry, jagged, or in slow motion. The audio portion of the feed may become unsynchronized with the video.

Video traffic tends to be unpredictable, inconsistent, and bursty compared to voice traffic. Compared to voice, video is less resilient to packet loss and has a higher volume of data per packet, as shown in Figure 6-5.

Notice how voice packets arrive every 20 ms and are a predictable 200 bytes each. In contrast, the number and size of video packets vary every 33 ms based on the content of the video. For example, if the video stream consists of content that is not changing much from frame to frame, the video packets will be small and fewer are required to maintain acceptable user experience. However, if the video stream consists of content that is rapidly changing, such as in an action sequence in a movie, the video packets will be larger and more are required per 33 ms time slot to maintain an acceptable user experience.

UDP ports, such as 554 used for the *Real-Time Streaming Protocol (RSTP)*, should be given priority over other, less time-sensitive, network traffic. Similar to voice, video can tolerate a certain amount of latency, jitter, and loss without any noticeable effects. Latency should be no more than 400 ms. Jitter should be no more than 50 ms, and video packet loss should be no more than 1 percent. Video traffic requires at least 384 kb/s of bandwidth.

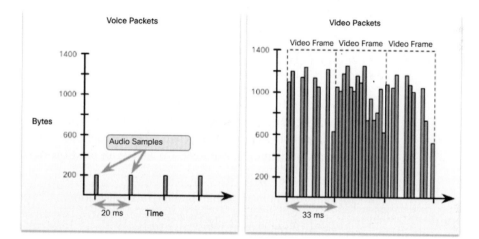

Figure 6-5   Voice and Video Sampling Comparison

The following summarizes video one-way requirements:

- Latency ≤ 200–400 ms
- Jitter ≤ 30–50 ms
- Loss ≤ 0.1–1.0%
- Bandwidth (384 kb/s – 20+Mb/s)

Data (6.1.2.4)

Most applications use either TCP or UDP. Unlike UDP, TCP performs error recovery. Data applications that have no tolerance for data loss, such as email and web pages, use TCP to ensure that, if packets are lost in transit, they will be resent. Data traffic can be smooth or bursty. Network control traffic is usually smooth and predictable. When there is a topology change, the network control traffic may burst for a few seconds. But the capacity of today's networks can easily handle the increase in network control traffic as the network converges.

However, some TCP applications can be very greedy, consuming a large portion of network capacity. FTP will consume as much bandwidth as it can get when you download a large file, such as a movie or game.

The following lists data traffic characteristics:

- Traffic can be smooth or bursty

- Traffic can be benign or greedy

- Traffic can be drop sensitive or drop insensitive

- Traffic can be delay sensitive or delay insensitive

- Traffic can be prone to TCP retransmits

Although data traffic is relatively insensitive to drops and delays compared to voice and video, a network administrator still needs to consider the quality of the user experience, sometimes referred to as quality of experience, or QoE. The two main factors a network administrator needs to ask about the flow of data traffic are as follows:

- Does the data come from an interactive application?

- Is the data mission critical?

Table 6-2 compares these two factors.

Table 6-2   Factors to Consider for Data Delay

Factor	Mission Critical	Not Mission Critical
Interactive	Prioritize for the lowest delay of all data traffic and strive for a 1- to 2-second response time.	Applications could benefit from lower delay.
Not interactive	Delay can vary greatly as long as the necessary minimum bandwidth is supplied.	Applications get any leftover bandwidth after all voice, video, and other data application needs are met.

Interactive
Graphic

Activity 6.1.2.6: Compare Traffic Characteristics

Refer to the online course to complete this activity.

Queueing Algorithms (6.1.3)

In this topic, you learn about the queuing algorithms used by networking devices.

Video Tutorial 6.1.3.1: QoS Algorithms

Refer to the online course to view this video.

Queuing Overview (6.1.3.1)

The QoS policy implemented by the network administrator becomes active when congestion occurs on the link. Queuing is a congestion management tool that can buffer, prioritize, and, if required, reorder packets before being transmitted to the destination. A number of queuing algorithms are available. For the purposes of this course, we focus on the following:

- *First-in, first-out (FIFO)*
- *Weighted Fair Queuing (WFQ)*
- *Class-Based Weighted Fair Queuing (CBWFQ)*
- *Low Latency Queuing (LLQ)*

First-In First-Out (FIFO) (6.1.3.2)

In its simplest form, FIFO queuing, also known as first-come, first-served queuing, involves buffering and forwarding of packets in the order of arrival.

FIFO has no concept of priority or classes of traffic and, consequently, makes no decision about packet priority. There is only one queue, and all packets are treated equally. Packets are sent out an interface in the order in which they arrive, as shown in Figure 6-6. Although some traffic is more important or time-sensitive based on the priority *classification*, notice that the traffic is sent out in the order it is received.

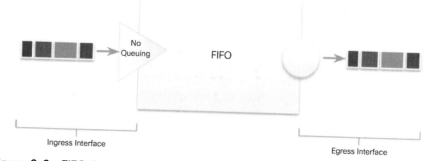

Figure 6-6   FIFO Queuing Example

When FIFO is used, important or time-sensitive traffic can be dropped when congestion occurs on the router or switch interface. When no other queuing strategies are configured, all interfaces except serial interfaces at E1 (2.048 Mb/s) and below use FIFO by default (serial interfaces at E1 and below use WFQ by default).

FIFO, which is the fastest method of queuing, is effective for large links that have little delay and minimal congestion. If your link has very little congestion, FIFO queuing may be the only queuing you need to use.

Weighted Fair Queuing (WFQ) (6.1.3.3)

WFQ is an automated scheduling method that provides fair bandwidth allocation to all network traffic. WFQ applies priority, or weights, to identified traffic and classifies it into conversations or flows, as shown in Figure 6-7.

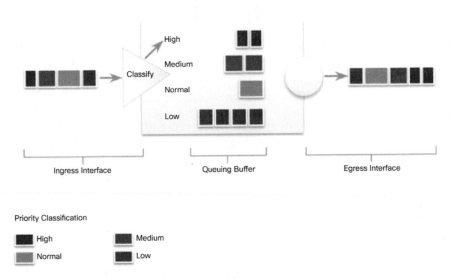

Figure 6-7 Weighted Fair Queuing Example

WFQ then determines how much bandwidth each flow is allowed relative to other flows. The flow-based algorithm used by WFQ simultaneously schedules interactive traffic to the front of a queue to reduce response time. It then fairly shares the remaining bandwidth among high-bandwidth flows. WFQ allows you to give low-volume, interactive traffic, such as Telnet sessions and voice, priority over high-volume traffic, such as FTP sessions. When multiple file transfer flows are occurring simultaneously, the transfers are given comparable bandwidth.

WFQ classifies traffic into different flows based on packet header addressing, including such characteristics as source and destination IP addresses, MAC addresses, port numbers, protocol, and *type of service (ToS)* value. The ToS value in the IP header can be used to classify traffic. ToS is discussed in more detail in the section "Marking at Layer 3 (6.2.2.5)."

Low-bandwidth traffic streams, which comprise the majority of traffic, receive preferential service, allowing their entire offered loads to be sent in a timely fashion. High-volume traffic streams share the remaining capacity proportionally among themselves.

Limitations

WFQ is not supported with tunneling and encryption because these features modify the packet content information required by WFQ for classification.

Although WFQ automatically adapts to changing network traffic conditions, it does not offer the degree of precision control over bandwidth allocation that CBWFQ offers.

Class-Based Weighted Fair Queuing (CBWFQ) (6.1.3.4)

CBWFQ extends the standard WFQ functionality to provide support for user-defined traffic classes. For CBWFQ, you define traffic classes based on match criteria including protocols, access control lists (ACLs), and input interfaces. Packets satisfying the match criteria for a class constitute the traffic for that class. A FIFO queue is reserved for each class, and traffic belonging to a class is directed to the queue for that class, as shown in Figure 6-8.

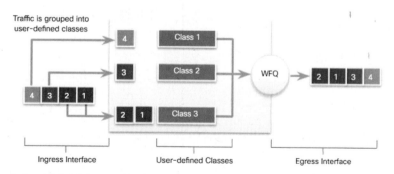

Figure 6-8   CBWFQ Example

When a class has been defined according to its match criteria, you can assign it characteristics. To characterize a class, you assign it bandwidth, weight, and maximum packet limit. The bandwidth assigned to a class is the guaranteed bandwidth delivered to the class during congestion.

To characterize a class, you also specify the queue limit for that class, which is the maximum number of packets allowed to accumulate in the queue for the class. Packets belonging to a class are subject to the bandwidth and queue limits that characterize the class.

After a queue has reached its configured queue limit, adding more packets to the class causes tail drop or packet drop to take effect, depending on how class policy is configured. Tail drop means a router simply discards any packet that arrives at the tail end of a queue that has completely used up its packet-holding resources. This is the default queuing response to congestion. Tail drop treats all traffic equally and does not differentiate between classes of service.

Low Latency Queuing (LLQ) (6.1.3.5)

The LLQ feature brings strict priority queuing (PQ) to CBWFQ. Strict PQ allows delay-sensitive data such as voice to be sent before packets in other queues. LLQ provides strict priority queuing for CBWFQ, reducing jitter in voice conversations, as shown in Figure 6-9.

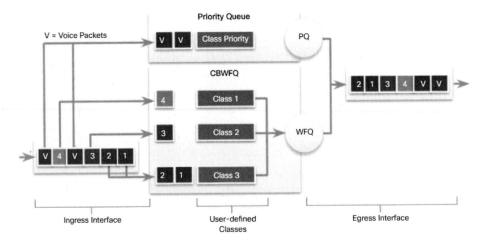

Figure 6-9   LLQ Example

Without LLQ, CBWFQ provides WFQ based on defined classes with no strict priority queue available for real-time traffic. The weight for a packet belonging to a specific class is derived from the bandwidth you assigned to the class when you configured it. Therefore, the bandwidth assigned to the packets of a class determines the order in which packets are sent. All packets are serviced fairly based on weight; no class of packets may be granted strict priority. This scheme poses problems for voice traffic that is largely intolerant of delay, especially variation in delay. For voice traffic, variations in delay introduce irregularities of transmission manifesting as jitter in the heard conversation.

With LLQ, delay-sensitive data is sent first, before packets in other queues are treated. LLQ allows delay-sensitive data such as voice to be sent first (before packets in other queues), giving delay-sensitive data preferential treatment over other traffic. Although it is possible to enqueue various types of real-time traffic to the strict priority queue, Cisco recommends that only voice traffic be directed to the priority queue.

Interactive Graphic	**Activity 6.1.3.7: Compare Queuing Algorithms**
	Refer to the online course to complete this activity.

QoS Mechanisms (6.2)

In this section, you learn how networking devices implement QoS.

QoS Models (6.2.1)

In this topic, you learn about the different QoS models.

Video	**Video Tutorial 6.2.1.1: QoS Models**
	Refer to the online course to view this video.

Selecting an Appropriate QoS Policy Model (6.2.1.1)

How can QoS be implemented in a network? Table 6-3 summarizes the three models for implementing QoS.

QoS is really implemented in a network using either IntServ or DiffServ. While IntServ provides the highest guarantee of QoS, it is very resource-intensive and, therefore, limited in scalability. In contrast, DiffServ is less resource-intensive and more scalable. The two are sometimes co-deployed in network QoS implementations.

Table 6-3   Models for Implementing QoS

Model	Description
Best-effort model	This model is not really an implementation because QoS is not explicitly configured.
	Use when QoS is not required.
Integrated services (IntServ)	This model provides very high QoS to IP packets with guaranteed delivery.
	It defines a signaling process for applications to signal to the network that they require special QoS for a period and that bandwidth should be reserved.
	However, IntServ can severely limit the scalability of a network.
Differentiated services (DiffServ)	This model provides high scalability and flexibility in implementing QoS.
	Network devices recognize traffic classes and provide different levels of QoS to different traffic classes.

Best Effort (6.2.1.2)

The basic design of the Internet provides for best-effort packet delivery and provides no guarantees. This approach is still predominant on the Internet today and remains appropriate for most purposes. The best-effort model treats all network packets in the same way, so an emergency voice message is treated the same way a digital photograph attached to an email is treated. Without QoS, the network cannot tell the difference between packets and, as a result, cannot treat packets preferentially.

The best-effort model is similar in concept to sending a letter using standard postal mail. Your letter is treated exactly the same as every other letter. With the best-effort model, the letter may never arrive, and unless you have a separate notification arrangement with the letter recipient, you may never know that the letter did not arrive.

Table 6-4 lists the benefits and drawbacks of the best-effort model.

Table 6-4   Benefits and Drawbacks of Best-Effort Model

Benefits	Drawbacks
The model is the most scalable.	There are no guarantees of delivery.
Scalability is limited only by bandwidth limits, in which case all traffic is equally affected.	Packets will arrive whenever they can and in any order possible, if they arrive at all.
No special QoS mechanisms are required.	No packets have preferential treatment.
It is the easiest and quickest model to deploy.	Critical data is treated the same as casual email is treated.

Integrated Services (6.2.1.3)

The needs of real-time applications, such as remote video, multimedia conferencing, visualization, and virtual reality, motivated the development of the IntServ architecture model in 1994 (RFC 1633, 2211, and 2212). IntServ is a multiple-service model that can accommodate multiple QoS requirements.

IntServ provides a way to deliver the end-to-end QoS that real-time applications require by explicitly managing network resources to provide QoS to specific user packet flows. It uses resource reservation and admission-control mechanisms as building blocks to establish and maintain QoS. This practice is similar to a concept known as "hard QoS." Hard QoS guarantees traffic characteristics, such as bandwidth, delay, and packet-loss rates, from end to end. Hard QoS ensures both predictable and guaranteed service levels for mission-critical applications.

Figure 6-10 is a simple illustration of the IntServ model.

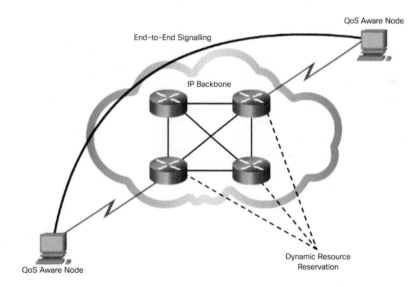

Figure 6-10   Simple IntServ Example

IntServ uses a connection-oriented approach inherited from telephony network design. Each individual communication must explicitly specify its traffic descriptor and requested resources to the network. The edge router performs admission control to ensure that available resources are sufficient in the network. The IntServ standard assumes that routers along a path set and maintain the state for each individual communication.

In the IntServ model, the application requests a specific kind of service from the network before sending data. The application informs the network of its traffic profile and requests a particular kind of service that can encompass its bandwidth and delay requirements. IntServ uses the *Resource Reservation Protocol (RSVP)* to signal the QoS needs of an application's traffic along devices in the end-to-end path through the network. If network devices along the path can reserve the necessary bandwidth, the originating application can begin transmitting. If the requested reservation fails along the path, the originating application does not send any data.

The edge router performs admission control based on information from the application and available network resources. The network commits to meeting the QoS requirements of the application as long as the traffic remains within the profile specifications. The network fulfills its commitment by maintaining the per-flow state and then performing packet classification, policing, and intelligent queuing based on that state.

Table 6-5 lists the benefits and drawbacks of the IntServ model.

Table 6-5   Benefits and Drawbacks of IntServ Model

Benefits	Drawbacks
Explicit end-to-end resource admission control	Resource intensive due to the stateful architecture requirement for continuous signaling
Per-request policy admission control	Flow-based approach not scalable to large implementations such as the Internet
Signaling of dynamic port numbers	

Differentiated Services (6.2.1.4)

The differentiated services (DiffServ) QoS model specifies a simple and scalable mechanism for classifying and managing network traffic and providing QoS guarantees on modern IP networks. For example, DiffServ can provide low-latency guaranteed service to critical network traffic such as voice or video while providing simple best-effort traffic guarantees to noncritical services such as web traffic or file transfers.

The DiffServ design overcomes the limitations of both the best-effort and IntServ models. The DiffServ model is described in RFCs 2474, 2597, 2598, 3246, and 4594. DiffServ can provide an "almost guaranteed" QoS while still being cost-effective and scalable.

The DiffServ model is similar in concept to sending a package using a delivery service. You request (and pay for) a level of service when you send a package. Throughout the package network, the level of service you paid for is recognized and your package is given either preferential or normal service, depending on what you requested.

DiffServ is not an end-to-end QoS strategy because it cannot enforce end-to-end guarantees. However, DiffServ QoS is a more scalable approach to implementing QoS. Unlike IntServ and hard QoS in which the end-hosts signal their QoS needs to the network, DiffServ does not use signaling. Instead, DiffServ uses a "soft QoS" approach. It works on the provisioned-QoS model, where network elements are set up to service multiple classes of traffic each with varying QoS requirements.

Figure 6-11 is a simple illustration of the DiffServ model.

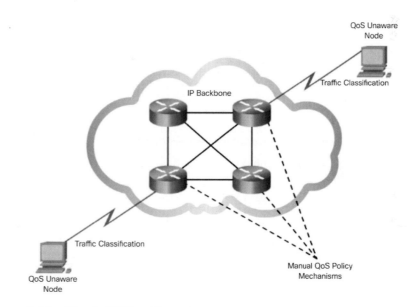

Figure 6-11   Simple DiffServ Example

As a host forwards traffic to a router, the router classifies the flows into aggregates (classes) and provides the appropriate QoS policy for the classes. DiffServ enforces and applies QoS mechanisms on a hop-by-hop basis, uniformly applying global meaning to each traffic class to provide both flexibility and scalability. For example, DiffServ could be configured to group all TCP flows as a single class, and allocate bandwidth for that class, rather than for the individual flows as IntServ would do. In addition to classifying traffic, DiffServ minimizes signaling and state maintenance requirements on each network node.

Specifically, DiffServ divides network traffic into classes based on business require-ments. Each of the classes can then be assigned a different level of service. As the packets traverse a network, each network device identifies the packet class and services the packet according to that class. It is possible to choose many levels of service with DiffServ. For example, voice traffic from IP phones is usually given preferential treat-ment over all other application traffic, email is generally given best-effort service, and nonbusiness traffic either can be given very poor service or blocked entirely.

Table 6-6 lists the benefits and drawbacks of the DiffServ model.

Table 6-6   Benefits and Drawbacks of DiffServ Model

Benefits	Drawbacks
Highly scalable	No absolute guarantee of service quality
Provides many different levels of quality	Requires a set of complex mechanisms to work in concert throughout the network

Note

Modern networks primarily use the DiffServ model; however, due to the increasing volumes of delay- and jitter-sensitive traffic, IntServ and RSVP are sometimes co-deployed.

Interactive Graphic

Activity 6.2.1.6: Compare QoS Models

Refer to the online course to complete this activity.

QoS Implementation Techniques (6.2.2)

In this topic, you learn how QoS uses mechanisms to ensure transmission quality.

Video

Video Tutorial 6.2.2.1: QoS Implementation Techniques

Refer to the online course to view this video.

Avoiding Packet Loss (6.2.2.1)

Packet loss is usually the result of congestion on an interface. Most applications that use TCP experience slowdown because TCP automatically adjusts to network congestion. Dropped TCP segments cause TCP sessions to reduce their window sizes. Some applications do not use TCP and cannot handle drops (fragile flows).

The following approaches can prevent drops in sensitive applications:

- Increase link capacity to ease or prevent congestion.
- Guarantee enough bandwidth and increase buffer space to accommodate bursts of traffic from fragile flows. Several mechanisms available in Cisco IOS QoS software can guarantee bandwidth and provide prioritized forwarding to drop-sensitive applications. Examples are WFQ, CBWFQ, and LLQ.

■ Prevent congestion by dropping lower-priority packets before congestion occurs. Cisco IOS QoS provides queuing mechanisms that start dropping lower-priority packets before congestion occurs. An example is *Weighted Random Early Detection (WRED)*.

QoS Tools (6.2.2.2)

The three categories of QoS tools are described in Table 6-7.

Table 6-7   Tools for Implementing QoS

QoS Tools	Description
Classification and marking tools	Sessions, or flows, are analyzed to determine what traffic class they belong to.
	Once class is determined, the packets are marked.
Congestion avoidance tools	Traffic classes are allotted portions of network resources as defined by the QoS policy.
	The QoS policy also identifies how some traffic may be selectively dropped, delayed, or re-marked to avoid congestion.
	The primary congestion avoidance tool is WRED and is used to regulate TCP data traffic in a bandwidth-efficient manner before tail drops caused by queue overflows occur.
Congestion management tools	When traffic exceeds available network resources, traffic is queued to await availability of resources.
	Common Cisco IOS-based congestion management tools include CBWFQ and LLQ algorithms.

See Figure 6-12 to help understand the sequence of how these tools are used when QoS is applied to packet flows.

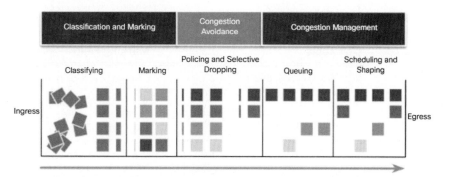

Figure 6-12   QoS Sequence

As shown in the figure, ingress packets (gray squares) are classified, and their respective IP header is marked (colored squares). To avoid congestion, packets are then allocated resources based on defined policies. Packets are then queued and forwarded out the egress interface based on their defined QoS shaping and policing policy.

Note

Classification and marking can be done on ingress or egress, whereas other QoS actions such as queuing and shaping are usually done on egress.

Classification and Marking (6.2.2.3)

Before a packet can have a QoS policy applied to it, the packet has to be classified. Classification and *marking* allows you to identify or "mark" types of packets. Classification determines the class of traffic to which packets or frames belong. Only after traffic is marked can policies be applied to it.

How a packet is classified depends on the QoS implementation. Methods of classifying traffic flows at Layers 2 and 3 include using interfaces, ACLs, and class maps. Traffic can also be classified at Layers 4 to 7 using *Network-Based Application Recognition (NBAR)*.

Note

NBAR is a classification and protocol discovery feature of Cisco IOS software that works with QoS features. NBAR is beyond the scope of this course.

Marking means that you are adding a value to the packet header. Devices receiving the packet look at this field to see whether it matches a defined policy. Marking should be done as close to the source device as possible. This establishes the trust boundary.

How traffic is marked usually depends on the technology. Table 6-8 describes some of the marking fields used in various technologies.

Table 6-8   Traffic Marking for QoS

QoS Tools	Layer	Marking Field	Width in Bits
Ethernet (802.1Q, 802.1p)	2	*Class of service (CoS)*	3
802.11 (Wi-Fi)	2	Wi-Fi Traffic Identifier (TID)	3
MPLS	2	Experimental (EXP)	3
IPv4 and IPv6	3	IP Precedence	3
IPv4 and IPv6	3	*Differentiated services code point (DSCP)*	6

The decision of whether to mark traffic at Layer 2 or 3 (or both) is not trivial and should be made after consideration of the following points:

- Layer 2 marking of frames can be performed for non-IP traffic.

- Layer 2 marking of frames is the only QoS option available for switches that are not "IP aware."

- Layer 3 marking will carry the QoS information end-to-end.

Marking at Layer 2 (6.2.2.4)

The IEEE standard that supports VLAN tagging at Layer 2 on Ethernet networks is 802.1Q. When it is implemented, two fields are added to the Ethernet frame. As shown in Figure 6-13, these two fields are inserted into the Ethernet frame following the source MAC address field.

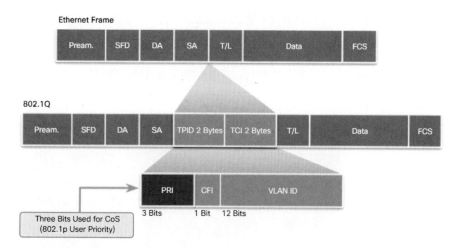

Figure 6-13   Ethernet Class of Service (CoS) Values

The 802.1Q standard also includes the QoS prioritization scheme known as *IEEE 802.1p*. The 802.1p standard uses the first three bits in the 802.1Q *Tag Control Information (TCI) field*. Known as the *Priority (PRI) field*, this 3-bit field identifies the class of service (CoS) markings. Three bits means that a Layer 2 Ethernet frame can be marked with one of eight levels of priority (values 0–7) as displayed in Table 6-9.

Table 6-9   Ethernet Class of Service (CoS) Markings

CoS Value	CoS Binary Value	Description
0	000	Best-Effort Data
1	001	Medium-Priority Data
2	010	High-Priority Data
3	011	Call Signaling
4	100	Video conferencing
5	101	Voice bearer (voice traffic)
6	110	Reserved
7	111	Reserved

Marking at Layer 3 (6.2.2.5)

IPv4 and IPv6 specify an 8-bit field in their packet headers to mark packets. As shown in Figure 6-14, both IPv4 and IPv6 support an 8-bit field for marking, the *Type of Service (ToS) field* for IPv4 and the *Traffic Class field* for IPv6.

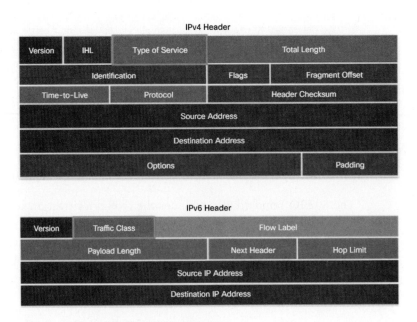

Figure 6-14   IPv4 and IPv6 Packet Headers

These fields are used to carry the packet marking as assigned by the QoS classification tools. Receiving devices then refer to the fields to forward the packets based on the appropriate assigned QoS policy.

Figure 6-15 displays the contents of the 8-bit field. In RFC 791, the original IP standard specified the *IP Precedence (IPP) field* to be used for QoS markings. However, in practice, these 3 bits did not provide enough granularity to implement QoS.

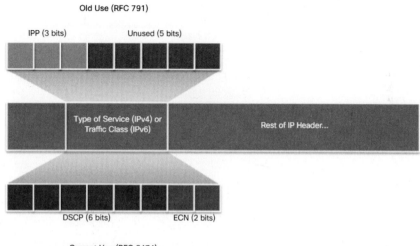

Figure 6-15   Type of Service/Traffic Class Field

RFC 2474 supersedes RFC 791 and redefines the ToS field by renaming and extending the IPP field. The new field, as shown in Figure 6-15, has 6 bits allocated for QoS. Called the Differentiated Services Code Point (DSCP) field, these 6 bits offer a maximum of 64 possible classes of service. The remaining two IP Extended Congestion Notification (ECN) bits can be used by ECN-aware routers to mark packets instead of dropping them. The ECN marking informs downstream routers that there is congestion in the packet flow.

The 64 DSCP values are organized into three categories:

- *Best effort (BE):* This is the default for all IP packets. The DSCP value is 0. The per-hop behavior is normal routing. When a router experiences congestion, these packets will be dropped. No QoS plan is implemented.

- *Expedited forwarding (EF):* RFC 3246 defines EF as the DSCP decimal value 46 (binary **101110**). The first three bits (101) map directly to the Layer 2 CoS value 5 used for voice traffic. At Layer 3, Cisco recommends that EF be used only to mark voice packets.

- *Assured forwarding (AF):* RFC 2597 defines AF to use the five most significant DSCP bits to indicate queues and drop preference. As shown in Figure 6-16, the first three most significant bits are used to designate the class. Class 4 is the best queue and Class 1 is the worst queue. The fourth and fifth most significant bits are used to designate the drop preference. The sixth most significant bit is set to zero.

The AFxy formula shows how the AF values are calculated. For example, AF32 belongs to class 3 (binary 011) and has a medium drop preference (binary 10). The full DSCP value is 28 because you include the sixth 0 bit (binary 011100).

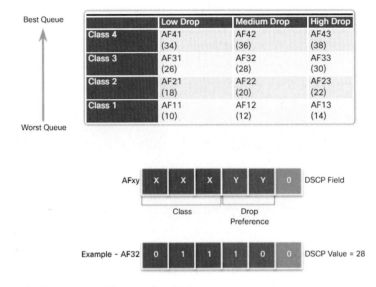

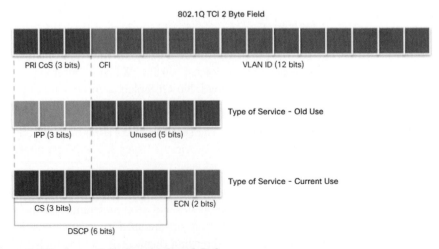

Figure 6-16   Assured Forwarding Values

Because the first 3 most significant bits of the DSCP field indicate the class, these bits are also called the Class Selector (CS) bits. As shown in Figure 6-17, these 3 bits map directly to the 3 bits of the CoS field and the IPP field to maintain compatibility with 802.1p and RFC 791.

Figure 6-17   Layer 2 CoS and Layer 3 ToS

The table in Figure 6-18 shows how the CoS values map to the Class Selectors and the corresponding DSCP 6-bit value. This same table can be used to map IPP values to the Class Selectors.

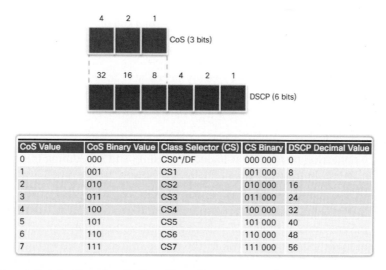

CoS Value	CoS Binary Value	Class Selector (CS)	CS Binary	DSCP Decimal Value
0	000	CS0*/DF	000 000	0
1	001	CS1	001 000	8
2	010	CS2	010 000	16
3	011	CS3	011 000	24
4	100	CS4	100 000	32
5	101	CS5	101 000	40
6	110	CS6	110 000	48
7	111	CS7	111 000	56

Figure 6-18 Mapping CoS to Class Selectors in DSCP

Trust Boundaries (6.2.2.6)

Where should markings occur? Traffic should be classified and marked as close to its source as technically and administratively feasible. This defines the trust boundary as shown in Figure 6-19 and described in the list that follows.

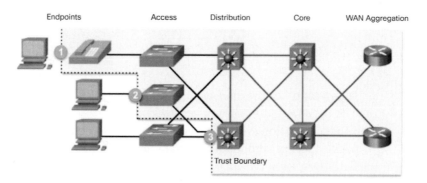

Figure 6-19 Various Trust Boundaries

- Trusted endpoints have the capabilities and intelligence to mark application traffic to the appropriate Layer 2 CoS and/or Layer 3 DSCP values. Examples of trusted endpoints include IP phones, wireless access points, video-conferencing gateways and systems, IP conferencing stations, and more.

- Secure endpoints can have traffic marked at the Layer 2 switch.

- Traffic can also be marked at Layer 3 switches/routers.

Re-marking of traffic is typically necessary. For example, re-marking CoS values to IP precedent or DSCP values.

Congestion Avoidance (6.2.2.7)

Congestion management includes queuing and scheduling methods where excess traffic is buffered or queued (and sometimes dropped) while it waits to be sent on an egress interface. Congestion avoidance tools are simpler. They monitor network traffic loads in an effort to anticipate and avoid congestion at common network and internetwork bottlenecks before congestion becomes a problem. These tools can monitor the average depth of the queue, as represented in Figure 6-20. When the queue is below the minimum threshold, there are no drops. As the queue fills up to the maximum threshold, a small percentage of packets are dropped. When the maximum threshold is passed, all packets are dropped.

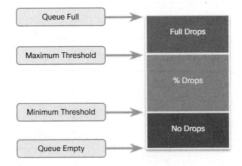

Figure 6-20   Congestion Avoidance Mechanisms

Some congestion avoidance techniques provide preferential treatment for which packets will get dropped. For example, Cisco IOS QoS includes Weighted Random Early Detection (WRED) as a possible congestion avoidance solution. The WRED algorithm allows for congestion avoidance on network interfaces by providing buffer management and allowing TCP traffic to decrease, or throttle back, before buffers are exhausted. Using WRED helps avoid tail drops and maximizes network use and TCP-based application performance. There is no congestion avoidance for

UDP-based traffic, such as voice traffic. In case of UDP-based traffic, methods such as queuing and compression techniques help reduce and even prevent UDP packet loss.

Shaping and Policing (6.2.2.8)

Traffic shaping and *traffic policing* are two mechanisms provided by Cisco IOS QoS software to prevent congestion.

Traffic shaping retains excess packets in a queue and then schedules the excess for later transmission over increments of time. The result of traffic shaping is a smoothed packet output rate, as shown in Figure 6-21.

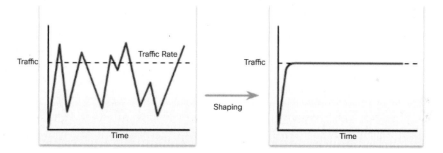

Figure 6-21   Shaping Traffic Example

Shaping implies the existence of a queue and of sufficient memory to buffer delayed packets, whereas policing does not.

Ensure that you have sufficient memory when enabling shaping. In addition, shaping requires a scheduling function for later transmission of any delayed packets. This scheduling function allows you to organize the shaping queue into different queues. Examples of scheduling functions are CBWFQ and LLQ.

Shaping is an outbound concept; packets going out an interface get queued and can be shaped. In contrast, policing is applied to inbound traffic on an interface. When the traffic rate reaches the configured maximum rate, excess traffic is dropped (or re-marked).

Policing is commonly implemented by service providers to enforce a contracted customer information rate (CIR). However, the service provider may also allow bursting over the CIR if the service provider's network is not currently experiencing congestion. Figure 6-22 shows a policing traffic example.

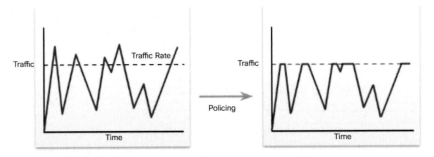

Figure 6-22   Policing Traffic Example

Activity 6.2.2.10: Identify QoS Mechanism Terminology

Refer to the online course to complete this activity.

Summary (6.3)

The quality of network transmission is impacted by the bandwidth of the links between the source and destination, the sources of delay as packets are routed to the destination, and jitter or the variation in delay of the received packets. Without QoS mechanisms in place, packets are processed in the order in which they are received. When congestion occurs, time-sensitive packets will be dropped with the same frequency as packets that are not time-sensitive.

Voice packets require latency of no more than 150 milliseconds (ms). Jitter should be no more than 30 ms, and voice packet loss should be no more than 1 percent. Voice traffic requires at least 30 kb/s of bandwidth.

Video packets require latency no more than 400 ms. Jitter should be no more than 50 ms, and video packet loss should be no more than 1 percent. Video traffic requires at least 384 kb/s of bandwidth.

For data packets, two factors impact the quality of experience (QoE) for end users:

- Does the data come from an interactive application?

- Is the data mission critical?

The four queuing algorithms discussed in this chapter are as follows:

- **First-in, first-out (FIFO):** Packets are forwarded in the order in which they are received.

- **Weighted Fair Queuing (WFQ):** Packets are classified into different flows based on header information including the ToS value.

- **Class-Based Weighted Fair Queuing (CBWFQ):** Packets are assigned to user-defined classes based on matches to criteria such as protocols, ACLs, and input interfaces. The network administrator can assign bandwidth, weight, and maximum packet limit to each class.

- **Low Latency Queuing (LLQ):** Delay-sensitive data such as voice is added to a priority queue so that it can be sent first (before packets in other queues).

The three queuing models discussed in the chapter are as follows:

- **Best effort:** This is the default queuing model for interfaces. All packets are treated in the same way. There is no QoS.

- **Integrated services (IntServ):** IntServ provides a way to deliver the end-to-end QoS that real-time applications require by explicitly managing network resources to provide QoS to specific user packet streams, sometimes called microflows.

- **Differentiated services (DiffServ):** DiffServ uses a soft QoS approach that depends on network devices that are set up to service multiple classes of traffic, each with varying QoS requirements. Although there is no QoS guarantee, the DiffServ model is more cost-effective and scalable than IntServ.

QoS tools include the following:

- **Classification and marking:** Classification determines the class of traffic to which packets or frames belong. Marking means that you are adding a value to the packet header. Devices receiving the packet look at this field to see whether it matches a defined policy.

- **Congestion avoidance:** Congestion avoidance tools monitor network traffic loads in an effort to anticipate and avoid congestion. As queues fill up to the maximum threshold, a small percentage of packets are dropped. When the maximum threshold is passed, all packets are dropped.

- **Shaping and policing:** Shaping retains excess packets in a queue and then schedules the excess for later transmission over increments of time. Shaping is used on outbound traffic. Policing either drops or re-marks excess traffic. Policing is often applied to inbound traffic.

Practice

There are no labs or activities for this chapter.

Check Your Understanding Questions

Complete all the review questions listed here to test your understanding of the topics and concepts in this chapter. The appendix "Answers to the 'Check Your Understanding' Questions" lists the answers.

1. Under which condition does congestion occur on a converged network with voice, video, and data traffic?

   A. If a user downloads a file that exceeds the file limitation that is set on the server

   B. If the request for bandwidth exceeds the amount of bandwidth available

   C. If video traffic requests more bandwidth than voice traffic requests

   D. If voice traffic latency begins to decrease across the network

2. What functionality is required on routers to provide remote workers with VoIP and video-conferencing capabilities?

   A. IPsec

   B. PPPoE

   C. QoS

   D. VPN

3. What happens when a router interface ingress queue is full and new network traffic is received?

    A. The router sends the received traffic immediately.

    B. The router will drop the arriving packets.

    C. The router drops all traffic in the queue.

    D. The router queues the received traffic while sending previously received traffic.

4. Which queuing method provides user-defined traffic classes where each traffic class has a FIFO queue?

    A. CBWFQ

    B. FIFO

    C. WFQ

    D. WRED

5. Which type of traffic does Cisco recommend be placed in the strict priority queue (PQ) when low latency queuing (LLQ) is being used?

    A. Data

    B. Management

    C. Video

    D. Voice

6. What is the default queuing method used on the LAN interfaces of Cisco devices?

    A. CBWFQ

    B. FIFO

    C. LLQ

    D. WFQ

7. What is the default queuing method used on the slower WAN interfaces of Cisco devices?

    A. CBWFQ

    B. FIFO

    C. LLQ

    D. WFQ

8. Which model is the only QoS model with no mechanism to classify packets?

    A. Best effort

    B. DiffServ

    C. Hard QoS

    D. IntServ

9. What happens when an edge router using IntServ QoS determines that the data pathway cannot support the level of QoS requested?

    A. Data is forwarded along the pathway using a best-effort approach.

    B. Data is forwarded along the pathway using DiffServ.

    C. Data is not forwarded along the pathway.

    D. Data is forwarded along the pathway using IntServ but not provided preferential treatment.

10. Which statement describes the QoS classification and marking tools?

    A. Classification is performed after traffic is marked.

    B. Classification should be done as close to the destination device as possible.

    C. Marking is the adding of a value to a packet header.

    D. Marking is the identification of which QoS policy should be applied to specific packets.

11. Which device would be classified as a trusted endpoint?

    A. Firewall

    B. IP conferencing station

    C. Router

    D. Switch

12. How many bits are used to identify the class of service (CoS) marking in a frame?

    A. 3

    B. 8

    C. 24

    D. 64

13. How many levels of priority are possible when using class of service (CoS) marking on frames?

    A. 3

    B. 8

    C. 24

    D. 64

CHAPTER 7

Network Evolution

Objectives

Upon completion of this chapter, you will be able to answer the following questions:

- What is the Cisco IoT System?

- What are the pillars of the Cisco IoT System?

- What is the importance of cloud computing?

- What is the importance of virtualization?

- What is the virtualization of network devices and services?

- What is software-defined networking?

- How are controllers used in network programming?

Key Terms

This chapter uses the following key terms. You can find the definitions in the Glossary.

private cloud   *Page 316*

hybrid cloud   *Page 316*

community cloud   *Page 316*

data center   *Page 316*

server operating system (OS)   *Page 318*

single point of failure   *Page 318*

server sprawl   *Page 318*

hypervisors   *Page 319*

virtual machines (VMs)   *Page 319*

management console   *Page 324*

*Cisco Unified Computing System
(UCS)*   *Page 324*

Cisco UCS Manager   *Page 324*

East-West traffic   *Page 325*

*Cisco Network Foundation Protection
(NFP)*   *Page 326*

control plane   *Page 326*

management plane   *Page 326*

data plane   *Page 326*

VMware   *Page 327*

*Cisco Application Centric Infrastructure
(ACI)*   *Page 328*

OpenFlow   *Page 328*

OpenStack   *Page 328*

Controller-based SDN   *Page 329*

northbound APIs   *Page 330*

southbound APIs   *Page 330*

North-South traffic   *Page 330*

SDN controllers   *Page 331*

*Transport Layer Security
(TLS)*   *Page 331*

flow table   *Page 332*

group table   *Page 332*

meter table   *Page 332*

*Application Network Profile
(ANP)*   *Page 332*

endpoint groups (EPGs)   *Page 332*

*Application Policy Infrastructure Controller
(APIC)*   *Page 333*

*Cisco Nexus 9000 Series
switches*   *Page 333*

spine-leaf topology   *Page 333*

policy-based SDN   *Page 335*

ACL Analysis   *Page 337*

ACL Path Trace   *Page 337*

Introduction (7.0.1.1)

Technology is constantly changing. Networks are always evolving.

The *Internet of Things (IoT)* is a phrase that denotes the billions of electronic devices that are now able to connect to our data networks and the Internet.

Cloud computing and *virtualization* are enabling individuals and organizations to store and access large amounts of data without worrying about the physical components.

Software-defined networking (SDN) is redefining how network administrators think about the architecture of their networks.

This chapter introduces you to these emerging trends in today's networks.

Internet of Things (7.1)

In this section, you learn the value of the Internet of Things.

IoT Elements (7.1.1)

In this topic, you learn about the Cisco IoT System.

What Is the IoT? (7.1.1.1)

In a very short time, the Internet has dramatically changed how we work, live, play, and learn. Yet, we have barely scratched the surface. Using existing and new technologies, we are connecting the physical world to the Internet. It is by connecting the unconnected that we transition from the Internet to the Internet of Things (IoT).

From its humble beginning as the Advanced Research Projects Agency Network (ARPANET) in 1969, when it interconnected a few sites, it is now predicted that the Internet will interconnect 50 billion things by 2020. The IoT refers to the network of these physical objects accessible through the Internet.

Fifty billion things provide trillions of gigabytes of data. How can they work together to enhance our decision making and interactions to improve our lives and our businesses? Enabling these connections are the networks that we use daily.

The Converged Network and Things (7.1.1.2)

Cisco estimates that 99 percent of things in the physical world are currently unconnected. Therefore, the IoT will experience tremendous growth as we connect more of the unconnected.

Many things are currently connected using a loose collection of independent, use-specific networks, as shown in Figure 7-1.

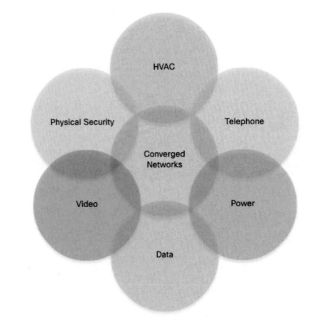

Figure 7-1   Converged Networks

For example, today's cars have multiple proprietary networks to control engine function, safety features, and communications systems. Converging these systems alone onto a common network would save over 50 lbs (23 kg) of cable in a modern full-size sedan. Other examples include commercial and residential buildings, which have various control systems and networks for heating, ventilation, and air conditioning (HVAC), telephone service, security, and lighting.

These dissimilar networks are converging to share the same infrastructure. This infrastructure includes comprehensive security, analytics, and management capabilities. The connection of the components into a converged network that uses IoT technologies increases the power of the network to help people improve their daily lives.

Challenges to Connecting Things (7.1.1.3)

The IoT connects smart objects to the Internet. It connects traditional computer devices as well as untraditional devices. Within the IoT, the communication is *Machine-to-Machine (M2M)*, enabling communication between machines without human intervention. For example, M2M occurs in cars with temperature and oil *sensors* communicating with an onboard computer.

Cisco Digital Solutions for Industries

Refer to the online course to view a video of how Cisco is developing digitization solutions for all types of industries. Digitization means connecting people and things, and making sense of the data in a meaningful and secure way.

The Six Pillars of the Cisco IoT System (7.1.1.4)

The challenge for IoT is to securely integrate millions of new things from multiple vendors into existing networks. To help address these challenges, Cisco introduced the *Cisco IoT System* to help organizations and industries adopt IoT solutions. Specifically, the Cisco IoT System reduces the complexities of digitization for manufacturing, utilities, oil and gas, transportation, mining, and public sector organizations.

The IoT system provides an infrastructure designed to manage large-scale systems of very different endpoints and platforms, and the huge amount of data that they create. The Cisco IoT System uses a set of new and existing products and technologies to help reduce the complexity of digitization.

The Cisco IoT System uses the concept of pillars to identify foundational elements. Specifically, the IoT System identifies the six technology pillars displayed in Figure 7-2.

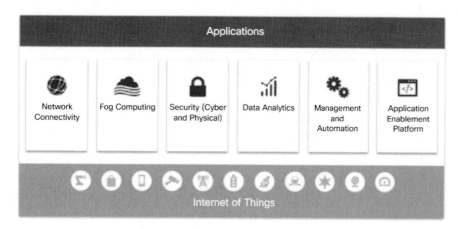

Figure 7-2   Six Pillars of IoT

IoT Pillars (7.1.2)

In this topic, you learn about the pillars of the Cisco IoT System.

The Network Connectivity Pillar (7.1.2.1)

There are many different types of networks: home networks, public Wi-Fi networks, small business networks, enterprise networks, service provider networks, data center networks, cloud networks, and IoT networks. Regardless of network type, they all need devices to provide network connectivity. However, network connectivity equipment varies depending on the type of network. For example, home networks typically consist of a wireless broadband router, while business networks will have multiple switches, APs, a firewall or firewalls, routers, and more.

The Cisco IoT System *network connectivity pillar* identifies devices that can be used to provide IoT connectivity to many diverse industries and applications.

What Is YOUR Ideal Building?

Video

Refer to the online course to view a video of how businesses can use the network to create ideal indoor environments. Using Cisco's Digital Ceiling, the network can manage lighting and air temperature seamlessly, based on the preferences of the occupants.

The Fog Computing Pillar (7.1.2.2)

Networking models describe how data flows within a network. The networking models include the following:

- **Client/server model (see Figure 7-3):** This is the most common model used in networks. Client devices request services of servers.

- *Cloud computing model* **(see Figure 7-4):** This is a newer model that supports cloud computing where servers and services are dispersed globally in distributed data centers. Cloud computing is discussed in more detail later in the section, "Cloud Computing (7.2.1)."

- *Fog computing model* **(see Figure 7-5):** This IoT network model identifies a distributed computing infrastructure closer to the network edge. It enables edge devices to run applications locally and make immediate decisions. This model reduces the data burden on networks because raw data does not need to be sent over network connections. It enhances resiliency by allowing IoT devices to operate when network connections are lost. It also enhances security by keeping sensitive data from being transported beyond the edge where it is needed.

These models are not mutually exclusive. Network administrators can use any combination of the three models to address the needs of the network users.

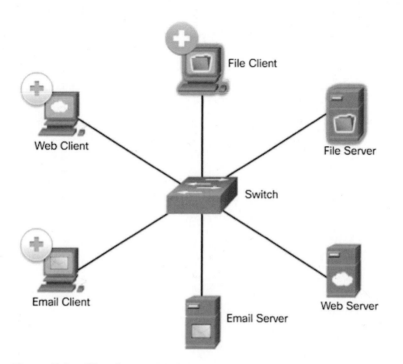

Figure 7-3   Client/server Model

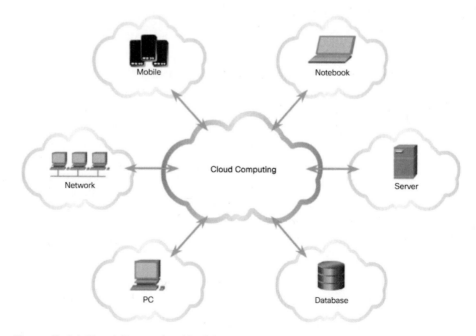

Figure 7-4   Cloud Computing Model

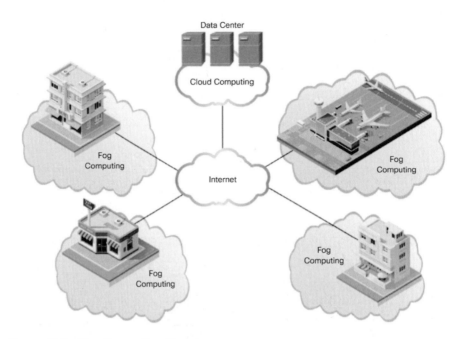

Figure 7-5   Fog Computing Model

The *fog computing pillar* basically extends cloud connectivity closer to the edge. It enables end devices, such as smart meters, industrial sensors, robotic machines, and others, to connect to a local integrated computing, networking, and storage system.

Fog applications are used to monitor or analyze real-time data from network-connected things and then take action such as locking a door, changing equipment settings, applying the brakes on a train, and more. For example, a traffic light can interact locally with a number of sensors that can detect the presence of pedestrians and bikers, and measure the distance and speed of approaching vehicles. The traffic light also interacts with neighboring lights, providing a coordinated effort. Based on this information, the smart light sends warning signals to approaching vehicles and modifies its own cycle to prevent accidents. The data collected by the smart traffic light system is processed locally to do real-time analytics. Coordinating with neighboring smart traffic light systems in the fog allows for any modification of the cycle. For example, it can change the timing of the cycles in response to road conditions or traffic patterns. The data from clusters of smart traffic light systems is sent to the cloud to analyze long-term traffic patterns.

Cisco predicts that 40 percent of IoT-created data will be processed in the fog by 2018.

The Security Pillar (7.1.2.3)

All networks need to be secured; however, the IoT introduces new attack vectors not typically encountered with normal enterprise networks. The Cisco IoT *security pillar* offers scalable cybersecurity solutions, enabling an organization to quickly and effectively discover, contain, and remediate an attack to minimize damage.

These cybersecurity solutions include the following:

- *Operational Technology (OT) security*: *Operational Technology (OT)* is the hardware and software that keeps power plants running and manages factory process lines. OT security includes the ISA 3000 industrial security appliance (see Figure 7-6) and fog data services.

Figure 7-6   Cisco Industrial Security Appliance 3000

- *IoT Network security*: This solution includes network and perimeter security devices such as switches, routers, ASA firewall devices, and Cisco FirePOWER Next-Generation Intrusion Prevention Services (NGIPS) (see Figure 7-7).

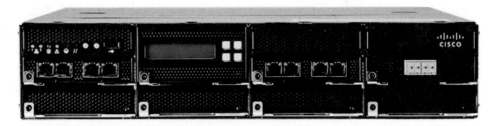

Figure 7-7   Cisco FirePOWER 8000 Series Appliance

■ *IoT Physical security*: This solution includes network surveillance video cameras such as the Cisco Video Surveillance IP Cameras (see Figure 7-8). These devices are feature-rich digital cameras that enable surveillance in a wide variety of environments. Available in standard and high definition, box and dome, wired and wireless, and stationary and pan-tilt-zoom (PTZ) versions, the cameras support MPEG-4 and H.264, and offer efficient network utilization while providing high-quality video.

Figure 7-8   Cisco Video Surveillance IP Cameras

Data Analytics Pillar (7.1.2.4)

The IoT can connect billions of devices capable of creating exabytes of data every day. To provide value, this data must be rapidly processed and transformed into actionable intelligence.

The Cisco IoT *data analytics pillar* consists of distributed network infrastructure components and IoT-specific *application programming interfaces (APIs)*.

Analytics and Automation: A New Approach

Video

Refer to the online course to view a video about Cisco data analytics solutions.

Management and Automation Pillar (7.1.2.5)

The IoT greatly expands the size and diversity of the network to include the billions of smart objects that sense, monitor, control, and react. Although networking these previously unconnected devices can deliver unparalleled levels of business and operational intelligence, it is essential to understand that operational environments are made up of multiple, disparate functional areas. Each of these areas also has distinctive requirements, including the need to track specific metrics. Operational technology systems can vary widely by industry, as well as by function in a given industry.

Cisco delivers a broad range of IoT management and automation capabilities throughout the extended network. Cisco management and automation products can be customized for specific industries to provide enhanced security and control and support.

The Cisco IoT *System management and automation pillar* includes management tools such as the Cisco IoT Field Network Director shown in Figure 7-9. Other management tools include Cisco Prime, Cisco Video Surveillance Manager, and more.

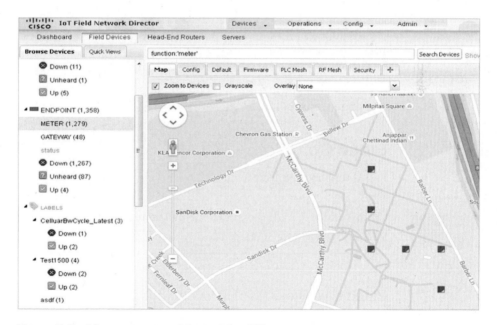

Figure 7-9 Management and Automation Pillar

Application Enablement Platform Pillar (7.1.2.6)

The *Application Enablement Platform pillar* provides the infrastructure for application hosting and application mobility between cloud and fog computing. The fog environment allows for multiple instances of the application across different end devices and sensors. These instances can communicate with each other for redundancy and data-sharing purposes to create business models such as pay-as-you-go consumption for objects, machines, and products.

For example, *Cisco IOx*, which is a combination of Cisco IOS and Linux, allows routers to host applications close to the objects they need to monitor, control, analyze, and optimize. Cisco IOx services are offered on multiple hardware devices that are customized for various industry needs and can therefore support applications specific to those industries.

Video	**Interview with Guido Jouret, VP/GM Internet of Things, Cisco** Refer to the online course to view a light-hearted interview about Cisco IOx.

Interactive Graphic	**Activity 7.1.2.7: Identify the IoT Pillars** Refer to the online course to complete this activity.

Cloud and Virtualization (7.2)

In this section, you learn why cloud computing and virtualization are necessary for evolving networks.

Cloud Computing (7.2.1)

In this topic, you learn the importance of cloud computing.

Video	**Video Tutorial 7.2.1.1: Cloud and Virtualization** Refer to the online course to view this video.

Cloud Overview (7.2.1.2)

Cloud computing involves large numbers of computers connected through a network that can be physically located anywhere. Providers rely heavily on virtualization to deliver their cloud computing services. Cloud computing can reduce operational costs by using resources more efficiently. Cloud computing supports a variety of data management issues:

- Enables access to organizational data anywhere and at any time
- Streamlines the organization's IT operations by subscribing only to needed services

- Eliminates or reduces the need for onsite IT equipment, maintenance, and management

- Reduces cost for equipment, energy, physical plant requirements, and personnel training needs

- Enables rapid responses to increasing data volume requirements

Cloud computing, with its "pay-as-you-go" model, allows organizations to treat computing and storage expenses more as a utility rather than as an investment in infrastructure. Capital expenditures are transformed into operating expenditures.

Cloud Services (7.2.1.3)

Cloud services are available in a variety of options, tailored to meet customer requirements. The three main cloud computing services defined by the *National Institute of Standards and Technology (NIST)* in its Special Publication (SP) 800-145 are as follows:

- *Software as a service (SaaS)*: The cloud provider is responsible for access to services, such as email, communication, and Office 365, that are delivered over the Internet. Users only need to provide their data.

- *Platform as a service (PaaS)*: The cloud provider is responsible for access to the development tools and services used to deliver the applications.

- *Infrastructure as a service (IaaS)*: The cloud provider is responsible for access to the network equipment, virtualized network services, and supporting network infrastructure.

Cloud service providers have extended this model to also provide *IT as a service (ITaaS)* to provide IT support for each of the cloud computing services. For businesses, ITaaS can extend the capability of IT without requiring investment in new infrastructure, training new personnel, or licensing new software. These services are available on demand and delivered economically to any device anywhere in the world without compromising security or function.

Cloud Models (7.2.1.4)

The four primary cloud models are

- *Public cloud*: Cloud-based applications and services offered in a public cloud are made available to the general population. Services may be free or are offered on a pay-per-use model, such as paying for online storage. The public cloud uses the Internet to provide services.

- *Private cloud*: Cloud-based applications and services offered in a private cloud are intended for a specific organization or entity, such as the government. A private cloud can be set up using the organization's private network, though this can be expensive to build and maintain. A private cloud can also be managed by an outside organization with strict access security.

- *Hybrid cloud*: A hybrid cloud is made up of two or more clouds (that is, private, community, or public), where each part remains a distinctive object, but both are connected using a single architecture. Individuals on a hybrid cloud would be able to have degrees of access to various services based on user access rights.

- *Community cloud*: A community cloud is created for exclusive use by a specific community. The differences between public clouds and community clouds are the functional needs that have been customized for the community. For example, healthcare organizations must remain compliant with policies and laws (for example, HIPAA) that require special authentication and confidentiality.

Cloud Computing versus Data Center (7.2.1.5)

The terms *data center* and *cloud computing* are often incorrectly used. These are the correct definitions:

- *Data center*: Typically, a data storage and processing facility run by an in-house IT department or leased offsite.

- **Cloud computing:** Typically, an off-premise service that offers on-demand access to a shared pool of configurable computing resources. These resources can be rapidly provisioned and released with minimal management effort.

Cloud computing is possible because of data centers. A data center is a facility used to house computer systems and associated components. A data center can occupy one room of a building, one or more floors, or an entire building. Data centers are typically very expensive to build and maintain. For this reason, only large organizations use privately built data centers to house their data and provide services to users. Smaller organizations that cannot afford to maintain their own private data center can reduce the overall cost of ownership by leasing server and storage services from a larger data center organization in the cloud.

Cloud computing is often a service that data centers provide, as shown Figure 7-10. Cloud service providers use data centers to host their cloud services and cloud-based resources. To ensure availability of data services and resources, providers often maintain space in several remote data centers.

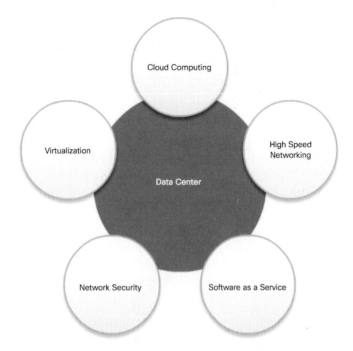

Figure 7-10   Cloud Computing in Relationship to Data Centers

Activity 7.2.1.6: Identify Cloud Computing Terminology

Refer to the online course to complete this activity.

Virtualization (7.2.2)

In this topic, you learn the importance of virtualization.

Cloud Computing and Virtualization (7.2.2.1)

The terms *cloud computing* and *virtualization* are often used interchangeably; however, they mean different things. Virtualization is the foundation of cloud computing. Without it, cloud computing, as it is most widely implemented, would not be possible.

Cloud computing separates the application from the hardware. Virtualization separates the OS from the hardware. Various providers offer virtual cloud services that can dynamically provision servers as required. For example, Amazon Elastic Compute cloud (Amazon EC2) web service provides a simple way for customers to dynamically provision the compute resources they need. These virtualized instances of servers are created on demand in Amazon's EC2.

Dedicated Servers (7.2.2.2)

To fully appreciate virtualization, you first need to understand some of the history of server technology. Historically, enterprise servers consisted of a *server operating system (OS)*, such as Windows Server or Linux Server, installed on specific hardware, as shown in Figure 7-11. All of a server's RAM, processing power, and hard drive space were dedicated to the service provided (for example, Web, email services, and so on)

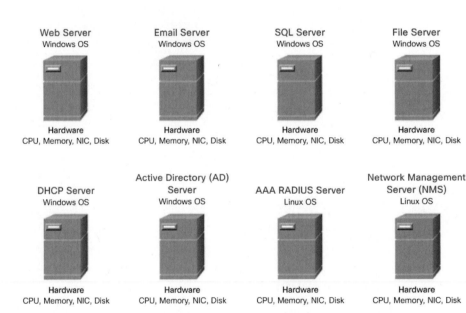

Figure 7-11   Dedicated Servers

The major problem with this configuration was that when a component failed, the service provided by this server became unavailable. This is known as a *single point of failure*. Another problem was that dedicated servers were underused. Dedicated servers often sat idle for long periods of time, waiting until there was a need to deliver the specific service they provided. These servers wasted energy and took up more space than was warranted by their amount of service. This is known as *server sprawl*.

Server Virtualization (7.2.2.3)

Server virtualization takes advantage of idle resources and consolidates the number of required servers. This also allows for multiple operating systems to exist on a single hardware platform.

For example, in Figure 7-12, the previous eight dedicated servers have been consolidated into two servers using *hypervisors* to support multiple virtual instances of the operating systems.

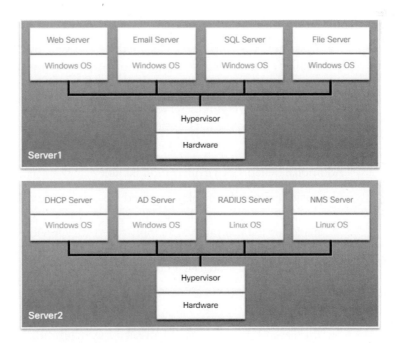

Figure 7-12   Hypervisor OS Installation

The hypervisor is a program, firmware, or hardware that adds an abstraction layer on top of the real physical hardware. The abstraction layer is used to create *virtual machines (VMs)* that have access to all the hardware of the physical machine such as CPUs, memory, disk controllers, and NICs. Each of these virtual machines runs a complete and separate operating system. With virtualization, enterprises can now consolidate the number of servers they require. For example, it is not uncommon for 100 physical servers to be consolidated as virtual machines on top of 10 physical servers that are using hypervisors.

The use of virtualization normally includes redundancy to protect from a single point of failure. Redundancy can be implemented in different ways. If the hypervisor fails, the VM can be restarted on another hypervisor. Also, the same VM can be run on two hypervisors concurrently, copying the RAM and CPU instructions between them. If one hypervisor fails, the VM continues running on the other hypervisor. The services running on the VMs are also virtual and can be dynamically installed or uninstalled, as needed.

Advantages of Virtualization (7.2.2.4)

One major advantage of virtualization is overall reduced cost because

- **Less equipment is required:** Virtualization enables server consolidation, which requires fewer physical servers, fewer networking devices, and less supporting infrastructure. It also means lower maintenance costs.

- **Less energy is consumed:** Consolidating servers lowers the monthly power and cooling costs. Reduced consumption helps enterprises achieve a smaller carbon footprint.

- **Less space is required:** Server consolidation with virtualization reduces the overall footprint of the data center. Fewer servers, network devices, and racks reduce the amount of required floor space.

Additional benefits of virtualization include

- **Easier prototyping:** Self-contained labs, operating on isolated networks, can be rapidly created for testing and prototyping network deployments. If a mistake is made, an administrator can simply revert to a previous version. The testing environments can be online but isolated from end users. When testing is completed, the servers and systems can be deployed to end users.

- **Faster server provisioning:** Creating a virtual server is far faster than provisioning a physical server.

- **Increased server uptime:** Most server virtualization platforms now offer advanced redundant fault-tolerance features, such as live migration, storage migration, high availability, and distributed resource scheduling.

- **Improved disaster recovery:** Virtualization offers advanced business continuity solutions. It provides hardware abstraction capability so that the recovery site no longer needs to have hardware that is identical to the hardware in the production environment. Most enterprise server virtualization platforms also have software that can help test and automate the failover before a disaster does happen.

- **Legacy support:** Virtualization can extend the life of OSs and applications, providing more time for organizations to migrate to newer solutions.

Abstraction Layers (7.2.2.5)

To help explain how virtualization works, it is useful to use layers of abstraction in computer architectures. A computer system consists of the abstraction layers illustrated in Figure 7-13.

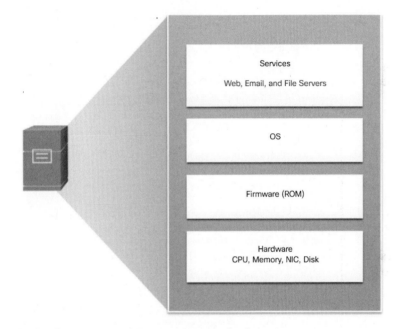

Figure 7-13   Computer Architecture Abstraction Layers

At each of these layers of abstraction, some type of programming code is used as an interface between the layer below and the layer above. For example, the C programming language is often used to program the firmware that accesses the hardware.

Figure 7-14 shows an example of virtualization. A hypervisor is installed between the firmware and the OS. The hypervisor can support multiple instances of OSs.

Type 2 Hypervisors (7.2.2.6)

A Type 2 hypervisor is software that creates and runs VM instances. The computer, on which a hypervisor is supporting one or more VMs, is a host machine. Type 2 hypervisors are also called hosted hypervisors. The reasons is that the hypervisor is installed on top of the existing OS, such as Mac OS X, Windows, or Linux. Then, one or more additional OS instances are installed on top of the hypervisor, as shown in Figure 7-15.

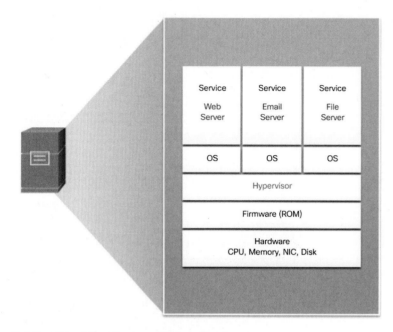

Figure 7-14   Virtual Architecture Abstraction Layers

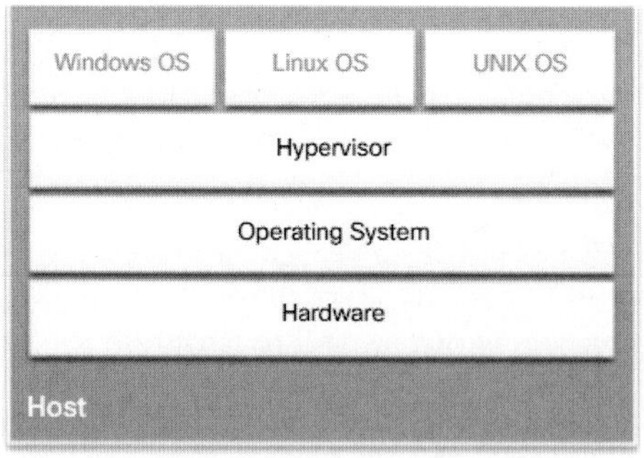

Figure 7-15   Type 2 Hypervisor: "Hosted" Approach

A big advantage of Type 2 hypervisors is that management console software is not required.

Type 2 hypervisors are popular with consumers and for organizations experimenting with virtualization. Common Type 2 hypervisors include

- Virtual PC
- VMware Workstation
- Oracle VM VirtualBox

- VMware Fusion

- Mac OS X Parallels

Many of these Type 2 hypervisors are free. Some offer more advanced features for a fee.

Note

It is important to make sure that the host machine is robust enough to install and run the VMs so that it does not run out of resources.

Interactive Graphic

Activity 7.2.2.7: Identify Virtualization Terminology

Refer to the online course to complete this activity.

Virtual Network Infrastructure (7.2.3)

In this topic, you learn about the virtualization of network devices and services.

Type 1 Hypervisors (7.2.3.1)

Type 1 hypervisors are also called the "bare metal" approach because the hypervisor is installed directly on the hardware. Type 1 hypervisors are usually used on enterprise servers and data center networking devices.

With Type 1 hypervisors, the hypervisor is installed directly on the server or networking hardware. Then, instances of an OS are installed on the hypervisor, as shown in Figure 7-16. Type 1 hypervisors have direct access to the hardware resources; therefore, they are more efficient than hosted architectures. Type 1 hypervisors improve scalability, performance, and robustness.

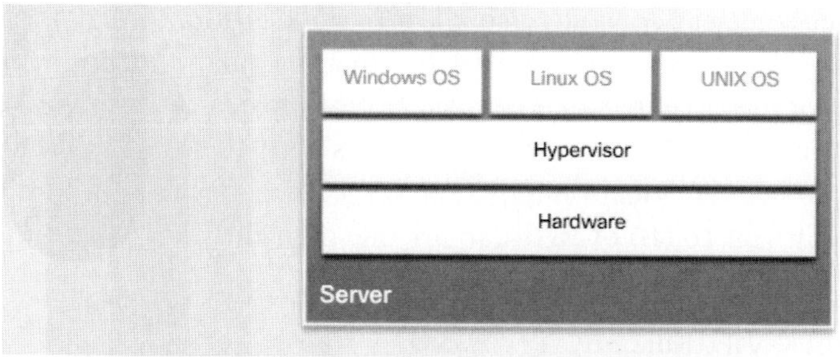

Figure 7-16   Type 1 Hypervisor: "Bare Metal" Approach

Installing a VM on a Hypervisor (7.2.3.2)

When a Type 1 hypervisor is installed, and the server is rebooted, only basic information is displayed, such as the OS version, the amount of RAM, and the IP address. An OS instance cannot be created from this screen. Type 1 hypervisors require a *management console* to manage the hypervisor. Management software is used to manage multiple servers using the same hypervisor. The management console can automatically consolidate servers and power on or off servers as required.

For example, assume that Server1 in Figure 7-17 becomes low on resources. To make more resources available, the management console moves the Windows instance to the hypervisor on Server2.

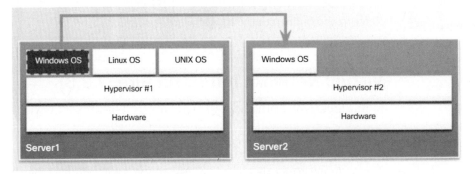

Figure 7-17   Moving an OS Instance Between Hypervisors

The management console provides recovery from hardware failure. If a server component fails, the management console automatically and seamlessly moves the VM to another server. The management console for the *Cisco Unified Computing System (UCS)* is shown in Figure 7-18. *Cisco UCS Manager* provides management for all software and hardware components in the Cisco UCS. It controls multiple servers and manages resources for thousands of VMs.

Some management consoles also allow overallocation. Overallocation occurs when multiple OS instances are installed, but their memory allocation exceeds the total amount of memory that a server has. For example, a server has 16 GB of RAM, but the administrator creates four OS instances with 10 GB of RAM allocated to each. This type of overallocation is a common practice because all four OS instances rarely require the full 10 GB of RAM at any one moment.

Network Virtualization (7.2.3.3)

Server virtualization hides server resources (for example, the number and identity of physical servers, processors, and OSs) from server users. This practice can create problems if the data center is using traditional network architectures.

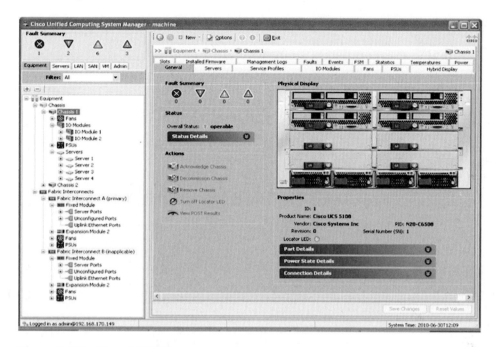

Figure 7-18   Cisco UCS Manager

For example, virtual LANs (VLANs) used by VMs must be assigned to the same switch port as the physical server running the hypervisor. However, VMs are movable, and the network administrator must be able to add, drop, and change network resources and profiles. This process is difficult to do with traditional network switches.

Another problem is that traffic flows differ substantially from the traditional client/server model. Typically, a data center has a considerable amount of traffic being exchanged between virtual servers (referred to as *East-West traffic*). These flows change in location and intensity over time, requiring a flexible approach to network resource management.

Existing network infrastructures can respond to changing requirements related to the management of traffic flows by using QoS and security-level configurations for individual flows. However, in large enterprises using multivendor equipment, each time a new VM is enabled, the necessary reconfiguration can be very time consuming.

Could the network infrastructure also benefit from virtualization? If so, then how?

The answer is found in how a networking device operates using a data plane and a control plane, as discussed in the section "Control Plane and Data Plane (7.3.1.1)," later in the chapter.

Activity 7.2.3.4: Identify Hypervisor Terminology

Refer to the online course to complete this activity.

Network Programming (7.3)

In this section, you learn why network programmability is necessary for evolving networks.

Software-Defined Networking (7.3.1)

In this topic, you learn about software-defined networking.

Video Tutorial 7.3.1.1: Network Programming, SDN, and Controllers

Refer to the online course to view this video.

Control Plane and Data Plane (7.3.1.1)

The *Cisco Network Foundation Protection (NFP)* framework logically divides routers and switches into three functional areas called "planes":

■ *Control plane*: This is typically regarded as the brains of a device. It is used to make forwarding decisions. The control plane contains Layer 2 and Layer 3 route forwarding mechanisms, such as routing protocol neighbor tables and topology tables, IPv4 and IPv6 routing tables, STP, and the ARP table. Information sent to the control plane is processed by the CPU.

■ *Data plane*: Also called the forwarding plane, this plane is typically the switch fabric connecting the various network ports on a device. The data plane of each device is used to forward traffic flows. Routers and switches use information from the control plane to forward incoming traffic out the appropriate egress interface. Information in the data plane is typically processed by a special data plane processor, such as a digital signal processor (DSP), without the CPU getting involved.

■ *Management plane*: Responsible for managing network elements. Management plane traffic is generated either by network devices or network management stations using processes and protocols such as Telnet, SSH, TFTP, FTP, NTP, AAA, SNMP, syslog, TACACS+, RADIUS, and NetFlow.

The example in Figure 7-19 illustrates how Cisco Express Forwarding (CEF) uses the control plane and data plane to process packets.

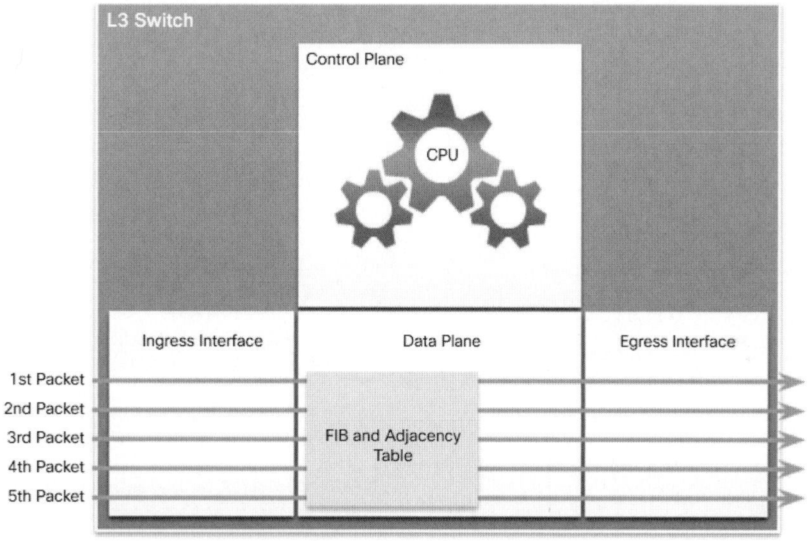

Figure 7-19 Cisco Express Forwarding (CEF), Control Plane, and Data Plane

CEF is an advanced, Layer 3 IP switching technology that enables forwarding of packets to occur at the data plane without consulting the control plane. In CEF, the control plane's routing table prepopulates the CEF Forwarding Information Base (FIB) table in the data plane. The control plane's ARP table prepopulates the adjacency table. Packets are then forwarded directly by the data plane based on the information contained in the FIB and adjacency table, without needing to consult the information in the control plane.

To virtualize the network, the control plane function is removed from each device and is performed by a centralized controller, as shown in Figure 7-20. The centralized controller communicates control plane functions to each device. Each device can now focus on forwarding data while the centralized controller manages data flow, increases security, and provides other services.

Virtualizing the Network (7.3.1.2)

In the late 1990s, *VMware* developed a virtualizing technology that enabled a host OS to support one or more client OSs. Most virtualization technologies are now based on this technology. The transformation of dedicated servers to virtualized servers has been embraced and is rapidly being implemented in data center and enterprise networks.

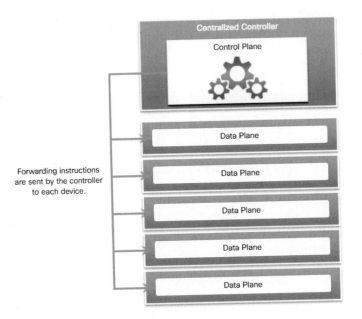

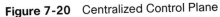

Figure 7-20 Centralized Control Plane

Two major network architectures have been developed to support network virtualization:

- **Software-defined networking (SDN):** A network architecture that virtualizes the network.

- *Cisco Application Centric Infrastructure (ACI)*: A purpose-built hardware solution for integrating cloud computing and data center management.

Some other network virtualization technologies are available, some of which are included as components in SDN and ACI:

- *OpenFlow*: This approach was developed at Stanford University to manage traffic between routers, switches, wireless access points, and a controller. The OpenFlow protocol is a basic element in building SDN solutions. The Open Networking Foundation is now responsible for maintaining the OpenFlow standard. Go to this website to learn more about OpenFlow: www.opennetworking.org/sdn-resources/openflow.

- *OpenStack*: This approach is a virtualization and orchestration platform available to build scalable cloud environments and provide an infrastructure as a service (IaaS) solution. OpenStack is often used with Cisco ACI. Orchestration in networking is the process of automating the provisioning of network components such as servers, storage, switches, routers, and applications. Go here to learn more about OpenStack: www.openstack.org/software/.

- **Other components:** Other components include Interface to the Routing System (I2RS), Transparent Interconnection of Lots of Links (TRILL), Cisco FabricPath (FP), and IEEE 802.1aq Shortest Path Bridging (SPB).

SDN Architecture (7.3.1.3)

In a traditional router or switch architecture, the control plane and data plane functions occur in the same device. Routing decisions and packet forwarding are the responsibility of the device operating system.

Software-defined networking (SDN) is a network architecture that has been developed to virtualize the network. For example, SDN can virtualize the control plane. Also known as *controller-based SDN*, SDN moves the control plane from each network device to a central network intelligence and policy-making entity called the SDN controller. Figure 7-21 shows the two architectures.

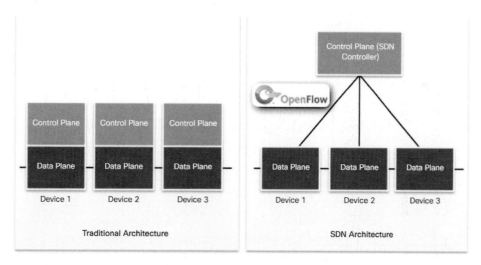

Figure 7-21   Traditional and SDN Architectures

The SDN controller is a logical entity that enables network administrators to manage and dictate how the data plane of virtual switches and routers should handle network traffic. It orchestrates, mediates, and facilitates communication between applications and network elements.

Figure 7-22 illustrates the SDN framework.

Note the use of application programming interfaces (APIs) within the SDN framework. An API is a set of standardized requests that define the proper way for an application to request services from another application.

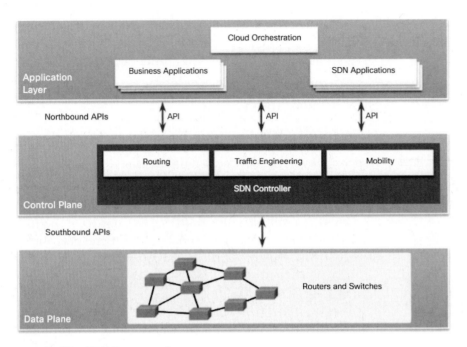

Figure 7-22   SDN Framework

The SDN controller uses *northbound APIs* to communicate with the upstream applications. These APIs help network administrators shape traffic and deploy services.

The SDN controller also uses *southbound APIs* to define the behavior of the downstream virtual switches and routers. OpenFlow is the original and widely implemented southbound API.

Note

Traffic in a modern data center is described as *North-South traffic* (going between external data center users and the data center servers) and East-West (going between data center servers).

Visit this website to learn more about SDN, OpenFlow, and the Open Networking Foundation: www.opennetworking.org/sdn-resources/sdn-definition.

Interactive Graphic

Activity 7.3.1.5: Identify Control Plane and Data Plane Characteristics

Refer to the online course to complete this activity.

Controllers (7.3.2)

In this topic, you learn about the *SDN controllers* used in network programming.

SDN Controller and Operations (7.3.2.1)

The SDN controller defines the data flows that occur in the SDN data plane. A flow is a sequence of packets traversing a network that share a set of header field values. For example, a flow could consist of all packets with the same source and destination IP addresses, or all packets with the same VLAN identifier.

Each flow traveling through the network must first get permission from the SDN controller, which verifies that the communication is permissible according to the network policy. If the controller allows a flow, it computes a route for the flow to take and adds an entry for that flow in each of the switches along the path.

The controller performs all complex functions. It populates flow tables. Switches manage the flow tables.

In Figure 7-23, an SDN controller communicates with OpenFlow-compatible switches using the OpenFlow protocol. This protocol uses *Transport Layer Security (TLS)* to securely send control plane communications over the network. Each OpenFlow switch connects to other OpenFlow switches. They can also connect to end-user devices that are part of a packet flow.

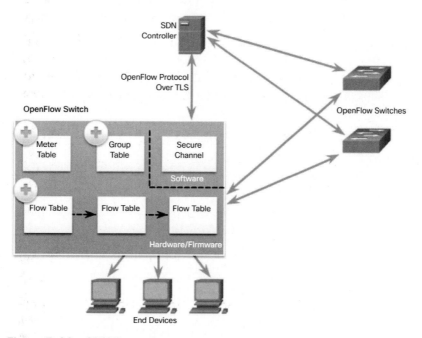

Figure 7-23   SDN Operation

Within each switch, a series of tables implemented in hardware or firmware are used to manage the flows of packets through the switch. To the switch, a flow is a sequence of packets that matches a specific entry in a flow table. A description of the tables in Figure 7-23 is as follows:

■ *Flow table*: This table matches incoming packets to a particular flow and specifies the functions that are to be performed on the packets. There may be multiple flow tables that operate in a pipeline fashion.

■ *Group table*: A flow table may direct a flow to a group table, which may trigger a variety of actions that affect one or more flows.

■ *Meter table*: This table triggers a variety of performance-related actions on a flow.

Cisco Application Centric Infrastructure (7.3.2.2)

Very few organizations actually have the desire or skill to program the network using SDN tools; however, the majority of organizations want to automate the network, accelerate application deployments, and align their IT infrastructures to better meet business requirements. Cisco developed the Application Centric Infrastructure (ACI) to meet these objectives in more advanced and innovative ways than earlier SDN approaches.

ACI is a data center network architecture that was developed by Insieme and acquired by Cisco in 2013. Cisco ACI is a purpose-built hardware solution for integrating cloud computing and data center management. At a high level, the policy element of the network is removed from the data plane. This simplifies the way data center networks are created.

To learn more about the differences between SDN and ACI, check out this blog: blogs.cisco.com/datacenter/is-aci-really-sdn-one-point-of-view-to-clarify-the-conversation.

Video

Fundamentals of ACI

Refer to the online course to view a video overview of the fundamentals of ACI.

Core Components of ACI (7.3.2.3)

The three core components of the ACI architecture are

■ *Application Network Profile (ANP)*: An ANP is a collection of *endpoint groups (EPGs)*, their connections, and the policies that define those connections. The EPGs shown in the figure, such as VLANs, Web services, and applications, are just examples. An ANP is often much more complex.

- *Application Policy Infrastructure Controller (APIC)*: The APIC is considered to be the brains of the ACI architecture. The APIC is a centralized software controller that manages and operates a scalable ACI clustered fabric. It is designed for programmability and centralized management. It translates application policies into network programming.

- *Cisco Nexus 9000 Series switches*: These switches provide an application-aware switching fabric and work with an APIC to manage the virtual and physical network infrastructure.

As shown in Figure 7-24, the APIC is positioned between the APN and the ACI-enabled network infrastructure. The APIC translates the application requirements into a network configuration to meet those needs.

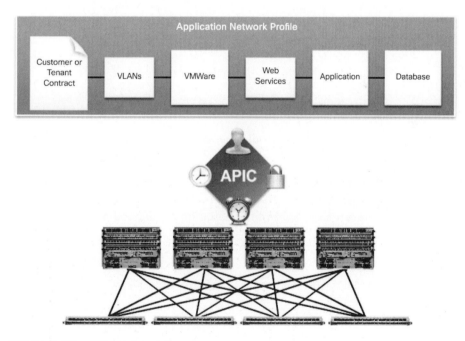

Figure 7-24   ACI Framework

Spine-Leaf Topology (7.3.2.4)

The Cisco ACI fabric is composed of the APIC and the Cisco Nexus 9000 series switches using two-tier *spine-leaf topology*, as shown in Figure 7-25. The leaf switches always attach to the spines, but they never attach to each other. Similarly, the spine switches attach only to the leaf and core switches (not shown). In this two-tier topology, everything is one hop from everything else.

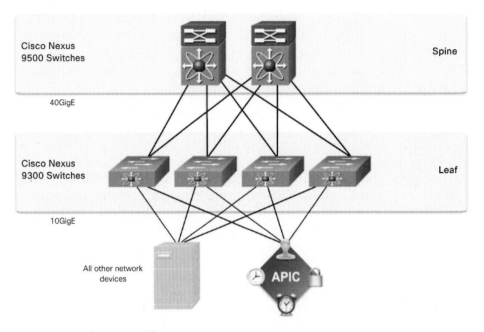

Figure 7-25   Spine-Leaf Topology

The Cisco APICs and all other devices in the network physically attach to leaf switches.

When compared to SDN, the APIC controller does not manipulate the data path directly. Instead, the APIC centralizes the policy definition and programs the leaf switches to forward traffic based on the defined policies.

For virtualization, ACI supports multivendor hypervisor environments that would connect to the leaf switches, including the following:

■ Microsoft (Hyper-V/SCVMM/Azure Pack)

■ Red Hat Enterprise Linux OS (KVM OVS/OpenStack)

■ VMware (ESX/vCenter/vShield)

SDN Types (7.3.2.5)

The Cisco Application Policy Infrastructure Controller-Enterprise Module (APIC-EM) extends ACI aimed at enterprise and campus deployments. To better understand APIC-EM, it is helpful to take a broader look at the three types of SDN:

■ **Device-based SDN:** In this type of SDN, the devices are programmable by applications running on the device itself or on a server in the network, as shown in

Figure 7-26. Cisco OnePK is an example of a device-based SDN. It enables programmers to build applications using C, and Java with Python, to integrate and interact with Cisco devices.

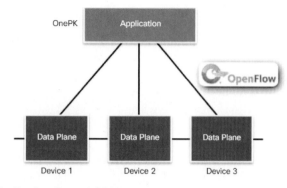

Figure 7-26 Device-Based SDN

■ **Controller-based SDN:** This type of SDN uses a centralized controller that has knowledge of all devices in the network, as shown in Figure 7-27. The applications can interface with the controller responsible for managing devices and manipulating traffic flows throughout the network. The Cisco Open SDN Controller is a commercial distribution of OpenDaylight.

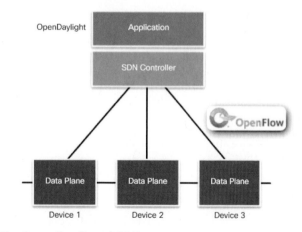

Figure 7-27 Controller-Based SDN

■ *Policy-based SDN:* This type of SDN is similar to controller-based SDN where a centralized controller has a view of all devices in the network, as shown in Figure 7-28. Policy-based SDN includes an additional Policy layer that operates at a higher level of abstraction. It uses built-in applications that automate advanced configuration tasks via a guided workflow and user-friendly GUI. No programming skills are required. Cisco APIC-EM is an example of this type of SDN.

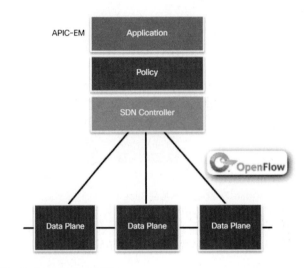

Figure 7-28   Policy-Based SDN

APIC-EM Features (7.3.2.6)

Each type of SDN has its own features and advantages. Policy-based SDN is the most robust, providing for a simple mechanism to control and manage policies across the entire network.

Cisco APIC-EM provides the following features:

- **Discovery:** Supports a discovery functionality that is used to populate the controller's device and host inventory database.

- **Device inventory:** Collects detailed information from devices within the network including device name, device status, MAC address, IPv4/IPv6 addresses, IOS/Firmware, platform, uptime, and configuration.

- **Host inventory:** Collects detailed information from hosts with the network including hostname, user ID, MAC address, IPv4/IPv6 addresses, and network attachment point.

- **Topology:** Supports a graphical view of the network (topology view). The Cisco APIC-EM automatically discovers and maps devices to a physical topology with detailed device-level data. In addition, autovisualization of Layer 2 and Layer 3 topologies on top of the physical topology provides a granular view for design planning and simplified troubleshooting. Figure 7-29 shows an example of a topology view generated by the Cisco APIC-EM.

- **Policy:** Enables you to view and control policies across the entire network including QoS.

- **Policy analysis:** Allows inspection and analysis of network access control policies. It also allows you to trace application-specific paths between end devices to quickly identify ACLs in use and problem areas. In addition, it enables ACL change management with easy identification of redundancy, conflicts, and incorrect ordering of access control entries. Incorrect ACL entries are known as *shadows*.

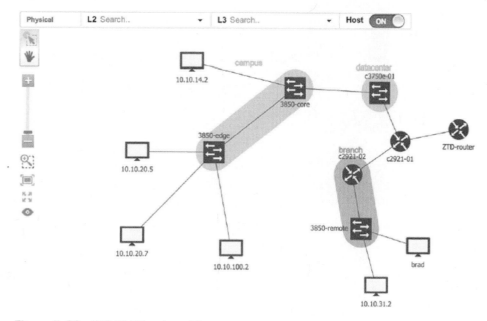

Figure 7-29 PIC-EM Topology View

APIC-EM ACL Analysis (7.3.2.7)

One of the most important features of the APIC-EM controller is the ability to manage policies across the entire network. Policies operate at a higher level of abstraction. Traditional device configuration applies to one device at a time, whereas SDN policies apply to the entire network.

APIC-EM *ACL Analysis* and *ACL Path Trace* provide tools to allow the administrator to analyze and understand ACL policies and configurations. Creating new ACLs or editing existing ACLs across a network to implement a new security policy can be challenging. Administrators are hesitant to change ACLs for fear of breaking them and causing new problems. ACL Analysis and Path Trace allow the administrator to easily visualize traffic flows and discover any conflicting, duplicate, or shadowed ACL entries.

APIC-EM provides the following tools to troubleshoot ACL entries:

- **ACL Analysis:** This tool examines ACLs on devices, searching for redundant, conflicting, or shadowed entries. ACL Analysis enables ACL inspection and interrogation across the entire network, exposing any problems and conflicts. Figure 7-30 provides a sample screenshot of this tool.

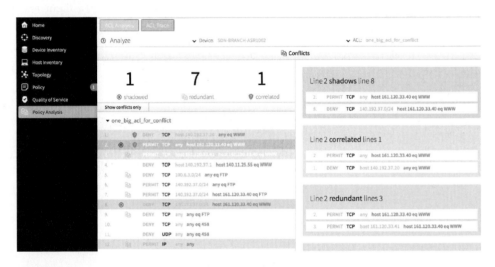

Figure 7-30   Sample ACL Analysis

- **ACL Path Trace:** This tool examines specific ACLs on the path between two end nodes, displaying any potential issues. Figure 7-31 provides a sample screenshot of this tool.

Figure 7-31 Sample ACL Path Trace

To learn more about ACL Analysis and ACL Path Trace, view the following video:
www.youtube.com/watch?v=-acUj5PVFLU.

Activity 7.3.2.8: Identify SDN Types

Refer to the online course to complete this activity.

Summary (7.4)

The IoT refers to the network of billons of physical objects accessible through the Internet as we continue to connect the unconnected. The challenge for IoT is to securely integrate new things from multiple vendors into existing networks. The six pillars of IoT are

- Network connectivity
- Fog computing
- Security
- Data analytics
- Management and automation
- Application enablement platform

Cloud computing involves large numbers of computers connected through a network that can be physically located anywhere. Cloud computing, with its "pay-as-you-go" model, allows organizations to treat computing and storage expenses more as a utility rather than as an investment in infrastructure. Cloud computing services include

- Software as a service (SaaS)
- Platform as a service (PaaS)
- Infrastructure as a service (IaaS)
- IT as a service (ITaaS)

Cloud models include

- Public clouds
- Private clouds
- Hybrid clouds
- Community clouds

Cloud computing is possible because of data centers. A data center is a facility used to house computer systems and associated components. Data centers rely heavily on virtualization to provide cloud computing services. Cloud computing separates the application from the hardware. Virtualization separates the OS from the hardware. This allows cloud computing customers to dynamically provision the compute resources they need when they need them.

Virtualized server hardware is managed through a hypervisor. Type 1 hypervisors are installed directly on the hardware. Then any OSs and VMs can be installed. Type 2 hypervisors, such as Mac OS X Parallels or Oracle VM VirtualBox, are installed on top of any existing OS.

SDN is a network architecture that has been developed to virtualize the network. For example, SDN can virtualize the control plane. Also known as controller-based SDN, SDN moves the control plane from each network device to a central network intelligence and policy-making entity called the SDN controller. The SDN controller defines the data flows that occur in the SDN data plane.

The three types of SDN are

- Device-based SDN

- Controller-based SDN

- Policy-based SDN

Policy-based SDN, such as Cisco's APIC-EM, is the most robust, providing for a simple mechanism to control and manage policies across the entire network. One of the most important features of the APIC-EM controller is the ability to manage policies across the entire network.

Practice

There are no labs or activities for this chapter.

Check Your Understanding Questions

Complete all the review questions listed here to test your understanding of the topics and concepts in this chapter. The appendix "Answers to the 'Check Your Understanding' Questions" lists the answers.

1. What is an example of an M2M connection in the IoT?

    A. A user sends an email over the Internet to a friend.

    B. An automated alarm system in a campus sends fire alarm messages to all students and staff.

    C. Redundant servers communicate with each other to determine which server should be active or standby.

    D. Sensors in a warehouse communicate with each other and send data to a server block in the cloud.

2. What is the term describing the extension of the Internet structure to billions of connected devices?

   A. BYOD

   B. Digitization

   C. IoT

   D. M2M

3. Which statement describes the Cisco IoT System?

   A. It is a router operating system combining IOS and Linux for fog computing.

   B. It is a switch operating system to integrate many Layer 2 security features.

   C. It is an advanced routing protocol for cloud computing.

   D. It is an infrastructure to manage large-scale systems of very different endpoints and platforms.

4. Which three network models are described in the fog computing pillar of the Cisco IoT System? (Choose three.)

   A. Client/server model

   B. Cloud computing model

   C. Enterprise WAN model

   D. Fog computing model

   E. P2P model

   F. Peer-to-peer model

5. Which IoT pillar extends cloud connectivity closer to the network edge?

   A. Management and automation pillar

   B. Application enablement platform pillar

   C. Network connectivity pillar

   D. Fog computing pillar

6. Which cybersecurity solution is described in the security pillar of the Cisco IoT System to address the security of power plants and factory process lines?

   A. IoT physical security

   B. IoT network security

   C. Cloud computing security

   D. Operational Technology specific security

7. Which cloud computing opportunity would provide the use of network hardware such as routers and switches for a particular company?

   A. Browser as a service (BaaS)

   B. Infrastructure as a service (IaaS)

   C. Software as a service (SaaS)

   D. Wireless as a service (WaaS)

8. What technology allows users to access data anywhere and at any time?

   A. Cloud computing

   B. Data analytics

   C. Micromarketing

   D. Virtualization

9. What statement describes fog computing?

   A. It creates a distributed computing infrastructure that provides services close to the network edge.

   B. It requires cloud computing services to support non-IP-enabled sensors and controllers.

   C. It supports larger networks than cloud computing does.

   D. It utilizes a centralized computing infrastructure that stores and manipulates big data in one very secure data center.

10. Which cloud computing service would be best for a new organization that cannot afford physical servers and networking equipment and must purchase network services on-demand?

    A. IaaS

    B. ITaaS

    C. PaaS

    D. SaaS

11. Which cloud model provides services for a specific organization or entity?

    A. A community cloud

    B. A hybrid cloud

    C. A private cloud

    D. A public cloud

12. How does virtualization help with disaster recovery within a data center?

   A. Guarantee of power

   B. Improvement of business practices

   C. Supply of consistent air flow

   D. Support of live migration

13. What is a difference between the functions of cloud computing and virtualization?

   A. Cloud computing provides services on web-based access, whereas virtualization provides services on data access through virtualized Internet connections.

   B. Cloud computing requires hypervisor technology, whereas virtualization is a fault-tolerance technology.

   C. Cloud computing separates the application from the hardware, whereas virtualization separates the OS from the underlying hardware.

   D. Cloud computing utilizes data center technology, whereas virtualization is not used in data centers.

14. Which is a characteristic of a Type 2 hypervisor?

   A. Best suited for enterprise environments

   B. Does not require management console software

   C. Has direct access to server hardware resources

   D. Installs directly on hardware

15. Which is a characteristic of a Type 1 hypervisor?

   A. Best suited for consumers and not for an enterprise environment

   B. Does not require management console software

   C. Installed directly on a server

   D. Installed on an existing operating system

16. Which technology virtualizes the control plane and moves it to a centralized controller?

   A. Cloud computing

   B. Fog computing

   C. IaaS

   D. SDN

17. Which two layers of the OSI model are associated with SDN network control plane functions that make forwarding decisions? (Choose two.)

    A. Layer 1
    B. Layer 2
    C. Layer 3
    D. Layer 4
    E. Layer 5

18. Which type of hypervisor would most likely be used in a data center?

    A. Nexus 9000 switch
    B. Oracle VM VirtualBox
    C. Type 1
    D. Type 2

19. Which type of hypervisor would most likely be used by a consumer?

    A. Nexus 9000 switch
    B. Oracle VM VirtualBox
    C. Type 1
    D. Type 2

20. What component is considered the brains of the ACI architecture and translates application policies?

    A. The Application Network Profile endpoints
    B. The Application Policy Infrastructure Controller
    C. The hypervisor
    D. The Nexus 9000 switch

CHAPTER 8

Network Troubleshooting

Objectives

Upon completion of this chapter, you will be able to answer the following questions:

- How is network documentation developed and used to troubleshoot network issues?

- What is the general troubleshooting process?

- What are the differences of troubleshooting methods that use a systematic, layered approach?

- How can you use an ICMP echo-based IP SLA to troubleshoot network connectivity issues?

- What are the different networking troubleshooting tools?

- How do you use a layered model to determine the symptoms and causes of network problems?

- How do you troubleshoot a network using the layered model?

Key Terms

This chapter uses the following key terms. You can find the definitions in the Glossary.

Introduction (8.0.1.1)

If a network or a portion of a network goes down, it can have a severe negative impact on the business. Network administrators must use a *systematic layered approach* for troubleshooting when network problems occur in order to bring the network back to full production as quickly as possible.

A network administrator's ability to resolve network problems quickly and efficiently is one of the most sought-after skills in IT. Enterprises need individuals with strong network troubleshooting skills, and the only way to gain these skills is through hands-on experience and by using systematic troubleshooting approaches.

This chapter describes general troubleshooting procedures, methods, tools, and the network documentation that should be maintained. Typical symptoms and causes at several layers of the OSI model are also discussed.

Class Activity 8.0.1.2: Network Breakdown

You have just moved into your new office, and your network is very small. After a long weekend of setting up the new network, you discover that it is not working correctly.

Some of the devices cannot access each other, and some cannot access the router that connects to the ISP.

It is your responsibility to troubleshoot and fix the problems. You decide to start with basic commands to identify possible troubleshooting areas.

Troubleshooting Methodology (8.1)

In this section, you learn troubleshooting approaches for various network problems.

Network Documentation (8.1.1)

In this topic, you learn how *network documentation* is developed and used to troubleshoot network issues.

Documenting the Network (8.1.1.1)

For network administrators to be able to monitor and troubleshoot a network, they must have a complete set of accurate and current network documentation. This documentation includes

- Configuration files, including *network configuration files* and *end-system configuration files*
- *Network topology diagrams*
- Baseline performance levels

Network documentation allows network administrators to efficiently diagnose and correct network problems, based on the network design and the expected performance of the network under normal operating conditions. All network documentation information should be kept in a single location either as hard copy or on the network on a protected server. Backup documentation should be maintained and kept in a separate location.

Network Configuration Files

Network configuration files contain accurate, up-to-date records of the hardware and software used in a network. Within the network configuration files, a table should exist for each network device used on the network, containing all relevant information about that device.

For example, Table 8-1 shows a sample network configuration table for two routers.

Table 8-1   Router Documentation

Device Name, Model	Interface Name	MAC Address	IPv4 Address	IPv6 Addresses	IP Routing Protocols
R1, Cisco 1941, c1900-universalk9-mz. SPA.154-3. M2.bin	Gig0/0	0007.8580. a159	192.168.10.1 /24	2001:db8:cafe:10::1/64 fe80::1	EIGRPv4 10 EIGRPv6 20
	Gig0/1	0007.8580. a160	192.168.11.1 /24	2001:db8:cafe:11::1/64 fe80::1	EIGRPv4 10 EIGRPv6 20
	Serial 0/0/0	N/A	10.1.1.1/30	2001:db8:acad:20::1/64 fe800::1	EIGRPv4 10 EIGRPv6 20
R2, Cisco 1941, c1900-universalk9-mz. SPA.154-3. M2.bin	Serial 0/0/0	N/A	10.1.1.2/30	2001:db8:acad:20::2/64 fe80::2	EIGRPv4 10 EIGRPv6 20

Table 8-2 shows similar information for a LAN switch.

Table 8-2 Switch Documentation

Switch Name, Model, Management IP Addresses, IOS Name	Port	Speed	Duplex	STP	Port-Fast	Trunk Status	Ether-Channel L2 or L3	VLANs	Key
S1 Cisco WS-2960-24TT 192.168.10.2/24 2001:db6: acad: 99::2 c2960-lanbasek9-mz.150-2S37.bin	G0/1	1000 Mb/s	Auto	Fwd	No	On	None	1	Connects to R1
	F0/2	100 Mb/s	Auto	Fwd	Yes	No	None	1	Connects to PC1

Information that could be captured within a device table includes

- Type of device, model designation
- IOS image name
- Device network hostname
- Location of the device (building, floor, room, rack, panel)
- If it is modular, include each module type and slot number
- Data link layer addresses
- Network layer addresses
- Any additional important information about physical aspects of the device

End-system Configuration Files

End-system configuration files focus on the hardware and software used in end-system devices, such as servers, network management consoles, and user workstations. An incorrectly configured end system can have a negative impact on the overall performance of a network. For this reason, having a sample baseline record of the hardware and software used on devices and recorded in end-system documentation, as shown in Table 8-3, can be useful when troubleshooting.

Table 8-3   End-System Documentation

Device Name, Purpose	Operating System	MAC Address	IP Address	Default Gateway	DNS Server	Network Appli-cations	High-Band-width Applica-tions
PC2	Windows 8	5475.D08E.9AD8	192.168.11.10 /24	192.168.11.1 /24	192.168.11.11 /24	HTTP, FTP	Video
			2001:DB8:ACAD:11::10/64	2001:DB8:ACAD:11::1	2001:DB8:ACAD:11::99		
SRV1	Linux	000C.D991.A138	192.168.20.254 /24	192.168.20.1 /24	192.168.11.1 /24	FTP, HTTP	
			2001:DB8:ACAD:4::100/64	2001:DB8:ACAD:4::1	2001:DB8:ACAD:11::99		

For troubleshooting purposes, the following information could be documented within the end-system configuration table:

- Device name (purpose)
- Operating system and version
- IPv4 and IPv6 addresses
- Subnet mask and prefix length
- Default gateway and DNS server
- Any high-bandwidth network applications used on the end system

Network Topology Diagrams (8.1.1.2)

Network topology diagrams keep track of the location, function, and status of devices on the network. As discussed in more detail in the sections that follow, the two types of network topology diagrams are the *physical topology diagram* and the *logical topology diagram*.

Physical Topology Diagram

A physical network topology shows the physical layout of the devices connected to the network. It is necessary to know how devices are physically connected to troubleshoot physical layer problems. Information recorded on the diagram typically includes

- Device type

- Model and manufacturer

- Operating system version

- Cable type and identifier

- Cable specification

- Connector type

- Cabling endpoints

Figure 8-1 shows a sample physical topology diagram.

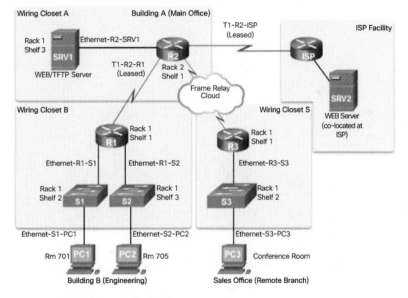

Figure 8-1   Physical Network Topology

Logical Topology Diagram

A logical network topology illustrates how devices are logically connected to the network, meaning how devices actually transfer data across the network when communicating with other devices. Symbols are used to represent network elements, such as routers, servers, hosts, VPN concentrators, and security devices. Additionally, connections between multiple sites may be shown but do not represent actual physical locations. Information recorded on a logical network diagram may include

- Device identifiers

- IP address and prefix lengths

- Interface identifiers

- Connection type

- Frame Relay DLCI for virtual circuits (if applicable)

- Site-to-site VPNs

- Routing protocols

- Static routes

- Data-link protocols

- WAN technologies used

Figure 8-2 shows a sample IPv4 network logical topology diagram. Although IPv6 addresses could also be displayed in the same topology, it may be clearer to create a separate IPv6 network logical topology diagram.

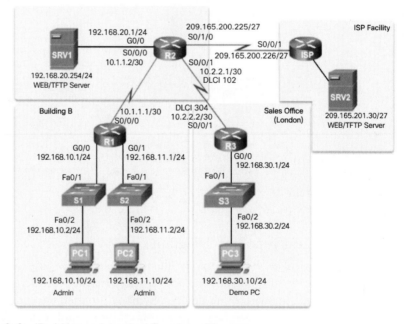

Figure 8-2   IPv4 Network Logical Topology Diagram

Establishing a Network Baseline (8.1.1.3)

The purpose of network monitoring is to watch network performance in comparison to a predetermined baseline. A *baseline* is used to establish normal network or system performance. Establishing a network performance baseline requires collecting performance data from the ports and devices that are essential to network operation. Figure 8-3 shows several questions that a baseline should answer.

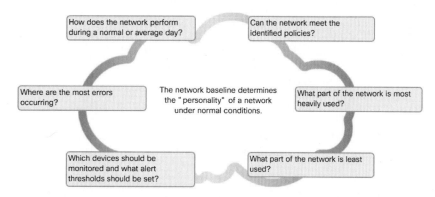

How does the network perform during a normal or average day?

Can the network meet the identified policies?

Where are the most errors occurring?

The network baseline determines the "personality" of a network under normal conditions.

What part of the network is most heavily used?

Which devices should be monitored and what alert thresholds should be set?

What part of the network is least used?

Figure 8-3   Questions That a Network Baseline Answers

Measuring the initial performance and availability of critical network devices and links allows a network administrator to determine the difference between abnormal behavior and proper network performance as the network grows or traffic patterns change. The baseline also provides insight into whether the current network design can meet business requirements. Without a baseline, no standard exists to measure the optimum nature of network traffic and congestion levels.

Analysis after an initial baseline also tends to reveal hidden problems. The collected data shows the true nature of congestion or potential congestion in a network. It may also reveal areas in the network that are underutilized and quite often can lead to network redesign efforts, based on quality and capacity observations.

Steps to Establish a Network Baseline (8.1.1.4)

The initial network performance baseline sets the stage for measuring the effects of network changes and subsequent troubleshooting efforts. Therefore, it is important to plan for it carefully.

To establish and capture an initial network baseline, perform the following steps:

Step 1. **Determine what types of data to collect.**

When conducting the initial baseline, start by selecting a few variables that represent the defined policies. If too many data points are selected, the amount of data can be overwhelming, making analysis of the collected data difficult. Start out simply and fine-tune along the way. Some good starting measures are interface utilization and CPU utilization.

Step 2. **Identify devices and ports of interest.**

Use the network topology to identify those devices and ports for which performance data should be measured. Devices and ports of interest include

- Network device ports that connect to other network devices

- Servers

- Key users

- Anything else considered critical to operations

A logical topology diagram can be useful in identifying key devices and ports to monitor. For example, in Figure 8-4 the network administrator has highlighted the devices and ports of interest to monitor during the baseline test. The devices of interest include PC1 (the Admin terminal) and SRV1 (the Web/TFTP server). The ports of interest include those ports on R1, R2, and R3 that connect to the other routers or to switches, and on R2, the port that connects to SRV1 (G0/0).

When the list of ports that are polled is shortened, the results are concise, and the network management load is minimized. Remember that an interface on a router or switch can be a virtual interface, such as a switch virtual interface (SVI).

Step 3. **Determine the baseline duration.**

The length of time and the baseline information being gathered must be sufficient for establishing a typical picture of the network. It is important that daily trends of network traffic are monitored. It is also important to monitor for trends that occur over a longer period of time, such as weekly or monthly. For this reason, when you are capturing data for analysis, the period specified should be, at a minimum, seven days long.

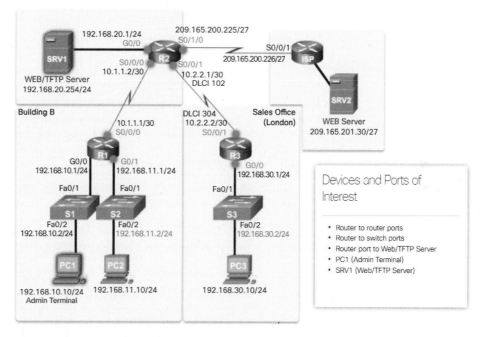

Figure 8-4 Planning for the First Baseline

Figure 8-5 shows examples of several screenshots of CPU utilization trends captured daily, weekly, monthly, and yearly.

In this example, notice that the workweek trends are too short to reveal the recurring utilization surge every weekend on Saturday evening, when a database backup operation consumes network bandwidth. This recurring pattern is revealed in the monthly trend. A yearly trend as shown in the Figure 8-5 may be too long of a duration to provide meaningful baseline performance details. However, it may help identify long-term patterns that should be analyzed further. Typically, a baseline needs to last no more than six weeks, unless specific long-term trends need to be measured. Generally, a two-to-four-week baseline is adequate.

Baseline measurements should not be performed during times of unique traffic patterns because the data would provide an inaccurate picture of normal network operations. Baseline analysis of the network should be conducted on a regular basis during normal work hours of an organization. Perform an annual analysis of the entire network or baseline different sections of the network on a rotating basis. Analysis must be conducted regularly to understand how the network is affected by growth and other changes.

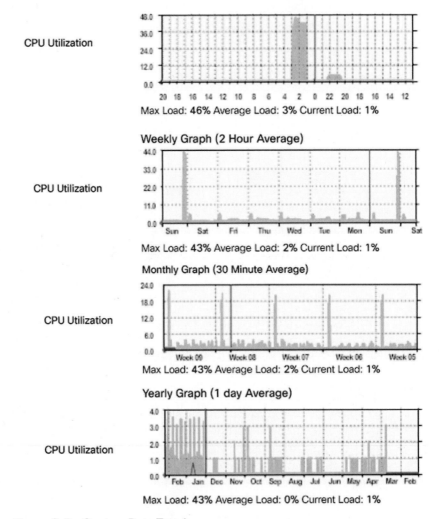

Figure 8-5   Capture Data Trends

Measuring Data (8.1.1.5)

When documenting the network, you often need to gather information directly from routers and switches. Obvious useful network documentation commands include **ping**, **traceroute**, and **telnet** as well as the following **show** commands:

- The **show ip interface brief** and **show ipv6 interface brief** commands are used to display the up or down status and IP address of all interfaces on a device.

- The **show ip route** and **show ipv6 route** commands are used to display the routing table in a router to learn the directly connected neighbors, more remote devices (through learned routes), and the routing protocols that have been configured.

- The **show cdp neighbors detail** command is used to obtain detailed information about directly connected Cisco neighbor devices.

Table 8-4 lists some of the most common Cisco IOS commands used for data collection.

Table 8-4 Commands for Data Collection

Command	Description
show version	Shows uptime version information for device software and hardware.
show ip interface [brief] show ipv6 interface [brief]	Shows all the configuration options that are set on an interface. Use the **brief** keyword to show only up/down status of IP interfaces and the IP address is of each interface.
show interface [*interface_type interface_num*]	Shows detailed output for each interface. To show detailed output for only a single interface, include the interface type and number in the command (for example, gigabitethernet 0/0).
show ip route show ipv6 route	Shows the contents of the routing table.
show arp show neighbors	Shows the contents of the ARP table (IPv4) and the neighbor table (IPv6).
show running-config	Shows current configuration.
show port	Shows the status of ports on a switch.
show vlan	Shows the status of VLANs on a switch.
show tech-support	This command is useful for collecting a large amount of information about the device for troubleshooting purposes. It executes multiple **show** commands, which can be provided to technical support representatives when reporting a problem.
show ip cache flow	Displays a summary of the *NetFlow* accounting statistics.

Manual data collection using **show** commands on individual network devices is extremely time-consuming and is not a scalable solution. Manual collection of data should be reserved for smaller networks or limited to mission-critical network devices. For simpler network designs, baseline tasks typically use a combination of manual data collection and simple network protocol inspectors.

Sophisticated network management software is typically used to baseline large and complex networks. These software packages enable administrators to automatically create and review reports, compare current performance levels with historical observations, automatically identify performance problems, and create alerts for applications that do not provide expected levels of service.

Establishing an initial baseline or conducting a performance-monitoring analysis may require many hours or days to accurately reflect network performance. Network management software or protocol inspectors and sniffers often run continuously over the course of the data collection process.

Interactive Graphic

Activity 8.1.1.6: Identify Benefits for Establishing a Network Baseline

Refer to the online course to complete this activity.

Interactive Graphic

Activity 8.1.1.7: Identify Commands Used for Measuring Data

Refer to the online course to complete this activity.

Packet Tracer ☐ Activity

Packet Tracer 8.1.1.8: Troubleshooting Challenge: Documenting the Network

This activity covers the steps to discover a network using primarily the **telnet**, **show cdp neighbors detail**, and **show ip route** commands. This is Part I of a two-part activity. Part II is Packet Tracer 8.2.4.15: Troubleshooting Challenge: Using Documentation to Solve Issues, which comes later in the chapter.

The topology you see when you open the Packet Tracer activity does not reveal all the details of the network. The details have been hidden using the cluster function of Packet Tracer. The network infrastructure has been collapsed, and the topology in the file shows only the end devices. Your task is to use your knowledge of networking and discovery commands to learn about the full network topology and document it.

Troubleshooting Process (8.1.2)

In this topic, you learn about the general troubleshooting process.

General Troubleshooting Procedures (8.1.2.1)

Troubleshooting takes a large portion of network administrators' and support personnel's time. Using efficient troubleshooting techniques shortens overall troubleshooting time when working in a production environment.

The troubleshooting process has three major stages, as shown in Figure 8-6:

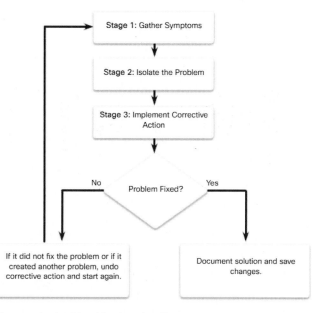

Figure 8-6   Stages in the Troubleshooting Process

Step 1.   **Gather symptoms:** Troubleshooting begins with gathering and documenting symptoms from the network, end systems, and users. In addition, the network administrator determines which network components have been affected and how the functionality of the network has changed compared to the baseline. Symptoms may appear in many different forms, including alerts from the network management system, console messages, and user complaints. While gathering symptoms, the network administrator needs to ask questions and investigate the issue to localize the problem to a smaller range of possibilities. For example, is the problem restricted to a single device, a group of devices, or an entire subnet or network of devices?

Step 2.   **Isolate the problem:** Isolating is the process of eliminating variables until a single problem or a set of related problems has been identified as the cause. To do this, the network administrator examines the characteristics of the problems at the logical layers of the network so that the most likely cause can be selected. At this stage, the network administrator may gather and document more symptoms, depending on the characteristics that are identified.

Step 3.   **Implement corrective action:** After identifying the cause of the problem, the network administrator works to correct the problem by implementing, testing, and documenting possible solutions. After finding the problem and determining a solution, the network administrator may need to decide if the solution can be implemented immediately or if it must be postponed. This depends on the impact of the changes on the users and the network. The severity of the problem should be weighed against the impact of the solution. For example, if a critical server or router must be offline for a significant amount of time, it may be better to wait until the end of the workday to implement the fix. Sometimes, a workaround can be created until the actual problem is resolved. This is typically part of a company's *change control procedures*.

If the corrective action creates another problem or does not solve the problem, the attempted solution is documented, the changes are removed, and the network administrator returns to gathering symptoms and isolating the issue.

These stages are not mutually exclusive. At any point in the process, it may be necessary to return to previous stages. For instance, the network administrator may need to gather more symptoms while isolating a problem. Additionally, when attempting to correct a problem, the network administrator could create another problem. In this instance, remove changes and begin troubleshooting again.

A troubleshooting policy, including change control procedures that document the change made and who made the change, should be established for each stage. A policy provides a consistent manner in which to perform each stage. Part of the policy should include documenting every important piece of information.

Communicate to the users and anyone involved in the troubleshooting process that the problem has been resolved. Other IT team members should be informed of the solution. Appropriate documentation of the cause and the fix will assist other support technicians in preventing and solving similar problems in the future.

Gathering Symptoms (8.1.2.2)

When gathering symptoms, the administrator needs to gather facts and evidence to progressively eliminate possible causes and eventually identify the root cause of the issue. By analyzing the information, the network administrator can formulate a hypothesis to propose possible causes and solutions, while eliminating others.

There are five information-gathering steps:

Step 1. **Gather information:** Gather information from the trouble ticket, users, or end systems affected by the problem to form a definition of the problem.

Step 2. **Determine ownership:** If the problem is within the control of the organization, move on to the next stage. If the problem is outside the boundary of the organization's control (for example, lost Internet connectivity outside the autonomous system), contact an administrator for the external system before gathering additional network symptoms.

Step 3. **Narrow the scope:** Determine if the problem is at the core, distribution, or access layer of the network. At the identified layer, analyze the existing symptoms and use your knowledge of the network topology to determine which piece of equipment is the most likely cause.

Step 4. **Gather symptoms from suspect devices:** Using a layered troubleshooting approach, gather hardware and software symptoms from the suspect devices. Start with the most likely possibility and use knowledge and experience to determine if the problem is more likely a hardware or software configuration problem.

Step 5. **Document symptoms:** Sometimes the problem can be solved using the documented symptoms. If not, begin the isolating stage of the general troubleshooting process.

To gather symptoms from a suspected malfunctioning networking device, use Cisco IOS commands and other tools, including

- **ping**, **traceroute**, and **telnet** commands

- **show** and **debug** commands

- Packet captures

- Device logs

Table 8-5 describes common Cisco IOS commands used to gather the symptoms of a network problem.

Table 8-5 Commands for Gathering Symptoms

Command	Description
ping {*host* | *ip-address*}	Sends an echo request packet to an address and waits for a reply. The *host* or *ip-address* variable is the IP alias or IP address of the target system.
traceroute {*destination*}	Identifies the path a packet takes through the networks. The *destination* variable is the hostname or IP address of the target system.
telnet {*host* | *ip-address*}	Connects to an IP address using the Telnet application. Alternatively, if SSH is enabled, use the **ssh - l** *username ip-address* command.
show ip interface brief **show ipv6 interface brief**	Displays a summary of the status of all interfaces on a device.

Command	Description
show ip route show ipv6 route	Displays contents of the currently running configuration file.
show running-config	Displays a list of options for enabling or disabling debugging events on a device.
[no] debug ?	Displays a list of options for enabling or disabling debugging events on a device.
show protocols	Displays the configured protocols and shows the global and interface-specific status of any configured Layer 3 protocol.

Note

Although the **debug** command is an important tool for gathering symptoms, it generates a large amount of console message traffic, and the performance of a network device can be noticeably affected. If the **debug** must be performed during normal working hours, warn network users that a troubleshooting effort is underway and that network performance may be affected. Remember to disable debugging when you are done.

Questioning End Users (8.1.2.3)

In many cases, an end user reports the problem. The information may often be vague or misleading, such as "The network is down" or "I cannot access my email." In these cases, the problem must be better defined. This may require asking questions of the end users.

Use effective questioning techniques when asking the end users about a network problem they may be experiencing. This will help you get the information required to document the symptoms of a problem.

Table 8-6 provides some guidelines and sample end-user questions.

Table 8-6   Questioning End Users

Guidelines	Sample End-User Questions
Ask questions that are pertinent to the problem.	What does not work?
Use each question as a means to either eliminate or discover possible problems.	Are the things that do work and the things that do not work related?
Speak at a technical level that the user can understand.	Has the thing that does not work ever worked?

Guidelines	Sample End-User Questions
Ask the user when the problem was first noticed.	When was the problem first noticed?
Determine whether anything unusual has happened since the last time it worked.	What has changed since the last time it did work?
Ask the user to re-create the problem, if possible.	Can you reproduce the problem?
Determine the sequence of events that took place before the problem happened.	When exactly does the problem occur?

Interactive Graphic

Activity 8.1.2.4: Identify Commands for Gathering Symptoms

Refer to the online course to complete this activity.

Isolating the Issue Using Layered Models (8.1.3)

In this topic, you compare troubleshooting methods that use a systematic, layered approach.

Using Layered Models for Troubleshooting (8.1.3.1)

After all symptoms are gathered, if no solution is identified, the network administrator compares the characteristics of the problem to the logical layers of the network to isolate and solve the issue.

Logical networking models, such as the OSI and TCP/IP models, separate network functionality into modular layers. These layered models can be applied to the physical network to isolate network problems when troubleshooting. For example, if the symptoms suggest a physical connection problem, the network technician can focus on troubleshooting the circuit that operates at the physical layer. If that circuit functions as expected, the technician looks at areas within another layer that could be causing the problem.

OSI Reference Model

The OSI reference model provides a common language for network administrators and is commonly used in troubleshooting networks. Problems are typically described in terms of a given OSI model layer.

The OSI reference model describes how information from a software application in one computer moves through a network medium to a software application in another computer.

The upper layers (5 to 7) of the OSI model deal with application issues and generally are implemented only in software. The application layer is closest to the end user. Both users and application layer processes interact with software applications that contain a communications component.

The lower layers (1 to 4) of the OSI model handle data-transport issues. Layers 3 and 4 are generally implemented only in software. The physical layer (Layer 1) and data link layer (Layer 2) are implemented in hardware and software. The physical layer is closest to the physical network medium, such as the network cabling, and is responsible for actually placing information on the medium.

Figure 8-7 shows some common devices and the OSI layers that must be examined during the troubleshooting process for that device. Notice that routers and multilayer switches are shown at Layer 4, the transport layer. Although routers and multilayer switches usually make forwarding decisions at Layer 3, ACLs on these devices can be used to make filtering decisions using Layer 4 information.

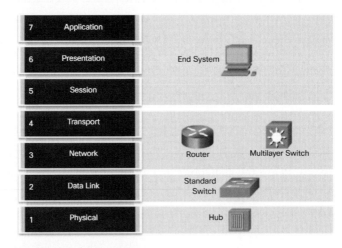

Figure 8-7   OSI Reference Model

TCP/IP Model

Similar to the OSI networking model, the TCP/IP networking model also divides networking architecture into modular layers. Figure 8-8 shows how the TCP/IP networking model maps to the layers of the OSI networking model. It is this close mapping that allows the TCP/IP suite of protocols to successfully communicate with so many networking technologies.

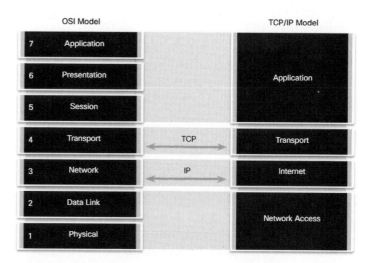

Figure 8-8   Comparing the OSI Model and the TCP Model

The application layer in the TCP/IP suite actually combines the functions of three OSI model layers: session, presentation, and application. The application layer provides communication between applications, such as FTP, HTTP, and SMTP on separate hosts.

The transport layers of TCP/IP and OSI directly correspond in function. The transport layer is responsible for exchanging segments between devices on a TCP/IP network.

The TCP/IP Internet layer relates to the OSI network layer. The Internet layer is responsible for addressing used for data transfer from source to destination.

The TCP/IP network access layer corresponds to the OSI physical and data link layers. The network access layer communicates directly with the network media and provides an interface between the architecture of the network and the Internet layer.

Troubleshooting Methods (8.1.3.2)

Using the layered models, a network administrator can use three primary methods for troubleshooting networks:

- *Bottom-up troubleshooting approach*
- *Top-down troubleshooting approach*
- *Divide-and-conquer troubleshooting approach*

Each approach has its advantages and disadvantages. This topic describes the three methods and provides guidelines for choosing the best method for a specific situation.

Bottom-Up Troubleshooting Method

In bottom-up troubleshooting, you start with the physical components of the network and move up through the layers of the OSI model until the cause of the problem is identified, as shown in Figure 8-9.

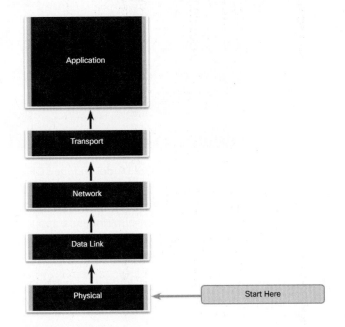

Figure 8-9   Bottom-Up Method

Bottom-up troubleshooting is a good approach to use when the problem is suspected to be a physical one. Most networking problems reside at the lower levels, so implementing the bottom-up approach is often effective.

The disadvantage of using the bottom-up troubleshooting approach is it requires that you check every device and interface on the network until the possible cause of the problem is found. Remember that each conclusion and possibility must be documented, so a lot of paperwork can be associated with this approach. A further challenge is to determine which devices to start examining first.

Top-Down Troubleshooting Method

In Figure 8-10, top-down troubleshooting starts with the end-user applications and moves down through the layers of the OSI model until the cause of the problem has been identified.

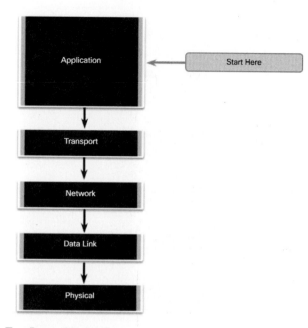

Figure 8-10   Top-Down Method

End-user applications of an end system are tested before tackling the more specific networking pieces. Use this approach for simpler problems or when you think the problem is with a piece of software.

The disadvantage with the top-down approach is it requires checking every network application until the possible cause of the problem is found. Each conclusion and possibility must be documented. The challenge is to determine which application to start examining first.

Divide-and-Conquer Troubleshooting Method

Figure 8-11 shows the divide-and-conquer troubleshooting approach to troubleshooting a networking problem. The network administrator selects a layer and tests in both directions from that layer.

In divide-and-conquer troubleshooting, the network administrator should start by collecting user experiences of the problem, document the symptoms and then, using that information, make an informed guess as to which OSI layer to start your investigation. When a layer is verified to be functioning properly, it can be assumed that the layers below it are functioning. The administrator can work up the OSI layers. If an OSI layer is not functioning properly, the administrator can work down the OSI layer model.

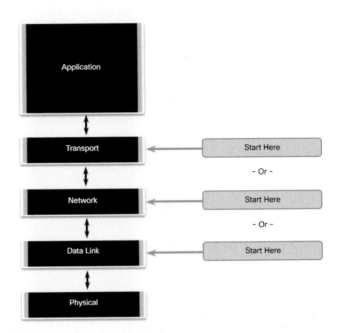

Figure 8-11   Divide-and-Conquer Method

For example, if users cannot access the web server, but they can ping the server, the problem is above Layer 3. If pinging the server is unsuccessful, the problem is likely at a lower OSI layer.

Other Troubleshooting Methods (8.1.3.3)

In addition to the systematic, layered approach to troubleshooting, there are also less-structured troubleshooting approaches.

One troubleshooting approach is built on an educated guess by the network administrator, based on the symptoms of the problem. This method is more successfully implemented by seasoned network administrators because they rely on their extensive knowledge and experience to decisively isolate and solve network issues. With a less-experienced network administrator, this troubleshooting method may be more like random troubleshooting.

Another approach involves comparing a working and nonworking situation and spotting significant differences, including

- Configurations
- Software versions
- Hardware and other device properties

Using this method may lead to a working solution, but without clearly revealing the cause of the problem. This method can be helpful when the network administrator is lacking an area of expertise or when the problem needs to be resolved quickly. After the fix has been implemented, the network administrator can do further research on the actual cause of the problem.

Substitution is another quick troubleshooting methodology. It involves swapping the problematic device with a known working one. If the problem is fixed, the network administrator knows the problem is with the removed device. If the problem remains, the cause may be elsewhere. In specific situations, this can be an ideal method for quick problem resolution, such as when a critical single point of failure, like a border router, goes down. It may be more beneficial to simply replace the device and restore service than to troubleshoot the issue.

Guidelines for Selecting a Troubleshooting Method (8.1.3.4)

To quickly resolve network problems, take the time to select the most effective network troubleshooting method. Figure 8-12 illustrates this process.

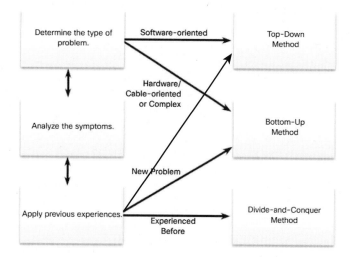

Figure 8-12 Guidelines for Selecting a Troubleshooting Method

The following is an example of how to choose a troubleshooting method based on a specific problem:

1. Two IP routers are not exchanging routing information. The last time this type of problem occurred, it was a protocol issue. Therefore, choose the divide-and-conquer troubleshooting method.

2. Analysis reveals that there is connectivity between the routers.

3. Start the troubleshooting process at the physical or data link layer.

4. Confirm connectivity and begin testing the TCP/IP-related functions at the next layer up in the OSI model, the network layer.

Interactive Graphic

Activity 8.1.3.5: Troubleshooting Methods

Refer to the online course to complete this activity.

Troubleshooting Scenarios (8.2)

In this section, you troubleshoot end-to-end connectivity in a small- to medium-sized business network, using a systematic approach.

Using IP SLA (8.2.1)

In this topic, you use an ICMP echo-based IP SLA to troubleshoot network connectivity issues.

IP SLA Concepts (8.2.1.1)

Network administrators must be proactive and continually monitor and test the network. The goal is to discover a network failure as early as possible. A useful tool for this task is the *Cisco IOS IP service-level agreement (SLA)*.

IP SLAs use generated traffic to measure network performance between two networking devices, multiple network locations, or across multiple network paths. In Figure 8-13, R1 is the IP SLA source that monitors the connection to the DNS server by periodically sending ICMP requests to the server.

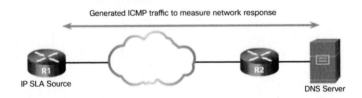

Figure 8-13 IP SLA Operation

Network engineers use IP SLAs to simulate network data and IP services to collect network performance information in real time. Performance monitoring can be done anytime, anywhere, without deploying a physical probe.

> **Note**
>
> Ping and traceroute are probe tools. A physical probe is different. It is a device that can be inserted somewhere in the network to collect and monitor traffic. The use of physical probes is beyond the scope of this course.

Measurements provided by the various IP SLA operations can be used for troubleshooting networks by providing consistent, reliable measurements that immediately identify problems and save troubleshooting time.

Additional benefits from using IP SLAs include

- Service-level agreement monitoring, measurement, and verification

- Network performance monitoring to provide continuous, reliable, and predictable measurements to measure the jitter, latency, or packet loss in the network

- IP service network health assessment to verify that the existing QoS is sufficient for new IP services

- Edge-to-edge network availability monitoring for proactive connectivity verification of network resources

Multiple IP SLA operations can be running on the network, or on a device, at any time. IP SLA information can be displayed using CLI commands or through SNMP.

> **Note**
>
> SNMP notifications based on the data gathered by an IP SLA operation are beyond the scope of this course.

IP SLA Configuration (8.2.1.2)

Instead of using **ping** manually, a network engineer can use the IP SLA ICMP echo operation to test the availability of network devices. A network device can be any device with IP capabilities (router, switch, PC, server, and so on).

The IP SLA ICMP echo operation provides the following measurements:

- Availability monitoring (packet loss statistics)

- Performance monitoring (latency and response time)

- Network operation (end-to-end connectivity)

To verify that the desired IP SLA operation is supported on the source device, use the **show ip sla application** privileged EXEC mode command. The output generated in Example 8-1 confirms that R1 is capable of supporting IP SLA. However, no sessions are currently configured.

Example 8-1 Available IP SLA Operations

```
R1# show ip sla application
      IP Service Level Agreements
Version: Round Trip Time MIB 2.2.0, Infrastructure Engine-III

Supported Operation Types:
      icmpEcho, path-echo, path-jitter, udpEcho, tcpConnect, http
      dns, udpJitter, dhcp, ftp, VoIP, icmpJitter
      802.1agEcho VLAN, Port, 802.1agJitter VLAN, Port, y1731Delay
      y1731Loss, udpApp, wspApp, mcast, generic

Supported Features:
      IPSLAs Event Publisher

IP SLAs low memory water mark: 61167610
Estimated system max number of entries: 44800

Estimated number of configurable operations: 44641
Number of Entries configured   : 0
Number of active Entries       : 0
Number of pending Entries      : 0
Number of inactive Entries     : 0
Time of last change in whole IP SLAs: *20:27:15.935 UTC Wed Jan 27 2016
```

To create an IP SLA operation and enter IP SLA configuration mode, use the **ip sla** *operation-number* global configuration command. The operation number is a unique number used to identify the operation being configured.

From IP SLA configuration mode, you can configure the IP SLA operation as an ICMP echo operation and enter ICMP echo configuration mode using the following command:

```
Router(config-ip-sla)# icmp-echo {dest-ip-address | dest-hostname} [source-ip
   {ip-address | hostname} | source-interface interface-id]
```

Next, set the rate at which a specified IP SLA operation repeats using the **frequency** *seconds* IP SLA echo configuration mode command. The range is from 1 to 604,800 seconds and the default is 60 seconds.

To schedule the IP SLA operation, use the following global configuration command:

```
Router(config)# ip sla schedule operation-number [life {forever | seconds}] [start-
   time {hh:mm [:ss] [month day | day month] | pending | now | after hh:mm:ss]
   [ageout seconds] [recurring]
```

Sample IP SLA Configuration (8.2.1.3)

To understand how to configure a simple IP SLA, refer to the topology in Figure 8-14.

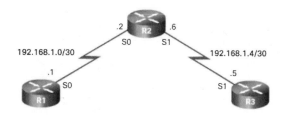

Figure 8-14 IP SLA ICMP Echo Configuration Topology

Example 8-2 shows a configuration for an IP SLA operation with an operation number of 1.

Example 8-2 IP SLA ICMP Echo Configuration

```
R1(config)# ip sla 1
R1(config-ip-sla)# icmp-echo 192.168.1.5
R1(config-ip-sla-echo)# frequency 30
R1(config-ip-sla-echo)# exit
R1(config)#
R1(config)# ip sla schedule 1 start-time now life forever
R1(config)# end
R1#
```

Multiple IP SLA operations may be configured on a device. Each operation can be referred to by its operation number. The **icmp-echo** command identifies the destination address to be monitored. In the example, it is set to monitor R3's S1 interface. The **frequency** command sets the IP SLA rate to 30-second intervals.

The **ip sla schedule** command schedules the IP SLA operation number 1 to start immediately (now) and continue until manually canceled (forever).

Note

Use the **no ip sla schedule** *operation-number* command to cancel the SLA operation. The SLA operation configuration is preserved and can be rescheduled when needed.

Verifying an IP SLA Configuration (8.2.1.4)

Use the **show ip sla configuration** *operation-number* command to display configuration values including all defaults for IP SLA operations or for a specific operation.

In Example 8-3, the **show ip sla configuration** command displays the IP SLA ICMP echo configuration.

Example 8-3 Verifying IP SLA Configuration

```
R1# show ip sla configuration
IP SLAs Infrastructure Engine-III
Entry number: 1
Owner:
Tag:
Operation timeout (milliseconds): 5000
Type of operation to perform: icmp-echo
Target address/Source address: 192.168.1.5/0.0.0.0
Type Of Service parameter: 0x0
Request size (ARR data portion): 28
Verify data: No
Vrf Name:
Schedule:
    Operation frequency (seconds): 30   (not considered if randomly scheduled)
    Next Scheduled Start Time: Start Time already passed
    Group Scheduled : FALSE
    Randomly Scheduled : FALSE
    Life (seconds): Forever
    Entry Ageout (seconds): never
    Recurring (Starting Everyday): FALSE
    Status of entry (SNMP RowStatus): Active
Threshold (milliseconds): 5000
Distribution Statistics:
    Number of statistic hours kept: 2
    Number of statistic distribution buckets kept: 1
    Statistic distribution interval (milliseconds): 20
Enhanced History:
History Statistics:
    Number of history Lives kept: 0
    Number of history Buckets kept: 15
    History Filter Type: None
```

Use the **show ip sla statistics** [*operation-number*] command to display the IP SLA operation monitoring statistics, as shown in Example 8-4.

Example 8-4 Verifying IP SLA Statistics

```
R1# show ip sla statistics
IPSLAs Latest Operation Statistics


IPSLA operation id: 1
      Latest RTT: 12 milliseconds
Latest operation start time: 00:12:31 UTC Wed Jan 27 2016
Latest operation return code: OK
Number of successes: 57
Number of failures: 0
Operation time to live: Forever
```

Lab 8.2.1.5: Configure IP SLA ICMP Echo

In this lab, you complete the following objectives:

- Build the Network and Verify Connectivity

- Configure IP SLA ICMP Echo on R1

- Test and Monitor the IP SLA Operation

Troubleshooting Tools (8.2.2)

In this topic, you learn about different networking troubleshooting tools.

Software Troubleshooting Tools (8.2.2.1)

A wide variety of software and hardware tools are available to make troubleshooting easier. These tools may be used to gather and analyze symptoms of network problems. They often provide monitoring and reporting functions that can be used to establish the network baseline.

Common software troubleshooting tools include *network management system tools*, *knowledge bases*, and *baselining tools*.

Network Management System Tools

Network management system (NMS) tools include device-level monitoring, configuration, and fault-management tools. Figure 8-15 shows a sample display from the WhatsUp Gold NMS software.

Figure 8-15   Network Management System

These tools can be used to investigate and correct network problems. Network monitoring software graphically displays a physical view of network devices, allowing network managers to monitor remote devices continuously and automatically. Device management software provides dynamic device status, statistics, and configuration information for key network devices.

Knowledge Bases

Online network device vendor knowledge bases have become indispensable sources of information. When vendor-based knowledge bases are combined with Internet search engines like Google, a network administrator has access to a vast pool of experience-based information.

Figure 8-16 shows the Cisco Tools & Resources page found at www.cisco.com.

This page provides information on Cisco-related hardware and software. It contains troubleshooting procedures, implementation guides, and original white papers on most aspects of networking technology.

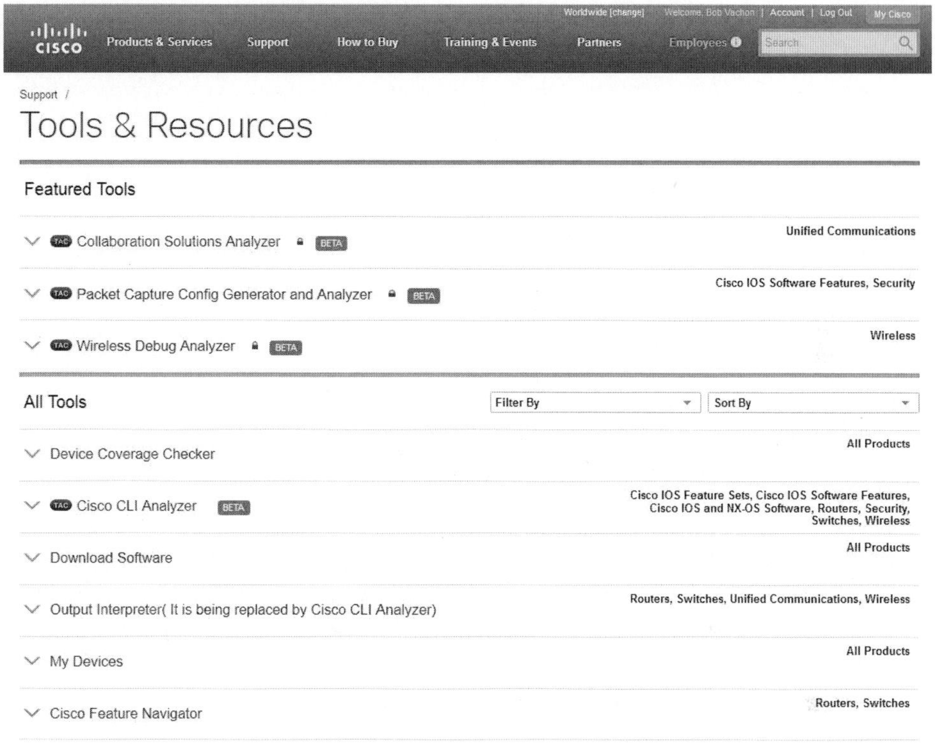

Figure 8-16 Cisco Tools and Resources

Baselining Tools

Many tools for automating the network documentation and baselining process are available. Figure 8-17 shows a screen capture of the SolarWinds Network Performance Monitor 12 baseline view.

Baselining tools help with common documentation tasks. For example, they can draw network diagrams, help keep network software and hardware documentation up-to-date, and help to cost-effectively measure baseline network bandwidth use.

Protocol Analyzers (8.2.2.2)

Protocol analyzers are useful to investigate packet content while flowing through the network. A protocol analyzer decodes the various protocol layers in a recorded frame and presents this information in a relatively easy-to-use format. Figure 8-18 shows a screen capture of the Wireshark protocol analyzer.

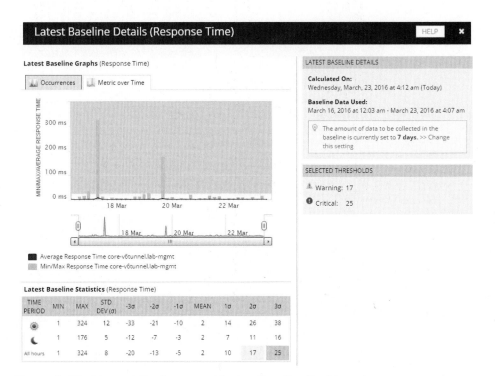

Figure 8-17   Network Performance Monitor Baseline Dashboard

The information displayed by a protocol analyzer includes the physical, data link, protocol, and descriptions for each frame. Most protocol analyzers can filter traffic that meets certain criteria so that, for example, all traffic to and from a particular device can be captured. Protocol analyzers such as Wireshark can help troubleshoot network performance problems. It is important to have both a good understanding of TCP/IP and how to use a protocol analyzer to inspect information at each TCP/IP layer.

Note

If you want to become more knowledgeable and skillful using Wireshark, an excellent resource is www.wiresharkbook.com.

Hardware Troubleshooting Tools (8.2.2.3)

Multiple types of hardware troubleshooting tools are available.

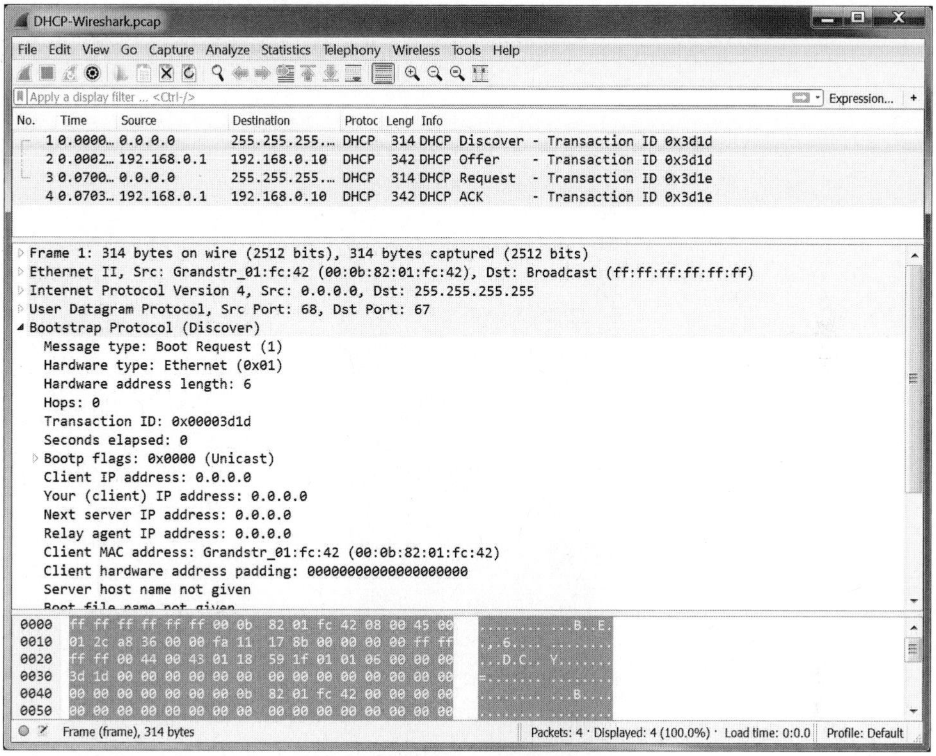

Figure 8-18   Wireshark Protocol Analyzer

Common hardware troubleshooting tools include

- *Digital multimeters (DMMs)*: DMMs, such as the Fluke 179 shown in Figure 8-19, are test instruments that are used to directly measure electrical values of voltage, current, and resistance. In network troubleshooting, most tests that would need a multimeter involve checking power supply voltage levels and verifying that network devices are receiving power.

- *Cable testers*: Cable testers are specialized, handheld devices designed for testing the various types of data communication cabling. Figure 8-20 displays the Fluke LinkRunner AT Network Auto-Tester. Cable testers can be used to detect broken wires, crossed-over wiring, shorted connections, and improperly paired connections. These devices can be inexpensive continuity testers, moderately priced data cabling testers, or expensive *time-domain reflectometers (TDRs)*. TDRs are used to pinpoint the distance to a break in a cable. These devices send signals along the cable and wait for them to be reflected. The time between sending the signal and receiving it back is converted into a distance measurement. The

TDR function is normally packaged with data cabling testers. TDRs used to test fiber-optic cables are known as *optical time-domain reflectometers (OTDRs)*.

Fluke 179 Digital Multimeter

Figure 8-19   Digital Multimeter

- *Cable analyzers*: Cable analyzers, such as the Fluke DTX Cable Analyzer in Figure 8-21, are multifunctional handheld devices that are used to test and certify copper and fiber cables for different services and standards. The more sophisticated tools include advanced troubleshooting diagnostics that measure the distance to a performance defect such as near-end crosstalk (NEXT) or return loss (RL), identify corrective actions, and graphically display crosstalk and impedance behavior. Cable analyzers also typically include PC-based software. After field data is collected, the data from the handheld device can be uploaded so that the network administrator can create up-to-date reports.

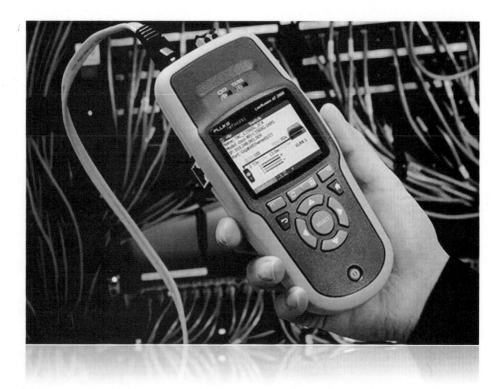

Figure 8-20   Cable Testers

Fluke Networks LinkRunner Pro
Tester

Fluke Networks CableIQ Qualification Tester

Figure 8-21   Cable Analyzer

■ *Portable network analyzers*: Portable devices like the Fluke OptiView in Figure 8-22 are used for troubleshooting switched networks and VLANs. By plugging the network analyzer in anywhere on the network, a network engineer can see the switch port to which the device is connected and see the average and peak utilization. The analyzer can also be used to discover VLAN configuration, identify top network talkers, analyze network traffic, and view interface details. The device can typically output to a PC that has network monitoring software installed for further analysis and troubleshooting.

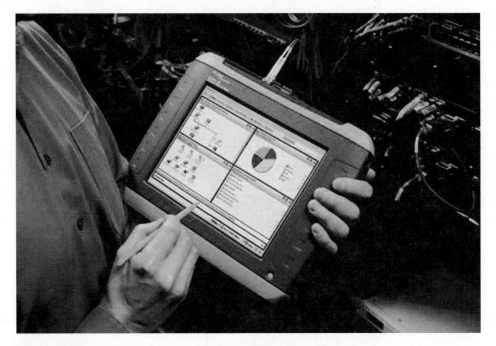

Figure 8-22   OptiView XG Network Analysis Tablet

■ *Network analysis module*: The Cisco NAM is a device or software, as shown in Figure 8-23. It provides an embedded browser-based interface that generates reports on the traffic that consumes critical network resources. It displays a graphical representation of traffic from local and remote switches and routers, such as seen in Figure 8-24. In addition, the NAM can capture and decode packets and track response times to pinpoint an application problem to a particular network or server.

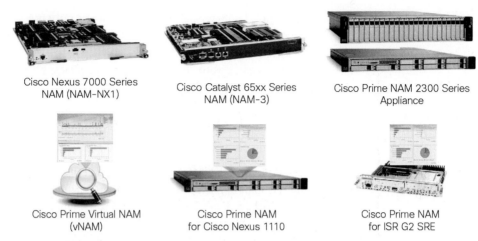

Figure 8-23   Cisco NAM Devices and Software

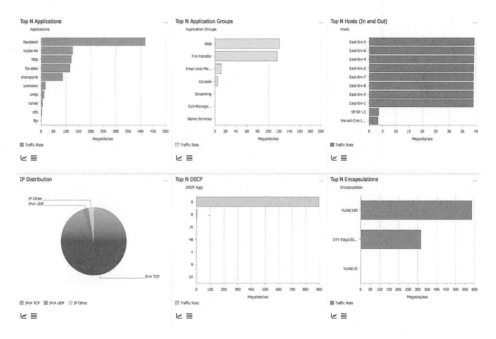

Figure 8-24   NAM Web Interface

Using a Syslog Server for Troubleshooting (8.2.2.4)

Syslog is a simple protocol used by an IP device known as a syslog client to send
text-based log messages to another IP device, the *syslog server*. Syslog is currently
defined in RFC 5424.

Implementing a logging facility is an important part of network security and for network troubleshooting. Cisco devices can log information regarding configuration changes, ACL violations, interface status, and many other types of events. Cisco devices can send log messages to several different facilities. Event messages can be sent to one or more of the following:

■ **Console:** Console logging is on by default. Messages log to the console and can be viewed when modifying or testing the router or switch using terminal emulation software while connected to the console port of the network device.

■ **Terminal lines:** Enabled EXEC sessions can be configured to receive log messages on any terminal lines. Similar to console logging, this type of logging is not stored by the network device and, therefore, is valuable only to the user on that line.

■ **Buffered logging:** Buffered logging is a little more useful as a troubleshooting tool because log messages are stored in memory for a time. However, log messages are cleared when the device is rebooted.

■ **SNMP traps:** Certain thresholds can be preconfigured on routers and other devices. Router events, such as exceeding a threshold, can be processed by the router and forwarded as SNMP traps to an external SNMP network management station. SNMP traps are a viable security logging facility but require the configuration and maintenance of an SNMP system.

■ **Syslog server:** Cisco routers and switches can be configured to forward log messages to an external syslog service. This service can reside on any number of servers or workstations, including Microsoft Windows and Linux-based systems. Syslog is the most popular message logging facility because it provides long-term log storage capabilities and a central location for all router messages.

Cisco IOS log messages fall into one of eight levels, shown in Figure 8-25.

	Level	Keyword	Description	Definition
Highest Level	0	emergencies	System is unusable	LOG_EMERG
	1	alerts	Immediate action is needed	LOG_ALERT
	2	critical	Critical conditions exist	LOG_CRIT
	3	errors	Error conditions exist	LOG_ERR
	4	warnings	Warning conditions exist	LOG_WARNING
	5	notifications	Normal (but significant) condition	LOG_NOTICE
	6	informational	Informational messages only	LOG_INFO
Lowest Level	7	debugging	Debugging messages	LOG_DEBUG

Figure 8-25 Severity Levels

The lower the level number, the higher the severity level. By default, all messages from levels 0 to 7 are logged to the console. While the ability to view logs on a central syslog server is helpful in troubleshooting, sifting through a large amount of data can be an overwhelming task. The **logging trap** *level* global configuration command limits messages logged to the syslog server based on severity. The *level* is the name or number of the severity level. Only messages equal to or numerically lower than the specified level are logged.

In Example 8-5, system messages from levels 0 (emergencies) to 5 (notifications) are sent to the syslog server at 209.165.200.225.

Example 8-5 Limiting Messages Sent to the Syslog Server

```
R1(config)# logging host 209.165.200.225
R1(config)# logging trap notifications
R1(config)# logging on
```

Interactive
Graphic

Activity 8.2.2.5: Identify Common Troubleshooting Tools

Refer to the online course to complete this activity.

Symptoms and Causes of Network Troubleshooting (8.2.3)

In this topic, you learn how to determine the symptoms and causes of network problems using a layered model.

Physical Layer Troubleshooting (8.2.3.1)

The physical layer transmits bits from one computer to another and regulates the transmission of a stream of bits over the physical medium. The physical layer is the only layer with physically tangible properties, such as wires, cards, and antennas.

Issues on a network often present as performance problems. Performance problems mean that a difference exists between the expected behavior and the observed behavior, and the system is not functioning as could be reasonably expected. Failures and suboptimal conditions at the physical layer not only inconvenience users but also can impact the productivity of the entire company. Networks that experience these kinds of conditions usually shut down. Because the upper layers of the OSI model depend on the physical layer to function, a network administrator must have the ability to effectively isolate and correct problems at this layer.

Figure 8-26 summarizes physical layer symptoms and causes.

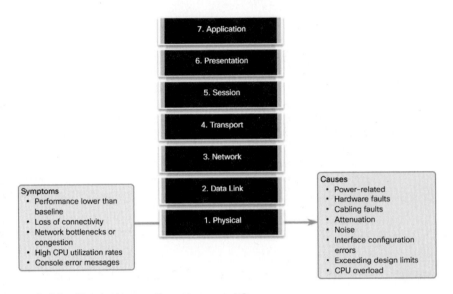

Figure 8-26   Physical Layer Symptoms and Causes

Common symptoms of network problems at the physical layer include

- **Performance lower than baseline:** The most common reasons for slow or poor performance include overloaded or underpowered servers, unsuitable switch or router configurations, traffic congestion on a low-capacity link, and chronic frame loss.

- **Loss of connectivity:** If a cable or device fails, the most obvious symptom is a loss of connectivity between the devices that communicate over that link or with the failed device or interface. This loss is indicated by a simple ping test. Intermittent loss of connectivity can indicate a loose or oxidized connection.

- **Network bottlenecks or congestion:** If a router, interface, or cable fails, routing protocols may redirect traffic to other routes that are not designed to carry the extra capacity. This can result in congestion or bottlenecks in those parts of the network.

- **High CPU utilization rates:** High CPU utilization rates are a symptom that a device, such as a router, switch, or server, is operating at or exceeding its design limits. If not addressed quickly, CPU overloading can cause a device to shut down or fail.

- **Console error messages:** Error messages reported on the device console could indicate a physical layer problem.

Issues that commonly cause network problems at the physical layer include

- **Power related:** Power-related issues are the most fundamental reason for network failure. Also, check the operation of the fans and ensure that the chassis intake and exhaust vents are clear. If other nearby units have also powered down, suspect a power failure at the main power supply.

- **Hardware faults:** Faulty network interface cards (NICs) can be the cause of network transmission errors due to late collisions, short frames, and *jabber*. Jabber is often defined as the condition in which a network device continually transmits random, meaningless data onto the network. Other likely causes of jabber are faulty or corrupt NIC driver files, bad cabling, or grounding problems.

- **Cabling faults:** Many problems can be corrected by simply reseating cables that have become partially disconnected. When performing a physical inspection, look for damaged cables, improper cable types, and poorly crimped RJ-45 connectors. Suspect cables should be tested or exchanged with a known functioning cable.

- *Attenuation*: Attenuation can be caused if a cable length exceeds the design limit for the media or when there is a poor connection resulting from a loose cable or dirty or oxidized contacts. If attenuation is severe, the receiving device cannot always successfully distinguish one bit in the data stream from another bit.

- **Noise:** Local *electromagnetic interference (EMI)* is commonly known as noise. Noise can be generated by many sources, such as FM radio stations, police radio, building security, and avionics for automated landing, crosstalk (noise induced by other cables in the same pathway or adjacent cables), nearby electric cables, devices with large electric motors, or anything that includes a transmitter more powerful than a cell phone.

- **Interface configuration errors:** Many things can be misconfigured on an interface to cause it to go down, such as incorrect clock rate, incorrect clock source, and interface not being turned on. This causes a loss of connectivity with attached network segments.

- **Exceeding design limits:** A component may be operating suboptimally at the physical layer because it is being utilized beyond specifications or configured capacity. When you are troubleshooting this type of problem, it becomes evident that resources for the device are operating at or near the maximum capacity and there is an increase in the number of interface errors.

- **CPU overload:** Symptoms include processes with high CPU utilization percentages, input queue drops, slow performance, SNMP timeouts, or no remote access, or services such as DHCP, Telnet, and ping are slow or fail to respond. On a switch, the following could occur: spanning tree reconvergence, EtherChannel links alternating up and down, or IP SLA failures. For routers, there could be no routing updates, route flapping, or HSRP flapping. One of the causes of CPU overload in a router or switch is high traffic. If one or more interfaces are regularly overloaded with traffic, consider redesigning the traffic flow in the network or upgrading the hardware.

Data Link Layer Troubleshooting (8.2.3.2)

Troubleshooting Layer 2 problems can be a challenging process. The configuration and operation of these protocols are critical to creating a functional, well-tuned network. Layer 2 problems cause specific symptoms that, when recognized, will help identify the problem quickly.

Figure 8-27 summarizes data link layer symptoms and causes.

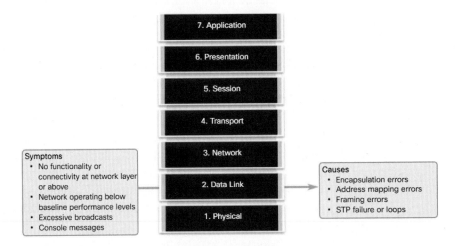

Figure 8-27   Data Link Layer Symptoms and Causes

The following are common symptoms of network problems at the data link layer:

- **No functionality or connectivity at the network layer or above:** Some Layer 2 problems can stop the exchange of frames across a link, whereas others only cause network performance to degrade.

- **Network is operating below baseline performance levels:** Two distinct types of suboptimal Layer 2 operation can occur in a network. First, the frames take a suboptimal path to their destination but do arrive. In this case, the network might experience high-bandwidth usage on links that should not have that level of traffic. Second, some frames are dropped. These problems can be identified through error counter statistics and console error messages that appear on the switch or router. In an Ethernet environment, an extended or continuous ping also reveals if frames are being dropped.

■ **Excessive broadcasts:** Operating systems use broadcasts and multicasts extensively to discover network services and other hosts. Generally, excessive broadcasts result from one of the following situations: poorly programmed or configured applications, large Layer 2 broadcast domains, or underlying network problems, such as STP loops or route flapping.

■ **Console messages:** In some instances, a router recognizes that a Layer 2 problem has occurred and sends alert messages to the console. Typically, a router does this when it detects a problem with interpreting incoming frames (encapsulation or framing problems) or when keepalives are expected but do not arrive. The most common console message that indicates a Layer 2 problem is a line protocol down message.

Issues at the data link layer that commonly result in network connectivity or performance problems include

■ **Encapsulation errors:** An encapsulation error occurs because the bits placed in a particular field by the sender are not what the receiver expects to see. This condition occurs when the encapsulation at one end of a WAN link is configured differently from the encapsulation used at the other end.

■ **Address mapping errors:** In topologies, such as point-to-multipoint or broadcast Ethernet, it is essential that an appropriate Layer 2 destination address be given to the frame. This ensures its arrival at the correct destination. To achieve this, the network device must match a destination Layer 3 address with the correct Layer 2 address using either static or dynamic maps. In a dynamic environment, the mapping of Layer 2 and Layer 3 information can fail because devices may have been specifically configured not to respond to ARP requests, the Layer 2 or Layer 3 information that is cached may have physically changed, or invalid ARP replies are received because of a misconfiguration or a security attack.

■ **Framing errors:** Frames usually work in groups of 8-bit bytes. A framing error occurs when a frame does not end on an 8-bit byte boundary. When this happens, the receiver may have problems determining where one frame ends and another frame starts. Too many invalid frames may prevent valid keepalives from being exchanged. Framing errors can be caused by a noisy serial line, an improperly designed cable (too long or not properly shielded), faulty NIC, duplex mismatch, or an incorrectly configured CSU/DSU line clock.

■ **STP failures or loops:** The purpose of the Spanning Tree Protocol (STP) is to resolve a redundant physical topology into a tree-like topology by blocking redundant ports. Most STP problems relate to forwarding loops that occur in a redundant topology. When ports in a redundant topology are not appropriately blocked, traffic is forwarded in circles indefinitely, causing excessive flooding because of a high rate of STP topology changes. A topology change should be a rare event in a well-configured network. For example, a topology change would occur when a link between two switches goes up or down. However, if a port is flapping (oscillating frequently between up and down states), this behavior causes repetitive topology changes and flooding, or slow STP convergence or reconvergence. This behavior can be caused by a mismatch between the real and documented topology; a configuration error, such as an inconsistent configuration of STP timers; an overloaded switch CPU during convergence; or a software defect.

Network Layer Troubleshooting (8.2.3.3)

Network layer problems include any problem that involves a Layer 3 protocol and both routed protocols (such as IPv4 or IPv6) and routing protocols (such as EIGRP, OSPF, and so on).

Figure 8-28 summarizes network layer symptoms and causes.

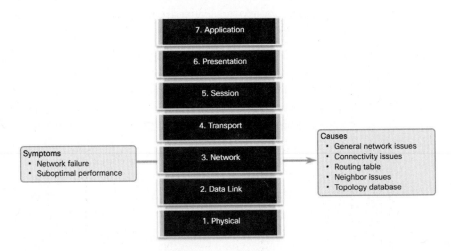

Figure 8-28   Network Layer Symptoms and Causes

Common symptoms of network problems at the network layer include

- **Network failure:** Network failure occurs when the network is nearly or completely nonfunctional, affecting all users and applications on the network. These failures, which are usually noticed quickly by users and network administrators, are obviously critical to the productivity of a company.

- **Suboptimal performance:** Network optimization problems usually involve a subset of users, applications, destinations, or a particular type of traffic. Optimization issues can be difficult to detect and even harder to isolate and diagnose because they usually involve multiple layers or even a single host computer. Determining that the problem is a network layer problem can take time.

In most networks, static routes are used in combination with dynamic routing protocols. Improper configuration of static routes can lead to less than optimal routing. In some cases, improperly configured static routes can create routing loops that make parts of the network unreachable.

Troubleshooting dynamic routing protocols requires a thorough understanding of how the specific routing protocol functions. Some problems are common to all routing protocols, whereas other problems are particular to the individual routing protocol.

There is no single template for solving Layer 3 problems. Routing problems are solved with a methodical process, using a series of commands to isolate and diagnose each problem.

Here are some areas to explore when diagnosing a possible problem involving routing protocols:

- **General network issues:** Often a change in the topology, such as a down link, may have effects on other areas of the network that might not be obvious at the time. This may include the installation of new routes, static or dynamic, or removal of other routes. Determine whether anything in the network has recently changed and if there is anyone currently working on the network infrastructure.

- **Connectivity issues:** Check for any equipment and connectivity problems, including power problems such as outages and environmental problems (for example, overheating). Also check for Layer 1 problems, such as cabling problems, bad ports, and ISP problems.

- **Routing table:** Check the routing table for anything unexpected, such as missing routes or unexpected routes. Use **debug** commands to view routing updates and routing table maintenance.

- **Neighbor issues:** If the routing protocol establishes an adjacency with a neighbor, check to see if there are any problems with the routers forming neighbor adjacencies.

- **Topology database:** If the routing protocol uses a topology table or database, check the table for anything unexpected, such as missing entries or unexpected entries.

Transport Layer Troubleshooting: ACLs (8.2.3.4)

Network problems can arise from transport layer problems on the router, particularly at the edge of the network where traffic is examined and modified. Two of the most commonly implemented transport layer technologies are access control lists (ACLs) and Network Address Translation (NAT), as shown in Figure 8-29.

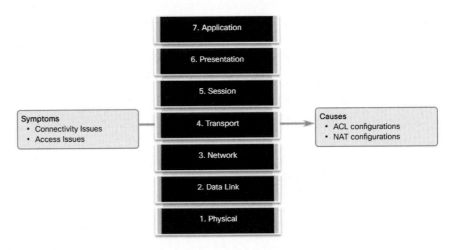

Figure 8-29   Transport Layer Symptoms and Causes

The most common issues with ACLs are caused by improper configuration, as shown in Figure 8-30.

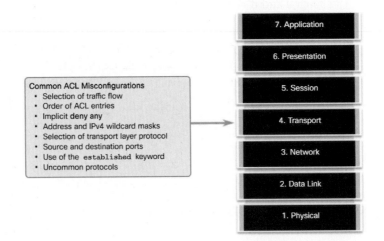

Figure 8-30   Common ACL Misconfigurations

Problems with ACLs may cause otherwise working systems to fail. Misconfigurations commonly occur in several areas:

- **Selection of traffic flow:** Traffic is defined by both the router interface through which the traffic is traveling and the direction in which this traffic is traveling. An ACL must be applied to the correct interface, and the correct traffic direction must be selected to function properly.

- **Order of access control entries:** The entries in an ACL should be from specific to general. Although an ACL may have an entry to specifically permit a particular traffic flow, packets never match that entry if they are being denied by another entry earlier in the list. If the router is running both ACLs and NAT, the order in which each of these technologies is applied to a traffic flow is important. Inbound traffic is processed by the inbound ACL before being processed by outside-to-inside NAT. Outbound traffic is processed by the outbound ACL after being processed by inside-to-outside NAT.

- **Implicit deny any:** When high security is not required on the ACL, this implicit access control element can be the cause of an ACL misconfiguration.

- **Addresses and IPv4 wildcard masks:** Complex IPv4 wildcard masks provide significant improvements in efficiency but are more subject to configuration errors. An example of a complex wildcard mask is using the IPv4 address 10.0.32.0 and wildcard mask 0.0.32.15 to select the first 15 host addresses in either the 10.0.0.0 network or the 10.0.32.0 network.

- **Selection of transport layer protocol:** When an administrator is configuring ACLs, it is important that only the correct transport layer protocols be specified. Many network administrators, when unsure whether a particular traffic flow uses a TCP port or a UDP port, configure both. Specifying both opens a hole through the firewall, possibly giving intruders an avenue into the network. It also introduces an extra element into the ACL, so the ACL takes longer to process, introducing more latency into network communications.

- **Source and destination ports:** Properly controlling the traffic between two hosts requires symmetric access control elements for inbound and outbound ACLs. Address and port information for traffic generated by a replying host is the mirror image of address and port information for traffic generated by the initiating host.

- **Use of the established keyword:** The **established** keyword increases the security provided by an ACL. However, if the keyword is applied incorrectly, unexpected results may occur.

- **Uncommon protocols:** Misconfigured ACLs often cause problems for protocols other than TCP and UDP. Uncommon protocols that are gaining popularity are VPN and encryption protocols.

The **log** keyword is a useful command for viewing ACL operation on ACL entries. This keyword instructs the router to place an entry in the system log whenever that entry condition is matched. The logged event includes details of the packet that matched the ACL element. The **log** keyword is especially useful for troubleshooting and also provides information on intrusion attempts being blocked by the ACL.

Transport Layer Troubleshooting: NAT for IPv4 (8.2.3.5)

Using NAT poses a number of problems, as summarized in Figure 8-31.

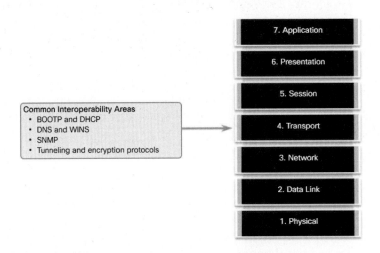

Figure 8-31 Common Interoperability Areas with NAT

These problems can include misconfigured NAT inside, NAT outside, or ACL. Other issues include interoperability with other network technologies, especially those that contain or derive information from host network addressing in the packet. Some of these technologies include

- **BOOTP and DHCP:** Both protocols manage the automatic assignment of IPv4 addresses to clients. Recall that the first packet that a new client sends is a DHCP-Request broadcast IPv4 packet. The DHCP-Request packet has a source IPv4 address of 0.0.0.0. Because NAT requires both a valid destination and source IPv4 address, BOOTP and DHCP can have difficulty operating over a router running either static or dynamic NAT. Configuring the IPv4 helper feature can help solve this problem.

- **DNS:** Because a router running dynamic NAT is changing the relationship between inside and outside addresses regularly as table entries expire and are re-created, a DNS server outside the NAT router does not have an accurate representation of the network inside the router. Configuring the IPv4 helper feature can help solve this problem.

- **SNMP:** Similar to DNS packets, NAT is unable to alter the addressing information stored in the data payload of the packet. Because of this, an SNMP management station on one side of a NAT router may not be able to contact SNMP agents on the other side of the NAT router. Configuring the IPv4 helper feature can help solve this problem.

- **Tunneling and encryption protocols:** Encryption and tunneling protocols often require that traffic be sourced from a specific UDP or TCP port, or use a protocol at the transport layer that cannot be processed by NAT. For example, IPsec tunneling protocols and generic routing encapsulation protocols used by VPN implementations cannot be processed by NAT.

Application Layer Troubleshooting (8.2.3.6)

Most of the application layer protocols provide user services. Application layer protocols are typically used for network management, file transfer, distributed file services, terminal emulation, and email. New user services are often added, such as VPNs and VoIP.

Figure 8-32 shows the most widely known and implemented TCP/IP application layer protocols, which are described in the list that follows.

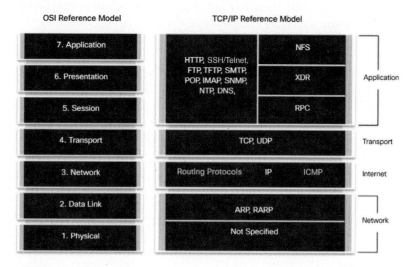

Figure 8-32   Application Layer

- **HTTP:** Supports the exchanging of text, graphic images, sound, video, and other multimedia files on the web.

- **SSH/Telnet:** Enables users to establish terminal session connections with remote hosts.

- **FTP:** Performs interactive file transfers between hosts.

- **TFTP:** Performs basic interactive file transfers typically between hosts and networking devices.

- **SMTP:** Supports basic message delivery services.

- **POP:** Connects to mail servers and downloads email.

- **SNMP:** Collects management information from network devices.

- **DNS:** Maps IP addresses to the names assigned to network devices.

The types of symptoms and causes depend on the actual application itself.

Application layer problems prevent services from being provided to application programs. A problem at the application layer can result in unreachable or unusable resources when the physical, data link, network, and transport layers are functional. It is possible to have full network connectivity, but the application simply cannot provide data.

Another type of problem at the application layer occurs when the physical, data link, network, and transport layers are functional, but the data transfer and requests for network services from a single network service or application do not meet the normal expectations of a user.

A problem at the application layer may cause users to complain that the network or the particular application that they are working with is sluggish or slower than usual when transferring data or requesting network services.

Interactive Graphic

Activity 8.2.3.7: Identify the OSI Layer Associated with a Network Issue

Refer to the online course to complete this activity.

Troubleshooting IP Connectivity (8.2.4)

In this topic, you troubleshoot a network using the layered model.

Components of Troubleshooting End-to-End Connectivity (8.2.4.1)

Diagnosing and solving problems are essential skills for network administrators. There is no single recipe for troubleshooting, and a particular problem can be diagnosed in many different ways. However, by employing a structured approach to the troubleshooting process, an administrator can reduce the time it takes to diagnose and solve a problem.

Throughout this topic, the following scenario is used: the client host PC1 is unable to access applications on Server SRV1 or Server SRV2. Figure 8-33 shows the topology of this network. PC1 uses SLAAC with EUI-64 to create its IPv6 global unicast address. EUI-64 creates the Interface ID using the Ethernet MAC address, inserting FFFE in the middle and flipping the seventh bit.

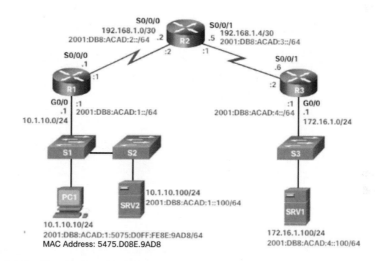

Figure 8-33   Troubleshooting Topology

When there is no end-to-end connectivity, and the administrator chooses to troubleshoot with a bottom-up approach, these are common steps the administrator can take:

Step 1.   Check physical connectivity at the point where network communication stops. This includes cables and hardware. The problem might be with a faulty cable or interface, or involve misconfigured or faulty hardware.

Step 2.   Check for duplex mismatches.

Step 3.   Check data link and network layer addressing on the local network. This includes IPv4 ARP tables, IPv6 neighbor tables, MAC address tables, and VLAN assignments.

Step 4.   Verify that the default gateway is correct.

Step 5.   Ensure that devices are determining the correct path from the source to the destination. Manipulate the routing information if necessary.

Step 6. Verify the transport layer is functioning properly. Telnet can also be used to test transport layer connections from the command line.

Step 7. Verify that no ACLs are blocking traffic.

Step 8. Ensure that DNS settings are correct. A DNS server should be accessible.

The outcome of this process is operational, end-to-end connectivity. If all the steps have been performed without any resolution, the network administrator may either want to repeat the previous steps or escalate the problem to a senior administrator.

End-to-End Connectivity Problem Initiates Troubleshooting (8.2.4.2)

Usually, what initiates a troubleshooting effort is the discovery that a problem has occurred with end-to-end connectivity. Two of the most common utilities used to verify a problem with end-to-end connectivity are **ping** and **traceroute**, as shown in Figure 8-34.

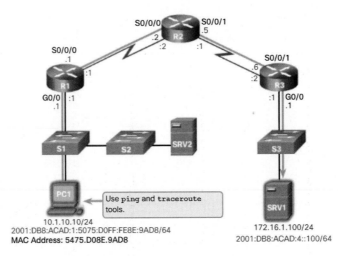

Figure 8-34 Verifying End-to-End Connectivity

Ping is probably the most widely known connectivity-testing utility in networking and has always been part of Cisco IOS Software. It sends out requests for responses from a specified host address. The **ping** command uses a Layer 3 protocol that is a part of the TCP/IP suite called ICMP. Ping uses the ICMP echo request and ICMP echo reply packets. If the host at the specified address receives the ICMP echo request, it responds with an ICMP echo reply packet. Ping can be used to verify end-to-end connectivity for both IPv4 and IPv6. Example 8-6 shows a successful ping from PC1 to SRV1, at address 172.16.1.100.

Example 8-6 Successful IPv4 **ping** from PC1 to Server1

```
PC1> ping 172.16.1.100

Pinging 172.16.1.100 with 32 bytes of data:
Reply from 172.16.1.100: bytes=32 time=8ms TTL=254
Reply from 172.16.1.100: bytes=32 time=1ms TTL=254
Reply from 172.16.1.100: bytes=32 time=1ms TTL=254
Reply from 172.16.1.100: bytes=32 time=1ms TTL=254

Ping statistics for 172.16.1.100:
    Packets: Sent = 4, Received = 4, Lost = 0 (0% loss),
Approximate round-trip times in milliseconds:
    Minimum = 1ms, Maximum = 8ms, Average = 2ms
```

The **traceroute** command in Example 8-7 illustrates the path the IPv4 packets take to reach their destination.

Example 8-7 Successful IPv4 **traceroute** from PC1 to Server1

```
C:\Windows\system32> tracert 172.16.1.100

Tracing route to 172.16.1.100 over a maximum of 30 hops

1    1 ms    <1 ms    <1 ms      10.1.10.1
2    2 ms     2 ms     1 ms      192.168.1.2
3    2 ms     2 ms     1 ms      192.168.1.6
4    2 ms     2 ms     1 ms      172.16.1.100
Trace complete.
```

Similar to the **ping** command, the Cisco IOS **traceroute** command can be used for both IPv4 and IPv6. The **tracert** command is used with the Windows operating system. The trace generates a list of hops, router IP addresses, and the final destination IP address that are successfully reached along the path. This list provides important verification and troubleshooting information. If the data reaches the destination, the trace lists the interface on every router in the path. If the data fails at some hop along the way, the address of the last router that responded to the trace is known. This address is an indication of where the problem or security restrictions reside.

As stated, the **ping** and **traceroute** utilities can be used to test and diagnose end-to-end IPv6 connectivity by providing the IPv6 address as the destination address. When using these utilities, the Cisco IOS utility recognizes whether the address is an IPv4 or IPv6 address and uses the appropriate protocol to test connectivity.

Example 8-8 shows the **ping** and **traceroute** commands on router R1 used to test IPv6 connectivity.

Example 8-8 Successful IPv6 **ping** and **traceroute** from R1 to Server1

```
R1# ping 2001:db8:acad:4::100

Type escape sequence to abort.
Sending 5, 100-byte ICMP Echos to 2001:DB8:ACAD:4::100, timeout is 2 seconds:
!!!!!
Success rate is 100 percent (5/5), round-trip min/avg/max = 56/56/56 ms
R1#
R1# traceroute 2001:db8:acad:4::100

Type escape sequence to abort.
Tracing the route to 2001:DB8:ACAD:4::100

  1 2001:DB8:ACAD:2::2 20 msec 20 msec 20 msec
  2 2001:DB8:ACAD:3::2 44 msec 40 msec 40 msec
R1#
```

Note

The **traceroute** command is commonly performed when the **ping** command fails. If the **ping** succeeds, the **traceroute** command is commonly not needed because the technician knows that connectivity exists.

Step 1: Verify the Physical Layer (8.2.4.3)

All network devices are specialized computer systems. At a minimum, these devices consist of a CPU, RAM, and storage space, allowing the device to boot and run the operating system and interfaces. This allows for the reception and transmission of network traffic.

When a network administrator determines that a problem exists on a given device and that the problem might be hardware-related, it is worthwhile to verify the operation of these generic components. The most commonly used Cisco IOS commands for this purpose are **show processes cpu**, **show memory**, and **show interfaces**. This topic discusses the **show interfaces** command.

When troubleshooting performance-related issues and hardware is suspected to be at fault, you can use the **show interfaces** command to verify the interfaces through which the traffic passes.

The output of the **show interfaces** command in Example 8-9 lists a number of important statistics that can be checked; they are described in the list that follows.

Example 8-9 Examining Input and Output Statistics on R1

```
R1# show interfaces GigabitEthernet 0/0
GigabitEthernet0/0 is up, line protocol is up
  Hardware is CN Gigabit Ethernet, address is d48c.b5ce.a0c0 (bia d48c.b5ce.a0c0)
  Internet address is 10.1.10.1/24
  <Output Omitted>
  Input queue: 0/75/0/0 (size/max/drops/flushes); Total output drops: 0
  Queueing strategy: fifo
  Output queue: 0/40 (size/max)
  5 minute input rate 0 bits/sec, 0 packets/sec
  5 minute output rate 0 bits/sec, 0 packets/sec
     85 packets input, 7711 bytes, 0 no buffer
     Received 25 broadcasts (0 IP multicasts)
     0 runts, 0 giants, 0 throttles
     0 input errors, 0 CRC, 0 frame, 0 overrun, 0 ignored
     0 watchdog, 5 multicast, 0 pause input
     10112 packets output, 922864 bytes, 0 underruns
     0 output errors, 0 collisions, 1 interface resets
     11 unknown protocol drops
     0 babbles, 0 late collision, 0 deferred
     0 lost carrier, 0 no carrier, 0 pause output
     0 output buffer failures, 0 output buffers swapped out
R1#
```

- **Input queue drops:** Input queue drops (and the related ignored and throttle counters) signify that at some point more traffic was delivered to the router than it could process. This does not necessarily indicate a problem. That could be normal during traffic peaks. However, it could be an indication that the CPU cannot process packets in time, so if this number is consistently high, it is worth trying to spot at which moments these counters are increasing and how this relates to CPU usage.

- **Output queue drops:** Output queue drops indicate that packets were dropped due to congestion on the interface. Seeing output drops is normal for any point where the aggregate input traffic is higher than the output traffic. During traffic peaks, packets are dropped if traffic is delivered to the interface faster than it can be sent out. However, even if this is considered normal behavior, it leads to packet drops and queuing delays, so applications that are sensitive to those, such as VoIP, might suffer from performance issues. Consistently seeing output drops can be an indicator that you need to implement an advanced queuing mechanism to implement or modify QoS.

- **Input errors:** Input errors indicate errors that are experienced during the reception of the frame, such as CRC errors. High numbers of CRC errors could indicate cabling problems, interface hardware problems, or, in an Ethernet-based network, *duplex mismatches.*

- **Output errors:** Output errors indicate errors, such as collisions, during the transmission of a frame. In most Ethernet-based networks today, *full-duplex* transmission is the norm, and *half-duplex* transmission is the exception. In full-duplex transmission, operation collisions cannot occur; therefore, collisions and especially late collisions often indicate duplex mismatches.

Step 2: Check for Duplex Mismatches (8.2.4.4)

Another common cause for interface errors is a mismatched duplex mode between two ends of an Ethernet link. In many Ethernet-based networks, point-to-point connections are now the norm, and the use of hubs and the associated half-duplex operation is becoming less common. This means that most Ethernet links today operate in full-duplex mode, and while collisions were seen as normal for an Ethernet link, collisions today often indicate that duplex negotiation has failed, and the link is not operating in the correct duplex mode.

The IEEE 802.3ab Gigabit Ethernet standard mandates the use of autonegotiation for speed and duplex. In addition, although it is not strictly mandatory, practically all Fast Ethernet NICs also use autonegotiation by default. The use of autonegotiation for speed and duplex is the current recommended practice.

However, if duplex negotiation fails for some reason, it might be necessary to set the speed and duplex manually on both ends. Typically, this would mean setting the duplex mode to full duplex on both ends of the connection. If this does not work, running half duplex on both ends is preferred over a duplex mismatch.

Duplex configuration guidelines include

- Autonegotiation of speed and duplex is recommended.

- If autonegotiation fails, manually set the speed and duplex on interconnecting ends.

- Point-to-point Ethernet links should always run in full-duplex mode.

- Half duplex is uncommon and typically encountered only when legacy hubs are used.

Troubleshooting Example

In the previous scenario, the network administrator needed to add additional users to the network. To incorporate these new users, the network administrator installed a second switch and connected it to the first. Soon after S2 was added to the network, users on both switches began experiencing significant performance problems connecting with devices on the other switch, as shown in Figure 8-35.

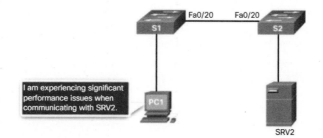

Figure 8-35   Duplex Mismatch Topology

The network administrator notices a console message on switch S2:

```
*Mar 1 00:45:08.756: %CDP-4-DUPLEX_MISMATCH: duplex mismatch discovered on FastEth-
   ernet0/20 (not half duplex), with Switch FastEthernet0/20 (half duplex).
```

Using the **show interfaces fa 0/20** command, the network administrator examines the interface on S1 used to connect to S2 and notices it is set to full duplex, as shown in Example 8-10.

Example 8-10   S1 Port Operating in Full Duplex

```
S1# show interface fa 0/20
FastEthernet0/20 is up, line protocol is up (connected)
  Hardware is Fast Ethernet, address is 0cd9.96e8.8a01 (bia 0cd9.96e8.8a01)
  MTU 1500 bytes, BW 10000 Kbit/sec, DLY 1000 usec,
     reliability 255/255, txload 1/255, rxload 1/255
  Encapsulation ARPA, loopback not set
  Keepalive set (10 sec)
  Full duplex, Auto-speed, media type is 10/100BaseTX
<Output omitted>
```

The network administrator now examines the other side of the connection, the port on S2. Example 8-11 shows that this side of the connection has been configured for half duplex.

Example 8-11 S2 Port Operating in Half Duplex

```
S2# show interface fa 0/20
FastEthernet0/20 is up, line protocol is up (connected)
  Hardware is Fast Ethernet, address is 0cd9.96d2.4001 (bia 0cd9.96d2.4001)
  MTU 1500 bytes, BW 100000 Kbit/sec, DLY 100 usec,
     reliability 255/255, txload 1/255, rxload 1/255
  Encapsulation ARPA, loopback not set
  Keepalive set (10 sec)
  Half duplex, Auto-speed, media type is 10/100BaseTX
<Output omitted>

S2(config)# interface fa 0/20
S2(config-if)# duplex auto
S2(config-if)#
```

The network administrator corrects the setting to **duplex auto** to automatically negotiate the duplex. Because the port on S1 is set to full duplex, S2 also uses full duplex. The users report that there are no longer any performance problems.

Step 3: Verify Layer 2 and Layer 3 Addressing on the Local Network (8.2.4.5)

When you are troubleshooting end-to-end connectivity, it is useful to verify mappings between destination IP addresses and Layer 2 Ethernet addresses on individual segments. In IPv4, this functionality is provided by ARP. In IPv6, the ARP functionality is replaced by the neighbor discovery process and ICMPv6. The neighbor table caches IPv6 addresses and their resolved Ethernet MAC (physical) addresses.

IPv4 ARP Table

The **arp** Windows command displays and modifies entries in the ARP cache that are used to store IPv4 addresses and their resolved MAC addresses. As shown in Example 8-12, the **arp** Windows command lists all devices that are currently in the ARP cache. The information that is displayed for each device includes the IPv4 address, MAC address (that is, Physical Address), and the type of addressing (static or dynamic).

Example 8-12 ARP Table on PC1

```
PC1> arp -a

Interface: 10.1.10.100 --- 0xd
  Internet Address      Physical Address    Type
  10.1.10.1             d4-8c-b5-ce-a0-c0   dynamic
  224.0.0.22            01-00-5e-00-00-16   static
  224.0.0.252           01-00-5e-00-00-fc   static
  255.255.255.255  ff-ff-ff-ff-ff-ff    static
```

The cache can be cleared by using the **arp -d** Windows command if the network administrator wants to repopulate the cache with updated information.

Note

The **arp** commands in Linux and MAC OS X have a similar syntax.

IPv6 Neighbor Table

As shown in Example 8-13, the **netsh interface ipv6 show neighbor** Windows command lists all devices that are currently in the neighbor table.

Example 8-13 Neighbor Table on PC1

```
PC1> netsh interface ipv6 show neighbor
Interface 13: LAB
Internet Address                           Physical Address  Type
----------------------------------------   ----------------  -----------
fe80::9c5a:e957:a865:bde9                  00-0c-29-36-fd-f7  Stale
fe80::1                                    d4-8c-b5-ce-a0-c0  Reachable (Router)
ff02::2                                    33-33-00-00-00-02  Permanent
ff02::16                                   33-33-00-00-00-16  Permanent
ff02::1:2                                  33-33-00-01-00-02  Permanent
ff02::1:3                                  33-33-00-01-00-03  Permanent
ff02::1:ff05:f9fb                          33-33-ff-05-f9-fb  Permanent
ff02::1:ffce:a0c0                          33-33-ff-ce-a0-c0  Permanent
ff02::1:ff65:bde9                          33-33-ff-65-bd-e9  Permanent
ff02::1:ff67:bae4                          33-33-ff-67-ba-e4  Permanent
```

The information that is displayed for each device includes the IPv6 address, MAC address, and the type of addressing. By examining the neighbor table, the network administrator can verify that destination IPv6 addresses map to correct Ethernet addresses. The IPv6 link-local addresses on all of R1's interfaces have been manually configured to FE80::1.

Note

The neighbor table for Linux and MAC OS X can be displayed using **ip neigh show** command.

Example 8-14 shows the neighbor table on the Cisco IOS router, using the **show ipv6 neighbors** command.

Example 8-14 Neighbor Table on R1

```
R1# show ipv6 neighbors
IPv6 Address                        Age   Link-layer Addr   State    Interface
FE80::21E:7AFF:FE79:7A81             8    001e.7a79.7a81    STALE    Gi0/0
2001:DB8:ACAD:1:5075:D0FF:FE8E:9AD8  0    5475.d08e.9ad8    REACH    Gi0/0
```

Note

The neighbor states for IPv6 are more complex than the ARP table states in IPv4. Additional information is contained in RFC 4861.

Switch MAC Address Table

When a destination MAC address is found in the switch MAC address table, the switch forwards the frame only to the port that has the device that has that particular MAC address. To do this, the switch consults its MAC address table.

The MAC address table lists the MAC address connected to each port. Use the **show mac address-table** command to display the MAC address table on the switch. Example 8-15 displays a sample switch MAC address table. Notice how the MAC address for PC1, a device in VLAN 10, has been discovered along with the S1 switch port to which PC1 attaches. Remember, a switch's MAC address table contains only Layer 2 information, including the Ethernet MAC address and the port number. IP address information is not included.

Example 8-15 MAC Address Table on Local LAN Switch

```
S1# show mac address-table
            Mac Address Table
-------------------------------------------
Vlan     Mac Address        Type      Ports
All      0100.0ccc.cccc     STATIC    CPU
All      0100.0ccc.cccd     STATIC    CPU
  10     d48c.b5ce.a0c0     DYNAMIC   Fa0/4
  10     000f.34f9.9201     DYNAMIC   Fa0/5
  10     5475.d08e.9ad8     DYNAMIC   Fa0/13
Total Mac Addresses for this criterion:  5
```

VLAN Assignment

Another issue to consider when troubleshooting end-to-end connectivity is VLAN assignment. In the switched network, each port in a switch belongs to a VLAN. Each VLAN is considered a separate logical network, and packets destined for stations that do not belong to the VLAN must be forwarded through a device that supports routing.

If a host in one VLAN sends a broadcast Ethernet frame, such as an ARP request, all hosts in the same VLAN receive the frame; hosts in other VLANs do not. Even if two hosts are in the same IP network, they will not be able to communicate if they are connected to ports assigned to two separate VLANs. Additionally, if the VLAN to which the port belongs is deleted, the port becomes inactive. All hosts attached to ports belonging to the VLAN that was deleted are unable to communicate with the rest of the network. Commands such as **show vlan** can be used to validate VLAN assignments on a switch.

Troubleshooting Example

Refer to the topology in Figure 8-36.

To improve the wire management in the wiring closet, the technician reorganized the cables connecting to S1. Almost immediately afterward, users started calling the support desk stating that they could no longer reach devices outside their own network.

An examination of PC1's ARP table using the **arp** Windows command shows that the ARP table no longer contains an entry for the default gateway 10.1.10.1, as shown in Example 8-16. There were no configuration changes on the router, so S1 is the focus of the troubleshooting.

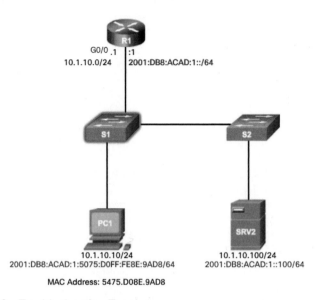

Figure 8-36   Troubleshooting Topology

Example 8-16 ARP Table on PC1

```
C:\> arp -a

Interface: 10.1.10.100 --- 0xd
  Internet Address      Physical Address      Type
  224.0.0.22            01-00-5e-00-00-16     static
  224.0.0.252           01-00-5e-00-00-fc     static
  255.255.255.255       ff-ff-ff-ff-ff-ff     static
```

The MAC address table for S1, as shown in Example 8-17, shows that the MAC address for R1 is on a different VLAN than the rest of the 10.1.10.0/24 devices, including PC1.

Example 8-17 MAC Address Table Reveals Wrong VLAN for Fa0/11

```
S1# show mac address-table
          Mac Address Table
-------------------------------------------
Vlan    Mac Address       Type       Ports
All     0100.0ccc.cccc    STATIC     CPU
All     0100.0ccc.cccd    STATIC     CPU
 1      d48c.b5ce.a0c0    DYNAMIC    Fa0/1
```

```
10        000f.34f9.9201        DYNAMIC    Fa0/5
10        5475.d08e.9ad8        DYNAMIC    Fa0/13
Total Mac Addresses for this criterion: 5
```

During the recabling, R1's patch cable was moved from Fa 0/4 on VLAN 10 to Fa 0/1 on VLAN 1. After the network administrator configured S1's Fa 0/1 port to be on VLAN 10, as shown in Example 8-18, the problem was resolved.

Example 8-18 Configuring the Correct VLAN

```
S1(config)# interface fa 0/1
S1(config-if)# switchport mode access
S1(config-if)# switchport access vlan 10
S1(config-if)#
```

As shown in Example 8-19, the MAC address table now includes an entry for R1 (that is, MAC address d48c.b5ce.a0c0) in VLAN 10 on port Fa 0/1.

Example 8-19 MAC Address Table on Local LAN Switch

```
S1# show mac address-table
              Mac Address Table
-------------------------------------------

Vlan      Mac Address          Type       Ports
All       0100.0ccc.cccc       STATIC     CPU
All       0100.0ccc.cccd       STATIC     CPU
10        d48c.b5ce.a0c0       DYNAMIC    Fa0/1
10        000f.34f9.9201       DYNAMIC    Fa0/5
10        5475.d08e.9ad8       DYNAMIC    Fa0/13
Total Mac Addresses for this criterion: 5
```

Step 4: Verify Default Gateway (8.2.4.6)

If there is no detailed route on the router or if the host is configured with the wrong default gateway, communication between two endpoints in different networks does not work. Figure 8-37 illustrates that PC1 uses R1 as its default gateway. Similarly, R1 uses R2 as its default gateway or gateway of last resort.

If a host needs access to resources beyond the local network, the default gateway must be configured. The default gateway is the first router on the path to destinations beyond the local network.

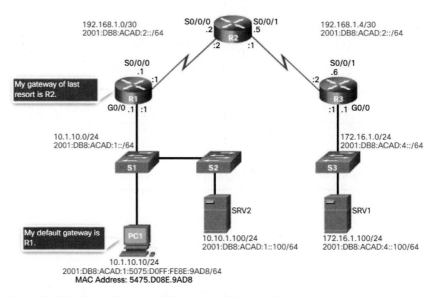

Figure 8-37   Identification of Current and Desired Path

Troubleshooting Example 1

Example 8-20 shows the **show ip route** Cisco IOS command and the **route print** Windows command to verify the presence of the IPv4 default gateway.

Example 8-20   Verify the IPv4 Default Gateway

```
R1# show ip route
<Output omitted>
Gateway of last resort is 192.168.1.2 to network 0.0.0.0


S*    0.0.0.0/0 [1/0] via 192.168.1.2
!------------------
C:\Windows\system32> route print
<Output omitted>
Network Destination      Netmask      Gateway      Interface        Metric
        0.0.0.0          0.0.0.0      10.1.10.2    10.1.10.100      11
```

In this example, the R1 router has the correct default gateway, which is the IPv4 address of the R2 router. However, PC1 has the wrong default gateway. PC1 should have the default gateway of R1 router 10.1.10.1. This must be configured manually if the IPv4 addressing information was manually configured on PC1. If the IPv4 addressing information was obtained automatically from a DHCPv4 server, the configuration on the DHCP server must be examined. A configuration problem on a DHCP server usually affects multiple clients.

Troubleshooting Example 2

In IPv6, the default gateway can be configured manually, using stateless autoconfiguration (SLAAC) or using DHCPv6. With SLAAC, the router advertises the default gateway to hosts using ICMPv6 Router Advertisement (RA) messages. The default gateway in the RA message is the link-local IPv6 address of a router interface. If the default gateway is configured manually on the host, which is very unlikely, the default gateway can be set either to the global IPv6 address or to the link-local IPv6 address.

As shown in Example 8-21, use the **show ipv6 route** Cisco IOS command to check for the IPv6 default route on R1 and use the **ipconfig** Windows command to verify if a PC has an IPv6 default gateway.

Example 8-21 Missing IPv6 Default Gateway

```
R1# show ipv6 route
<Output omitted>
S    ::/0 [1/0]
     via 2001:DB8:ACAD:2::2
!------------------
C:\Windows\system32> ipconfig
Windows IP Configuration
   Connection-specific DNS Suffix . :
   Link-local IPv6 Address . . . . . : fe80::5075:d0ff:fe8e:9ad8%13
   IPv4 Address. . . . . . . . . . . : 10.1.1.100
   Subnet Mask . . . . . . . . . . . : 255.255.255.0
   Default Gateway . . . . . . . . . : 10.1.10.1
```

R1 has a default route via router R2, but notice the **ipconfig** command reveals the absence of an IPv6 global unicast address and an IPv6 default gateway. PC1 is enabled for IPv6 because it has an IPv6 link-local address. The link-local address is automatically created by the device. Checking the network documentation, the network administrator confirms that hosts on this LAN should be receiving their IPv6 address information from the router using SLAAC.

Note

In this example, other devices on the same LAN using SLAAC would also experience the same problem receiving IPv6 address information.

Using the **show ipv6 interface GigabitEthernet 0/0** command in Example 8-22, you can see that although the interface has an IPv6 address, it is not a member of the All-IPv6-Routers multicast group FF02::2.

Example 8-22 Verify IPv6 Addresses on Interface G0/0

```
R1# show ipv6 interface GigabitEthernet 0/0
GigabitEthernet0/0 is up, line protocol is up
  IPv6 is enabled, link-local address is FE80::1
  No Virtual link-local address(es):
  Global unicast address(es):
    2001:DB8:ACAD:1::1, subnet is 2001:DB8:ACAD:1::/64
  Joined group address(es):
    FF02::1
    FF02::1:FF00:1
<Output Omitted>
```

This means the router is not enabled as an IPv6 router. Therefore, it is not sending out ICMPv6 RAs on this interface. In Example 8-23, R1 is enabled as an IPv6 router using the **ipv6 unicast-routing** command.

Example 8-23 R1 Configured as an IPv6 Router

```
R1(config)# ipv6 unicast-routing
R1(config)# end
R1#
R1# show ipv6 interface GigabitEthernet 0/0
GigabitEthernet0/0 is up, line protocol is up
  IPv6 is enabled, link-local address is FE80::1
  No Virtual link-local address(es):
  Global unicast address(es):
    2001:DB8:ACAD:1::1, subnet is 2001:DB8:ACAD:1::/64
  Joined group address(es):
    FF02::1
    FF02::2
    FF02::1:FF00:1
<Output Omitted>
```

The **show ipv6 interface GigabitEthernet 0/0** command now reveals that R1 is a member of FF02::2, the All-IPv6-Routers multicast group.

To verify that PC1 has the default gateway set, use the **ipconfig** command on a Microsoft Windows PC or the **ifconfig** command on Linux and Mac OS X. In Example 8-24, PC1 has an IPv6 global unicast address and an IPv6 default gateway. The default gateway is set to the link-local address of router R1, FE80::1.

Example 8-24 Verify the IPv6 Default Gateway

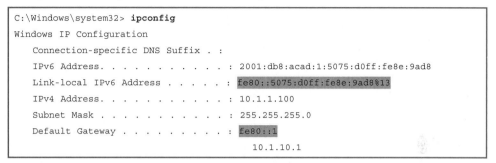

```
C:\Windows\system32> ipconfig
Windows IP Configuration
    Connection-specific DNS Suffix . :
    IPv6 Address. . . . . . . . . . . : 2001:db8:acad:1:5075:d0ff:fe8e:9ad8
    Link-local IPv6 Address . . . . . : fe80::5075:d0ff:fe8e:9ad8%13
    IPv4 Address. . . . . . . . . . . : 10.1.1.100
    Subnet Mask . . . . . . . . . . . : 255.255.255.0
    Default Gateway . . . . . . . . . : fe80::1
                                        10.1.10.1
```

Step 5: Verify Correct Path (8.2.4.7)

When you are troubleshooting, it is often necessary to verify the path to the destination network.

Troubleshooting the Network Layer

Figure 8-38 shows the reference topology indicating the intended path for packets from PC1 to SRV1.

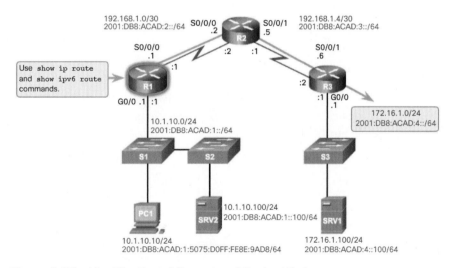

Figure 8-38 Identification of Current and Desired Path

In Example 8-25, the **show ip route** command is used to examine the IPv4 routing table.

Example 8-25 Examining the IPv4 Routing Table on R1

```
R1# show ip route | include Gateway

Gateway of last resort is 192.168.1.2 to network 0.0.0.0

S*     0.0.0.0/0 [1/0] via 192.168.1.2
       10.0.0.0/8 is variably subnetted, 2 subnets, 2 masks
C         10.1.10.0/24 is directly connected, GigabitEthernet0/0
L         10.1.10.1/32 is directly connected, GigabitEthernet0/0
       172.16.0.0/24 is subnetted, 1 subnets
D         172.16.1.0 [90/41024256] via 192.168.1.2, 05:32:46, Serial0/0/0
       192.168.1.0/24 is variably subnetted, 3 subnets, 2 masks
C         192.168.1.0/30 is directly connected, Serial0/0/0
L         192.168.1.1/32 is directly connected, Serial0/0/0
D         192.168.1.4/30 [90/41024000] via 192.168.1.2, 05:32:46, Serial0/0/0
R1#
```

The IPv4 and IPv6 routing tables can be populated by the following methods:

- Directly connected networks
- Local host or local routes
- Static routes
- Dynamic routes
- Default routes

The process of forwarding IPv4 and IPv6 packets is based on the longest bit match or longest prefix match. The routing table process will attempt to forward the packet using an entry in the routing table with the greatest number of far left matching bits. The number of matching bits is indicated by the route's prefix length.

Example 8-26 shows a similar scenario with IPv6. To verify that the current IPv6 path matches the desired path to reach destinations, use the **show ipv6 route** command on a router to examine the routing table.

Example 8-26 Examining the IPv6 Routing Table on R1

```
R1# show ipv6 route
IPv6 Routing Table - default - 7 entries
Codes: C - Connected. L - Local. S - Static. U - Per-user Static route
       B - BGP, R - RIP, I1 - ISIS L1, I2 - ISIS L2
       IA - ISIS interarea, IS - ISIS summary, D - EIGRP, EX - EIGRP external
       ND - ND Default, NDp - ND Prefix, DCE - Destination, NDr - Redirect
```

```
           O - OSPF Intra, OI - OSPF Inter, OE1 - OSPF ext 1, OE2 - OSPF ext 2
           ON1 - OSPF NSSA ext 1, ON2 - OSPF NSSA ext 2
S    ::/0 [1/0]
     via 2001:DB8:ACAD:2::2
C    2001:DB8:ACAD:1::/64 [0/0]
     via GigabitEthernet0/0, directly connected
L    2001:DB8:ACAD:1::1/128 [0/0]
     via GigabitEthernet0/0, receive
C    2001:DB8:ACAD:2::/64 [0/0]
     via Serial0/0/0, directly connected
L    2001:DB8:ACAD:2::1/128 [0/0]
     via Serial0/0/0, receive
D    2001:DB8:ACAD:3::/64 [90/41024000]
     via FE80::2, Serial0/0/0
D    2001:DB8:ACAD:4::/64 [90/41024256]
     via FE80::2, Serial0/0/0
L    FF00::/8 [0/0]
     via Null0, receive
R1#
```

After you examine the IPv6 routing table, you can see that R1 does have a path to 2001:DB8:ACAD:4::/64 via R2 at FE80::2.

The following list, along with Figure 8-39, describes the process for both the IPv4 and IPv6 routing tables.

If the destination address in a packet

- Does not match an entry in the routing table, the default route is used. If a default route is not configured, the packet is discarded.

- Matches a single entry in the routing table, the packet is forwarded through the interface that is defined in this route.

- Matches more than one entry in the routing table and the routing entries have the same prefix length, the packets for this destination can be distributed among the routes that are defined in the routing table.

- Matches more than one entry in the routing table and the routing entries have different prefix lengths, the packets for this destination are forwarded out of the interface that is associated with the route that has the longer prefix match.

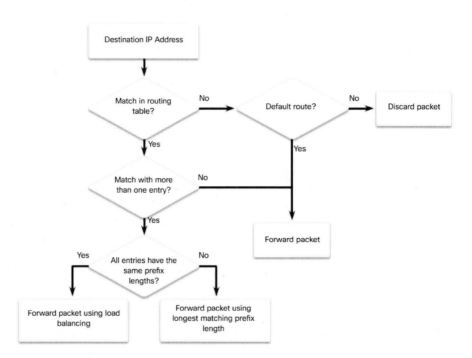

Figure 8-39   Troubleshooting Decision Tree

Troubleshooting Example

Devices are unable to connect to the server SRV1 at 172.16.1.100. Using the **show ip route** command, the administrator should check to see whether a routing entry exists to network 172.16.1.0/24. If the routing table does not have a specific route to SRV1's network, the network administrator must then check for the existence of a default or summary route entry in the direction of the 172.16.1.0/24 network. If none exists, the problem may be with routing, and the administrator must verify that the network is included within the dynamic routing protocol configuration or add a static route.

Step 6: Verify the Transport Layer (8.2.4.8)

If the network layer appears to be functioning as expected, but users are still unable to access resources, the network administrator must begin troubleshooting the upper layers. Two of the most common issues that affect transport layer connectivity include ACL configurations and NAT configurations. A common tool for testing transport layer functionality is the Telnet utility.

Caution

While Telnet can be used to test the transport layer, for security reasons, SSH should be used to remotely manage and configure devices.

Troubleshooting the Transport Layer

A network administrator is troubleshooting a problem where someone cannot send email through a particular SMTP server. The administrator pings the server, and it responds. This means that the network layer and all layers below the network layer between the user and the server are operational. The administrator knows the issue is with Layer 4 or up and must start troubleshooting those layers.

Telnet server application runs on its own well-known port number 23, and Telnet clients connect to this port by default. However, Telnet can also be used as a troubleshooting tool by using the command with any TCP port that must be tested. Telnet output indicates whether the connection is accepted (as indicated by the word "Open" in the output), is refused, or times out. From any of those responses, further conclusions can be made concerning the connectivity. Certain applications, if they use an ASCII-based session protocol, might even display an application banner; it may be possible to trigger some responses from the server by typing in certain keywords, such as with SMTP, FTP, and HTTP.

Given the previous scenario, the administrator telnets from PC1 to the server HQ, using IPv6, and the Telnet session is successful, as shown in Example 8-27.

Example 8-27 Successful Telnet Connection Over IPv4

```
C:\> telnet 2001:DB8:172:16::100
HQ#
```

In Example 8-28, the administrator attempts to telnet to the same server, using port 80.

Example 8-28 Testing the Transport Layer over IPv4 Using Port 80 (HTTP)

```
C:\> telnet 2001:DB8:172:16::100 80
HTTP/1.1 400 Bad Request
Date: Wed, 26 Sep 2012 07:27:10 GMT
Server: cisco-IOS
Accept-Ranges: none
400 Bad Request
Connection to host lost.
```

The output verifies that the transport layer is connecting successfully from PC1 to HQ. However, the server is not accepting connections on port 80.

Example 8-29 shows a successful Telnet connection from R1 to R3 over IPv6.

Example 8-29 Successful Telnet Connection Over IPv6

```
R1# telnet 2001:db8:acad:3::2
Trying 2001:DB8:ACAD:3::2 ... Open

User Access Verification

Password:
R3>
```

Example 8-30 is a similar Telnet attempt using port 80. Again, the output verifies a successful transport layer connection, but R3 refuses the connection using port 80.

Example 8-30 Testing the Transport Layer over IPv6 Using Port 80 (HTTP)

```
R1# telnet 2001:db8:acad:3::2 80
Trying 2001:DB8:ACAD:3::2, 80 ...
% Connection refused by remote host

R1#
```

Step 7: Verify ACLs (8.2.4.9)

On routers, ACLs may be configured to prohibit protocols from passing through the interface in the inbound or outbound direction.

Use the **show ip access-lists** command to display the contents of all IPv4 ACLs and the **show ipv6 access-list** command to show the contents of all IPv6 ACLs configured on a router. The specific ACL can be displayed by entering the ACL name or number as an option for this command; you can display a specific ACL. The **show ip interfaces** and **show ipv6 interfaces** commands display IPv4 and IPv6 interface information that indicates whether any IP ACLs are set on the interface.

Troubleshooting Example

To prevent spoofing attacks, the network administrator decided to implement an ACL preventing devices with a source network address of 172.16.1.0/24 from entering the inbound S0/0/1 interface on R3, as shown in Figure 8-40. All other IP traffic should be allowed.

However, shortly after implementing the ACL, users on the 10.1.10.0/24 network were unable to connect to devices on the 172.16.1.0/24 network, including SRV1. The **show ip access-lists** command shows that the ACL is configured correctly, as shown in Example 8-31.

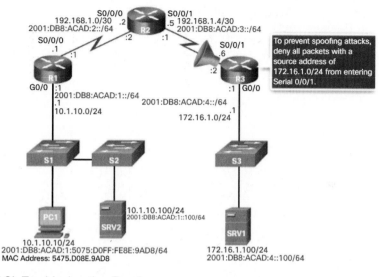

To prevent spoofing attacks, deny all packets with a source address of 172.16.1.0/24 from entering Serial 0/0/1.

Figure 8-40 ACL Troubleshooting Topology

Example 8-31 Display ACLs and ACL Placement on R1

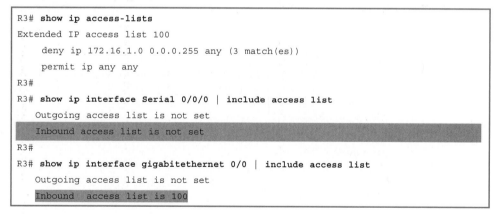

```
R3# show ip access-lists
Extended IP access list 100
    deny ip 172.16.1.0 0.0.0.255 any (3 match(es))
    permit ip any any
R3#
R3# show ip interface Serial 0/0/0 | include access list
    Outgoing access list is not set
    Inbound access list is not set
R3#
R3# show ip interface gigabitethernet 0/0 | include access list
    Outgoing access list is not set
    Inbound  access list is 100
```

The **show ip interfaces serial 0/0/1** command reveals that the ACL was never applied to the inbound interface on Serial 0/0/1. Further investigation reveals that the ACL was accidentally applied to the G0/0 interface, blocking all outbound traffic from the 172.16.1.0/24 network.

After the IPv4 ACL is correctly placed on the Serial 0/0/1 inbound interface, as shown in Example 8-32, devices are able to successfully connect to the server.

Example 8-32 Changing ACL Placement

```
R3(config)# interface gigabitethernet 0/0
R3(config-if)# no ip access-group 100 in
R3(config-if)# exit
R3(config)#
R3(config)# interface serial 0/0/1
R3(config-if)# ip access-group 100 in
```

Step 8: Verify DNS (8.2.4.10)

The DNS protocol controls the DNS, a distributed database with which you can map hostnames to IP addresses. When you configure DNS on the device, you can substitute the hostname for the IP address with all IP commands, such as **ping** or **telnet**.

To display the DNS configuration information on the switch or router, use the **show running-config** command. When no DNS server is installed, it is possible to enter names to IP mappings directly into the switch or router configuration. Use the **ip host** global configuration command to enter name-to-IPv4 mapping to the switch or router. The **ipv6 host** command is used for the same mappings using IPv6. These commands are demonstrated in Example 8-33. Because IPv6 network numbers are long and difficult to remember, DNS is even more important for IPv6 than for IPv4.

Example 8-33 Creating Name-to-IP Mappings

```
R1(config)# ip host ipv4-server 172.16.1.100
R1(config)# ipv6 host ipv6-server 2001:db8:acad:4::100
R1(config)# exit
R1#
R1# ping ipv4-server
Type escape sequence to abort.
Sending 5, 100-byte ICMP Echos to 172.16.1.100, timeout is 2 seconds:
!!!!!
Success rate is 100 percent (5/5), round-trip min/avg/max = 52/56/64 ms
R1#
R1# ping ipv6-server
Type escape sequence to abort.
Sending 5, 100-byte ICMP Echos to 2001:DB8:ACAD:4::100, timeout is 2 seconds:
!!!!!
Success rate is 100 percent (5/5), round-trip min/avg/max = 52/54/56 ms
R1#
```

To display the name-to-IP-address mapping information on the Windows-based PC, use the **nslookup** command.

Troubleshooting Example

The output in Example 8-34 indicates that either the client was unable to reach the DNS server or the DNS service on the 10.1.1.1 device was not running. At this point, the troubleshooting needs to focus on communications with the DNS server or to verify the DNS server is running properly.

Example 8-34 Unable to Reach DNS Server

```
C:\> nslookup Server
*** Request to 10.1.1.1 timed-out
```

To display the DNS configuration information on a Microsoft Windows PC, use the **nslookup** command. DNS should be configured for IPv4, IPv6, or both. DNS can provide IPv4 and IPv6 addresses at the same time, regardless of the protocol that is used to access the DNS server.

Because domain names and DNS are a vital component of accessing servers on the network, many times the user thinks that the network is down when the problem is actually with the DNS server.

Interactive Graphic

Activity 8.2.4.11: Identify Commands to Troubleshoot a Network Issue

Refer to the online course to complete this activity.

Packet Tracer Activity

Packet Tracer 8.2.4.12: Troubleshooting Enterprise Networks 1

This activity uses a variety of technologies you have encountered during your CCNA studies, including VLANs, STP, routing, inter-VLAN routing, DHCP, NAT, PPP, and Frame Relay. Your task is to review the requirements, isolate and resolve any issues, and then document the steps you took to verify the requirements.

Packet Tracer Activity

Packet Tracer 8.2.4.13: Troubleshooting Enterprise Networks 2

This activity uses IPv6 configurations, including DHCPv6, EIGRPv6, and IPv6 default routing. Your task is to review the requirements, isolate and resolve any issues, and then document the steps you took to verify the requirements.

Packet Tracer Activity

Packet Tracer 8.2.4.14: Troubleshooting Enterprise Networks 3

This activity uses a variety of technologies you have encountered during your CCNA studies, including routing, port security, EtherChannel, DHCP, NAT, PPP, and Frame

Relay. Your task is to review the requirements, isolate and resolve any issues, and then document the steps you took to verify the requirements.

Packet Tracer 8.2.4.15: Troubleshooting Challenge: Using Documentation to Solve Issues

This is Part II of a two-part activity. Part I is Packet Tracer 8.1.1.8: Troubleshooting Challenge: Documenting the Network, which you should have completed earlier in the chapter. In Part II, you use your troubleshooting skills and documentation from Part I to solve connectivity issues between PCs.

Summary (8.3)

Class Activity 8.3.1.1: Documentation Development

As the network administrator for a small business, you want to implement a documentation system to use with troubleshooting network-based problems.

After much thought, you decide to compile simple network documentation information into a file to be used when network problems arise. You also know that if the company gets larger in the future, this file can be used to export the information to a computerized network software system.

To start the network documentation process, you include

- A physical diagram of your small business network

- A logical diagram of your small business network

- Network configuration information for major devices, including routers and switches.

Packet Tracer
☐ Activity

Packet Tracer 8.3.1.2: CCNA Skills Integration Challenge

In this comprehensive CCNA skills activity, the XYZ Corporation uses a combination of eBGP and PPP for WAN connections. Other technologies include NAT, DHCP, static and default routing, EIGRP for IPv4, inter-VLAN routing, and VLAN configurations. Security configurations include SSH, port security, switch security, and ACLs.

For network administrators to be able to monitor and troubleshoot a network, they must have a complete set of accurate and current network documentation, including configuration files, physical and logical topology diagrams, and a baseline performance level.

The three major stages to troubleshooting problems are gathering symptoms, isolating the problem, and then correcting the problem. It is sometimes necessary to temporarily implement a workaround to the problem. If the intended corrective action does not fix the problem, the change should be removed. In all process steps, the network administrator should document the process. A troubleshooting policy, including change control procedures, should be established for each stage. After the problem is resolved, it is important to communicate this information to the users, anyone involved in the troubleshooting process, and to other IT team members.

The OSI model or the TCP/IP model can be applied to a network problem. A network administrator can use the bottom-up method, the top-down method, or the divide-and-conquer method. Less structured methods include shoot-from-the-hip, spot-the-differences, and move-the-problem.

Common software tools that can help with troubleshooting include network management system tools, knowledge bases, baselining tools, host-based protocol analyzers, and Cisco IOS EPC. Hardware troubleshooting tools include a NAM, digital multimeters, cable testers, cable analyzers, and portable network analyzers. Cisco IOS log information can also be used to identify potential problems.

There are characteristic physical layer, data link layer, network layer, transport layer, and application layer symptoms and problems of which the network administrator should be aware. The administrator may need to pay particular attention to physical connectivity, default gateways, MAC address tables, NAT, and routing information.

Practice

The following activities provide practice with the topics introduced in this chapter. The Labs and Class Activities are available in the companion *Connecting Networks v6 Labs & Study Guide* (ISBN 9781587134296). The Packet Tracer Activity instructions are also in the *Labs & Study Guide*. The PKA files are found in the online course.

Class Activities

Class Activity 8.0.1.2: Network Breakdown

Class Activity 8.3.1.1: Documentation Development

Labs

Lab 8.2.1.5: Configure IP SLA ICMP Echo

Packet Tracer
☐ Activity

Packet Tracer Activities

Packet Tracer 8.1.1.8: Troubleshooting Challenge: Documenting the Network

Packet Tracer 8.2.4.12: Troubleshooting Enterprise Networks 1

Packet Tracer 8.2.4.13: Troubleshooting Enterprise Networks 2

Packet Tracer 8.2.4.14: Troubleshooting Enterprise Networks 3

Packet Tracer 8.2.4.15: Troubleshooting Challenge: Using Documentation to Solve Issues

Packet Tracer 8.3.1.2: CCNA Skills Integration Challenge

Check Your Understanding Questions

Complete all the review questions listed here to test your understanding of the topics and concepts in this chapter. The appendix "Answers to the 'Check Your Understanding' Questions" lists the answers.

1. Which statement describes the physical topology for a LAN?

   A. It defines how hosts and network devices connect to the LAN.

   B. It depicts the addressing scheme that is employed in the LAN.

   C. It describes whether the LAN is a broadcast or token-passing network.

   D. It shows the order in which hosts access the network.

2. When should a network performance baseline be measured?

   A. After normal work hours to reduce possible interruptions

   B. During normal work hours of an organization

   C. Immediately after the main network devices are restarted

   D. When a denial-of-service attack to the network is detected and blocked

3. In which step of gathering symptoms does the network engineer determine if the problem is at the core, distribution, or access layer of the network?

   A. Determine ownership.

   B. Determine the symptoms.

   C. Document the symptoms.

   D. Gather information.

   E. Narrow the scope.

4. A network technician is troubleshooting an email connection problem. Which question to the end user will provide clear information to better define the problem?

   A. How big are the emails you tried to send?

   B. Is your email working now?

   C. What kind of equipment are you using to send emails?

   D. When did you first notice your email problem?

5. A team of engineers has identified a solution to a significant network problem. The proposed solution is likely to affect critical network infrastructure components. What should the team follow while implementing the solution to avoid interfering with other processes and infrastructure?

   A. Change-control procedures

   B. Knowledge base guidelines

   C. One of the layered troubleshooting approaches

   D. Syslog messages and reports

6. A network engineer is troubleshooting a network problem and can successfully ping between two devices. However, Telnet between the same two devices does not work. Which OSI layers should the administrator investigate next?

   A. All the layers

   B. From the network layer to the application layer

   C. From the network layer to the physical layer

   D. Only the network layer

7. Which troubleshooting method begins by examining cable connections and wiring issues?

   A. Bottom-up

   B. Divide-and-conquer

   C. Substitution

   D. Top-down

8. An administrator is troubleshooting an Internet connectivity problem on a router. The output of the **show interfaces gigabitethernet 0/0** command reveals higher than normal framing errors on the interface that connects to the Internet. At what layer of the OSI model is the problem likely occurring?

   A. Layer 1

   B. Layer 2

   C. Layer 3

   D. Layer 4

   E. Layer 7

9. Users report that the new website http://www.company1.biz cannot be accessed. The helpdesk technician checks and verifies that the website can be accessed with http://www.company1.biz:90. Which layer in the TCP/IP model is involved in troubleshooting this issue?

   A. Application

   B. Internet

   C. Network access

   D. Transport

10. A user reports that after an OS patch of the networking subsystem has been applied to a workstation, it performs very slowly when connecting to network resources. A network technician tests the link with a cable analyzer and notices that the workstation sends an excessive number of frames smaller than 64 bytes and also other meaningless frames. What is the possible cause of the problem?

   A. Cabling faults

   B. Corrupted application installation

   C. Corrupted NIC driver

   D. Ethernet signal attenuation

11. A networked PC is having trouble accessing the Internet, but it can print to a local printer and ping other computers in the area. Other computers on the same network are not having any issues. What is the problem?

   A. The default gateway router does not have a default route.

   B. The link between the switch to which the PC connects and the default gateway router is down.

   C. The PC has a missing or incorrect default gateway.

   D. The switch port to which the PC connects has an incorrect VLAN configured.

12. Which three pieces of information are typically recorded in a logical topology diagram? (Choose three.)

   A. Cable specifications

   B. Device locations

   C. Device models and manufacturers

   D. IP address and prefix lengths

   E. Routing protocols

   F. Static routes

13. A company is setting up a website with SSL technology to protect the authentication credentials required to access the website. A network engineer needs to verify that the setup is correct and that the authentication is indeed encrypted. Which tool should be used?

   A. Baselining tool

   B. Cable analyzer

   C. Fault-management tool

   D. Protocol analyzer

14. Which number represents the most severe level of syslog logging?

   A. 0

   B. 1

   C. 6

   D. 7

Answers to the "Check Your Understanding" Questions

Chapter 1

1. A. For this small office, an appropriate connection to the Internet would be through a common broadband service called digital subscriber line (DSL), available from the company's local telephone service provider. Because the company has so few employees, bandwidth is not a significant problem. If the company were bigger, with branch offices in remote sites, private lines would be more appropriate. VSATs are used to provide connectivity to remote locations and typically used only when no other connectivity options are available.

2. D. When traveling employees need to connect to a corporate email server through a WAN connection, the VPN will create a secure tunnel between an employee laptop and the corporate network over the WAN connection. Obtaining dynamic IP addresses through DHCP is a function of LAN communication. Sharing files among separate buildings on a corporate campus is accomplished through the LAN infrastructure. A DMZ is a protected network inside the corporate LAN infrastructure.

3. D. WANs are used to interconnect the enterprise LAN to remote branch site LANs and telecommuter sites. A WAN is owned by a service provider. Although WAN connections are typically made through serial interfaces, not all serial links are connected to a WAN. LANs, not WANs, provide end-user network connectivity in an organization.

4. B and D. Digital leased lines require a channel service unit (CSU) and a data service unit (DSU). An access server concentrates dialup modem dial-in and dial-out user communications. Dialup modems are used to temporarily enable the use of analog telephone lines for digital data communications. A Layer 2 switch is used to connect a LAN.

5. C. A connection-oriented system predetermines the network path, creates a virtual circuit for the duration of the packet delivery, and requires that each packet only carry an identifier. A connectionless packet-switched network, such as the Internet, requires each data packet to carry addressing information.

6. B. Unlike circuit-switched networks which typically require expensive permanent connections, packet-switched networks can take alternate paths if available to reach the destination.

7. B. ISDN (Integrated Services Digital Network), ATM (Asynchronous Transfer Mode), and MPLS (Multiprotocol Label Switching) do not describe fiber-optic technologies.

8. D. ISDN and ATM are Layer 1 and 2 technologies that are typically used on private WANs. Municipal Wi-Fi is a wireless public WAN technology. Corporate communications over public WANs should use VPNs for security.

9. D and E. ATM (Asynchronous Transfer Mode) is a Layer 2 technology. ANSI (American National Standards Institute) and ITU (International Telecommunication Union) are standards organizations.

10. D. A leased link establishes a dedicated constant point-to-point connection between two sites. ATM is cell-switched. ISDN is circuit-switched. Frame Relay is packet-switched.

11. A. A private WAN solution that involves dedicated links between sites offers the best security and confidentiality. Both private and public WAN solutions offer comparable connection bandwidth, depending on the technology chosen. Connecting multiple sites with private WAN connections could be very expensive. The website and file exchange service support is not relevant.

12. B and D. VPNs over the Internet provide low-cost, secure connections to remote users. VPNs are deployed over the Internet public infrastructure.

13. A. LTE, or Long-Term Evolution, is a fourth-generation cellular access technology that supports Internet access.

14. B. The equipment located at a cable service provider office, the cable modem termination system (CMTS), sends and receives digital cable modem signals on a cable network to provide Internet services to cable subscribers. A DSLAM performs a similar function for DSL service providers. A CSU/DSU is used in leased-line connections. Access servers are needed to process multiple simultaneous dial-up connections to a central office (CO).

15. B. MPLS can use a variety of underlying technologies such as T- and E-carriers, Carrier Ethernet, ATM, Frame Relay, and DSL, all of which support lower speeds than an Ethernet WAN. Neither a circuit-switched network, such as the public switched telephone network (PSTN) or Integrated Service Digital Network (ISDN), nor a packet-switched network is considered high speed.

Chapter 2

1. B. The **show controllers** command enables an administrator to view the type of cable attached to a serial interface such as a V.35 DCE.

2. B. The **show interfaces** privileged EXEC mode command shows the state of the interfaces, along with other information that related to them. "Serial 0/0/0 is down, line protocol is down" is displayed if there is no cable connected because there is no Layer 1 or Layer 2 activity going on. The interface has been turned on by the use of the **no shutdown** command; otherwise, the "Serial 0/0/0 is administratively down, line protocol is down" message would be displayed, whether or not a cable has been connected.

3. C. Authentication, multilink, and compression are options on PPP that are advantages over HDLC.

4. D. PPP can support multiple network layer protocols, such as IPv4, IPv6, IPX, and AppleTalk. It handles the interface with various network layer protocols via separate NCPs. There is a protocol field in a PPP frame to specify the network layer protocol that is being used. The information

field in a PPP frame is the data payload. LCP sets up and terminates a link. It does not check which network layer protocol is used for the data.

5. C, D, and F. Link-establishment frames establish and configure a link. Link-maintenance frames manage and debug a link. Link-termination frames terminate a link.

6. D. LCP terminates a link after exchange of data is complete by exchanging link-termination packets. The link may terminate for various reasons before the data exchange is complete. NCP will only terminate the network layer and NCP link. IPCP and IPXCP are specific network control protocols.

7. B, E, and F. PPP can be used on slower legacy asynchronous serial lines and faster synchronous serial interfaces. PPP LCP is responsible for negotiating PPP options and for the link establishment and link quality monitoring. PPP is an open standard and is not Cisco specific. Network protocols are carried in NCPs, and the default encapsulation of serial interfaces on Cisco routers is HDLC.

8. D. The **show ppp multilink** command displays the multilink interface, the hostnames for the endpoints, and the serial interfaces assigned to the multilink bundle. The **show interfaces** command will display the IP address, the LCP and NCP (IPCP) status, and the queuing type.

9. A. Issuing the **ppp quality 70** command will reduce the link quality threshold before it shuts down from 90 percent of packets received that were sent, to a drop rate of 70 percent before shutting down. Setting the threshold to 100 percent will shut down the link if 100 percent of packets are not received. Lowering the clock rate will not help a link that is going down. The **bandwidth** command is used for routing protocol calculations, not link quality.

10. C. Sometimes PAP should be used instead of CHAP. When a plaintext password is needed to simulate login at a remote host, PAP is preferable because passwords are not sent in clear text with CHAP.

Chapter 3

1. C. The term *SOHO* refers to small offices and home offices from which many telecommuters work. VPN is a virtual private network and provides a secure connection between the SOHO and the headquarters office. PPPoE is a point-to-point technology over Ethernet, and WiMax is a broadband wireless technology.

2. B and C. To enable the secure management of teleworkers who connect to the corporate network via VPN, a VPN server or concentrator, an authentication server, and multifunction security appliances are necessary components at the corporate end. They are not client requirements.

3. C. Unlike cable technology, DSL is not a shared medium. Each user has a separate connection to the DSLAM. Different varieties of DSL provide both symmetrical and asymmetrical connections. Generally, the local loop is limited to 3.39 miles using DSL.

4. A. A digital subscriber line (DSL) delivers high-speed connections over existing copper wires (PSTN).

5. C. PPPoE provides the authentication, accounting, and link management features inherent with PPP. QoS refers to the capability to provide better service to selected network traffic. DSL is a broadband technology, and ISDN is a dialup technology.

6. A. The default maximum data field of an Ethernet frame is 1500 bytes. However, in PPPoE the Ethernet frame payload includes a PPP frame that has also has a header. This reduces the available data MTU to 1492 bytes.

7. D and E. PPP, CHAP, an IP address, the dialer pool number, and the MTU size are all configured on the dialer interface. The customer router CHAP username and password must match what is configured the ISP router. The **pppoe-client** command, not the **dialer pool** command, is applied to the Ethernet interface to link it to the dialer interface.

8. A and F. The dialer pool number configured on both the dialer and Ethernet interfaces must match. The interface numbers and the username and the password do not have to match.

9. D. A GRE IP tunnel does not provide authentication or security. A leased line is not cost effective when compared to using high-speed broadband technology with VPNs. A dedicated ISP is not required when utilizing VPNs between multiple sites.

10. B. Site-to-site VPNs are statically defined VPN connections between two sites that use VPN gateways. The internal hosts do not require VPN client software and send normal, unencapsulated packets onto the network where they are encapsulated by the VPN gateway.

11. B. The GRE tunneling protocol is used for site-to-site VPNs, not for remote-access VPNs for mobile users. GRE alone does not provide any encryption, so the traffic is not secure between the endpoints.

12. A and F. BGP is the only interdomain routing protocol that routes between autonomous systems. It does not use cost or hop count as its metric but instead is policy-based, which means it makes its routing decision based on configurable policies.

13. D. BGP routers can establish adjacencies only with other BGP routers identified by the **neighbor** router configuration command.

14. B. BGP updates are encapsulated over TCP on port 179. In BGP, every AS is assigned a unique 16-bit or 32-bit AS number (ASN). BGP is an Exterior Gateway Protocol (EGP) used for the exchange of routing information between autonomous systems. BGP should not be used when there is a single connection to the Internet or another AS.

15. B. An External BGP (eBGP) relationship configured between two routers in different autonomous systems uses this **neighbor** router configuration command.

Chapter 4

1. A, D, and E. If the information in a packet header and an ACL statement match, the rest of the statements in the list are skipped, and the packet is permitted or denied as specified by the matched statement. If a packet header does not match an ACL statement, the packet is tested against the next statement in the list. This matching process continues until the end of the list is reached. At the end of every ACL statement is an implicit **deny any** statement which is applied to all packets for which conditions did not test true and results in a "deny" action.

2. B and D. ACLs can be configured as a simple firewall that provides security using basic traffic filtering capabilities. ACLs are used to filter host traffic by allowing or blocking matching packets to networks.

3. D. An outbound ACL should be utilized when the same ACL filtering rules will be applied to packets coming from more than one inbound interface before exiting a single outbound interface. The outbound ACL will be applied on the single outbound interface.

4. C and E. Standard ACLs filter traffic based solely on a specified source IP address. Extended ACLs can filter by source or destination, protocol, or port. Both standard and extended ACLs contain an implicit deny as a final ACE. Standard and extended ACLs can be identified by either names or numbers.

5. A and B. To permit or deny one specific IP address, you can use either the wildcard mask **0.0.0.0** (used after the IP address) or the wildcard mask keyword **host** (used before the IP address).

6. A, D, and E. Extended ACLs should be placed as close as possible to the source IP address so that traffic that needs to be filtered does not cross the network and use network resources. Because standard ACLs do not specify a destination address, they should be placed as close to the destination as possible. Placing a standard ACL close to the source may have the effect of filtering all traffic and limiting services to other hosts. Filtering unwanted traffic before it enters low-bandwidth links preserves bandwidth and supports network functionality. Decisions on placing ACLs inbound or outbound are dependent on the requirements to be met.

7. D. The **access-list 110 permit tcp 172.16.0.0 0.0.0.255 any eq 22 ACE** will match traffic on port 22, which is SSH, that is sourced from network 172.16.0.0/24 with any destination.

8. B. With an inbound ACL, incoming packets are processed before they are routed. With an outbound ACL, packets are first routed to the outbound interface, and then they are processed. Thus, processing inbound is more efficient from the router perspective. The structure, filtering methods, and limitations (on an interface, only one inbound and one outbound ACL can be configured) are the same for both types of ACLs.

9. B. IPv4 and IPv6 ACLs can be configured on the same device as long as they utilize different ACL names. IPv6 ACLs provide the same functionality as named IPv4 extended ACLs but cannot have the same name as any IPv4 ACLs.

10. D. A network administrator will use the **ipv6 traffic-filter** command within interface configuration mode to apply an IPv6 ACL.

11. B. The IPv6 access list statement, **permit tcp any host 2001:DB8:10:10::100 eq 25**, will allow IPv6 packets from any host to the SMTP server at 2001:DB8:10:10::100. The source of the packet is listed first in the ACL, which in this case is any source, and the destination is listed second, in this case the IPv6 address of the SMTP server. The port number is last in the statement, port 25, which is the well-known port for SMTP.

12. B. One of the major differences between IPv6 and IPv4 ACLs are two implicit permit ACEs at the end of any IPv6 ACL. These two permit ACEs allow neighbor discovery operations to function on the router interface.

13. C, D, and E. All IPv6 ACLs automatically include two implicit **permit** statements; **permit icmp any any nd-ns** and **permit icmp any any nd-na.** These statements allow the router interface to perform neighbor discovery operations. An implicit **deny ipv6 any any** is also automatically included at the end of any IPv6 ACL that blocks all IPv6 packets not otherwise permitted.

14. A. Unlike IPv4, IPv6 has only one type of access list and that is the named extended access list.

Chapter 5

1. B. An SNMP agent that resides on a managed device collects and stores information about the device and its operation. This information is stored by the agent locally in the MIB. An NMS periodically polls the SNMP agents that are residing on managed devices by using the get request to query the devices for data. A set request is used by the NMS to change the configuration in the agent device or to initiate actions within a device.

2. D. To solve the issue of the delay that exists between when an event occurs and the time it is noticed via polling by the NMS, you can use SNMP trap messages. SNMP trap messages are generated from SNMP agents and are sent to the NMS immediately to inform it of certain events without having to wait for the device to be polled by the NMS.

3. A. SNMPv1 and SNMPv2 use community strings to control access to the MIB. SNMPv3 uses encryption, message integrity, and source validation.

4. B. Both SNMPv1 and SNMPv2c use a community-based form of security, and community strings are plaintext passwords. Plaintext passwords are not considered a strong security mechanism. Version 1 is a legacy solution and not often encountered in networks today.

5. A and E. The command **snmp-server user admin1 admin v3 encrypted auth md5 abc789 priv des 256 key99** creates a new user and configures authentication with MD5. The command does not use a secret encrypted password on the server. The command **snmp-server community** *string access-list-number-or-name* restricts SNMP access to defined SNMP managers.

6. A. The **snmp-server enable traps** command enables SNMP to send trap messages to the NMS at 10.10.50.25. This *notification-types* argument can be used to specify what specific type of trap is sent. If this argument is not used, all trap types are sent. If the *notification-types* argument is used, repeated use of this command is required if another subset of trap types is desired.

7. B. Port security limits the number of source MAC addresses allowed through a switch port. This feature can prevent an attacker from flooding a switch with many spoofed MAC addresses.

8. C. To mitigate a VLAN hopping attack, disable Dynamic Trunking Protocol (DTP) and set the native VLAN of trunk links to a VLAN not in use.

9. C. DHCP starvation attacks are launched by an attacker with the intent to create a DoS situation for DHCP clients. To accomplish this goal, the attacker uses a tool that sends many DHCPDISCOVER messages to lease the entire pool of available IP addresses, thus denying them to legitimate hosts.

10. A. Both discovery protocols can provide hackers with sensitive network information. They should not be enabled on edge devices and should be disabled globally or on a per-interface basis if not required. CDP is enabled by default.

11. A. The SPAN feature copies or mirrors traffic between an ingress and egress port.

12. A. The **show monitor** command enables you to verify the SPAN session. The command displays the type of the session, the source ports for each traffic direction, and the destination port.

Chapter 6

1. B. Traffic requires enough bandwidth to support services. When there is not enough bandwidth, congestion occurs and typically results in packet loss.

2. C. Quality of service (QoS) needs to be enabled on routers to provide support for VoIP and video conferencing. QoS refers to the capability of a network to provide better service to selected network traffic, as required by voice and video applications.

3. B. When the volume of traffic is greater than what can be transported across the network, devices queue, or hold, the packets in memory until resources become available to transmit them. If the number of packets to be queued continues to increase, the memory within the device fills up and packets are dropped.

4. A. CBWFQ extends the standard WFQ functionality to provide support for user-defined traffic classes. A FIFO queue is reserved for each class, and traffic belonging to a class is directed to the queue for that class.

5. D. With LLQ, delay-sensitive data is sent first, before packets in other queues are treated. Although it is possible to enqueue various types of real-time traffic to the strict priority queue, Cisco recommends that only voice traffic be directed to the priority queue.

6. B. When no other queuing strategies are configured, all interfaces except serial interfaces at E1 (2.048 Mb/s) and below use FIFO by default. Serial interfaces at E1 and below use WFQ by default.

7. D. When no other queuing strategies are configured, all interfaces except serial interfaces at E1 (2.048 Mb/s) and below use FIFO by default. Serial interfaces at E1 and below use WFQ by default.

8. A. The best-effort model has no way to classify packets; therefore, all network packets are treated the same way. Without QoS, the network cannot tell the difference between packets and, as a result, cannot treat packets preferentially.

9. C. IntServ uses the Resource Reservation Protocol (RSVP) to signal the QoS needs of an application's traffic along devices in the end-to-end path through the network. If network devices along the path can reserve the necessary bandwidth, the originating application can begin transmitting. If the requested reservation fails along the path, the originating application does not send any data.

10. C. Marking means that you are adding a value to the packet header. Devices receiving the packet look at this field to see whether it matches a defined policy. Marking should be done as close to the source device as possible. This establishes the trust boundary.

11. B. Trusted endpoints have the capabilities and intelligence to mark application traffic to the appropriate Layer 2 CoS and/or Layer 3 DSCP values. Examples of trusted endpoints include IP phones, wireless access points, video-conferencing gateways and systems, IP conferencing stations, and more.

12. A. The 802.1p standard uses the first three bits in the Tag Control Information (TCI) field. Known as the Priority (PRI) field, this 3-bit field identifies the class of service (CoS) markings. Three bits means that a Layer 2 Ethernet frame can be marked with one of eight levels of priority (values 0–7).

13. D. RFC 2474 redefines the ToS field with a new 6-bit Differentiated Services Code Point (DSCP) QoS field. Six bits offers a maximum of 64 possible classes of service.

Chapter 7

1. D. Within the IoT, the communication is Machine-to-Machine (M2M), enabling communication between machines without human intervention. For example, M2M occurs in cars with temperature and oil sensors communicating with an onboard computer.

2. C. The Internet of Things (IoT) is a phrase that denotes the billions of electronic devices that are now able to connect to our data networks and the Internet.

3. D. The Cisco IoT System uses a set of new and existing products and technologies to reduce the complexities of digitization for all industries. It provides an infrastructure designed to manage

large-scale systems of very different endpoints and platforms, and the huge amount of data that they create.

4. A, B, and D. The fog computing pillar describes the client/server model, the cloud computing model, and the fog computing model.

5. D. The fog computing pillar basically extends cloud connectivity closer to the edge. It enables end devices, such as smart meters, industrial sensors, robotic machines, and others, to connect to a local integrated computing, networking, and storage system.

6. D. The Cisco IoT security pillar cybersecurity solutions include Operational Technology (OT) security, IoT Network security, and IoT Physical security. OT is the hardware and software that keeps power plants running and manages factory process lines.

7. B. With IaaS, the cloud provider is responsible for access to the network equipment, virtualized network services, and supporting network infrastructure.

8. A. Cloud computing enables access to organizational data anywhere and at any time; streamlines the organization's IT operations by subscribing only to needed services; eliminates or reduces the need for onsite IT equipment, maintenance, and management; reduces cost for equipment, energy, physical plant requirements, and personnel training needs; and enables rapid responses to increasing data volume requirements.

9. A. This IoT network model identifies a distributed computing infrastructure closer to the network edge. It enables edge devices to run applications locally and make immediate decisions. This reduces the data burden on networks because raw data does not need to be sent over network connections. It enhances resiliency by allowing IoT devices to operate when network connections are lost. It also enhances security by keeping sensitive data from being transported beyond the edge where it is needed.

10. A. IaaS would be the best solution because the cloud provider is responsible for access to the network equipment, virtualized network services, and supporting network infrastructure.

11. C. Private cloud applications and services are intended for a specific organization or entity, such as the government.

12. D. A benefit of virtualization is increased server uptime with advanced redundant fault-tolerance features including live migration, storage migration, high availability, and distributed resource scheduling.

13. C. The terms *cloud computing* and *virtualization* are often used interchangeably; however, they mean different things. Virtualization is the foundation of cloud computing. Without it, cloud computing, as it is most widely implemented, would not be possible. Cloud computing separates the application from the hardware. Virtualization separates the OS from the hardware.

14. B. A Type 2 hypervisor, also called a hosted hypervisor, is software that creates and runs VM instances. A big advantage of Type 2 hypervisors is that management console software is not required.

15. C. With Type 1 hypervisors, the hypervisor is installed directly on the server or networking hardware. Then instances of an OS are installed on the hypervisor. Type 1 hypervisors have direct access to the hardware resources; therefore, they are more efficient than hosted architectures. Type 1 hypervisors improve scalability, performance, and robustness.

16. D. Software-defined networking (SDN) is a network architecture that has been developed to virtualize the network. For example, SDN can virtualize the control plane. Also known as controller-based SDN, SDN moves the control plane from each network device to a central network intelligence and policy-making entity called the SDN controller.

17. B and C. The control plane contains Layers 2 and 3 route forwarding mechanisms, such as routing protocol neighbor tables and topology tables, IPv4 and IPv6 routing tables, STP, and the ARP table. Information sent to the control plane is processed by the CPU.

18. C. Type 1 hypervisors are also called the "bare metal" approach because the hypervisor is installed directly on the hardware. Type 1 hypervisors are usually used on enterprise servers and data center networking devices.

19. D. Type 2 hypervisors are very popular with consumers and for organizations experimenting with virtualization. Common Type 2 hypervisors include Virtual PC, VMware Workstation, Oracle VM VirtualBox, VMware Fusion, and Mac OS X Parallels.

20. B. The APIC is considered to be the brains of the ACI architecture. The APIC is a centralized software controller that manages and operates a scalable ACI clustered fabric. It is designed for programmability and centralized management. It translates application policies into network programming.

Chapter 8

1. A. A physical topology defines the way in which computers and other network devices are connected to a network.

2. B. Baseline measurements should not be performed during times of unique traffic patterns because the data would provide an inaccurate picture of normal network operations. Baseline analysis of the network should be conducted on a regular basis during normal work hours of an organization. Perform an annual analysis of the entire network or baseline different sections of the network on a rotating basis. Analysis must be conducted regularly to understand how the network is affected by growth and other changes.

3. E. In the "narrow the scope" step of gathering symptoms, a network engineer will determine if the network problem is at the core, distribution, or access layer of the network. After this step is complete and the layer is identified, the network engineer can determine which pieces of equipment are the most likely cause.

4. D. To efficiently establish exactly when the user first experienced email problems, the technician should ask an open-ended question so that the user can state the day and time that the problem was first noticed. Closed questions require only a yes or no answer, which will require further questions to determine the actual time of the problem.

5. A. Change-control procedures should be established and applied for each stage to ensure a consistent approach to implementing the solutions and to enable changes to be rolled back if they cause other unforeseen problems.

6. B. A successful ping indicates that everything is working on the physical, data link, and network layer. All of the other layers should be investigated.

7. A. In bottom-up troubleshooting, you start with the physical components of the network and move up through the layers of the OSI model until the cause of the problem is identified, as shown in Figure 8-9.

8. B. Framing errors are symptoms of problems at the data-link layer, Layer 2, of the OSI model.

9. D. The issue is that the new website is configured with TCP port 90 for HTTP, which is different from the normal TCP port 80. Therefore, this is a transport layer issue.

10. C. The symptom of excessive runt packets and jabber is typically a Layer 1 issue, such as caused by a corrupted NIC driver, which could be the result of a software error during the NIC driver upgrade process. Cable faults would cause intermittent connections, but in this case, the network is not touched and the cable analyzer has detected frame problems, not signal problems. Ethernet signal attenuation is caused by an extended or long cable, but in this case, the cable has not been changed. A NIC driver is part of the operating system; it is not an application.

11. C. Because other computers on the same network work properly, the default gateway router has a default route, and the link between the workgroup switch and the router works. An incorrectly configured switch port VLAN would not cause these symptoms

12. D, E, and F. Information recorded on a logical network diagram may include device identifiers, IP address and prefix lengths, interface identifiers, connection type, Frame Relay DLCI for virtual circuits (if applicable), site-to-site VPNs, routing protocols, static routes, data-link protocols, and WAN technologies used.

13. D. Protocol analyzers are useful to investigate packet content while flowing through the network. A protocol analyzer decodes the various protocol layers in a recorded frame and presents this information in a relatively easy-to-use format.

14. A. The lower the level number, the higher the severity level. By default, all messages from level 0 to 7 are logged to the console.

3G/4G wireless Cellular/mobile broadband standards supporting speeds of up to 5 Mb/s.

A

access control entries (ACEs) A single line in an ACL. Also known as and ACL statement.

access control list (ACL) A series of IOS commands that control whether a router forwards or drops packets based on information found in the packet header.

access server A communications processor that connects asynchronous devices to a LAN or WAN through network and terminal emulation software. It performs both synchronous and asynchronous routing of supported protocols. Sometimes called a network access server.

ACL Analysis Cisco APIC-EM troubleshooting tool used to examine ACLs on devices, searching for redundant, conflicting, or shadowed entries. ACL Analysis enables ACL inspection and interrogation across the entire network, exposing any problems and conflicts.

ACL Path Trace Cisco APIC-EM troubleshooting tool used to examine specific ACLs on the path between two end nodes and display any potential issues.

amplifier Cable service provider term describing a device that regenerates an incoming signal to extend further through the network. Cable networks use various types of amplifiers in their transportation and distribution networks.

antenna site Cable provider term describing the location of the main receiving antennas and satellite dishes.

application enablement platform pillar One of the six Cisco IoT System pillars. This pillar provides the infrastructure for application hosting and application mobility between cloud and fog computing. For example, Cisco IOx can run an industry-specific application on the router that collects the data from various sensors, enabling the router to support fog computing. Compare with network connectivity pillar, fog computing pillar, security pillar, data analytics pillar, and system management and automation pillar.

Application Network Profile (ANP) A core component of Cisco ACI architecture, the ANP is a collection of endpoint groups (EPGs), their connections, and the policies that define those connections.

Application Policy Infrastructure Controller (APIC) Considered to be the brains of the Cisco ACI, the APIC is a centralized software controller that manages and operates a scalable and clustered ACI fabric. It is designed for programmability and centralized management and translates application policies into network programming.

application programming interfaces (APIs) Special subroutines used by an application program to communicate with the operating system or some other control program. APIs use special function calls to provide the linkage to the required subroutine for execution. Open and standardized APIs are used to ensure the portability of the application code and the vendor independence.

AS number (ASN)   A 16-bit or 32-bit number used in BGP configuration to uniquely identify an organization on the Internet. The AS numbers are managed by the IANA.

assured forwarding (AF)   A category of DSCP values consisting of four classes to provide differing levels of forwarding assurances. Compare with best effort (BE) and expedited forwarding (EF).

asymmetric DSL (ADSL)   A type of DSL service used to connect home users and SOHO sites to Internet service providers (ISPs). ADSL supports higher downstream speeds and slower upstream speeds. Compare with symmetric DSL (SDSL).

asynchronous circuits   Serial lines that transmit one byte at a time and each byte is preceded by a start bit and a stop bit. An asynchronous serial interface does not need a clock rate and is typically slower than synchronous circuits. Compare with synchronous circuits.

Asynchronous Transfer Mode (ATM)   An international standard for cell relay in which multiple service types (such as voice, video, or data) are conveyed in fixed-length (53-byte) cells. Fixed-length cells allow cell processing to occur in hardware, thereby reducing transit delays.

attenuation   The gradual loss in signal intensity that occurs while transmitting analog or digital signals over long distances, such as when a UTP cable exceeds the design limit of 100 meters.

Authentication, Authorization, and Accounting (AAA)   A network security service that provides the primary framework to set up access control on a network device (for example, router, switch). AAA is a way to control who is permitted to access a network (authenticate) and what they can do while they are there (authorize), and to audit what actions they performed while accessing the network (accounting).

authenticator   IEEE 802.1X term to describe a switch or wireless access point that controls physical access to the network based on the authentication status of the client. The switch acts as an intermediary (proxy) between the client and the authentication server. It requests identifying information from the client, verifies that information with the authentication server, and relays a response to the client. The switch uses a RADIUS software agent, which is responsible for encapsulating and de-encapsulating the Extensible Authentication Protocol (EAP) frames and interacting with the authentication server.

B

baseline   A reference used to establish normal network or system performance by collecting performance data from the ports and devices that are essential to network operation.

baselining tools   Tools that are used to help establish and measure the network's behavior.

Basic Rate Interface (BRI)   An ISDN interface composed of two 64-kb/s B channels and one D 16-bit channel for circuit-switched communication of voice, video, and data.

best effort (BE)   A category of DSCP values with a value of 0. When a router experiences congestion, these packets will be dropped. No QoS plan is implemented. Compare with expedited forwarding (EF) and assured forwarding (AF).

best-effort model   Default model when QoS is not explicitly configured. Compare with IntServ model and differentiated services (DiffServ).

BGP peers   BGP term used to describe two BGP routers that have formed an adjacency and are exchanging routing information.

bit-oriented   A class of data link layer communication protocols that can transmit frames regardless of frame content. Compared with byte-oriented protocols, bit-oriented protocols provide full-duplex operation and are more efficient and reliable.

Border Gateway Protocol (BGP)   An exterior gateway routing protocol used by ISPs to propagate routing information.

bottom-up troubleshooting approach   Troubleshooting method that starts with the physical components of the network and moves up through the layers of the OSI model until the cause of the problem is found. Bottom-up troubleshooting is a good approach to use when you suspect a physical problem. Compare with the top-down troubleshooting approach and the divide-and-conquer troubleshooting approach.

broadband connections   The wide bandwidth characteristics of a transmission medium and its capability to transport multiple signals and traffic types simultaneously. The medium can be coax, optical fiber, twisted pair, or wireless.

broadband modem   A type of digital modem used with broadband communications such as DSL or cable Internet service.

broadband service   Technology that provides Internet access using broadband connections. Broadband service technologies include DSL, cable, and satellite access.

C

cable analyzers   Multifunctional handheld devices that are used to test and certify copper and fiber cables for different services and standards. The more sophisticated tools include advanced troubleshooting diagnostics that measure distance to performance defect (NEXT, RL), identify corrective actions, and graphically display crosstalk and impedance behavior.

cable modem (CM)   Device located at the customer premise; it is used to convert an Ethernet signal from the user device to broadband cable frequencies, which are transmitted to the headend.

cable modem termination system (CMTS)   A component that exchanges digital signals with cable modems on a cable network. A headend CMTS communicates with cable modems that are located in the subscriber homes.

cable testers   Specialized handheld devices designed to test the various types of data communication cabling. Cabling testers can be used to detect broken wires, crossed-over wiring, shorted connections, and improperly paired connections.

Carrier Detect (CD) signal   A serial line signal that is used to see whether a neighbor device is connected.

Carrier protocol   Term used in GRE to describe the protocol (for example, GRE) that encapsulates the Passenger protocol. Compare with Passenger protocol and Transport protocol.

CDP reconnaissance attacks   Type of LAN attack that occurs when a cybercriminal uses CDP to discover network infrastructure vulnerabilities. Compare with Telnet attacks,

MAC address table flooding attacks, VLAN attacks, and DHCP spoofing attacks.

cellular/mobile   Wireless communication using radio waves to communicate through nearby cell towers.

central office (CO)   A local telephone company office to which all local loops in a given area connect and in which circuit switching of subscriber lines occurs.

Challenge Handshake Authentication Protocol (CHAP)   A security feature supported on lines using PPP encapsulation that prevents unauthorized access. CHAP does not itself prevent unauthorized access; it merely identifies the remote end. The router or access server then determines whether that user is allowed access.

change control procedures   Troubleshooting policies that should be established and applied for each stage to ensure a consistent approach to implementing the solutions, and to enable changes to be rolled back if they cause other unforeseen problems.

channel service unit/data service unit (CSU/DSU)   A digital interface device that connects end-user equipment to the local digital telephone loop. Often mentioned with DSU as CSU/DSU.

circuit-switched network   A type of communication in which two network nodes establish a dedicated communications channel (circuit) through the network before the nodes may communicate.

Cisco AnyConnect Secure Mobility Client   VPN software that is installed on a host to securely establish a remote-access VPN.

Cisco Application Centric Infrastructure (ACI)   A data center architecture solution originally developed by Insieme and acquired by Cisco in 2013 for integrating cloud computing and data center management. ACI is the Cisco SDN solution that includes a data center fabric built with Nexus 9000 switches running ACI Fabric OS, a cluster of Application Policy Infrastructure Controllers (APICs), and an ecosystem of integrated solutions.

Cisco Application Policy Infrastructure Controller-Enterprise Module (APIC-EM)   A policy-based SDN for enterprise and campus deployments.

Cisco Discovery Protocol (CDP)   A Cisco proprietary Layer 2 link discovery protocol enabled on all Cisco devices by default. It is used to discover other CDP-enabled devices for autoconfiguring connections and to troubleshoot network devices. Compare with Link Layer Discovery Protocol (LLDP).

Cisco IOS IP service-level agreement (SLA)   Feature used to continually monitor and test a network.

Cisco IoT System   Solution provided by Cisco to simplify the complexities of digitization for manufacturing, utilities, oil and gas, transportation, mining, and public sector organizations. The IoT system provides an infrastructure designed to manage large-scale systems of very different endpoints and platforms, and the huge amount of data that they create. The Cisco IoT System uses a set of new and existing products and technologies to help reduce the complexity of digitization.

Cisco IOx   This IOS combines Cisco IOS and Linux and enables routers to host applications close to the objects they need to monitor, control, analyze, and optimize. Cisco IOx services are offered on multiple hardware devices that are customized for various industry needs and can therefore support applications specific to those industries.

Cisco Network Foundation Protection (NFP)   Framework developed by Cisco that logically divides router and switch operations into three functional areas; the Control plane, Management plane, and Data plane (also called the Forwarding plane).

Cisco Nexus 9000 Series switches   Core components of Cisco ACI architecture that provide an application-aware switching fabric and work with an APIC to manage the virtual and physical network infrastructure.

Cisco UCS Manager   Application used to manage all software and hardware components in the Cisco UCS. Cisco UCS Manager can control multiple servers and manage resources for thousands of VMs.

Cisco Unified Computing System (UCS)   A product line developed specifically for a data center to manage the computing hardware, virtualization, and switching fabric. Cisco UCS is managed by Cisco UCS Manager.

Cisco Visual Networking Index (VNI)   Group within Cisco that performs projections, estimates and forecasts, and direct data collection for broadband connections, video subscribers, mobile connections, and more.

Class-Based Weighted Fair Queuing (CBWFQ)   QoS queuing method that permits custom policies per class of traffic, such as specifying web traffic more bandwidth than email traffic. All other unspecified traffic uses WFQ. Compare with first-in, first-out (FIFO), Weighted Fair Queuing (WFQ), and Low Latency Queuing (LLQ).

classification   QoS term to describe the action of sorting types of packets so they can be marked and have policies applied to them.

class of service (CoS)   QoS marking that exists in the Layer 2 header of a frame, which a switch can identify.

clock skew   A clock's frequency difference, or the first derivative of its offset with respect to time.

cloud computing   The use of computing resources (hardware and software) that are delivered as a service over a network. An enterprise typically accesses the processing power, storage, software or other computing services, often via a web browser, from a provider for a fee. The provider is usually an external company that hosts and manages the cloud resources.

cloud computing model   Network model that supports cloud computing where servers and services are dispersed globally in distributed data centers.

community cloud   A cloud model created for exclusive use by a specific community. Compare with public cloud, private cloud, and hybrid cloud.

community string   A text string that acts as a password and is used to authenticate messages sent between a management station and a router containing an SNMP agent. The community string is sent in every packet between the manager and the agent.

congestion avoidance   QoS tool to monitor network traffic loads in an effort to anticipate and avoid congestion. As queues fill up to the maximum threshold, a small percentage of packets are dropped. When the maximum threshold is passed, all packets are dropped.

control plane   One of the Cisco NFP functional areas that consists of managing device-generated packets required for the operation of the network itself, such as ARP message exchanges or OSPF routing advertisements. Compare with management plane and data plane.

controller-based SDN   One of three types of SDN implementations. This type of SDN uses a centralized controller that has knowledge of all devices in the network. The applications can interface with the controller responsible for managing devices and manipulating traffic flows throughout the network. Compare with device-based SDN and policy-based SDN.

customer premises equipment (CPE)   Terminating equipment, such as terminals, telephones, and modems, supplied by the telephone company, installed at customer sites, and connected to the telephone company network.

D

data analytics pillar   One of the six Cisco IoT System pillars. This pillar provides the infrastructure and tools for enterprises to combine IoT analytics with business analytics by using APIs that can run directly on Cisco IOx fog nodes. Compare with network connectivity pillar, fog computing pillar, security pillar, system management and automation pillar, and application enablement platform pillar.

data center   A facility used to house computer systems and associated components, including redundant data communications connections, high-speed virtual servers, redundant storage systems, and security devices. Only large organizations use privately built data centers. Smaller organizations lease server and storage services from data center organizations.

data communications equipment (DCE)   An EIA term. The ITU refers to this device as the data circuit-terminating equipment (DCE). The devices and connections of a communications network that comprise the network end of the user-to-network interface. The DCE provides a physical connection to the network, forwards traffic, and provides a clocking signal used to synchronize data transmission between DCE and DTE devices. Broadband modems and interface cards are examples of DCE.

data-link connection identifier (DLCI)   A value that specifies a PVC or SVC in a Frame Relay network. In the basic Frame Relay specification, DLCIs are locally significant (connected devices might use different values to specify the same connection). In the LMI extended specification, DLCIs are globally significant (DLCIs specify individual end devices).

Data over Cable Service Interface Specification (DOCSIS)   An international standard developed by CableLabs, a nonprofit research and development consortium for cable-related technologies. CableLabs tests and certifies cable equipment vendor devices, such as cable modems and cable modem termination systems, and grants DOCSIS-certified or qualified status.

data plane (forwarding plane)   One of the Cisco NFP functional areas, it is responsible for forwarding data. Data plane traffic normally consists of user-generated packets being forwarded between end devices. Most traffic travels through the router, or switch, via the data plane. Compare with control plane and management plane.

data terminal equipment (DTE)   A device at the user end of a user-network interface that serves as a data source, destination, or both. DTE connects to a data network through a DCE device (such as a modem) and typically uses clocking signals generated by the DCE. DTE includes such devices as computers, protocol translators, and multiplexers.

dedicated lines   A communications line that is indefinitely reserved for transmissions rather than switched as transmission is required.

delay   QoS term used to describe the time it takes for a packet to travel from the source to the destination. Fixed delay is a specific amount of time a specific process takes. A variable delay takes an unspecified amount of time and is affected by factors such as how much traffic is being processed.

demarcation point   The point where the service provider or telephone company network ends and connects with the customer's equipment at the customer's site.

demodulates   The process of taking an analog signal such as sound and converting it to a digital signal such as when a modem receives data over telephone lines.

denial-of-service (DoS) attack   Any attack that is used to overload specific devices and network services with illegitimate traffic, thereby preventing legitimate traffic from reaching those resources.

dense wavelength-division multiplexing (DWDM)   An optical technology used to increase bandwidth over existing fiber-optic backbones. DWDM works by combining and transmitting multiple signals simultaneously at different wavelengths on the same fiber.

DHCP snooping   Cisco switch security feature that is enabled on an interface or VLAN. If a switch receives a DHCP packet on an untrusted port, the switch compares the source packet information with that held in the DHCP Snooping Binding Database. The switch will deny unauthorized DHCP messages incoming on untrusted port.

DHCP Snooping Binding Database   The table that is populated by the DHCP snooping feature. It contains IP to MAC address lease information.

DHCP spoofing attacks   Attacks in which a cybercriminal installs a fake DHCP server on the network. Legitimate clients acquire their IP confirmation from the bogus server. These types of attacks force the clients to use both a false Domain Name System (DNS) server and a computer that is under the control of the attacker as their default gateway.

DHCP starvation attack   Type of attack in which the cybercriminal floods the DHCP server with bogus DHCP requests and eventually leases all the available IP addresses in the DHCP server pool. After these IP addresses are issued, the server cannot issue any more addresses, and this situation produces a denial-of-service (DoS) attack because new clients cannot obtain network access.

dialer interface   A virtual interface used by dial-up, ISDN, PPP, and more.

dialup modem   An older type of modem that connects a computer to the Internet via a standard telephone line.

differentiated services (DiffServ)   QoS model that provides high scalability and flexibility. QoS differentiates between multiple traffic flows. Network devices recognize traffic classes and provide different levels of QoS to different traffic classes. DiffServ is less resource-intensive and more scalable than IntServ. Compare with best-effort model and IntServ model.

differentiated services code point (DSCP)   Defined in RFC 2474 to redefine the ToS field by renaming and extending the IP Precedence (IPP) field. The new field has 6 bits allocated for the Differentiated Services Code Point (DSCP) field, offering a maximum of 64 possible classes of service. The 64 DSCP values are organized into three categories consisting of best effort (BE), expedited forwarding (EF), and assured forwarding (AF).

digital multimeters (DMMs)   Test instruments that directly measure electrical values of voltage, current, and resistance. In network troubleshooting, most multimedia tests involve checking power-supply voltage levels and verifying that network devices are receiving power.

digital signal level (DS)   The series of standard digital transmission rates or levels based on DS0, a transmission rate of 64 kb/s. This originated from the bandwidth normally used for one telephone voice channel.

digital signal processor (DSP)   QoS algorithm used in voice networks when small packet loss is experienced. DSP analyzes and re-creates what the lost audio signal should be.

digital subscriber line (DSL)   An always-on connection technology that uses existing twisted-pair telephone lines to transport high-bandwidth data and that provides IP services to subscribers. A DSL modem converts an Ethernet signal from the user device into a DSL signal, which is transmitted to the central office.

distribution network   Cable service provider term describing the network segment from the provider headend to cable subscribers. Sometimes referred to as the distribution area.

divide-and-conquer troubleshooting approach   Troubleshooting approach that starts by collecting users' experiences with the problem and documenting the symptoms. Then, using that information, you make an informed guess about the OSI layer at which to start your investigation. After you verify that a layer is functioning properly, assume that the layers below it are functioning, and work up the OSI layers. If an OSI layer is not functioning properly, work your way down the OSI layer model. Compare with the bottom-up troubleshooting approach and top-down troubleshooting approach.

downstream   Service provider term used when describing traffic from the provider network to the subscriber network. Compare with upstream.

DSL access multiplexer (DSLAM)   The device located at the provider's central office (CO). It concentrates connections from multiple DSL subscribers.

DSL micro filter   DSL device used to enable analog devices (that is, phones, fax machines) to communicate with the CO PSTN switch.

DSL modem   DSL device located at the customer premises. The modem converts Ethernet signals from the internal network to DSL signals, which are transmitted to the central office.

DSL transceiver   DSL provider term used to describe equipment to connect the subscriber network to DSL. The DSL transceiver is typically a dedicated DSL modem or an interface added to a router.

dual-homed topology   Topology that provides redundancy such as when spoke routers are connected to two hub routers across a WAN cloud. Contrast with point-to-point, hub-and-spoke, and full-mesh topologies.

duplex mismatch   Term used in Ethernet to describe a situation in which one end of the link is set to full duplex and the other end of the link is set to half duplex.

Dynamic ARP inspection (DAI)   Cisco Catalyst switch security feature that prevents ARP spoofing and ARP poisoning attacks.

Dynamic Multipoint VPN (DMVPN)   Cisco software solution that simplifies the configuration for building multiple VPNs in an easy, dynamic, and scalable manner. It provides increased flexibility when connecting central office sites with branch sites in a hub-and-spoke configuration.

Dynamic Trunking Protocol (DTP)   A Cisco proprietary protocol that negotiates both the status and encapsulation of trunk ports.

E

E1   A type of leased line available from service providers in Europe providing bandwidth of up to 2.048 Mb/s. Contrast with T1, T3, and E3 leased lines.

E3   A type of leased line available from service providers in Europe providing bandwidth of up to 34.368 Mb/s. Contrast with T1, T3, and E1 leased lines.

East-West traffic   Term used in virtualization to describe traffic being exchanged between virtual servers. Compare with North-South traffic.

electromagnetic interference (EMI)   Interference by magnetic signals caused by the flow of electricity. EMI can cause reduced data integrity and increased error rates on transmission channels. The physics of this process are that electrical current creates magnetic fields, which in turn cause other electrical currents in nearby wires. The induced electrical currents can interfere with proper operation of the other wire.

Electronic Industries Alliance (EIA)   Best known for its standards related to electrical wiring, connectors, and the 19-inch racks used to mount networking equipment. EIA standards are often combined with TIA standards and referred to as TIA/EIA standards.

end-point groups (EPGs)   Term used in Cisco ACI to describe endpoints (for example, VLANs, Web server, application).

end-system configuration table   Type of table that contains baseline records of the hardware and software used in end-system devices such as servers, network management consoles, and desktop workstations. An incorrectly configured end system can have a negative impact on a network's overall performance.

enterprise network   A large and diverse network connecting most major points in a company or other organization. It differs from a WAN in that it is privately owned and maintained.

Ethernet over MPLS (EoMPLS)   Type of Ethernet WAN service that works by encapsulating Ethernet PDUs in MPLS packets and forwarding them across the MPLS network. Each PDU is transported as a single packet.

expedited forwarding (EF)   A category of DSCP values with a value of 46 (binary 101110). The first 3 bits (101) map directly to the Layer 2 CoS value 5 used for voice traffic. At Layer 3, Cisco recommends that EF only be used to mark voice packets. Compare with best effort (BE) and assured forwarding (AF).

extended ACLs   IOS feature that filters traffic based on multiple attributes, including protocol type, source IPv4 addresses, destination IPv4 addresses, source ports, and destination ports.

Extensible Authentication Protocol (EAP)   IEEE 802.1X protocol used between a supplicant and a RADIUS authentication server.

external BGP (eBGP)   A BGP configuration between two peers in different autonomous systems. For example, eBGP would be used to connect an enterprise AS to a service provider AS. Compare with Internal BGP (iBGP).

F

firewall   A router or access server designated as a buffer between any connected public network and a private network. A firewall router uses access lists and other methods to ensure the security of the private network.

first-in, first-out (FIFO)   QoS queuing method that is often the default queuing method for a faster interface. FIFO has no concept of priority or classes of traffic and, consequently, makes no decision about packet priority. FIFO forwards packets in the order they arrived. Compare with Weighted Fair Queuing (WFQ), Class-Based Weighted Fair Queuing (CBWFQ), and Low Latency Queuing (LLQ).

flow table   One of three SDN tables implemented in data center switches. This table matches incoming packets to a particular flow and specifies the functions that are to be performed on the packets. Multiple flow tables may operate in a pipeline fashion. Compare with group table and meter table.

fog applications   Applications developed to run on fog-enabled devices (for example, Cisco IOx routers and switches) and process data locally. Examples of deployed fog applications include site asset management, energy monitoring, and smart parking.

fog computing model   Network model that distributes the computing infrastructure to extend cloud connectivity closer to the network edge. It enables edge devices to run fog applications locally and make immediate decisions. This reduces network traffic because raw data is not sent over network connections and enhances resiliency by allowing IoT devices to operate when network connections are lost. The model also enhances security by keeping sensitive data from being transported beyond the edge where it is needed.

fog computing pillar   One of the six Cisco IoT System pillars. This pillar supports the fog computing model. Compare with network connectivity pillar, security pillar, data analytics pillar, system management and automation pillar, and application enablement platform pillar.

Frame Relay   An industry-standard WAN Layer 2 protocol that handles multiple virtual circuits between connected devices.

full duplex   Operation in which both devices can transmit and receive on the media at the same time.

full-mesh topology   A network in which each network node has either a physical circuit or a virtual circuit connecting it to every other network node. A full mesh provides a great deal of redundancy, but because it can be prohibitively expensive to implement, it is usually reserved for network backbones. Contrast with point-to-point, hub-and-spoke, and dual-homed topologies.

G

generic routing encapsulation (GRE)   A tunneling protocol developed by Cisco that can encapsulate a wide variety of protocol packet types inside IP tunnels. GRE creates a virtual point-to-point link to Cisco routers at remote points, over an IP internetwork. GRE is designed to manage the transportation of multiprotocol and IP multicast traffic between two or more sites that may have only IP connectivity. It can encapsulate multiple protocol packet types inside an IP tunnel.

get request   Type of request used by the SNMP manager to query a device for data.

group table   One of three SDN tables implemented in data center switches. A flow table may direct a flow to a group table, which may trigger a variety of actions that affect one or more flows. Compare with flow table and meter table.

H

half duplex   A situation in which both devices can transmit and receive on the media but cannot do so simultaneously.

headend   Cable provider term describing where signals are first received, processed, formatted, and then distributed downstream to the cable network. The headend facility is usually unmanned, under security fencing, and is similar to a telephone company central office.

High-Level Data Link Control (HDLC)   An ISO bit-oriented Layer 2 WAN serial line protocol that supports router-to-router connections. It is the default encapsulation of serial interfaces on Cisco routers. Contrast with Point-to-Point Protocol (PPP).

hub   Generally, a device that serves as the center of a star topology network.

hub-and-spoke topology   A topology in which stub routers (spokes) are connected to a central hub router. A single interface to the hub can be shared by all spoke circuits. For example, spoke sites can be interconnected through the hub site using virtual circuits and routed subinterfaces at the hub. A hub-and-spoke topology is also an example of a single-homed topology. Sometimes referred to as a hub-to-spoke topology. Contrast with point-to-point, full-mesh, and dual-homed topologies.

hybrid cloud   A cloud model that combines two or more cloud models (that is, private, community, or public). Individuals on a hybrid cloud would be able to have degrees of access to various services based on user access rights. Compare with public cloud, private cloud, and community cloud.

hybrid fiber-coaxial (HFC)   A telecommunications industry term for a broadband network that combines optical fiber and coaxial cable. It is commonly used by cable service providers.

hypervisors   Programs, firmware, or hardware that is used to create instances of virtual machines (VMs), which are emulated hardware including CPU, memory, storage, and networking settings in one OS. A hypervisor adds an abstraction layer on top of the real physical hardware to create VMs. Each VM runs a complete and separate operating system.

I

IEEE 802.1p   IEEE standard that is used with the IEEE 802.1Q protocol to define traffic class expediting and dynamic multicast filtering. The 802.1p standard uses the first three bits in the 802.1Q Tag Control Information (TCI) field to create the Priority (PRI) field which identifies the Class of Service (CoS) markings.

IEEE 802.1X   IEEE standard defines a port-based access control and authentication protocol.

infrastructure as a service (IaaS)   Cloud service in which the cloud provider is responsible for access to the network equipment, virtualized network services, and supporting network infrastructure. IaaS provides processing, storage, networking, or other fundamental computing resources to customers. Compare with software as a service (SaaS) and platform as a service (PaaS).

Institute of Electrical and Electronics Engineers (IEEE)   Organization of electrical engineering and electronics dedicated to advancing tech-nological innovation and creating standards in a wide area of industries including power and energy, healthcare, telecommunications, and networking.

integrated services (IntServ)   QoS model that is sometimes called hard QoS; it provides guaranteed QoS to IP packets. However, IntServ is considered to be a legacy QoS model because it is very resource intensive and therefore limited in scalability. Compare with best-effort model and differentiated services (DiffServ).

Integrated Services Digital Network (ISDN)   A communication protocol, offered by telephone companies, that permits telephone net-works to carry data, voice, and other source traffic.

internal BGP (iBGP)   A BGP configuration between two peers in the same autonomous system. For example, iBGP would be used between routers in a service provider AS. Compare with external BGP (eBGP).

International Organization for Standardization (ISO)   An international standard-setting body with members from global national standards organizations. The ISO is responsible for multiple standards including the OSI reference model.

Internet of Things (IoT)   The architecture that connects billions of smart objects to the Internet.

Internet Protocol Security (IPsec)   See *IPsec*.

intrusion prevention system (IPS)   A network security feature typically deployed as a service on an ISR G2 router or by using a dedicated device (such as an IPS sensor). An IPS captures and analyzes incoming and outgoing traffic to detect traffic anomalies, detect network attacks, issue alerts, block malicious packets, and more.

IoT Network security   A Cisco IoT security pillar cybersecurity solution that includes network and perimeter security devices such as switches, routers, ASA firewall devices, and

Cisco FirePOWER Next-Generation Intrusion Prevention Services (NGIPS).

IoT Physical security   A Cisco IoT security pillar cybersecurity solution that includes Cisco video surveillance IP cameras.

IP Control Protocol (IPCP)   The PPP NCP for IPv4 traffic.

IP Preference (IPP) field   Field defined in the original IP standard RFC 791 to be used for QoS markings. It has now been replaced with the Differentiated Services Code Point (DSCP) defined in RFC 2474.

IPsec   A framework of open standards that spells out the rules for secure communications. IPsec works at the network layer, protecting and authenticating IP packets between participating IPsec peers.

IP Source Guard   Cisco Catalyst switch security feature that prevents MAC and IP address spoofing attacks.

IPv6 Control Protocol (IPv6CP)   The PPP NCP for IPv6 traffic.

IT as a service (ITaaS)   Cloud service in which the cloud provider provides IT support for the cloud computing service. ITaaS can extend the capability of IT without requiring investment in new infrastructure, training new personnel, or licensing new software.

J

jabber   The condition in which a network device continually transmits random, meaningless data onto the network.

jitter   The variation in delay (that is, latency). Ideal network conditions have little variation in the time it takes to receive packets, whereas a network experiencing congestion could have a lot of variation in latency.

K

keepalives   Messages used by various protocols to ensure the other peer is still connected.

Kiwi syslog server   GUI SNMP manager software available from SolarWinds to collect, filter, display, alert, archive, forward, and react to syslog and SNMP traps.

knowledge bases   Information databases used to assist in the use or troubleshooting of a product. Online network device vendor knowledge bases have become indispensable sources of information. When vendor-based knowledge bases are combined with Internet search engines such as Google, a network administrator has access to a vast pool of experience-based information.

L

last-mile   See local loop.

latency   The time (in milliseconds or seconds) it takes for a packet to get from its source to its destination. Higher bandwidths typically have lower latency. Latency is sometimes displayed as RTT (round trip time) in command output.

leased line   A type of dedicated line provided by a service provider to a client network. Leased lines are often referred to by different names such as leased circuits, serial link, serial line, point-to-point link, and T1/E1 or T3/E3 lines. Leased lines are available in different capacities and are generally priced based on the bandwidth required and the distance between the two connected points. In North America, service providers use the T-carrier system to define the digital transmission capability of a serial copper media link, while Europe uses the E-carrier system. For instance, a T1 link supports 1.544 Mb/s, an E1 supports 2.048 Mb/s, a T3 supports 43.7 Mb/s, and an E3 connection supports 34.368 Mb/s.

light-emitting diodes (LEDs)   A semiconductor light source. LEDs are used as indicator lamps in many devices and are increasingly used for general lighting.

Link Access Procedure, Balanced (LAPB) A data link layer protocol that was used with legacy X.25.

Link Control Protocol (LCP)   A protocol that establishes, configures, and tests data-link connections for use by PPP.

link-establishment frames   PPP LCP frames (Configure-Request, Configure-Ack, Configure-Nak, and Configure-Reject) used to establish and configure a link.

Link Layer Discovery Protocol (LLDP)   A vendor-neutral Layer 2 link discovery protocol used to discover other LLDP-enabled devices for autoconfiguring connections and to troubleshoot network devices. Compare with Cisco Discovery Protocol (CDP).

link-maintenance frames   PPP LCP frames (Code-Reject, Protocol-Reject, Echo-Request, Echo-Reply, and Discard-Request) used to manage and debug a link.

link-termination frames   PPP LCP frames (Terminate-Request and Terminate-Ack) used to terminate a link.

link quality management (LQM)   A PPP feature that monitors the quality of the link. It can be used with the **ppp quality** interface configuration command to define a threshold to enable and disable the PPP link.

Local AAA Authentication   AAA authentication method that uses a local database for authentication. This method is sometimes known as self-contained authentication. This method stores usernames and passwords locally in the Cisco router, and users authenticate against the local database. Local AAA is ideal for small networks. Compare with Server-Based AAA Authentication.

local loop   A line from the premises of a telephone subscriber to the telephone company CO. Also referred to as the last-mile.

local SPAN   A term used when traffic on a switch is mirrored to another port on that switch. Compare with RSPAN.

logical topology diagram   Diagram that includes symbols to represent routers, servers, hosts, VPN concentrators, and security devices. It also includes symbols representing the type of link used to interconnect these devices, including interfaces and IP addressing. Compare with physical topology diagram.

Long-Term Evolution (LTE)   Usually marketed as 4G LTE; it is a standard for wireless communication.

Low Latency Queuing (LLQ)   QoS queuing method that is sometimes referred to as PQ-CBWFQ (Priority Queuing CBWFQ).

LLQ guarantees PQ assigned traffic bandwidth and sent first. LLQ is typically used in voice networks. Compare with first-in, first-out (FIFO), Weighted Fair Queuing (WFQ), and Class-Based Weighted Fair Queuing (CBWFQ).

M

MAC address table flooding attack   A type of LAN attack that occurs when a cybercriminal exploits a default switch behavior to create a MAC address flooding attack. MAC address tables are limited in size. MAC flooding attacks exploit this limitation with fake source MAC addresses until the switch MAC address table is full and the switch is overwhelmed. Compare with CDP reconnaissance attacks, Telnet attacks, VLAN attacks, and DHCP spoofing attacks.

Machine-to-Machine (M2M)   IoT term describing communication between machines without human intervention. For example, M2M occurs in cars with temperature and oil sensors communicating with an onboard computer.

management console   Application used with Type 1 hypervisors to manage multiple VM servers. The management console can automatically consolidate multiple servers and power on or off servers as required. It also provides recovery from hardware failure and can automatically and seamlessly move an unresponsive VM to another server.

Management Information Base (MIB)   A database of the objects that can be managed on a device. The managed objects, or variables, can be set or read to provide information on the network devices and interfaces.

management plane   One of the Cisco NFP functional areas; it is responsible for managing network elements. Management plane traffic is generated either by network devices or network management stations using processes and protocols such as Telnet, SSH, TFTP, FTP, NTP, AAA, SNMP, syslog, TACACS+, RADIUS, and NetFlow. Compare with control plane and data plane.

marking   QoS term to describe adding a value to the packet header. Devices receiving the packet look at this field to see if it matches a defined policy. Marking should be done as close to the source device as possible. This establishes the trust boundary.

maximum segment size (MSS)   The maximum size of the data portion in the TCP segment; it is determined by subtracting the IP and TCP headers from the Ethernet maximum transmission unit (MTU).

maximum transmission unit (MTU)   The largest size of packets that an interface can transmit without the need to fragment.

message digest 5 (MD5)   A popular cryptographic hash function producing a 128-bit (16-byte) hash value, typically expressed in text format as a 32-digit hexadecimal number. MD5 has been utilized in a wide variety of cryptographic applications and is also commonly used to verify data integrity. Contrast with SHA message-digest algorithm.

meter table   One of three SDN tables implemented in data center switches. The table triggers a variety of performance-related actions on a flow. Compare with flow table and group table.

Metropolitan Ethernet (MetroE)   Also called Ethernet MAN or metro Ethernet. This metropolitan area network (MAN) is based on Ethernet standards. It is commonly used to connect subscribers to a larger service network or the Internet.

modulates   The process of taking digital signals and converting them to an analog signal such as when a modem sends data over telephone lines.

multihomed   Term used to describe an enterprise with connections to two or more service providers. Compare with single-homed.

Multilink PPP   A PPP option that provides load balancing over the router interfaces that PPP uses. Also referred to as MP, MPPP, MLP, or Multilink, it provides a method for spreading traffic across multiple physical WAN links while providing packet fragmentation and reassembly, proper sequencing, multivendor interoperability, and load balancing on inbound and outbound traffic.

multiplex   A communication method by which multiple analog or digital signals are combined into one signal over a shared medium.

Multipoint Generic Routing Encapsulation (mGRE)   A variation of GRE used with DMVPN. An mGRE tunnel interface allows a single GRE interface to support multiple IPsec tunnels. With mGRE, dynamically allocated tunnels are created through a permanent tunnel source at the hub and dynamically allocated tunnel destinations, created as necessary, at the spokes. This reduces the size and simplifies the complexity of the configuration.

Multiprotocol Label Switching (MPLS)   MPLS is a packet-forwarding technology that uses labels to make data-forwarding decisions. With MPLS, the Layer 3 header analysis is done just once (when the packet enters the MPLS domain). Label inspection drives subsequent packet forwarding.

municipal Wi-Fi   Cities that provide wireless Internet access for free or for a nominal fee. Most implementations use a mesh topology, which is a series of interconnected access points located throughout a city.

N

named ACLs   ACLs identified in a configuration by a descriptive name. Standard named ACLs are created using the **ip access-list standard acl-name** global configuration command. Extended named ACLs are created using the **ip access-list extended acl-name** global configuration command. Compare with numbered ACLs.

National Institute of Standards and Technology (NIST)   A U.S. Department of Commerce standards agency that promotes innovation and industrial competitiveness. It is defined in "Special Publication (SP) 800-145, The NIST Definition of Cloud Computing," which defines software as a service (SaaS), platform as a service (PaaS), and infrastructure as a service (IaaS).

Neighbor Advertisement (NA)   ICMPv6 message used by an interface to announce its presence on the local link. NA is used in the IPv6 Neighbor Discovery (ND) feature.

Neighbor Discovery (ND)   IPv6 feature used to resolve a MAC address to an IPv6 address to perform a similar function to IPv4 ARP. ND utilizes the ICMPv6 Neighbor Solicitation (NS) and Neighbor Advertisement (NA) messages to accomplish this function.

Neighbor Solicitation (NS)   ICMPv6 message used to discover other IPv6 hosts on the local link. NS is used in the IPv6 Neighbor Discovery (ND) feature.

NetFlow   NetFlow efficiently provides a key set of services for IP applications, including network traffic accounting, usage-based network billing, network planning, security, denial-of-service monitoring capabilities, and network monitoring. NetFlow creates an environment where administrators have the tools to understand who, what, when, where, and how network traffic is flowing.

Network Address Translation (NAT)   Only globally unique in terms of the public Internet. A mechanism for translating private addresses into publicly usable addresses to be used within the public Internet. An effective means of hiding actual device addressing within a private network.

Network Analysis Module (NAM)   The NAM is an embedded browser-based interface that generates reports on the traffic that consumes critical network resources. It can be installed in Cisco Catalyst 6500 series switches and Cisco 7600 series routers to provide a graphical representation of traffic from local and remote switches and routers. In addition, the NAM can capture and decode packets and track response times to pinpoint an application problem to the network or server.

Network-Based Application Recognition (NBAR)   QoS classification method that classifies traffic at Layers 4 to 7. NBAR is a classification and protocol discovery feature of Cisco IOS software that works with QoS features.

network baseline   A reference used to efficiently diagnose and correct network problems. A network baseline documents what the network's expected performance should be under normal operating conditions. This information is captured in documentation such as configuration tables and topology diagrams.

network configuration files   Files that contain accurate, up-to-date records of the hardware and software used in a network. Within the network configuration files, a table should exist for each network device used on the network, containing all relevant information about that device.

network connectivity pillar   One of the six Cisco IoT System pillars. It is designed to meet existing and new network IoT demands by providing built-in scalability, integrated cybersecurity, and convergence by supporting IT and operational technology (OT) standards and protocols. Compare with fog computing pillar, security pillar, data analytics pillar, system management and automation pillar, and application enablement platform pillar.

Network Control Protocols (NCPs)   Protocols used to establish and configure different network layer protocols.

network documentation   A logical diagram of the network and detailed information about each component. This information should be kept in a single location, either as hard copy or on the network on a protected website. Network documentation should include a network configuration table, an end-system configuration table, and a network topology diagram.

network management system (NMS)   Generally, a reasonably powerful and well-equipped computer, such as an engineering workstation. It is responsible for managing parts of a network. NMSs communicate with agents to help keep track of network statistics and resources.

network management system tools   Tools that help simplify network management; they include device-level monitoring, configuration, and fault-management tools. These tools can be used to investigate and correct network problems.

network topology diagrams   A graphical representation of a network that illustrates how each device is connected and its logical architecture. A topology diagram has many of the same components as the network configuration table. Each network device should be represented on the diagram with consistent notation or a graphical symbol. Also, each logical and physical connection should be represented using a simple line or other appropriate symbol. Routing protocols also can be shown.

Next Hop Clients (NHCs)   The name given to spoke routers using NHRP in a hub-and-spoke DMVPN configuration. Compare with Next Hop Server (NHS).

Next Hop Resolution Protocol (NHRP)   A Layer 2 resolution and caching protocol similar to Address Resolution Protocol (ARP). NHRP creates a distributed mapping database of public IP addresses for all tunnel spokes. NHRP is a client server protocol consisting of the NHRP hub known as the Next Hop Server (NHS) and the NHRP spokes known as the Next Hop Clients (NHCs).

Next Hop Server (NHS)   The name given to the hub router using NHRP in a hub-and-spoke DMVPN configuration. Compare with Next Hop Clients (NHCs).

node   Cable service provider term describing the devices that convert optical signals to RF signals.

nonbroadcast multi-access (NBMA)   A multi-access network that does not support broadcasting (such as X.25) or in which broadcasting is not feasible (for example, an SMDS broadcast group or an extended Ethernet that is too large).

northbound APIs   Subroutines used by an SDN controller to communicate with the upstream applications. These APIs help network administrators shape traffic and deploy services.

North-South traffic   Term used in virtualization to describe traffic being exchanged between external data center users and the data center server. Compare with East-West traffic.

numbered ACLs   ACLs identified in the configuration by a number. The number also designates the type of ACL. For instance, ACLs numbered between 1 and 99 and between 1300 and 1999 are standard ACLs, whereas ACLs numbered between 100 and 199 and between 2000 and 2699 are extended ACLs. Numbered ACLs are configured using the **access-list** global configuration command. Compare with named ACLs.

O

Object ID (OID)   SNMP term to describe a variable (that is, object) in the MIB. OIDs uniquely identify managed objects in the MIB hierarchy that organizes the OIDs based on RFC standards into a hierarchy of OIDs, usually displayed as a tree.

OpenFlow   Protocol developed at Stanford University that is a foundational element for building SDN solutions. The OpenFlow standard is now maintained by the Open Networking Foundation.

OpenStack   A cloud operating system that is used in data centers to control large pools of compute, storage, and networking resources. OpenStack uses a web dashboard to build scalable cloud environments and provide an infrastructure as a service (IaaS) solution. OpenStack is often used with Cisco ACI.

Operational Technology (OT)   Hardware and software that detects or causes a change through the direct monitoring and/or control of physical devices, processes, and events in the enterprise. For example, OT is the hardware and software that keeps power plants running and manages factory process lines.

Operational Technology (OT) security   A cybersecurity solution (for example, Cisco ISA 3000 industrial security appliance and fog data services) provided by the Cisco IoT security pillar.

optical carrier (OC)   Term used by service providers to identify a standardized set of specifications for transmission bandwidths used with SONET fiber networks. For example, OC-1 supports bandwidths of 51.84 Mb/s, OC-3 supports 155.52 Mb/s, OC-768 supports 40 Gb/s.

optical time-domain reflectometers (OTDRs)   TDRs used to test fiber-optic cables.

P

packet analyzer   Network monitoring software that is also known as a sniffer, packet sniffer, or traffic sniffer. A packet analyzer such as Wireshark captures packets entering and exiting a network interface card (NIC).

packet loss   QoS term used to refer to packets that did not reach their destination because of network congestion, an invalid QoS policy that is dropping packets, physical cable problems, and more.

packet-switched network (PSN)   A type of network that splits traffic data into packets that are routed over a shared network. Routers determine the links that packets must be sent over based on the addressing information in each packet. Packet-switching networks do not require a circuit to be established, and they allow many pairs of nodes to communicate over the same channel.

parallel connection   A connection that uses multiple wires running parallel to each other to transfer data on all the wires simultaneously. Contrast with parallel connection.

parallel ports   Legacy connectors on computers that used parallel connections such as a legacy printer. Parallel ports have been replaced by USB interfaces. Contrast with RS-232 serial ports and universal serial bus (USB) interfaces.

Passenger protocol   Term used in GRE to describe the original IPv4, IPv6, or legacy protocol (that is, AppleTalk, DECnet, or IPX) packet that will be encapsulated by a Carrier protocol. Compare with Carrier protocol and Transport protocol.

Password Authentication Protocol (PAP)   An authentication protocol that allows PPP peers to authenticate one another. The remote router attempting to connect to the local router is required to send an authentication request. Unlike CHAP, PAP passes the password and username in the clear (unencrypted). PAP does not itself prevent unauthorized access but merely identifies the remote end. The router or access server then determines if that user is allowed access. PAP is supported only on PPP lines.

path vector routing protocol   The way BGP makes its loop-free routing decisions.

permanent virtual circuits (PVCs)   Type of virtual circuit used in Frame Relay that is always ready and available for data transfer. PVCs are used to carry both voice and data traffic between a source and destination, and support data rates up to 4 Mb/s or more.

physical topology diagram   Diagram documenting the mapping of a network by showing the physical layout of equipment, cables, and interconnections. Compare with logical topology diagram.

platform as a service (PaaS)   Cloud service in which the cloud provider is responsible for access to the development tools and services used to deliver the applications. Compare with software as a service (SaaS) and infrastructure as a service (IaaS).

playout delay buffer   QoS term for the mechanism that compensates for jitter by buffering packets and then plays them out in a steady stream.

point of presence (POP)   A point of interconnection between the communications facilities provided by the telephone company and the building's main distribution facility.

Point-to-Point Protocol (PPP)   A Layer 2 WAN protocol that provides router-to-router and host-to-network connections over synchronous and asynchronous circuits. It should be used on Cisco routers when connecting to other vendor routers. It also supports options such as authentication, compression, multilinking, and more. Contrast with High-Level Data Link Control (HDLC).

point-to-point topology   In this topology, connections used to connect LANs to service provider WANs and to connect LAN segments within an enterprise network. Contrast with full-mesh, hub-and-spoke, and dual-homed topologies.

policy-based SDN   One of three types of SDN implementations. This is the most robust type of SDN and is similar to controller-based SDN but includes an additional policy layer that operates at a higher level of abstraction. It uses a built-in intuitive GUI application to help automate advanced configuration tasks. Cisco APIC-EM is an example of this type of SDN. Compare with device-based SDN and controller-based SDN.

portable network analyzers   A portable device that is used to troubleshoot switched networks and VLANs. By plugging in the network analyzer anywhere on the network, a network engineer can see the switch port to which the device is connected and the average and peak utilization.

port mirroring   A switch traffic forwarding feature that copies traffic flowing between ingress and egress ports to another port usually connected to a packet analyzer. Cisco Catalyst switches implement port mirroring using the Switched Port Analyzer (SPAN) feature.

port security   A generic term meaning procedures and configurations performed on a switch interface to protect the network from attacks and unauthorized wired devices.

PPP callback   PPP option used to enhance security and reduce toll charges by making a Cisco router act as a callback client or a callback server. The client makes the initial call, requests that the server call it back, and terminates its initial call. The callback router answers the initial call and makes the return call to the client based on its configuration statements.

PPP over Ethernet (PPPoE)   PPPoE combines two widely accepted standards, Ethernet and PPP, to provide an authenticated method of assigning IP addresses to client systems. PPPoE clients are typically personal computers connected to an ISP over a remote broadband connection, such as DSL or cable service. ISPs deploy PPPoE because it supports high-speed broadband access using their existing remote access infrastructure and because it is easier for customers to use.

Primary Rate Interface (PRI)   An ISDN interface to primary rate access. Primary rate access consists of a single 64-kb/s D channel plus 23 (T1) or 30 (E1) B channels for voice or data.

Priority (PRI) field   A 3-bit field in the 802.1Q Tag Control that identifies the class of service (CoS) markings of the frame.

private cloud   A cloud model where all cloud-based applications and services offered are intended for an enterprise only. A private cloud can be provisioned internally but would be expensive to build and maintain. A private cloud can also be provisioned strict access security by a cloud provider. Compare with public cloud, hybrid cloud, and community cloud.

private WAN infrastructure   Dedicated point-to-point leased lines, circuit-switched links, such as PSTN or ISDN, and packet-switched links, such as Ethernet WAN, ATM, or Frame Relay.

protocol analyzer   Decodes the various protocol layers in a recorded frame and presents this information in a relatively easy-to-use format. WireShark is a protocol analyzer.

public cloud   A cloud model where all cloud-based applications and services offered publically to anyone. Services may be free or are offered on a pay-per-use model, such as paying for online storage. The public cloud uses the Internet to provide services. Compare with private cloud, hybrid cloud, and community cloud.

public switched telephone network (PSTN)   A general term referring to the variety of telephone networks and services in place worldwide. Also called the plain old telephone service (POTS).

public WAN infrastructure   Broadband Internet access using digital subscriber line (DSL), cable, and satellite access. Broadband connection options are typically used to connect small offices and telecommuting employees to a corporate site over the Internet. Data traveling between corporate sites over the public WAN infrastructure should be protected using VPNs.

R

radio frequency (RF)   A generic term referring to frequencies that correspond to radio transmissions. Cable TV and broadband networks use RF technology.

Real-Time Streaming Protocol (RSTP)   Protocol used for establishing and controlling media streaming sessions between endpoints.

remote-access VPNs   Type of VPN network that enables remote VPN clients (remote host) to gain secure access to the enterprise network via a VPN server device at the network edge.

Remote Authentication Dial-In User Service (RADIUS)   An open standard AAA protocol used to provide remote-access authentication, authorization, and accounting. RADIUS encrypts only the password message. RADIUS does not encrypt usernames, accounting information, or any other information carried in the RADIUS message. Compare with Terminal Access Controller Access Control System (TACACS+).

Remote SPAN (RSPAN)   RSPAN allows source and destination ports to be in different switches and is useful in situations when the packet analyzer or IPS is on a different switch than the traffic being monitored. Compare with Local SPAN.

Resource Reservation Protocol (RSVP)   A network-control protocol used in an IntServ QoS model that enables end devices to request specific QoS from IntServ-enabled devices.

RS-232 serial ports   Legacy EIA connectors on computers that used serial connections such as legacy mice. RS-232 ports have been replaced by USB interfaces. Contrast with parallel ports and universal serial bus (USB) interfaces.

S

satellite Internet   Internet connection typically used by rural users where cable and DSL are not available. A VSAT provides two-way (upload and download) data communications. The upload speed is about one-tenth of the 500-kb/s download speed. Cable and DSL have higher download speeds, but satellite systems are about 10 times faster than an analog modem. To access satellite Internet services, subscribers need a satellite dish, two modems (uplink and downlink), and coaxial cables between the dish and the modem.

SDN controllers   Controllers that perform all complex functions. They define the data flows that occur in the SDN Data plane and populate

the data center switches forwarding flow tables. Each flow traveling through the network must first get permission from the SDN controller, which verifies that the communication is permissible according to the network policy. If the controller allows a flow, it computes a route for the flow to take and adds an entry for that flow in each of the switches along the path.

Secure Sockets Layer (SSL)   A cryptographic protocol designed to provide communication security over the Internet. It has since been replaced by Transport Layer Security (TLS).

security pillar   One of the six Cisco IoT System pillars. This pillar offers scalable cybersecurity solutions, enabling an organization to quickly and effectively discover, contain, and remediate an attack to minimize damage. Compare with network connectivity pillar, fog computing pillar, data analytics pillar, system management and automation pillar, and application enablement platform pillar.

sensors   IoT devices that convert a physical, biological, or chemical parameter into an electrical signal. For example, the temperature and oil sensors in cars that communicate with an onboard computer.

serial connection   A connection that uses a single wire to transfer the data bits one at a time. Contrast with parallel connection.

Serial Line Internet Protocol (SLIP)   Legacy serial line protocol that has been replaced by PPP.

Server-Based AAA Authentication   AAA server authentication method that is much more scalable than local AAA Authentication. With server-based method, the router communicates with a central AAA server using TACACS+ or RADIUS. The AAA server contains the usernames and passwords for all users and serves as a central authentication system for all infrastructure devices.

server operating system (OS)   Operating system developed for servers such as Windows Server or Linux Server. All of a server's RAM, processing power, and hard drive space were dedicated to the service (for example, web, email services) provided.

server sprawl   Term used to describe dedicated servers that sit idle for long periods of time, wasting energy and taking up more space than is warranted by their amount of service.

service provider   A company that provides access to other networks or the Internet to its subscribers.

set request   A type of request used by the SNMP manager to change the configuration in the agent device. A set request can also initiate actions within a device.

Simple Network Management Protocol (SNMP)   Network management protocol used to manage devices (that is, SNMP agents) on an IP network. The SNMP manager, which is part of the network management system (NMS), communicates with SNMP agents to monitor and manage network performance and to help find and solve network problems.

single-homed   Term used to describe an enterprise with one connection to a service provider. Compare with multihomed.

single-homed topology   A topology that provides one connection to a hub router across a WAN cloud. Contrast with dual-homed, point-to-point, hub-and-spoke, and full-mesh topologies.

single point of failure   A device (for example, a router, switch, server) that is a part of a network that, if it fails, will stop the entire system from working. A single point of failure is undesirable in any system with a goal of high availability or reliability.

site-to-site VPNs   VPNs that connect entire networks to each other; for example, they can connect a branch office network to a company headquarters network.

SNMP agents   Agents that reside on managed devices. SNMP agents collect and store information about the device and its operation.

snmpget   Freeware utility used to quickly retrieve real-time information from the MIB. The snmpget utility requires that the SNMP version, the correct community, the IP address of the network device to query, and the OID number are set.

SNMP manager   An application running on a network management system (NMS). The SNMP manager runs SNMP management software that is used to poll SNMP agents and query the MIB of SNMP agents using UDP port 161.

SNMP traps   Alert messages sent from an SNMP agent to the SNMP manager. SNMP agents send SNMP traps to the SNMP manager using UDP port 162.

software as a service (SaaS)   Cloud service in which the cloud provider is responsible to provide consumers to fully functional applications. The cloud provider manages the underlying hardware or software infrastructure and is responsible for access to services, such as email, communication, and Office 365 that are delivered over the Internet. Users only need to provide their data.

Compare with platform as a service (PaaS) and infrastructure as a service (IaaS).

software-defined networking (SDN)   An architecture that decouples network control (control plane) from the network devices (forwarding plane). SDN brings automation and programmability into data center, campus, backbone, and wide-area networks.

southbound APIs   Routines used by an SDN controller to define the behavior of the downstream virtual switches and routers. OpenFlow is the original and widely implemented southbound API.

spine-leaf topology   Two-tier data center topology consisting of spine switches and leaf switches. Leaf switches always attach to the spines, but they never attach to each other and spine switches only attach to the leaf and core switches.

spoke-to-spoke   A DMVPN hub-and-spoke topology in which endpoints (i.e., spokes) can establish point-to-point links with other endpoints (i.e., spokes) using the Next Hop Resolution Protocol (NHRP).

standard ACL   IOS feature used to filter traffic based on source IPv4 addresses.

subscriber drop   Cable service provider term used to describe the connection from distribution network feeder to the subscriber's cable modem.

supplicant   IEEE 802.1X term used to describe an 802.1X-enabled port on the client device. The device requests access to LAN and switch services and then responds to requests from the switch. The client device can be a PC running 802.1X-compliant client software.

Switched Port Analyzer (SPAN)   A feature on Cisco switches that is used to enable port mirroring of incoming and outgoing traffic. As traffic flows through a switch, the frames are also copied to a designated SPAN port connected to a packet analyzer or Intrusion Prevention System (IPS) device to collect and analyze traffic.

symmetric DSL (SDSL)   A type of DSL service used to connect corporate sites to service providers. SDSL provides the same downstream and upstream capacity in both directions. Compare with asymmetric DSL (ADSL).

synchronous circuits   Serial lines that require a clock signal and are typically faster than asynchronous circuits. Compare with asynchronous circuits.

Synchronous Data Link Control (SDLC)   An SNA data link layer communications protocol. A bit-oriented, full-duplex protocol that has spawned numerous similar protocols, including HDLC and LAPB.

Synchronous Digital Hierarchy (SDH)   A standard that defines how to transfer multiple data, voice, and video traffic over optical fiber using lasers or light-emitting diodes (LEDs) over great distances. SDH is a European-based ETSI and ITU standard, whereas SONET is an American-based ANSI standard. Both are essentially the same and, therefore, often listed as SONET/SDH.

Synchronous Optical Networking (SONET)   A high-speed (up to 2.5 Gb/s) synchronous network specification developed by Bellcore and designed to run on optical fiber. STS-1 is the basic building block of SONET. Approved as an international standard in 1988, SONET is an American-based ANSI standard, whereas SDH is a European-based ETSI and ITU standard. Both are essentially the same and, therefore, often listed as SONET/SDH.

syslog   A protocol that was developed for UNIX systems in the 1980s but was first documented as RFC 3164 by IETF in 2001. Syslog uses UDP port 514 to send event notification messages across IP networks to event message collectors.

syslog server   A server that receives and stores syslog messages that can be displayed with a syslog application.

systematic layered approach   A troubleshooting method that analyzes the network as a whole rather than in a piecemeal fashion. A systematic approach minimizes confusion and cuts down on time that would be wasted with trial and error.

system management and automation pillar One of the six Cisco IoT System pillars. This pillar provides tools to simplify the integration of different systems. Cisco delivers a broad range of IoT management and automation products that can be customized for specific industries to provide enhanced security and control and support. Compare with network connectivity pillar, Fog computing pillar, security pillar, data analytics pillar, and Application Enablement Platform pillar.

T

T1   A type of leased line available from service providers in North America providing bandwidth of up to 1.54 Mb/s. Contrast with T3, E1, and E3 leased lines.

T3   A type of leased line available from service providers in North America providing bandwidth of up to 44.7 Mb/s. Contrast with T1, E1, and E3 leased lines.

Tag Control Information (TCI) field   A 16-bit field in the 802.1Q header. The first three bits of the User Priority field are defined by the IEEE 802.1p specification. The next bit is the Canonical Format Indicator (CFI) field followed by 12 bits for the VLAN identifier.

Telecommunications Industry Association (TIA)   Organization responsible for developing communication standards in a variety of areas, including radio equipment, cellular towers, voice over IP (VoIP) devices, satellite communications, and more. TIA standards are often combined with EIA standards and referred to as TIA/EIA standards.

telecommuters   See *teleworker*.

teleworker   A user using teleworking services. Also referred to as a telecommuter.

teleworking   Working from a nontraditional workplace such as at home; it offers many benefits to the worker and to the business.

Telnet attacks   One of two types of attacks. In the first type, a cybercriminal attempts to connect remotely to a device using brute-force password attacks. In the second type, a cybercriminal creates a Telnet DoS attack to deny administrative access to the Telnet lines. Compare with CDP reconnaissance attacks, MAC address table flooding attacks, VLAN attacks, and DHCP spoofing attacks.

Terminal Access Controller Access Control System (TACACS+)   A Cisco proprietary AAA protocol used to provide remote-access authentication, authorization, and accounting. TACACS+ message exchanges are encrypted. Compare with Remote Authentication Dial-In User Service (RADIUS).

time-division multiplexing (TDM)   A technique in which information from multiple channels can be allocated bandwidth on a single wire based on preassigned time slots. Bandwidth is allocated to each channel regardless of whether the station has data to transmit.

time-domain reflectometers (TDRs)   Special type of cable tester that can pinpoint the distance to a break in a cable by sending signals and measuring the time it takes the break to reflect the signal.

toll network   Network that consists of the long-haul, all-digital, fiber-optic communications lines, switches, routers, and other equipment inside the WAN provider network. There is a fee to use the services of a toll network.

top-down troubleshooting approach   A troubleshooting approach that starts with the end-user applications and moves down through the layers of the OSI model until the cause of the problem is found. You test end-user applications of an end system before tackling the more specific networking pieces. Use this approach for simpler problems or when you think the problem is with a piece of software. Compare with the bottom-up troubleshooting approach and the divide-and-conquer troubleshooting approach.

Traffic Class field   IPv6 equivalent of the IPv4 Type of Service (ToS) field.

traffic policing   QoS mechanism that limits the amount of bandwidth that certain network traffic can use. Policing typically drops (discards) excess traffic. Compare with traffic shaping.

traffic shaping   QoS mechanisms for preventing congestion by queueing (that is, delaying) excess traffic and sending it later. Traffic shaping retains excess packets in a queue and then schedules the excess for later transmission over increments of time. Compare with traffic policing.

transportation network   Service provider term describing the network link between an antenna site and the headend or the headend and distribution network. The transportation network can be microwave, coaxial, or fiber optic.

Transport Layer Security (TLS)   A cryptographic protocol that replaces Secure Sockets Layer (SSL) but is still frequently referred to as "SSL." It provides secure communications over a computer network and is commonly used to secure web access with HTTPS.

Transport protocol   Term used in GRE to describe the delivery protocol that encapsulates the Carrier protocol. Compare with Carrier protocol and Passenger protocol.

trunk lines   Telephone lines that are switched over a telephone carrier network and provide voice and data transfer between two customers.

Type 1 hypervisors   Also called the "bare metal" approach because the hypervisor is installed directly on the hardware. Instances of an OS are then installed on the server, giving Type 1 hypervisors direct access to the hardware resources. Type 1 hypervisors improve scalability, performance, and robustness and are therefore usually used on enterprise servers and data center networking devices.

Type 2 hypervisors   Also called "hosted hypervisors" because the hypervisors are installed on top of the existing OS (for example, Mac OS X, Windows, or Linux). Many are available at no cost and therefore popular with consumers and for organizations experimenting with virtualization.

type of service (ToS) See Type of Service (ToS) field.

Type of Service (ToS) field QoS marking that exists in the Layer 3 header of a packet, which a router can identify.

U

universal serial bus (USB) interface Common connectors on computers that have replaced parallel and serial ports due to their fast speeds and universal acceptance. Contrast with parallel and RS-232 serial ports.

upstream Service provider term used when describing traffic from the subscriber network to the provider network. Compare with downstream.

V

very small aperture terminal (VSAT) A solution that creates a private WAN using satellite communications. A VSAT is a small satellite dish similar to those used for home Internet and TV. VSATs create a private WAN while providing connectivity to remote locations.

virtual circuit (VC) A logical circuit created to ensure reliable communication between two network devices. A virtual circuit is defined by a VPI/VCI pair, and it can be either permanent (PVC) or switched (SVC). Virtual circuits are used in Frame Relay. In ATM, a virtual circuit is called a virtual channel.

virtualization The creation of a virtual version of something, such as a hardware platform,

operating system (OS), storage device, or network resources. Virtualization separates the OS from the hardware.

virtual machines (VMs) Instances of an OS running on top of another OS. VMs run a complete and separate operating system and have access to all the resources (that is, CPUs, memory, disk controllers, and NICs) of the host OS. VMs are the result of virtualization.

Virtual Private LAN Service (VPLS) A class of VPN that supports the connection of multiple sites in a single bridged domain over a managed IP/MPLS network. VPLS presents an Ethernet interface to customers, simplifying the LAN/WAN boundary for service providers and customers, and enabling rapid and flexible service provisioning, because the service bandwidth is not tied to the physical interface. All services in a VPLS appear to be on the same LAN, regardless of location.

virtual private networks (VPNs) Networks that extend a private network across a public network, such as the Internet. They enable a computer to send and receive data across shared or public networks as if it were directly connected to the private network, while benefiting from the functionality, security, and management policies of the private network. This is done by establishing a virtual point-to-point connection through the use of dedicated connections, encryption, or a combination of the two.

VMware Commercial cloud and virtualization software and services on the x86 architecture pioneered by VMware, Inc., a subsidiary of Dell Technologies.

voice over IP (VoIP) A voice technology that uses traditional telephones to establish telephone calling privileges over the Internet. VoIP uses voice-enabled routers that convert analog voice from traditional telephone signals into IP packets. After the signals are converted into IP packets, the router sends those packets between corresponding locations.

VPN client software   Software that is installed on a host and used to establish a remote-access VPN connection.

VPN gateway   An enterprise device that is responsible for encapsulating, encrypting, and sending outbound traffic through a VPN tunnel over the Internet to a peer VPN gateway that strips the headers, decrypts the content, and relays the packet toward the target host inside its private network. The VPN gateway could be a router, a firewall, or a Cisco Adaptive Security Appliance (ASA).

W

WAN switch   A multiport internetworking device used in service provider networks. These devices typically switch traffic, such as Frame Relay or ATM, and operate at Layer 2.

Weighted Fair Queuing (WFQ)   QoS queuing method that attempts to balance available bandwidth between incoming flows. WFQ is often the default method applied to serial interfaces. Compare with first-in, first-out (FIFO), Class-Based Weighted Fair Queuing (CBWFQ), and Low Latency Queuing (LLQ).

Weighted Random Early Detection (WRED)   A QoS congestion avoidance tool that is used by TCP to regulate data traffic in a bandwidth-efficient manner before tail drops caused by queue overflows occur. WRED provides buffer management and allows TCP traffic to decrease, or throttle back, before buffers are exhausted.

wildcard masks   A string of 32 binary digits used by the router to determine which bits of the address to examine for a match.

WiMAX (Worldwide Interoperability for Microwave Access)   Type of access described in the IEEE standard 802.16. WiMAX offers high-speed broadband service with wireless access. It provides broad coverage like a cell phone network rather than using small Wi-Fi hotspots.

X

X.25   Legacy WAN protocol that worked with the Link Access Procedure, Balanced (LAPB) data link layer protocol. X.25 was replaced by Frame Relay.

Index